Practitioner's Guide
to Business Impact Analysis

Internal Audit and IT Audit

Series Editor: Dan Swanson

Practitioner's Guide
to Business Impact Analysis

Priti Sikdar

CRC Press
Taylor & Francis Group
Boca Raton London New York

CRC Press is an imprint of the
Taylor & Francis Group, an informa business

AN AUERBACH BOOK

CRC Press
Taylor & Francis Group
6000 Broken Sound Parkway NW, Suite 300
Boca Raton, FL 33487-2742

First issued in paperback 2021

Printed on acid-free paper

ISBN-13: 978-1-4987-5066-0 (hbk)
ISBN-13: 978-0-367-56792-7 (pbk)

Visit the Taylor & Francis Web site at
http://www.taylorandfrancis.com

and the CRC Press Web site at
http://www.crcpress.com

I dedicate this book to my Daddy, Samares Sikdar, who was a constant source of inspiration and encouragement for me throughout my career and writing. I pray to God, may he rest in peace and continue to bless me and my endeavors to spread knowledge and expertise!

Contents

Foreword

I have great pleasure in penning this foreword. I have known Priti for several years and not only has she written very interesting articles but has also indulged in imparting on the job training to her colleagues and peers on matters relating to IT and business risks. Her passion for her subjects, her commitment to research and her love for innovation, differentiates her from other authors and writers.

I have read the first few chapters of this publication and believe that the seamless flow of the content would even enable a non-technical person to understand and appreciate the subject matter. I am also impressed by the diagrams and the illustrations given, which further supports easy understanding of the content. I am confident that this book will be a "must have" for every library. While knowledge knows no end, dissemination of knowledge and knowledge sharing are of utmost importance. Although we may reside and operate from one place, we have become global professionals and in this context, Priti's endeavour to practically apply her education, knowledge, and her experience to guide other professionals across the globe, is indeed commendable! I wish Priti and this publication, lots of luck and success.

Khushroo Panthaky

(Khushroo Panthaky is a friend, ex-colleague, and a global assurance professional for the past three decades. He is heading the Audit & Assurance function in a global consulting firm in India)

Preface

My book, *Practitioner's Guide to Business Impact Analysis* is an effort to translate my years of experience in enterprise risk, internal audit, business resilience, and business continuity management into a useful guide for Practitioners. In this ever-changing business, anything can make impact. Recently there was a demonetization policy introduced by our Government by which some big notes got out of circulation. For not less than 50 days it caused a huge impact on business. In fact, it gave it a new shape and it led to losses for some kinds of businesses. So, question is, are businesses aware of such impacts, are they prepared to absorb sudden changes?

There are several standards on risk, security, and business continuity across the globe. I remember that in the process of doing a business impact analysis, we realized that there was no prescribed methodology to perform a Business Impact Analysis or BIA. At that time, Gartner had a preliminary template which served as a guideline and the rest based on experience previously taken, the assignment was concluded. Many times, we know what is to be done, but have little knowledge of how it is to be performed. My book is full of illustrations, diagrams, tables, templates that can set the reader going!

Business impact analysis is a necessary process for any risk and gap assessment as well as a security implementation under globally accepted standards such as ISO 27001. I have attempted to bring out commonalities in all global standards and have put global risk models with due permission of the certifying agencies like British Standards Institute. This will enable organizations to pitch for multiple standards while preparing their security and BCM infrastructure and obtain these certifications simultaneously by this integrated approach.

At the end, there is a flip through gallery of illustrations, tables, templates, and so on, which is for walkthrough and if reader needs any one of these they can easily use them in their work. This was a book I had conceptualized for quite some time and to make my journey successful, my children Kunal and Saloni have helped convert my hand diagrams into photoshop. I am also thankful to the British Standards Institute where I was invited to attend the "train the trainer" batch for BS 25999 standard and obtain my eligibility certificate to perform BCM audits and analysis.

I have preferred to make the book lucid and informative especially sections on risk and BIA and I am sure that readers will find it informative and useful. It is prescribed that organizations and practitioners engaged to implement a business impact analysis, have a read of the book and take a hint for implementing methodology for BIA.

About the Author

Priti Sikdar, (FCA, DISA, CISA, CISM, CRISC, ISO 27001 LA, BCCS, BS 25999 LA, PRINCE 2 [FC]) has over 23 years of experience in the risk, assurance, business resilience, IT governance, and internal audit. She has been ranked amongst the top 15 talent global professionals by BCMi in 2007. She is a recognized trainer and speaker and author of two books on her subject. She has worked as Head of Finance for Shipping and Logistics Company. She has been Partner with Ray & Co Chartered Accountants where she performed many bank audits relating to risk based, IS audits and data migration and post-implementation audits. She was also into Sarbanes Oxley Compliance where she was performing ITGC and Revenue modules of SOX.

She owned ISA Tutorials where she was teaching Chartered Accountants IT audit, IS systems and how to audit in complex technology environments. Ms. Sikdar has worked with Grant Thornton as Manager Business Risk Services where she has initiated a BS 25999 rollout, SAS 70 assignments and Enterprise Risk assessments. She was with KPMG London where she was doing IT internal audit for Financial Services sector and was spearheading a big in-house Technology Global Services Project for six divisions of Technology within Risk and Assurance function.

Ms. Sikdar has written two books; *Information Systems Audit & Security* and *Management Information Systems for Final C.A.* published by Lawpoint Publishers India. Besides, she writes articles and white papers on IS Audit and Business Continuity Planning as well as speaks at international conferences and ISACA local chapters. Her articles are carried in Indo-Swiss and Indo-U.S. magazines and she does a lot of online mentoring for students appearing for CISA and CISM examinations. Ms. Sikdar gives online consulting for U.S. and South Africa regions on third-party assurance, secure infrastructure building, writing of security policies and rolling out an information systems management system in line with ISO 27001 and ISO 22301 standards. As subject matter expert, she is consulted for complex IT audit and control assignments and she is involved in risk assessments and gap analysis for her clients in India. She is also Vice President of the Global Forum of Disaster Reduction.

Chapter 1

Understanding Organizational Context

Practitioners are versatile; they are conversant with a large number of organizations having varied technological environments, different management structures, and diverse geographical expanses. Business environment is increasingly becoming complex; new styles of business are emerging; and e-commerce is coming up in a big way that affects styles of managing business and marketing of products.

Conducting a business impact analysis (BIA) for an organization makes it imperative for a practitioner to understand the business and the manifold dependencies and relationships and to study the enterprise as an extended enterprise (Figure 1.1).

The Internet provides a good means of obtaining information about organizations, which includes news stories, articles, and financial data published by organizations. Increasing velocity of data makes mining of information really difficult!

Business environment is dynamic and is constantly evolving to realize benefits through optimizing the resources. Every organization aims at carrying on business perpetually and being able to serve its customers almost on a 24/7 basis. We live in customer-centric markets operating in different time zones, and it is critical to keep our systems up and running to meet the requirements of all stakeholders.

A preclude to *business impact analysis* is understanding the organizational context. Some of the trends impacting the business landscape include globalization, electronic commerce, enterprise resource planning, outsourcing business operations, and increasing legal and regulatory norms and crossborder laws for international businesses. In understanding the organizational context, it is important to consider external vendors, business partners, regulatory bodies, and customers as a part of "Extended Enterprise."

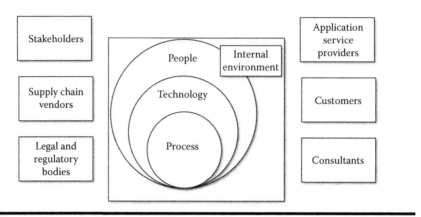

Figure 1.1   Extended enterprise.

Where to Begin?

When a practitioner gets introduced to a new organization for BIA, he or she will first exercise his or her energies in getting information about the business organization from industry publications, company web site, and published information to get a first-hand idea of the size, geographical expanse, and management of the organization.

Use of Work Breakdown Structure (WBS)

In large multinational organizations, there are multiple products and many diverse processes; some are linked and some are independent. The presence of huge workflows in different geographical and global locations makes the determination of the impact on these business processes indeed a challenge! Understanding business processes is important in studying the organizational context. Hence a *work breakdown structure* will be useful.

A *work breakdown structure* is a key project deliverable that organizes the team's *work* into manageable sections. It can be applied in breaking complex organizational structures into manageable sections and in studying complex processes (Figure 1.2).

A business continuity management process is considered as a project and will follow the same principles as followed under project management. The Project Management Body of Knowledge (PMBOK) defines the *work breakdown structure* as a "deliverable oriented hierarchical decomposition of the *work* to be executed by the project team."* In this process, complex business functions are broken down

---

* http://www.workbreakdownstructure.com/how-to-make-a-work-breakdown-structure.php.

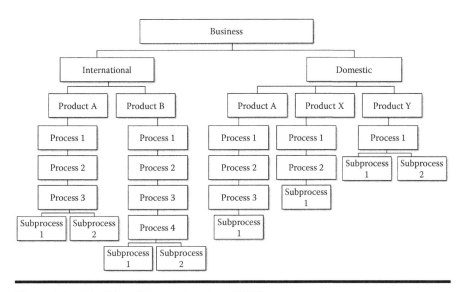

Figure 1.2 Work breakdown structure (WBS).

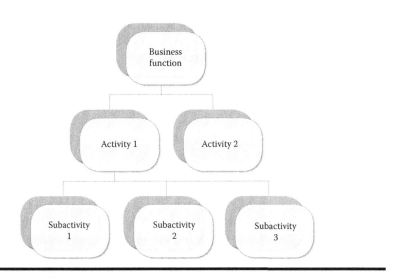

Figure 1.3 Factoring of processes.

into activities and subactivities in order to better comprehend each part and its relevant importance to the overall business function (Figure 1.3).

The culture and management philosophy gets reflected in the vision, mission, policies, and procedures adopted by the organization. *As-is* documentation is a big tool while attempting an organization-wide exercise. Our best assumption is that

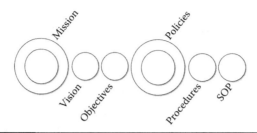

Figure 1.4 Understanding mission, vision, and policies.

we are doing the BIA at the behest of top management, and the intent of top management can be easily read in existing vision, mission, and policy documentation (Figure 1.4).

Generally, the objects clause present in the Memorandum of Association (company formation documents) of the company designates the boundary of business that may be conducted by the organization. Vision and mission statements throw light on the long-term proposed planning and management foresight in relation to the business. The team leader (TL) will be able to grasp the tone at the top and plan his or her activities accordingly.

A mission statement expresses the organization's purpose in a manner that solicits support and continuous commitment. It lays a basis to set the tone of the company and to outline its concrete goals.

Let us have a few examples of published mission/vision statements:

1. *Nike*: "To bring inspiration and innovation to every athlete in the world."
2. *Starbucks*: "To inspire and nurture the human spirit—one person, one cup, and one neighbourhood at a time."
3. *eBay*: "Provide a global trading platform where practically anyone can trade practically anything."
4. *Oxfam*: "A just world without poverty."

Vision statements on the other hand are short one liners that outline the primary goals of the company. When you go through the vision, mission, and objectives, it will answer a few vital questions:

1. What are the opportunities and needs that the organization wants to address?
2. What is the current business of the organization? Does it address the needs outlined in the mission statement? In the case of Starbucks, it is to have a coffee chain in every neighborhood.
3. How does the organization address change in the mission or vision as originally drafted?
4. What levels of service are being provided?

5. What are the underlying principles that guide the business? In the case of Nike, it is to cater to the needs of athletes. In case of Oxfam, a nonprofit-making organization, it is striving to fight poverty.

A statement should express the organization's purpose in a way that inspires support and ongoing commitment. It is up to the mission statement to set the tone of the company and to outline concrete goals. A good mission gives employees something to bind them together in terms of common goals and, at the same time, helps brand building to influence public perception of the enterprise.

The TL who initiates the business impact analysis determines whether the mission and vision are duly exhibited and communicated to all key stakeholders: management, staff, suppliers, partners, customers, and outsourced vendors. According to a recent study conducted by *Harvard Business Review*, up to 70% of employees do not understand their company's strategy. Communicating the mission/vision can serve to guide employees/executives in taking day-to-day decisions. A comparison chart shown in Table 1.1 depicts the significance of the mission and vision projected by the enterprise and throws light on why it is advantageous to start with examining them when performing a BIA.

Table 1.1 Queries on Vision-Mission Statements

Vision Statement	Questions Addressed by Vision Statement	Mission Statement	Questions Addressed by Mission Statement
Denotes purpose and value of business	Where do you want to be?	States primary objectives for customer needs and corporate values	How do you want to get where you want to be?
It is futuristic	It helps answer the question why you are working here	It talks of present leading to future, it can form the base for long-term planning	Where do we aspire to be say in the next five years?
It influences how the world views your organization, it is image building	It helps prospective customers to decide whether they will like to do business with you	It gives direction to middle management and employees to carry on day-to-day activities of business	Why do we do things? What for and for whom?

Policies are high-level statements; they are directive controls formulated by top management. Resultant procedures are an outline of boundaries, giving clear rules of authority and delegation of responsibility and accountability. For instance, a policy can be as follows: "The entire office area on first and second floors will remain a nonsmoking zone." Workplace policies deal with operational practices and ongoing management and administration. It removes doubts and misunderstanding in respect of work and provides transparency and consistency at work.

Organization may have different types of policies. It may include the following:

1. Code of conduct policy for employees
2. Communication policy
3. Health and safety policy
4. Staff recruitment policy
5. Termination of employment policy
6. Nondisclosure policy, which may include employees signing a Nondisclosure Agreement (NDA) at the time of joining the organization
7. IT security policy, e-mail policy, social media policy, and so on

Please note the above is not a comprehensive list. Organizations may make policies for the following two reasons:

1. Necessitated by legislative or regulatory requirement. For instance, in many countries, BCM is mandated by regulators, and hence organizations need to have the BCM policy and procedures in place.
2. Policies for running the administration of the company and forming a framework for business planning.

Policy is a top-down control, and all procedures in line with these policies will be strictly adhered to and will be interwoven into the work culture of the organization. TL should determine that the policies and procedures are clear and concise and are actually communicated to appropriate recipients either through e-mail, through posters, or through the intranet of the company.

A well-documented set of policies and procedures serves as a good assurance tool to determine compliance and assess performance. Benefits from initial reference to policies and procedures are that the uniformity in organizational procedures is made visible, and it serves as a benchmark to check compliance to organizational values and legislation.

The TL has to ascertain that policies deal with ongoing management and administration, and it should

- Be clear and concise.
- Be communicated to all employees.
- Delineate clear responsibilities for tasks.

- Indicate the means of solving new problems.
- Give framework for business planning.

Illustration: During audit of a hotel chain, it was discovered that branch outlets were stacking old machines without scrapping them. When the site manager was questioned, it was learned that he or she was not aware of the procedure and of the person to whom he or she was supposed to escalate this matter. The impact was that there was a cost of storage of nonfunctional assets as well as the burden of insuring those assets. These factors had been overlooked.

Look for *SOPs* (*Standard Operating Procedures*): As policies are high-level statements and hence crisp and short, a set of operating procedures can be developed that delineates how to follow the policy by giving end-to-end procedures for each business process. These are referred to as standard operating procedures (SOPs) and give a clear indication of the origin and the end of the procedure and the authorities for approving and validating the respective procedures. TL should ask for SOPs if the organization has them, and this will help them study the end-to-end flow of operations. Use of data flow diagrams (DFDs) will save a lot of time in the study of organizational processes.

A *point to note* for the TL here is that many times, the team for operational excellence/quality assurance within the organization is already maintaining DFDs of processes for monitoring performance because they must adhere to prespecified turnaround times (TATs), and obtaining a copy of these documents for reference will save a lot of time and will stop the TL from reinventing the wheel! In the absence of documented SOPs, a TL can use DFDs to document processes from end to end. DFD can be drawn using any one or combination of the symbols shown in Figures 1.5 and 1.6.

But in reality, modern organizational processes are complex, diverse, interlinked, and wearing a global cap. People working with long workflows themselves have little knowledge of the start–finish of the processes of which they are also a part. Business process workflows may originate from the entry at an outsourced vendor's installation through different locations and then may join the organizational

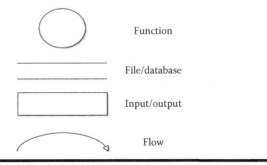

Figure 1.5   DFD symbols.

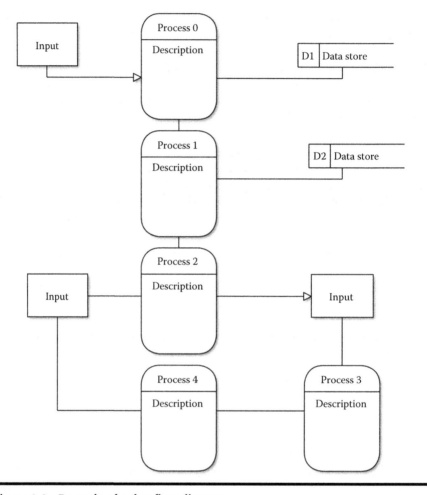

Figure 1.6 Example of a dataflow diagram.

network to complete a task. Hence procedure documentation may be a difficult task involving intrabusiness and intradepartmental interchange of information in order to complete the task.

Understanding of Organization Structure

Every organization has its unique structure, and it is important that the TL delves into the structure and get to the "who-is-who" of the organization. This helps determine the authority–responsibility relationships and understand the span of control. It will further help identify the people whom you want to interview during the BIA exercise. Basically an organization structure is a hierarchy of people and its functions.

Business continuity is organization wide; it has to be embedded into the culture and practiced continuously. Hence it is imperative for a practitioner to understand organizational structure since it will help him or her to study the values and bonding within the organization. It is possible that a big and diversified organization may have different structures for different lines of business or different products, and this diversity has to be understood in the beginning of the project.

Types of Organizational Structures

1. *Flat organizational structure*: In many small organizations (generally 20 employees or less), a flat structure with a few levels of management exists; executives, analysts, secretaries, and lower level employees are in close coordination with management. It facilitates quick decision making (Figure 1.7).
2. *Bureaucratic structures*: In well-organized organizations that are sizable, a bureaucratic structure may exist. The characteristics of such an organization are
   a. The use of standard methods and procedures for performing work.
   b. A high degree of control to ensure standard performance.
   c. Existence of tall structure or hierarchies (Figure 1.8).
   They maintain strict hierarchies of positions and form a tall structure. Bureaucratic organizations tend to be slightly standardized, and the postbureaucratic structures reflect some flexibility and modern ideas and methodologies. It may introduce a total quality management (TQM) system within it.
3. *Functional structure*: This is based on job functions such as marketing, research and development, and finance (Figure 1.9).
   Small companies should use a functional organization when they want to arrange their organizational structure by department. For example, a small company may have a director, two managers, and two analysts in the marketing department. The director would likely report to the chief executive officer (CEO), and both managers would report to the director. In addition, each manager may have an analyst reporting to him or her. A functional organizational structure works well when small companies are heavily project focused. Directors can assign certain projects to managers, who can then divide tasks with their analysts. The department can then more effectively meet their project deadlines.

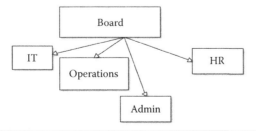

Figure 1.7   Flat organization structure.

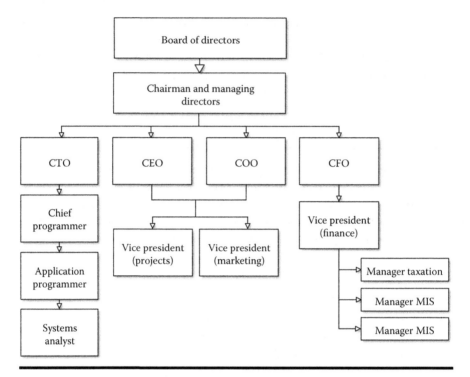

Figure 1.8   Bureaucratic structure.

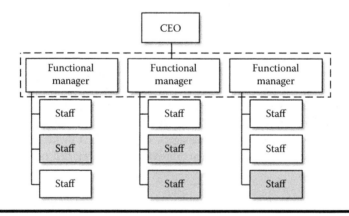

Figure 1.9   Functional structure.

4. *Divisional structure*: This is generally used in large organizations that are widespread over geographical locations having different types of products or market areas. To illustrate, an engineering company can have a projects division, a products division, and many subdepartments within each division. Again, each division may have a domestic business and international

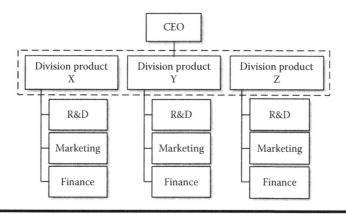

Figure 1.10 Divisional structure.

business. The advantage is the ease of administration, but employees do not interact between divisions, and sometimes the optimum use of resources cannot be made (Figure 1.10).

A disadvantage of divisional structure is that it is costly because of its size and scope. Small businesses can use a divisional structure on a smaller scale, having different offices in different parts of the city, for example, or assigning different sales teams to handle different geographic areas. Divisions can be formed on geographical basis, product/service line basis, or on any other criterion deemed fit by the management.

5. *Matrix organization*: A *matrix organizational structure* is a company structure in which the reporting relationships are set up as a grid, or matrix, rather than in the traditional hierarchy. In other words, employees have dual reporting relationships—generally to both a functional manager and a product manager. It is a hybrid of functional and divisional structures. In a team-based architecture, teams are based on functions or projects. The matrix organizational structure divides authority both by function and by project.

In a matrix structure, each employee reports to two immediate supervisors: one functionally and another administratively. The best talent required from each division is sought for the purpose of working on projects with common objectives. An advantage is the deployment of optimum resources from within the organization to work on organizational projects (Figure 1.11).

In a BIA, it is necessary to understand the current organization structure. It will make administering BIA and collecting information from each section simpler. One thing to note would be that interdependencies exist in every organization. Any part of the organization needs other parts in order to function smoothly.

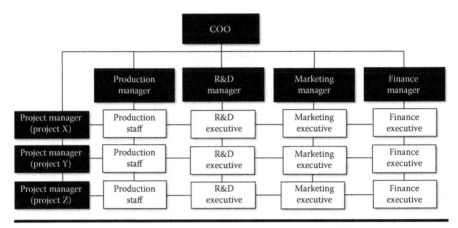

Figure 1.11 Matrix organization.

Understanding the People Culture

Associated with every organization structure are the people who fill those structures. A practitioner's experience of people in different organizations they visit is varied. There is one lot that is not so knowledgeable but that respects the practitioner's subject expertise and is willing to learn. There is one lot that is indifferent and does not want to go beyond its normal duties. There is one section who readily answers your queries and another section that is tight lipped and does not reveal much. Amid all these different mind-sets, a practitioner has to conduct an organization-wide exercise.

A first assessment of culture and a few handshakes will make him or her ready for what lies ahead; it will help him or her frame approach roads and methodology for using his further steps. Knowledge of *who-is-who* matrix sets the stage for persons to contact during the BIA, and it saves on time by enabling prescheduling of meetings and interviews or for circulation of a questionnaire.

Understanding the IT Infrastructure of the Organization

Information technology is all pervasive and penetrates each and every segment of the organization. The rapid pace of business and technology changes coupled with increasing performance expectations from customers, employees, and management applies constant pressure on IT infrastructures and supporting teams to provide around-the-clock availability and to minimize planned and unplanned disruptions. Enterprises are now adopting technologies that enable high-availability systems, real-time communications, and faster recovery times while minimizing IT cost. Technology is a dynamic function in every organization.

Information technology can be broadly divided into the following:

1. IT infrastructure
2. IT applications

IT infrastructure is in the form of the hardware, telecommunications, and other infrastructure necessary to house information assets of the organization, and this should be flexible to accommodate growth and expansion of the organization. A customized IT control infrastructure fulfills the following objectives:

1. Internal control
2. Business continuity needs
3. Compliance to best practices/standards
4. Scope for self-assessments and continuous improvement
5. Reduction in security incidents/downtime/disruptions
6. Release of resources for productive business purposes
7. Ease of audits

A clear understanding of IT infrastructure is as important as understanding the business that the organization is into. IT is an enabler, a service department within the business environment. Every organization has an IT profile with a blend of IT infrastructure, services, and applications that govern the day-to-day business of the organization. Assessing IT infrastructure at the onset facilitates planning for ITDR at a later stage.

As a practitioner, a round with IT generally involves a probe into the following areas:

1. Hardware infrastructure and viewing where the information assets are placed (the network diagram, Figure 1.12).
2. Applications used by different departments and sections and utilities deployed to ease operations.
3. Location of data center and server rooms, UPS, storage of backups, and whether there exists a process for offsite or online transfer of data to backup site, if any.
4. Existence of program development within the organization and segregation of environments.
5. Modes for telecommunication and connectivity including remote connectivity to enterprise systems.

Increasing demands on storage, data protection, processing priorities, and reporting have brought in applications of emerging technologies (virtualization, cloud computing, mobile devices, and social networks) that have introduced new challenges, risk, and opportunities that must be either addressed or exploited.

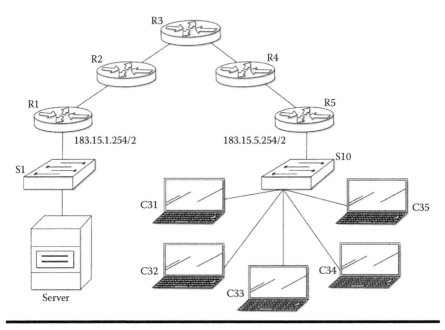

Figure 1.12 Illustrative network diagram.

Advances in telecommunications, user-friendly technology, improved data storage solutions, cost-effective virtualized environments, and cloud computing are enabling enterprises to increase data storage capabilities, to become agile, and to improve business resilience. They can also be mobilized to serve the business continuity objectives of an organization. Technology can provide a vehicle for channelizing business at alternate locations. Mobile devices and social networks can provide channels for communication in a crisis. There is always a need to interact and collaborate with customers, suppliers, employees, government agencies, and peers during a business disruption.

To adapt and respond to such demands under both normal and adverse conditions, the enterprise is incorporating robust technology that supports policies and procedures and recovery solutions that are tested periodically as part of the BCM program. IT as an enabler has to support complex business relationships, multifarious products, and diverse business interests that change as per opportunities and have a heavy pressure on the IT infrastructure and applications to give support and timely modification.

IT applications that run the business, the application development process, where they are maintained from, change management process, compatibility with other applications, computing environment, and all other associated factors have to be considered in order to ascertain the accuracy, reliability, and authenticity of the information systems existing in the organization.

Data storage facilities are revolutionized, and data vaulting, backup to disk, deduplication, and so on are used for backup and data controls. Advances in telecommunication and lowering of cost of facilities that enable higher bandwidth have enabled organizations to increase data storage and replication. This gives the disaster recovery a boost by electronically replicating data and programs offsite.

Capability to access enterprise resources using laptops, tablets, and smart phones represents a significant advantage for employees who cannot travel to the physical location of the enterprise; use of VPN is rampant. It has led to saving in space and computing resources by advocating a *work from home* culture.

TL has to understand how the organization is enhancing its resilience by using server virtualization and cloud computing and moving applications to temporary environments during planned outages or system maintenance. Planning for business continuity is planning for disaster recovery. IT plays a pivotal role in providing for resources and alternate processing facilities in the form of ITDR.

ITDR requires immense resources, and, in order to achieve resource optimization, it will do good to identify existing resources that can be channelized toward ITDR activities. A simple VPN and work from home facility granted to your executives can be a business continuity arrangement already tested and already live! In an era of strict budgetary constraints, looking at utilization of existing resources is always advantageous.

Study the Geographical Dispersion of Business

Whenever we visit an organization for any type of consultancy/internal audit/other work, it is important to note the total expanse of business. Today organizations have gone global, with one leg in one continent and other leg in anther continent. In this case, scoping of work becomes difficult. It may not be possible to visit all locations or countries. Although it is excluded from scope, responsibility from identification of risks to business arising from interdependencies existing between locations cannot be absolved (Figure 1.13).

To illustrate, during one such BIA exercise, it was discovered that some of the applications used by the organization were controlled from an overseas location. On probing, it was discovered that the overseas location had no provision for IT DR, and hence there was a reverse risk that the organization faced; in the event of overseas location being down, the current location of the organization would be down till the overseas location was restored.

Transborder laws are applicable for the transfer of data from one country to another. Privacy laws are different, and there is no standard or global cyber law. The risk of breach of information security exists in the absence of controls, and hence understanding the laws governing all related locations is significant in the BIA exercise.

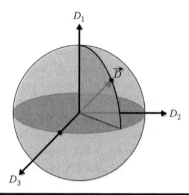

Figure 1.13 Business dispersion across the globe.

Understanding Applicable Compliance Requirements of the Organization

Listing of applicable global regulations, mandatory standards, and business specific regulations stipulated by regulators of the industry will serve the practitioner to cover the legal and regulatory risks faced by the organization. Information on the same can be gathered on the initial meetings and discussions with the client and confirmed by checking on the official web sites of the regulatory bodies.

Understanding Third-Party Service Providers

As part of the extended enterprise, third-party service providers hold organizational dependencies, and hence it will be beneficial for the practitioner to look at service level agreements (SLAs) to check whether it contains a "right to audit clause," which empowers the client organization to conduct an audit of the physical security and continuity arrangements at the provider's installation to ensure the continued service from the provider even during a disaster or outage. Alternatively, receiving third-party audit independent reports, SSAE 16 audit or ISAE 3402, regularly will be the evidence of controls exercised at the provider's installation.

Most common services outsourced are data center, payroll processing, data entry operators, and so on. The importance of each activity covered and the impact on nonreceipt of services from each such provider during a disaster need to be assessed, and hence preparation of a department-wise chart will ease out the BIA process. In the illustration in Table 1.2, the payroll-processing service is significant as employees' morale is at stake, and furthermore many employees may have to pay off their monthly installments on housing loans, car loans, and so on.

Table 1.2   Querying for Third-Party Services Provider

Name of Service Provider	Department(s) Utilizing the Service	Nature of Service	Periodicity of Service	SLA Contains "Right to Audit Clause?"	Provider has ITDR in Place?	Is Service Considered to be Vital for Organizational Continuity?
Ascon payroll services	HR/admin	Payroll processing	Monthly	Yes	Yes	Yes

Refer to Audit Reports

In the present context, an organization undergoes manifold audits: some are mandated by regulators, some by management, and some others by vendors. A quick look at the content or qualifying content can be useful for understanding the controls and the way of working of the organization.

1. *Internal audit*: The internal audit function takes care of all mandatory standards, implementation, and audits that go on almost throughout the year. A risk-based approach to audit is beneficial in identifying control gaps and remedial measures to remove these control gaps. But even an internal audit team working within the organization has to understand different functions, business units, people, and so on in order to carry out the relevant audits effectively. These audit reports help practitioners to make a first overview of operational risks and regulatory noncompliance issues faced by the organization.

    Understanding which sector the business falls is important to determine regulatory and compliance to standards and procedures as Policy and Procedures manual will also help determine rules and internal compliances. Sometimes it will pay to look at the existing documentation; for instance, at one place I found that business had a business excellence division where it had data flow diagrams of individual processes along with turnaround times (TATs), and this document can be used to determine the RTOs and list critical processes.

2. *Management audits*: For management audits, the focus is more on the planning process and people process. At the onset, planning process involves setting of vision, mission, policies, and procedures. Auditors look at Policy Manual, Standard Operating Procedures manual, and other documents existing with the client and make a document review, which will assist them in further business impact analysis exercise.

    The existence of policy documents and mission statements that express management philosophy must be coupled with employees being aware of mission, vision, policies, and procedures and having an understanding of their roles and responsibilities in the organizational setup. This can be witnessed by the inclusion of a presentation in the induction procedure and a sign off from individual employees, who after reading and understanding the documents have an undertaking to abide by them.

    TL can assess job descriptions and supporting documents that relate to management communication and documentation of key result areas (KRAs) to understand the spread of the organization and the segregation of duties.

3. *Operational audits*: Auditors will assess revenue streams, inventory details, quality stipulations, and turnaround time (TAT), inspection reports, third-party suppliers, third-party assurance (SSAE 16) reports, list of alternate suppliers in case of emergency, and so on. Auditors cover the procurement process, production process, distribution process, trading module, sales process, advertising, promotion processes, and so on. TL doing a BIA needs to read industry publications, economic, regulatory environment, business trends, benchmark competitor products, and study standards set by the organization for operational excellence.

4. *Financial auditors*: Financial auditors have assurance agenda over financial statements, budgets, cost variations, MIS, pay outs and income, and the factors that impact the profitability of the organization. Elements to be assessed include the following:
   – Bookkeeping
   – Costing
   – Budgeting
   – Loans
   – Financial analysis

5. *Technology auditors*: This is emerging as an important field as technology is entwined into the fabric of every organization wherefrom it serves as a chief enabler to business and acts as a chief channel for communication and integration among all business units. The major areas to see comprise
   a. Chief applications that help run business.
   b. IT general controls that protect the applications.
   c. Interfaces and utilities used by the people.
   d. Network architecture and firewalls, IDS, and so on.

Compliance is an important business function and auditor to enlist the compliances required to be met by the organization and all supporting documentation, recent management assertions, and audit reports. Before initiating a BIA, it helps to get the audit points that may have bearing on the criticality analysis and the gaps to be identified in an attempt to treat risks that the organization faces.

Understanding the organizational context in terms of internal and external dependencies and listing down the vendors, suppliers, and service providers associated with the organization lay a foundation for conducting the business impact analysis. A fair idea of business and the organization structure will help further activities in the process. Viewing the organization in extended form helps perform a comprehensive analysis of recovery objectives.

Information is the key to success in almost all fields, so doing proper groundwork, exploring external sources such as industry publications, trade journals, and annual reports, and gaining knowledge on the organization and the business conducted by the organization are essential steps in initiating the BIA exercise. The Federal Financial Institutions Examination Council (FFIEC) has said that "the institution's first step in building a business continuity plan (BCP) is to perform a BIA."* To get the BIA right, we need to get our facts right! Authenticity of information is gained in its source and the effort that has gone in building up the information. In addition, well begun is half done; a good BIA results when the practitioner has a fair understanding of the organization and its complexity in terms of people, process, and technology.

---

* D. J. Cougias, *Federal Financial Institutions Examination Council (FFIEC) Information Technology (IT) Examination Handbook* series.

Chapter 2

Business Impact Analysis

Introduction to Business Impact Analysis (BIA)

In Chapter 1, "Understanding Organizational Context," practitioners have understood the business of the client, their organizational structure, their geographical boundaries, and the internal/external people with whom the organization is associated. Performing a business impact analysis involves going a step further in ascertaining what impact the risks can have on the sustained availability of the business! To begin with, let us have a look at some of the definitions of BIA.

Definitions

Business impact analysis can be defined as the process of studying and analyzing business functions so as to study the effect that these disruptions have on them. Consequences of a disruption can include financial loss, reputational loss, and loss of competitive position; these are in addition to the potential loss of staff, loss of data, and even loss of access to buildings.

Gartner defines business impact analysis (BIA) as a process that identifies and evaluates the potential effects (financial, life and safety, regulatory, legal and contractual, reputation, and so forth) of natural and man-made events on business operations (Gartner IT Glossary[*]).

BIA can be best described as a process that examines business processes, identifies critical processes, takes stock of all interdependencies internal or external, lists down stakeholder requirements, and identifies areas of high risk by adopting techniques of data gathering and data analysis in order to study

---

[*] Gartner IT Glossary, Business Impact Analysis, http://www.gartner.com/it-glossary/bia-business-impact-analysis.

the probable impact of natural or man-made adverse incidents on the smooth running of the business.

The key considerations in a BIA are as follows:

1. What are the key service objectives of the organization?
2. What resources (products or services) will be required to meet these objectives? (Deliverables)
3. How to achieve organizational objectives? (Activities)
4. Who needs to be engaged (internal and external entities) in the performance of organizational entities?
5. Time frame within which the activities that go toward the fulfilment of organizational objectives should be performed?

Top Management Commitment

A business impact analysis may be used for multiple purposes, but it is always undertaken at the behest of top management. An effective BCM is driven from the top of the organization, which is fully endorsed and actively promoted by the Board or Executive Committee. The overall accountability of building a business continuity management system commensurate to the size, location, nature of business, and complexity of organizational business lies with the board, although it may be administered at the organizational and operational levels.

The way resilience is viewed in an organization depends to a large extent on the style of organizational governance and the level of awareness among its employees. Even when an outside consultant steps in for conducting a BIA, he or she faces the following challenges:

■ Lack of a framework or policy for conducting a business impact analysis
■ Lack of formal BIA procedures
■ Lack of risk acceptance as a process
■ Lack of organizational responsibility in respect of business resilience

In these conditions, it becomes extremely important to incorporate the BIA into the culture of the organization. BIA is an effective tool that is used in many disciplines. BIA can be used in governance for management, monitoring, and oversight for internal audit and for gap analysis and compliance checking as a part of external audit. Business impact is an area of interest for all the above three functions, and hence there is commonality of objectives in carrying out a business impact analysis in the following areas (Table 2.1):

1. Enterprise risk management
2. Business continuity management
3. Third-party risk management

Table 2.1 Commonality of Objectives

Enterprise Risk Management (ERM)	Business Service Continuity	Third-Party Assessments
BIA emphasis on operational risks-identifying risks and gap analysis	BIA for identifying critical processes, upstream and downstream dependencies and judging severity against time criticality	BIA to inventory critical third-party service providers involved in provision of services to critical functions.
Business process focussed	Purpose is to plan for incident escalation	All main suppliers of goods for conducting critical business processes to be listed.
Operational risk mitigation	It aids in estimating resource requirements	SLAs to be examined to check right to audit clause is present.
Regulatory and standards integration	Business resumption strategies	Arrange visits to third-party or arrange conference calls to discuss their business continuity arrangements.
Resilience and continuity solutions	Testing and awareness	Obtain confidence on continuity of third-party vendors by visiting installation or in some cases obtaining a copy of SSAE 16 reports.

An integrated approach is to incorporate

- Better process prioritization.
- More effective risk mitigation techniques.
- More efficient investment in risk management.

It is recommended to build a cross-functional core team and define other extended teams who will participate in business continuity activities. As a prework exercise, it will do good to organize different tools, training, and a BIA implementation plan before initiating a BIA exercise.

For a more elaborate discussion and illustration on BIA for other standards and applications, refer to Chapter 8.

Geographical Scope of a BIA

In a highly-dispersed organization with offices all around the country and also over-seas offices, the BIA scope needs to be well defined. The following considerations hold true for the following:

1. The whole organization where various overseas locations and national offices are highly interdependent.
2. Homogenous units where the composition of offices is similar in function and spread.

You can even circulate a sheet to collect BIA information.

The most important consideration here is the management intent, which determines whether the BCM function is to be centralized or kept decentralized with regular exchanges of reports.

BCM and incident response strategies will be in line with the management intent and will make practitioner's task easier by predefining it in scope. But sometimes, the inability to visit outstation installations may pose difficulties as data collection from that installation may not be accurately performed or may remain inadequate to justify the BIA of the enterprise.

Let us look at the chief objectives of a BIA:

1. Examine business processes and functions, assess the impact on business, and calculate the financial impact for each based on a worst-case scenario.
2. Estimate intangible operational impacts for each process or function.
3. Define the necessary resources that will be required for recovery of these processes or functions.
4. Identify the organization's need to recover critical processes and functions over a defined time frame and to build an appropriate business case for providing resources from the top management.

Note: BIA does not assess the risks that could negatively impact the business func-tions; a risk assessment (RA) needs to be conducted before completing a BIA.

Once you step into the initiation stage, you have to treat the BIA as a project management and divide it into manageable phases with preassigned time frame and estimated deliverables (Figure 2.1). A practitioner will get clarity on a few things as follows:

What it is we are trying to achieve?

The *answer* is we are trying to ascertain critical business processes, give them severity levels based on time criticality, and rank them in the order of impor-tance. In doing so, whom we have to deal with? What is our geographical coverage as per scope?

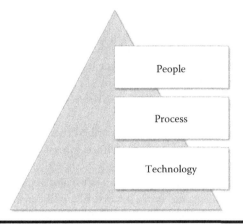

Figure 2.1 Components of business.

What components of business shall we focus on?

The *answer* is that we shall focus on the three main components of business such as people, process, and technology. We need to interact with business functions, involve people in our activities, get input from them, and, above all, we need to perform critical business functions during an outage. Technology is a major role player in planning the disaster recovery plan (ITDR). Once our areas of focus are delineated, our BIA can be planned accordingly.

How do we carry out the BIA?

The *answer* is that we shall *customize* the BIA according to the business, scope, mission, and values of the people, so as to achieve accurate deliverables that can form a part of the management report to obtain management commitment on necessary resources to build the business continuity management system in the organization.

BIA will be performed in the following three phases:

■ Data collection
■ Data analysis
■ BIA report

As per our understanding, business continuity is an organization-wide exercise, and it is undertaken by top management. It has also to be understood that management is instigated to give the mandate since BIA is mandated or requisitioned by other entities such as

1. Regulator.
2. Shareholder.
3. Auditors.
4. Customers.

Our main deliverable at this stage would be a detailed BIA report along with the risk assessment working jotting the criticality, time severity, and resource requirement list for the recovery to the management in the form of a PowerPoint Presentation or Word Document. Based on this report, the top management will take a decision on budget for recovery, commitment of people, IT, and other resources for building the BCMS for the organization. BIA helps to drive informed and better investment decisions.

A point to note is that there is no prescribed methodology for conducting it apart from best practices, and there is no defined format for reporting. But we shall develop formats for different purposes to help us smoothen our task.

Business resilience is a subject of almost all major regulators in the financial services, banking insurance, and other sectors. BIA will continue to hold a place of importance. So let us minutely study the different aspects of BIA with its alternate approaches and customize it to a few major industries to illustrate better and to make a realistic business case.

Data Gathering for the Business Impact Analysis

Data collection for conducting a BIA will include all activities necessary to study and document the following:

- The business functions performed by an organization
- The resources required to support each business function performed
- Interdependencies between business functions (the information flow)
- The impact(s) of not performing a specific business function
- The criticality of each process
- A recovery time objective (RTO) for each business function
- A recovery point objective (RPO) for the data that support each business function

Once we understand what we want to collect, we shall go into how to collect data/information for BIA.

Treat BIA as a (mini) project: Define the person's responsible for BIA (facilitator) implementation and his or her authority. A BIA facilitator must have a pleasant personality and excellent communication skills. He or she should have convincing skills to explain his or her concept and get buy-in from his or her audience. Further he or she should follow project management techniques, should have defined deliverables, and should follow preset timelines.

Conduct a control self-assessment (CSA): In organizations where a level of awareness and understanding of BIA requirements exists, a control self-assessment (CSA) can be conducted before the BIA as a preparedness measure. The objective of the

CSA is to get managers at the shop floor level to participate and identify key business processes. It is meant to cover the following areas:

- Vital records and documents
- Resources and equipment
- Physical access to facility
- Skills and knowledge required to run processes
- Stakeholders
- Legal and regulatory obligations to be met if business interrupts

The BIA facilitator can participate as an observer to get an insight into current risks and control lacuna pointed by the operations staff. Alternatively, a standard questionnaire can be circulated to all line staff, and results can be collated to feed into the BIA information.

In many organizations, the level of awareness of business continuity and concept of BIA is low. Hence employees have to be educated on this topic before we can obtain effective results in our BIA collection exercise. In such cases, we have started weekly training and awareness programs at this stage itself to increase the interaction with people and trigger favourable response from them.

As a practitioner, penetrating an enterprise information system, the primary component is going to be access. Access to the following resources will be needed:

1. Data and documents
2. Application system documents
3. Facilities

This can be enabled by issue of *entry passes* for physical access to the installations in scope and temporary *User ID/password* to access system and applications where necessary.

BIA project for a practitioner is also time critical. His choice of people and source of information have to be appropriate. For instance, it is possible to browse enterprise *web site* to ascertain the nature of business; the *vision, mission, and goals* of the enterprise; and also the *geographical expanse* of business; it will take only a *kickoff meeting* to meet the personnel connected to the BIA and the persons who are going to be a "Single Points of Contact" (SPOCs) in the BCM project. Also the geographical extent to be covered within the country and visit to overseas office can only be ascertained at the time of initial discussions with management.

Management philosophy can best be gauged by reading of *policies and procedures*. In some places, the business excellence cell has maintained a *Standard Operating Procedures* document, which contains data flow diagrams of processes, and if these are made available, it will make comprehending processes from end to end easier. There is no need to reinvent the wheel!

Everybody knows the methods of collection of data/information; the real expertise of a practitioner lies in the choice of methods used for collection of data as customized to the needs of the enterprise. Methods/techniques should be linked to purpose and objective. For instance, when you ask for the *organization chart* to find out "who is who" in the organization.

The success of a business impact analysis is in the effectiveness of its data gathering exercise. Although it is easy to collect information from various sources, it is important to consider the appropriateness of the source of information from where it is solicited from. Source of information for BIA can be from

1. Top management.
2. PR/external agencies.
3. Finance.
4. Marketing.
5. Insurance.
6. Others.

Again, choice of source depends on type of data to be collected as follows:

1. *Primary data*, which are collected by the data collector from various sources. These may be done through questionnaires, interviews, focus groups, and observation.
2. *Secondary data* are the data that are available. It includes data maintained by hospitals, health departments, public databases, Federal Agencies, and so on. It will also, include the "as-is" documents such as organizational charts, policies, procedures manual, and so on.

All data collection methodologies are dependent on credibility accorded to data collected. An objective way of data collection is preferred over a subjective process since the latter may contain personal bias.

Some Golden Rules for Data Collection for BIA

- Invite as many people from each department to participate and give their opinion to practitioner during initiation of the assignment.
- Participation from business and IT is advisable since each will play a role in the BCM function of the enterprise.
- Keep the facilitator to be a good communicator who can keep the atmosphere light, reach out to the quietest and indifferent person, and spark an interest in the crowd toward the BIA initiative.
- Consistent approach for sessions with various segments will give standardized results, which can be comparable, and will give the participants a similar frame of reference for future discussions.

Note: BIA focuses on processes and not procedures. It interrogates different functions for what they do, not how they do it.

A BIA facilitator may consider triangulation techniques to give more credibility to his or her data collection.

Triangulation techniques involve collection of the same information through different methods and validating. For instance, you may include geographical expanse in questionnaire, and you may like to confirm when you are interviewing the executive. This is a good way for validating data.

Triangulation techniques are of two types:

1. *Triangulation of sources*: This involves gathering information from different sources. You may have collected a piece of information from web site that you may like to confirm during interview with concerned department.
2. *Triangulation of evaluations*: It involves more than one person gathering the same information to confirm it. Use of triangulation techniques serve as a cross check to validate information collected during a BIA exercise. Getting the organization into the BCM culture right at the onset is going to create an atmosphere of acceptability for the practitioner. We have even ventured into installing a BCM Suggestions Box at strategic location and weekly gifts to the employees contributing constructive suggestions. This makes BIA interactive and a collective process.

Since data and information gathered by BIA will be referred for further stages in the BCM exercise, the authenticity of data is extremely important. BIA practitioner may consider use of triangulation techniques.

Key Deliverables from Data Collection for BIA

- Identification of all critical assets of the enterprise.
- Identification of all critical business processes.
- Identification of time within which critical processes have to be recovered for maintaining continuity of operations.
- Mapping of all IT resources that are deployed and all applications running on enterprise systems.
- Identifying the recovery point objective (the time to which transactions or data must be recovered).
- Identifying vital materials and records necessary for recovery or continuance.
- Identifying the organization's risk appetite.
- Listing of all threats and mapping impacts to enterprise either qualitative or quantitative.
- Identifying the financial and nonfinancial costs.

The criteria for data collection will be based on situation and context. Let us have a look at some common means of data gathering.

Observation

Every organization has a work culture and a lot of things can be gathered merely by observing people at work. It is believed that observation is the best audit tool! How can we use this technique in a BIA? Much of BIA and RA are dependent on researcher's instinct and capacity to gather information through use of senses. It is critical to have credible information, so careful consideration must be given to who is doing the observation.

BIA facilitator can use any of the following techniques to observe business processes and culture:

a. *Covert collector*: Here the observer keeps himself or herself under cover and knows what he or she wants and carries on his or her work secretly. We are familiar with concept of *mystery shopper, mystery customer* in a restaurant that management utilizes to assess level of service given by staff. For instance, overhearing employee conversations during lunch hour can give input on level of confidence they have for management. Observing discipline level and enterprise attitude toward policy compliance is possible using this technique.

b. *Nonparticipant collector* is not a part of the team but is merely an observer and notes his observations, which feed into the data used for BIA. For instance, a facilitator may be an observer in a table top exercise that enterprise is currently running to get an insight into level of BCM knowledge among the participants of the exercise (Figure 2.2).

Apart from these, it is possible to use observation technique to observe the following:

i. Data traffic patterns
ii. Performance of business process
iii. Human behavior for culture
iv. Technology infrastructure

Advantages of observation technique are:

■ This technique can be used for first-hand information; it is not retrospective.
■ Nature of products or services make observation more meaningful.
■ It can be used to estimate the culture and BCM awareness.

Figure 2.2   Study of existing business processes.

Limitations of observation technique are:

- Observer bias.
- Selected sample is unrepresentative.
- Respondents do not give favorable response to this technique.
- It requires more resources to conduct this technique.

Surveying

Surveying is the most popular technique of collecting information from individuals through *questionnaire*. It can be used effectively to obtain information from sites not visited by the BCM facilitator either domestically or from overseas offices.

The questionnaire should be clear, concise, easy to understand, and fast to fill out. It is also important to explain the purpose of the questionnaire to the participants in order to procure a buy-in for the BIA process.

BIA questionnaires must be carefully designed to ask the right questions and be easily understood and must not open to wide variances in interpretation. If there is a markets cell within the client organization that develops market surveys or questionnaires, they may be approached to vet the questionnaire before circulating it. It is advisable to collectively improvise the document before circulation to get maximum results.

The questionnaires can be distributed by e-mail or requested on web sites. It is a good practice to hold a kick off meeting/conference call to introduce a questionnaire, to explain its significance to respondents, and to give guidance on how to fill it.

Illustration:

BIA Questionnaire for XYZ Corporation Inc.

………………….. Department   Location…….…………….

Name of HOD……………….……   Date: mm/dd/yy

Business process	What are the key IT resources needed?	Who are the key people needed?	What are the key support services needed?	RTO	RPO	Any turnaround procedures?
Activity 1	2 laptops, 1 server, 1 printer	2 people during critical period	HR-to get contract people	24 hours	30-minutes data backup	No
Activity 2	1 laptop, 1 printer, server, application "endure"	1 person during time of outage	HR, admin, IT	24 hours	40-minutes data backup	No

Advantages of surveying technique:

- It can lead to generation of standardized qualitative and comparable data from many of respondents.
- Questionnaires can be effectively utilized to get data from subject matter experts (SMEs) within the enterprise who otherwise have little time to contribute toward the BCM initiative. It enables them to fill out the questionnaires regarding their business units, business functions, and business processes at a time that are convenient for them (within a specified time frame), thereby giving consistent, focused, and concise information for analysis.
- A well-structured questionnaire will save you a lot of time and will lead to more accurate response from participants. It is also a good practice to use both qualitative and quantitative questions to identify impacts.

Limitations of questionnaires are as follows:

- Employees cannot be easily motivated to take time out of their schedule to fill up questionnaires.
- Level of respondents is not known, which is based on varying education levels and sometimes may not give correct response.
- Follow-up may be a challenge if one has to go back and verify something. This may be problem if the questionnaires have been filled by participants from outstation or overseas office.

Questionnaires have to have a signoff feature at the end so that it is authenticated by the person filling it. This brings in a sense of responsibility and gives credibility to the information collected by it. Facilitator has to ensure that a completeness check on the document is performed by person collecting it so that data from all centres are consistent, and collation of data becomes easy for the purpose of BIA analysis.

Note: It is not right to put complete reliance on information collected from surveys alone, and face-to-face interviews can be scheduled to obtain a more objective insight into specific areas.

Focus Groups: A focus group survey is a method wherein the respondents are put in a single group and interviewed in an interactive manner. The participants in a focus group are given the opportunity to freely talk about and discuss their ideas and opinions toward the object of the survey.

Focus groups can also be conducted over a telephonic network or made online on web network. There are certain free video providers that help connecting to respondents over a geographical distance. Here the interviewer serves as a moderator, and he or she has the responsibility to control and steer the discussion.

To get maximum results from group sessions, it is necessary to

1. *Involve as many people as possible*: Get everyone from each department to participate, including every function. Encourage all to contribute their opinions. This will give each person a sense of ownership and commitment and will allow you to tease out more complete information.
2. *Include both business people and IT people*: These two groups must communicate to align business requirements to available or new technology so as to provide a viable continuity to the enterprise. Facilitator can make session interesting and short to get maximum output between busy work schedules and pressures faced by client team members.
3. *Be consistent*: It is important to conduct the sessions with different departments in the same way to maintain consistency. This will make the experience common across the organization and will give everyone a reference for future discussion.
4. *Keep focussed on processes*: When you are developing recovery strategies, you will then identify alternative procedures for accomplishing processes, such as using failover data centres or switching to manual procedures until your technology is back up. Yet another goal of a BIA is to identify the relationships and dependencies in a business function. This includes internal dependencies on support functions, such as HR, admin, and IT, and on vendors and supply chains.
5. *Ensure there is no language barrier*: The respondents have to understand the language in which discussions are to be conducted and have to understand the moderator the way he or she wants them to understand and give accurate answers to questions.

Face-to-Face Key Informant Interviews

Face-to-face key informant interviews are the most frequently used technique for data collection. Information we collect by means of questionnaires can be endorsed by face-to-face interviews. Generally, HODs can be interviewed by the BIA facilitator to get a first-hand overview of business processes carried on by the department, personnel working in the department, dependencies on external suppliers, service providers, operational risks faced by the department, and other information required for BIA.

A point to note here is that the interviewer should do his homework well, he or she should be ready with the questions in, and ideally interview should be conducted by two persons; one who does interviewing, and the other who is recording responses. Alternatively, audio recording of interviews can be made to be played on later to check on responses.

Telephonic Interviews

Telephonic interviews are also common considering modern enterprise is highly dispersed across geographical boundaries. Telephone interviews are cost effective since it saves on travel cost of visiting overseas offices.

The following points have to be kept in mind for an effective interview:

1. *Interviewer should be a good listener*: It is generally found that in the attempt to get all questions through, the stress on listening is missed. As a result, the executive gets irritated and gives a negative feedback or sometimes may walk out of the interview.
2. *Focus on core areas*: Idea is to focus on subject matter and solicit main input required for BIA. To illustrate if the finance manager is being interviewed, discussion should be focussed on financial impact in case a disaster strikes the enterprise. Also in the time allotted for the interview, he or she has to get requisite information. So the facilitator has to have good communication skills to politely keep the conversation to the subject and not allow the conversation to stray on unnecessary details.
3. *Put the interviewee at ease*: For better results, it is necessary to build a rapport with the interviewee. Interviewer has to explain the purpose of the interview and slowly build a light atmosphere, yet stick to relevant questions in order to solicit useful answers for BIA. Choice of open questions and close questions (respondent has to choose from given choices only) that may chiefly be used to get quantitative response for the interviewee should be used prudently.

Group Interviews

Group interviews are where a number of key informants are interviewed together if they belong to the same function; for example, operations, finance, IT, and so on. Group interviews can be used for listing out criticality of business operations. Once one key informant has made a point, the others can just quickly agree or disagree with it.

Disadvantage of this technique is that it may produce a biased picture which can be offset by supplementing group. If a questionnaire or a checklist is prepared in advance and carried for the interview, it will support both the interviewer and the interviewee in keeping the flow of questions steady and logical and obtaining relevant answers.

Document Analysis

Document analysis is analysis of documents in order to extract information in respect of the topic being evaluated. This can include all types of documents such as formal reports, minutes of meetings, memos and print media reports, or electronic media transcripts. It can be a generic examination or scrutiny of say service level agreements to ascertain whether the service entity has a fully documented and functional disaster recovery plan, and also there is a provision for a right to audit's clause in the SLAs that accord auditability of these facilities. The criteria for review and analysis should be documented in advance and if documents need rating, the names of the rater or raters, in case dual rating has to be performed, must be documented.

Workshops

Data collection workshops can be an effective method of gathering needed data. We need to still prepare a questionnaire so as to cover all data points. Participants for the workshop need to be chosen on some logical basis; same function, same location, and so on. Location and time for the workshop need to be communicated to all respondents.

Before workshop, take care to ensure all amenities such as papers, white board, projector, or flip chart are installed and provision for water and tea/coffee arrangements are in place.

A clear agenda should be stated and distributed to participants. Identify workshop completion criteria so the facilitator and participants are clear about what is expected, what the required outcomes are, and how the workshop will conclude.

The facilitator's job is to ensure the workshop objectives are met, participants stay on main agenda items, and show a readiness to tackle difficult issues if they arise during the workshop. Some companies use the concept of a "parking lot," where issues are written up on note cards and collected or written on sticky notes and posted on a white board or an empty wall. It would be a good idea to encourage participants to write issues on sticky notes that can be stuck on a white board and taken up at fixed intervals so as not to interrupt the proceedings of the workshop.

After the workshop, the results should be documented and shared with the participants by way of e-mail or physical documents so as to give them a chance to review them, and any errors or omissions are corrected before the results are finalized.

Delphi Technique

Delphi technique is a quantitative option aimed at gaining consensus. It solicits response from a group of respondents in an iterative round where results from one round are reviewed till final round where consensus is obtained.

Applicability can be in getting response on recovery time objectives (RTOs) and recovery point objectives (RPOs). It is also used to identify trends and probability for threat materialization for the enterprise can be fixed using this technique.

Drawbacks include the following:

■ May not be representative, leaves out extreme positions
■ Absence of time and commitment from respondents
■ Habit of twisting facts and theories in respondents

A relationship of trust is built between members of the group; there are no inhibitions and no influence from any other group. These sessions are useful to actively engage participants to reach consensus on the information being collected. For instance, fixing RTOs for different processes.

Exploring the collective intelligence of participants and giving them a sense of ownership and pride in arriving at a combined consensus are very effective for BIA. Having discussed techniques of data collection, we need to go back to recapitulating what we want to collect for an effective analysis of the business.

Checklist for effective data collection

1. Are all locations where enterprise has its business been covered and a list has been prepared for the same? (document analysis, kickoff meeting, interview, questionnaires)
2. Were questionnaires and interview data consistent and succeeded in obtaining desired results? (conference calls, interviews, questionnaires, workshops)
3. Are processes relevant to the BIA and are samples representative of the population? (triangulation methods, cross checks, interview, group discussion, workshop)
4. Has there been a validity check on data collected such as signoff by HODs? Triangulation methods, cross checks, interview, group discussion, workshop)
5. Remove bias from data by proper validation and then proceed for final collation of data and for putting BIA results into the BIA report.

Note: (Data collection methods suggested against each item are illustrative only)

We need the following information for BIA.

- Number of customers, transactions, total revenue, purpose of business unit, and critical operations performed
- Financial (quantitative) and intangible (qualitative) costs associated with a business outage on a daily basis, and how it changes when projected over a period of time
- Key personnel required to support the business unit's functions after a disruptive event
- List of critical systems and applications, including computing platforms and software
- Recovery time objective (RTO), that is, time in which systems, activities, applications, or functions must be recovered after an outage to resume critical functions
- Recovery point objective (RPO), that is, the maximum amount of data loss the business unit can sustain during an event
- Critical deadlines associated with various business units and business functions
- Alternate processing contingencies, such as relying on manual-based systems until systems are up and running
- Seasonal or period of year (end of financial year) or last few days of the month for payroll-processing jobs' urgencies need to be documented

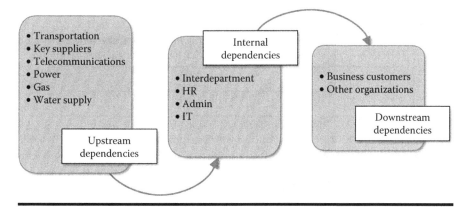

Figure 2.3   Interdependencies with external and internal entities.

- Contact numbers for key personnel, management, and key vendors to be contacted in case of emergency must be documented and kept at hand
- Office space, equipment, and staff list to be determined that have to be arranged for during a contingency
- Documentation such as service level agreements and legal contracts, which have to be kept handy as part of vital records listings
- Interdepartmental dependencies and external dependencies for workflow (Figure 2.3)

Collecting Dependency Data

A significant element of data gathering exercise is determination of *internal and external interdependencies*. Although it is easy to map internal dependencies that exist interdepartmental or with support functions such as HR, Admin, IT, and so on, dependencies on external upstream and downstream are more significant.

Note: It is recommended to collect dependency data by way of a dependency workshop. Refer to Annexure A at the end of this subsection for details.

Upstream Dependencies   The loss suffered when key suppliers get affected by disaster is termed as "upstream losses." If you are a trader and depend on goods and services from suppliers, you could be inconvenienced if the area from where your supplies arrive is affected by disaster.

In case of a manufacturing company, continued supply of raw materials is critical to uninterrupted production and supply of enterprise goods. There may be instances that part of fabrication for your product is performed by an ancillary unit and that unit is affected by disaster. It also leads to upstream losses and will have to be considered during impact analysis. Today's business is a part of the supply chain, and any one unit not performing can cause unanticipated losses to the business.

Table 2.2 Key Personnel Chart

Business Function	Key Personnel	Fall-back Identified	Contact of Key Person	Contact of Fall-back

Downstream Dependencies   In case your business supplies spare parts to a big industrial house, there will be huge losses suffered if the big industry shuts down or is hit with a major disaster due to some reason. This is because a lot of investment in terms of people, machines, and raw material has been made, and if the finished goods cannot be delivered, there will be additional expenses in storage of these goods. You may have to shut down if you were only supplying to one customer or will have to absorb these downstream losses, although your business has not suffered impact from disaster directly.

Understanding the People Dependency   People are the most important resource not only from a point of view of planning and implementation of BCM initiative but as major players in the business of the enterprise. In a natural disaster, it is possible that employees will be affected and may be seriously injured or shall lose their lives. Although we do not want to think of extremes, we need to plan for the same.

List of key personnel with contact (Table 2.2).

Succession Planning

It is necessary to identify key positions, key knowledge, and key skills needed for business continuity. Succession planning in companies covers many areas, but typically it is discussed in terms of replacing key employees as well as how to transfer the reins of the company from one leader to the next.

From a risk management perspective, it can also address who will replace key employees in the event of a planned or unplanned departure. Succession planning can include training employees to promote to higher positions and take leadership roles.

In publicly traded companies or high profile start-ups, the company often purchases what is called *key man insurance*. This insurance covers the cost of losing a high-ranking executive in the company, the assumption being that if someone at that level were suddenly unavailable to carry out that function, the business would suffer financial losses. In many enterprises, the core management team refrains from taking the same flight in order to ensure that if there is a plane crash, the entire team does not get wiped out together. This is bound by policy and is a good preventive control.

Another example is when an employee is nearing retirement, he or she identifies his successor who can take up the role. Technology systems (expert systems) can capture the knowledge and problem-solving qualities in a sort of a decision support system to help the successor take certain predefined decisions.

Data collected must be tabulated and arranged logically in order to facilitate analysis for deciding recovery strategies. Once an inventory of business processes is made, it can go through a classification exercise. First, a list of all critical business processes will have to be made. They can be ascertained on the following criteria:

- Provide vital support to critical functions
- Mandatory functions (are critical)
- Functions that cannot suffer significant interruption

In the next section, we shall understand business impact factors and recovery time objectives. Please refer to **Chapter 9** for more illustrations.

Appendix

Conducting an Interdependencies' Workshop

Background

The shift of some services, such as IT services, payroll processing, telemarketing, call center operations, to specialized third-party service providers gives the benefit of greater utilization, economy, and efficiency. Given a better resource and infrastructure mix for greater financial and operational performances, through outsourcing or offshoring options, there are risks, complexities, and vulnerabilities that emerge from these growing interdependencies.

The effective mapping of these interdependencies during the initial stage will help the TL gauge criticality of these processes and include them in their analysis during the BIA exercise. Interdependencies in an enterprise are relationships that are both internal and external, domestic and offshore, which may affect an enterprise's ability to recover from an incident and sustain its business.

The objective of this workshop would be to

- Increase the awareness of the extent of reliance on private and public organizations for essential/critical operations.
- Determine steps to mitigate impact of disruption among interdependent entities.
- Lay down a process of periodic evaluation of external interdependencies.
- Lay down a standard for factoring resiliency clause and right to audit clause in the Service Level Agreements with external vendors.
- Identify the impact of interdependencies on recovery time objective and recovery point objectives.

Time taken for workshop: five to seven hours.

Attendees to the Interdependencies' Workshop

- Representatives from each business function.
- Representatives from information technology department.
- Representatives from administration department.
- Representatives from human resources department.
- Representatives from data center.
- Representatives from security.
- Representatives from business continuity function.

Steps for Conducting Interdependencies Workshop

Step 1—Orientation of objectives of workshop: Orientation of objectives of workshop and defining internal/external dependencies. Ask attendees to fill the following form:

Particulars	Core Business Function	Internal Dependency	External Dependency
Operations	Storage of Documents	IT for Backup	XYZ Corporation

Note: Internal dependency is the reliance of business on other departments for carrying out their core functions. For example, dependence on finance for claims payout.

External dependency is the reliance on third-party to perform or complete the performance of business functions. For example, payroll processing.

Step 2—Define geographical area to be covered: Since business is spread over continents and management of servers and applications may be from country other than the one in which the organization operates from, it is necessary to define the scope of the inclusions of interdependencies from a location perspective.

For example, many organizations have mainframes housed in the United States. Many U.S. organizations have call centers in India, Philippines, or other countries. Although it would be worthwhile to explore the dependency for scenarios where the outage may hit the area where servers are located and bring organizational systems to a standstill, such decisions to cover reverse risks need to be taken only by the management of the organization in question.

Let us take the following illustration. ABC & Co has its head office in London. It has 56 branches all over UK. It is in the business of providing health insurance products in the United Kingdom, Asia, and Europe.

They are heavily dependent on third-party vendors for provision of following services:

a. Thomas & Co for data center based on outskirts of London.
b. Ellis & Co for processing of payroll based out of Peterborough.
c. Contact us services for tele calling based out of Bath.
d. Panache is the sole vendor for printing of policies (London).
e. Bennett & Co is based in London, and they do document storage for them (London).
f. KPZ manages their medical testing for all centres in the United Kingdom (London).
g. William Blake associates do the tax computation for them (London).
h. Normans Limited do their claims processing (Bath).

Now let us assume some scenarios–facilitators to the interdependency workshop should take scenarios that involve interaction with public agencies, suppliers, and all types of external and other dependencies.

i. Terrorist event
ii. Man-made event such as a malfunction, deliberate disruption to operations.

Step 3—Identify Interdependencies: You can circulate a blank form to every participant, and let them enter the interdependency in the table. It will be beneficial to tabulate list of vendors, their location, and function performed vis-à-vis the disaster scenario chosen to find out which service can be affected and to study what mitigation measures exist to take care of such incidents at the vendor's installation.

The following what-if questions can be asked:

a. Does the enterprise have interdependencies that can become critical in times of crisis?
b. What is the existing arrangement with these dependency agencies to deal with emergency?
c. Are contractual arrangements (SLAs) in place and vetted by legal department?
d. What are the RTOs for processes that have such dependencies?
e. Do any of the dependency pose a threat of single point of failure? Only one vendor or vendor in only one location?

f. Have the major interfaces, data entry points, and systems that will be affected identified?

g. Is the person or contact points in external agencies been identified?

Again you need to identify if services outsourced are critical to business considering the time to recover that has been defined in which the function has to be up and about.

Business managers can fill a form mapping vendors on whom they depend (upstream) and who depend on their services (downstream), but it is more significant to concentrate on upstream dependencies than downstream dependencies (Table 2.3).

Note: In a large complex organization, we could design separate columns for public dependency internal dependency and external dependencies or have separate columns as per your requirement. This will help in analyzing the impact of interdependency that individually helps prioritize public and other dependencies for further action. Idea is to plan for mitigation measures to reduce impact from these dependencies (Table 2.4).

Step 4—Prioritize interdependencies: Workshop mode is ideal to finalize and give a priority to every dependency so as to arrive at a list of critical dependencies for which detailed planning needs to be done.

Step 5—Consider possibilities: After you choose top priority dependencies, have a round table discussion on actions to be taken to get the product/service during an outage. Sharing of recovery plans at a later stage with external agencies especially fire department could prove useful. A course of action for all interdependency has to be discussed, chosen, and documented.

Step 6—Remediation: Plan to remediate; once identification of critical interdependencies has been made, look into contractual agreements, and see all the clauses for service continuity have been incorporated.

Benefits of Dependency Workshop

The major benefit from the workshop is collaborative effort on the part of concerned people having knowledge of their processes and the connection that these processes have with other entities. It leads to first-hand information on vendor dependencies, both upstream and downstream, and also identifies criticality of such relationships.

Conclusion

Chief deliverable from the dependency workshop is a documented table for enterprise-wide dependencies (mainly upstream), their criticality, and recommendations for action points to reduce single dependencies and other obstacles

Table 2.3 Vendor Dependency Table

Vendor	Service	Location	Scenario 1 (Snowstorm)	Scenario 2 (Tube strike)	Scenario 3 (Fire)	Comment
Thomas & Co	Data center	London				
Ellis & Co	Processing payroll	London				
Contact us services	Tele calling	Bath				
Panache	Printing policies	London				
Bennet & Co	London	Document storage				
KPZ	London	Medical tests				
William Blake Associates	London	Tax computation				
Normans limited	Bath	Claims processing				
Remarks	London vendors will be affected by city outage	Identify whether services are critical for business recovery	City outage	Partial city outage	Building outage	This table will form input for BIA analysis

Table 2.4 Contact List of Authorities

Public Agencies	Service Required	Under Which Scenario	Criticality Level	Whether Alternative Existed?
Emergency management agencies, hospitals, and medical centers				
Federal government agencies				
State government agencies				
Local government agencies				
Utilities gas, water, and telecom				
Police, fire, and transportation				

identified during the workshop. This deliverable will be backed by collaborative consensus, and it renders a lot of credibility and authenticity to the information. This helps in building alternatives and bring in resilience for the enterprise.

Business Impact Factors

In the previous section, we dealt with data/information collection on an enterprise-wide basis. It gave us an insight into the assets of the enterprise including facilities, processes, applications, vendor dependencies, and so on.

In this section, we will discuss factors that impact business. An impact can be defined as any consequence whether tangible or intangible of any event or an entity's action or influence (Figure 2.4).

Downtime is undesirable and cost of downtime has to be ascertained in terms of cost per hour, cost per day, and cost per peak period where cost will be accelerated. Some of the tangible costs of downtime include the following:

■ *Lost revenue*: With 24/7 e-commerce applications, problem is accentuated since sales depending fully on system availability. This means there is 24/7 customer support, mobile work place, and need for the Internet and exchange of e-mails. One way to estimate loss is to calculate normal hourly sales multiplied by number of hours of downtime.

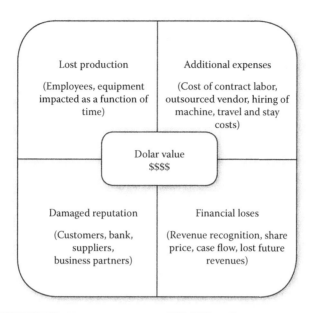

Figure 2.4   Loss impacts chart.

- *Lost productivity*: There is idle time when system is down. Employees have to be paid for the idle time, which becomes additional burden.
- *Late fees and penalties*: When delivery is delayed, the SLA has provision for fines and penalties. Noncompliance to regulatory norms also leads to payment of fines.

Modern business environments are complex; they are an extended enterprise where they are interlinked with many other entities (Figure 2.5).

Chief Impact Factors on Business

1. Financial Impact
   a. Lost sales and income
   b. Increased expenses (outsourced resources, hiring of equipment, etc.)
   c. Fines and penalties
2. Operational impact
   a. Customer dissatisfaction
   b. Delay of business plans
   c. Decrease in sales
3. Reputational impact
4. Legal and regulatory impact

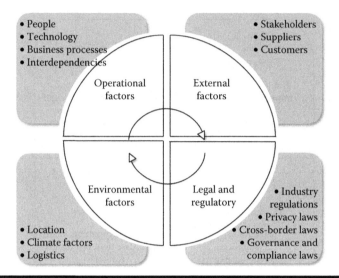

Figure 2.5   Impact factors in an extended enterprise.

Some Emerging Trends in Global Business Environment

Global business is faced with challenges. We must take some insight into the following:

1. World population will double in the next 40 years.

    Impact: Hence globally, agriculture will be required to supply as much food as has been produced during all of human history to meet needs over the next 40 years. Again distribution of world population is going to be as shown in Figure 2.6.

    You will observe in chart 2.6 that the population in developed countries has a steep fall.

    Potential business impact

    a. Developed nations will find that retirees will have to remain on the job to remain competitive. Developed nations will begin to increase immigration limits to allow workers/professionals from more populated countries.

    b. Demand for personnel in distant countries will increase the need for foreign language training and employee incentives suited to other cultures.

2. The growth in information industries is creating a knowledge-dependent global society.

    Potential business impact

    a. Pace of technological innovation is increasing.

    b. E-business and the Internet will reduce the cost of doing business.

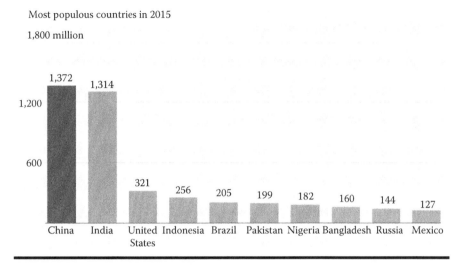

Most populous countries in 2015

Figure 2.6   Distribution of population in the next few years.

    c. Top managers must be computer literate to retain their jobs and achieve success.

    d. Knowledge workers are generally higher paid, and their proliferation is increasing overall prosperity.

    e. Entry-level and unskilled positions are requiring a growing level of education.

    f. Information now flows from front-office workers to higher management for analysis.

    g. Downsizing, restructuring, reorganization, outsourcing, and layoffs will continue.

In the backdrop of all these rapidly changing factors, there is a threat of an economic downturn that will have global repercussions.

Economic downturn: An economic downturn is a general slowdown in economic activity over a sustained period. It can happen in a specific region (e.g., the Asian financial crisis in the late 1990s) or on a global scale (e.g., the global financial crisis in the late 2000s). The main features of an economic downturn include *rising unemployment, falling share and house prices, low consumer confidence, and declining investment.*

Although you may not be able to completely protect your business from an economic downturn, understanding how it could affect you will help you develop a plan to minimize its impact. You may also be able to identify new business opportunities.

Planning, reviewing, and monitoring your business should give you the information you need to make changes to help you stay financially viable. This should make it easier for your business to respond to, and recover from, an economic downturn.

Decline in profits has direct financial impact. Typically, the share price of a corporation suffering a disaster falls by around 5% to 8% within the first few days after a disaster. Recovery of the share price depends on organizational resilience and capacity to resume operations. Such organizations can make their recovery a case study and use it to enhance stakeholder value.

Those who are unable to do so must accept a drip in their share prices and loss of customer confidence. Empirical research has shown that in such cases, organization hit by a major disaster may have to close business at the end of two years.

An organization has to survive in this situation. Identifying major areas where they can get hit is crucial to an impact analysis:

1. Inability to conduct critical customer services
2. Damage to reputation or brand
3. Reduction in market share
4. Failure to protect organization's assets including intellectual property and personnel
5. Noncompliance to legal and regulatory norms

External Factors That Impact Business

Stakeholders have invested their money in the enterprise, and their chief concerns are good governance and benefit realization through enhanced return on investment (ROI). They have a right to involve themselves in strategy formulation and would be interested in a comprehensive impact analysis.

1. *Customers* are mainly interested in continued availability of goods and services, quality of customer service support, and quality of goods and services. Every enterprise is highly sensitive to customer-facing activities and applications as they cannot afford to lose customers in this highly competitive market.
2. *Suppliers* are interested in removing logistics hassles, in ensuring a steady business from the enterprise, and in ensuring that downstream losses do not occur which cut the part of business that they are currently getting from this enterprise.

A point to note here is that just as our business continuity affects the supplier, the suppliers' business continuity and disaster recovery plan is of interest to us to get assurance of continued services in case of disaster (Table 2.5).

Hence the service level agreement (SLA) with supplier needs to contain a "right to audit" clause whereby our auditors can visit their installation and check their business continuity arrangements to obtain a level of confidence on the supplier's capacity to provide uninterrupted service during a disaster.

Table 2.5   Single Points of Failure

Business Units	Internal Single Point of Failure	External Single Point of Failure
Printing of policies for customers		Vendor X (monopoly vendor)
Underwriting department at single office	Single point of concentration	
Legal documents (only paper copies, not scanned)	Stored hard copies at one place	
Research analyst	Single person incharge	

Legal and Regulatory Factors

Every business has to adhere to the laws of the country in which it does business. A global business, having offices across the globe, is also governed by the laws of those countries. Industry to which the enterprise belongs is sometimes governed by regulators who are very strict in norms of compliance. For instance, regulators in insurance, banking, and financial services are very active.

The major category of legal and regulatory factors is

1. Industry regulations.
2. Privacy laws.
3. Cross-border laws.
4. Governance and compliance laws.

Industry regulations such as the Basel III Accord for Capital Adequacy for the Banking sector, the Solvency II norms set for the insurance industry, cross-border laws are varied and are different for different countries. Impact can be *financial* where the fines have to be paid, and *loss of reputation* since the enterprise has defaulted in statutory dues. For BIA analysis, list down the compliances and the penalties for noncompliance as shown in Table 2.6.

Financial services industry is governed by privacy regulations where the card details of customers are a valuable asset that has to be safeguarded at all cost. Also governed by the PCI DSS standard, there has to be compliance to the norms, and periodic audits are undertaken to check continued compliance to the PCI DSS standard.

Various other governance laws may be prevalent in the location where the enterprise is situated or conducts business. Tabulating the requirements and considering them in the business continuity analysis and strategy will ensure reduction in the financial, legal, and reputational impacts that noncompliance of these laws can have for the enterprise.

Table 2.6   Table for Compliances to be Met per Department

Department	Compliances Applicable	Person Responsible	Time of Submitting Return or Compliance	Penalty for Late Submission or Noncompliance
X	A, C	Ms. Blue	8th of every month	A-$10 per day C-$50 per day
Y	B, D, I	Mr. Red	15th of every month	B-$25 D-$100 I-$125
Z	C, E, F	Mrs. Black	Quarterly on 1st day of next quarter	C-$10 per day E-$75 for every instance F-$135 per quarter

Environmental Factors

An organization coexists along with other businesses, and it is necessary to understand the trends in environment and their relevance/significance on organizational operations and competitiveness. Internal and external factors affecting business have to be enlisted, and an environment analysis is done in order to adapt policies and processes of organizational operations and products to environment.

Environmental factors include climate, weather, location, and other factors. Let us look at some of the environmental factors that impact business:

1. *Location of the business* is one of the environmental factors since it determines ease of access to resources such as raw materials, labour, power, markets, people, and essential services such as banking, transportation, communication, insurance, and warehousing. Organizations prepare siting reports which checks a checklist of required features in a new office/factory that the organization wishes to obtain or lease. BIA facilitator can browse through such reports for a few purchases/new leases to check what criteria are utilized for the same.

   Geography is important to decision-making. It has been observed that highly dispersed organizations are less employee friendly. Dismissal of employees is less in areas near to head office; this may be due to the fact that those in close proximity can influence management and executives keep them in observation. Hence appraisal of such employees is more favourable.

   Sometimes, dispersed teams do not perform due to the following factors:
   a. Absence of common goals
   b. Cultural differences

    c. Difference in time zones

    d. Lack of communication

Mitigating controls include the following:

    a. Communication protocols document standards and time management standards. Periodic conference call meetings can be made mandatory to ensure smooth communication.

    b. Arrangement of few face-to-face meetings by having annual or semiannual programmes that involves a mix of management staff and employees to interact in a nonformal mode in order to exchange views and ideas and voice difficulties in operations.

    c. Encourage shared folders for information exchange and creation of informal what's app for communication.

    d. Since team is dispersed, a slightly more time should be factored for such a team so that task completion is properly done.

2. *Climatic factors* include major disasters such as earthquakes, storms, tornados, floods, and the like. Certain seismic zones have high probability of earthquakes, whereas certain other areas are vulnerable to floods, storms, hurricanes, or other natural disasters. Again these factors will be considered when we discuss incident response plans to respond to climatic exposures.

3. *Logistics* is an environmental factor that determines whether essential services and people will continue to be available. It will be good to invest in supply chain contingency planning. BIA facilitator has to interrogate the interviewees about recent instances of supply chain disruption and encourage them to identify areas where such disruptions can pose a threat to business continuity.

Operational Factors

Business Processes

During BIA, a substantial percentage of time is devoted to the data collection phase, where the practitioner learns about the business, processes, people, and technology, which runs together to keep the business going.

After dividing the organization into logical units according to geographical location or line of business or functional units, the common techniques used for data collection are interviews, surveys/questionnaires, and workshops.

During this stage, business processes are examined, and their level of importance is ascertained along with their association with different other links within and outside the enterprise (Table 2.7).

A point to note here is how to categorize what is critical? Criteria for setting criticality benchmarks have to be explained to respondents so that the response is consistent.

Table 2.7 Business Process Criticality

Business Process	Criticality Level	RTO	RPO

Categories of Business Processes based on "Criticality":

1. *Mission-critical processes* are those processes that are the baseline to be performed in any condition to keep the business going. They have the greatest impact on operations and potential for recovery. A convenient way to collect details about mission-critical operations within the department is either through questionnaire, interview, or workshops.

   From a technology perspective, the network, system, or application outage that is mission critical would cause extreme disruption to the business. Such an outage often has serious legal and financial ramifications. This type of outage may threaten the health, well-being, and safety of individuals (hospital systems come to mind). These systems may require significant efforts to restore, and these efforts are almost always disruptive to the rest of the business (in the case that any other parts of the business are able to function during such an outage).

   The special feature of these processes is that an outage becomes time critical and is inflexible to time lapse in recovery of the same. Hence the recovery time objective for these processes will be low.

2. *Vital* functions are functions that have to be performed immediately after the mission-critical functions are recovered. Vital functions might include things like payroll, which on the face of it might not be mission critical in terms of being able to get the business back up and running immediately but which can be vital to the company's ability to function beyond the disaster recovery stage.

3. *Important* functions and processes will not affect business operations in the short term but will have a long-term impact if they are missing or disabled. They may cause legal or financial impact and may be related to functional business units across the organization. For instance, these systems may include e-mail, Internet access, databases, and other business tools used in a support functions in IT or business. If disabled, these systems take a moderate amount of time and effort (as compared to mission critical) to restore to a fully functioning state. The recovery time requirement for important business processes often is measured in days or weeks.

4. *Minor* business processes are often those that have been developed over time to deal with small, recurring issues or functions. They are not necessary for recovery and will should be recovered only in the long term. Parsing of business processes in order of importance leads to discarding of redundant processes that business can do without (Tables 2.8 and 2.9).

Rating points: You could give some rating points on the basis of some predefined criteria. For example, you may according 40 points to mission-critical process, and every process in this category can be given points as per the following suggested manner (Tables 2.10 and 2.11).

Table 2.8   Categories of Business Processes

- **Category 1**: Mission-Critical—0–12 hours
- **Category 2**: Vital—13–24 hours
- **Category 3**: Important—1–3 days
- **Category 4**: Minor—more than 3 days

Table 2.9   Recovery Priorities of Business Processes

Critical Activity	Ranking	RTO	Recovery Priority	Recovery Sequence
IT applications	Critical	11 hours	High	1
Investment function	Vital	23 hours	High	2
Customer service e-mail systems	Important	25–48 hours	Medium	3
Fax, copier	Minor	Up to 7 days	Low	4
Marketing	Minor	Up to 25 days	Low	5

Table 2.10   Recovery Priorities of Business Processes

- **Category 1**: Mission-Critical—40 points
- **Category 2**: Vital—10 points
- **Category 3**: Important—3 points
- **Category 4**: Minor—1 point

Table 2.11   Risk Levels

Level 1: Less than 6 points
Level 2: 7–15 points
Level 3: 16–39 points
Level 4: 40 points or more

54 ■ *Practitioner's Guide to Business Impact Analysis*

Please note that above points and risk levels are illustrated for understanding and you may have your own levels defined. Once criticality categories are fixed, you can fill the column in Table 2.9. It becomes essential to establish critical functions, their recovery priorities, and interdependencies to develop acceptable recovery time objectives (RTOs) and recovery point objective (RPO). It would be wrong to calculate RTO/RPO without considering the interdependencies between processes, people, and other resources.

Dependencies on internal and external entities impact routine working of the Department, and hence it is necessary to tabulate key dependencies.

Person-specific dependency: The information provided should list any internal individuals within the department on whom there is a key dependency, such as specific skills, expertise, or access not shared with others in the department, for example, user access to specific system (Table 2.12).

Suppliers: The information provided should list down internal departments and external organizations on which the primary department is dependent to provide a service, product, or goods (Table 2.13).

Customers: The information provided should list any internal departments and external organizations which receive a service, product, or goods listed alphabetically to undertake prioritized activities (Table 2.14).

Table 2.12   Person Dependencies

Name of Individual/ Title of Role	Nominated Deputy	Skills/Expertise Not Shared with Colleagues

Table 2.13   Dependency on Suppliers

Service Activity	Internal Supplier	External Supplier	Product/Service Provided

Table 2.14   Dependency of Customers

Service Activity	Internal Customer	External Customer	Product/Service Provided

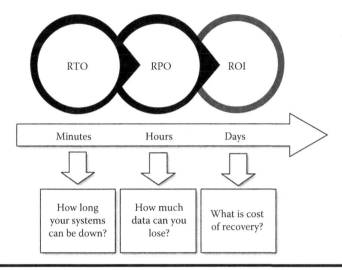

Figure 2.7 Time criticality in business.

Time-critical periods/service priority: The aim of this section is to agree what impact a disruption to the delivery of a service/product would have over time, so that the priority for service restoration can be established (Figure 2.7). A rating for each of the impact priorities over time should be given for each of the services, products, and activities using the following definitions:

  RTO (*recovery time objective*) indicates allowable downtime or the earliest point in time at which the business operations must resume after disaster.

  RPO (*recovery point objective*) signifies the amount of data that are acceptable to have been lost and subsequently recovered once the service is restored.

Work recovery time (*WRT*) indicates the duration of time needed to recover lost data (based on RPO) and to enter data resulting from work backlogs (manual data generated during system outage that must be entered). If your MTD is three days, Day 1 might be your RTO, and Days 2 to 3 might be your WRT. It takes time to get critical business functions back up and running once the systems (hardware, software, and configuration) are restored.

Recovery point is the exact point in time you will be returned to after all your recovery processing activities have been completed successfully. This is the point from which you will resume normal business operations.

MTPOD is also known as maximum allowable outage and maximum acceptable outage. It is the time window during which a recovery must become effective before an outage compromises the organizational capability to achieve its business objectives and ultimately endangers its survival.

Maximum allowable downtime (*MAD*) determines the minimum acceptable level of operations that are required for this business process/function within the RTO. For example, if the RTO is four to seven days, does this business process/

function need to be restored at 100% of normal capacity? In times of disaster, organization cannot operate in a "business as usual" mode. Critical business operations identified above will be recovered, and slowly resumption of processes to normal mode can be restored.

Maximum allowable outage/maximum acceptable outage (MAO) or maximum tolerable period of disruption (MTPOD/MTPD): All of these mean that beyond a certain time, the impact from a disaster becomes unacceptable to the business. It is a useful metric that determines how much unavailability an organization can stand before the continuing failure to carry on the activity, which will create intolerable impacts. It is also known as the *point of survival*.

Each business creates a prioritized summary of recovery objectives; at the department level, should the business experience a loss of facility, loss of staff, or loss of IT capabilities? Critical business processes and applications are linked to maximum allowable outage (MAO) that drives strategic recommendations for increased business availability and resiliency (Figure 2.8).

MTPOD is determined by the following factors:

a. Stakeholders suffering impact can be internal stakeholders such as directors and employees or external stakeholders such as customers, competitors, suppliers, and so on. There are stakeholders with financial interest such as bankers, insurers, financiers, and some others such as media, pressure groups, and politicians.
b. Nature and size of impact.
c. Rate of increase in impact over passage of time.

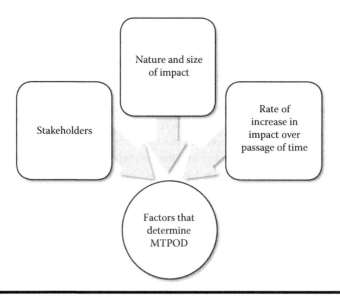

Figure 2.8　Factors determining MTPOD.

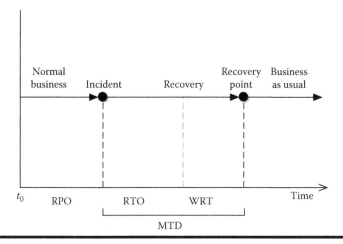

Figure 2.9 MTD = The duration of the RTO plus the WRT.

Maximum tolerable downtime (MTD): Let us understand these concepts viewing the Figure 2.9. Normal business prevailed till the point where the incident or event strikes. But even though backups were being transferred to the backup site at intervals of 30 minutes, there was data loss of 30 minutes when the incident occurred. This was our RPO.

Our RTO has been defined, say 24 hours. So our critical business processes would be up in around 24 hours. So it will leave a backlog of activities not performed as also the lost data to be reentered. This will take up the recovery time shown under WRT above.

Sum of RTO and WRT is the MTPD, that is, the maximum tolerable period of disruption shown above. Beyond this point, the business resumption should be done, and business should commence to be as usual. MTD denotes the point of survival and beyond that point, you should conclude your business resumption.

People

People are the most important asset of every enterprise. They drive business initiatives and are responsible for wealth creation. Hence continuous availability of management staff, workers, employees, and support staff is the key to its success and continuity.

Impact Factors affecting people continuity

■ *Management crisis*: In enterprises where management is at daggers end with each other and constantly having disagreement among themselves **creating silos** in the work environment. It makes people insecure, and employees are

Table 2.15   Table for Mapping Special/Rare Skills for Business Operations

Department	Special Skill	Time to Hire	Number of Skill Workers	Whether Business Process can Operate Without this Role?
Underwriting	Underwriting	5 months	20	No
Dealer	Trading in securities	4 months	2	No

worried about their career progression leading to an increase in the level of attrition. Major impact is *employee morale and attrition* and the costs associated with hiring. Efficiency of work also falls down leading to *customer dissatisfaction.*

■ *Lack of skilled and trained personnel*: Sometimes it is difficult to find people with some specialized competencies. For instance, actuaries, underwriters, and so on. During the data collection exercise, it is necessary to identify such roles and tabulate that so that they may be considered while we do final analysis and strategy planning.

■ In the example if a special skill takes time to appoint and if this role is critical to the business process, then it is imperative that the persons should not sit in one geographical location but are distributed at different locations in order to avoid *a single point of failure* (Table 2.15).

■ In a very big financial services company, who had installed a sophisticated enterprise resource-planning software, we found that there was only one person who had knowledge about the software. All people were totally dependent on this one person to resolve their queries and for troubleshooting. This was a typical people dependency case, which could lead to a *single point of failure* if this person quit or was unavailable due to some reason.

■ In yet another case in a bank, where the trading room trader was a one-man show, a brilliant person was handling in a very professional way, they said. On interviewing the person, we learned that he had no time even for a biological break! He was having his meal after trading hours were over, and he had to do a lot of multitasking in the absence of a fall back.

■ In this case, there was a risk that health of that employee would fall due to such pressure at work. Also, the efficiency level could fall after some time, and most important is it could be a sure case of *single point of failure.* If he was handling a critical process, he had to have a fall back who could handle the work jointly and manage when one is absent or unavailable due to some reason.

■ Advantage of preparing a table for special skills is that we must *factor the lead time for replacement* and have HR consider how he or she can arrange for these skills at alternate processing location.

- *Disgruntled employees in the organization*: In some enterprises, there is a section of employees who are not happy with the organization or its management. There can be various reasons for the same.
- But the impact on the enterprise is that they may *try to make the good workers biased* or *spread bad name* for the enterprise by *prejudicing customers* or stakeholders. They may even adopt an a "go slow attitude" whereby they will delay performance of critical processes deliberately.
- The BIA facilitator cannot do much in this instance, but he or she can educate the people to identify such disgruntled employees, assign them to noncritical tasks immediately, and encourage them to leave the organization. Alternatively, HR can counsel them and try to remove their grievances and win them over.
- *Pandemic/epidemic*: Disease may strike a geographical location in the form of epidemic or pandemic. In this case, impact would be *mass absenteeism*. Work will suffer, and there will be delay in the capability to provide goods and services. In this instance, our BIA attempts should cover whether
  - Fall-back personnel have been given *cross training* in carrying out the duties of the absentee personnel.
  - Whether there exists a possibility of temporarily *hiring contract personnel* through some HR agencies.
- *Strikes and lockouts*: This is a serious industrial relation issue when it affects the working of the industry by causing a lockout. Impact is that business operations are disrupted, which has direct bearing on *revenue, on customer's goodwill on stakeholders' confidence*, and *profit margins*. During BIA, it has to be enquired as to whether efforts at *maintaining good and cordial relations* with the Labour Union and its representatives exist and that there have been no past precedents of such issues happening in the organization.

Technology

Technology is all pervasive and infiltrates into every function of the enterprise. At the time of individual interviews and questioning rounds, it becomes necessary to understand the applications that support business processes (Figure 2.10).

Technology supports processing of business transactions and accounting for the same. Applications require a hardware platform to house its data, and these data have to be preserved and protected.

Inventory of all desktop applications and local databases including standalone critical systems used within the enterprise has to be mapped with the business processes using them. Also, regular backup arrangements existing at the enterprise should be documented and checked against business requirements with reference to time criticality and note shortfall if any in meeting the requirements (Table 2.16).

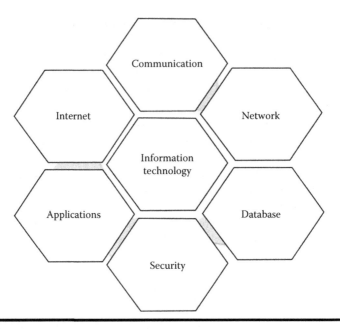

Figure 2.10 Components of technology.

Table 2.16 Inventorying of Technology Assets

Department/ Process	Hardware	IT Application Software (Version No.)	Telephony

Determine the legal and regulatory implications and impact on goodwill of the enterprise if customer facing applications suffer a downtime.

Proprietary corporate information assets: If the enterprise has trade secrets or proprietary designs, plans holding copyright, or patent, then it is necessary to prepare a list of such approved proprietary trade secrets or sensitive information and to review it to ensure that everything on the list which has value is protected. Measures are there to reduce potential risks from their loss, modification, or destruction.

Operational factors (iv)-vital records: Storage and recovery of original documents and vital records are crucial to save unfavorable financial, reputational, or other impacts. The impact of loss on account of not storing original documents in fireproof cabinet or not having scanned copies in electronic form should be examined. Vital documents may include the following:

1. Corporate papers
2. Contracts and legal papers
3. Insurance policies

Operational factors (v)-upstream and downstream: Dependencies (already discussed before RTO discussion above) The cost of disaster is in recovering critical business processes and then working toward full recovery of functions to reinstate business as usual. Needless to say, that the more time an organization takes to recover, the costs of recovery will increase. Causes of loss are causes of cost, and they can take the shape of

- Brand image recovery cost.
- Loss of customers (lifetime value of each) and market share.
- Training/retraining costs for staff.
- Fines and penalties for noncompliance.
- Liability claims.
- Recruitment costs for new staff on staff turnover.
- Salaries paid to staff to recover work backlog and maintain deadlines.
- Loss of profits.
- Cost of replacement of equipment and software.
- Cost of replacement of facilities.
- Penalties on nonperformance of service contracts.
- Loss on loss of bidding for new contracts.
- Cost of recreating data and records.
- Additional cost of working, administrative costs, travel, and subsistence, and so on.
- Additional advertising and communication costs.

Some of these costs may be insured but experience shows that only around 40% of actual loss is covered by insurance. Hence it is better to review what went wrong in your organization:

- Did you experience unavailability of power supply?
- Did you suffer from no access to the Internet?
- Did anything drastic happened to premises?
- Were your key documents destroyed in fire?
- Did you lose one of the best staff members?
- Any key supplier went out of business?
- Were services such as roads were closed due to civil disturbance?

If the answer is yes, then adjust strategies to prepare for such contingencies if not done earlier. Once you understand severity of impacts and high costs of recovery, the significance of putting preventive controls for possible impacts will be proven, and appropriate planning will be undertaken.

Business Impact Analysis

In this book, we have viewed the business continuity management from a practitioner's viewpoint. But no matter what type of industry we deal with, it is certain that it will be the people in the client organization who will ultimately take ownership of the business continuity management system (BCMS).

BCMS is a top management initiative, and hence it is essential to adopt a top—down approach and involve the following members of management in the business impact exercise:

- Chief financial officer (CFO)
- Chief information officer (CIO)
- Vice-president of operations (VP-Operations)
- Chief risk officer (CRO)
- Chief security officer (CSO)
- Facilities manager
- Senior management from key business areas

A BCM coordinator is usually identified at the commencement of the BCM project, and he or she should be completely involved in the BIA along with the facilitator who guides every step by giving his subject matter expertise to the project. The role of the BCP/DR coordinator is to manage the process, ensuring its effectiveness within the DR planning project. A time commitment and specific resources are needed for successful compilation of a business impact analysis.

In the previous subsections, we have considered the following:

1. Set the BIA objectives
2. Understood the organizational context
3. Conducted interviews, survey, and questionnaire to collect BIA information
4. Documented dependencies
5. Listed vital records
6. Taken tentative estimates of recovery time objectives and recovery point objectives
7. Business impact factors that can cause financial, operational, reputational, or legal and regulatory impact (Figure 2.11)

Cost of downtime (unavailability of systems): Information is the lifeblood of every business. Business systems suffer from a chronic ailment, downtime. Business processes are obstructed, and there is delay in processing of transactions. Tangible costs to be incurred on disruption for all lines of business consolidated together are called tangible cost of downtime. It is a very important part of our BIA analysis.

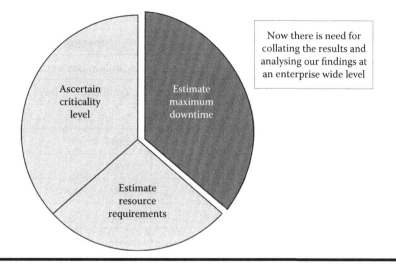

Figure 2.11 Estimate of maximum allowable downtime.

Let us look at some illustrations on the costs due to downtime:

■ Lost revenue
■ Lost customers
■ Interim workers' salaries
■ Inventory lost
■ Penalties paid
■ SLA issues
■ Lost brand image

Downtime can be both planned downtime and unplanned downtime. Approximately 10% to 12% of systems face unplanned downtime. The causes of unplanned downtime can be

■ A power outage.
■ Human error or program failure.
■ Unprotected disk or multiple-disk failure.
■ Other hardware failure.

Planned events account for 90% of downtime. Causes of planned downtime can be (Table 2.17)

■ Daily/weekly/monthly saves.
■ Software installation/upgrade (OS, application, or middleware).
■ Operating systems upgrades.
■ Hardware upgrades.

According to a statistic given by Dun & Bradstreet, 59% of the Fortune 500 companies experience a downtime of 1.7 hours a week, which includes both planned as well as unplanned downtime.

Table 2.17 Downtime Cost Some Estimates

S. No.	Industry	Cost ($)
1	Finance broking	5.5 million per hour
2	Finance credit card authorities	3.10 million per hour
3	Telecom	2 million per hour
4	Online retail	613,000
5	Internet service provider	90,000
6	Transport	89,500
7	Media	90,000
8	Shipping	28,000

Source: Meta Group & Contingency Planning Research table.

A complete business impact analysis provides the insight needed to quantify the costs of unplanned and planned downtime. Understanding this cost is essential because this helps prioritize your high availability investment and has a direct influence on the high availability technologies chosen to minimize the downtime risk.

Loss Impact Analysis

We need to examine critical impacts identified from the data collected. Gartner Group Inc. has predicted that 93% of companies that experience a significant data loss go out of business within five years. How to identify critical impact? There has to be a means of measuring an impact, such as any dollar value that can be assigned or any loss of reputation or intangible outcome. We also need to understand that criticality benchmarks will keep changing, and hence the critical impacts will also undergo a change. Hence conducting a loss impact analysis is a continuous process, and business strategy has to be modified with changes in impact.

A business impact analysis is undertaken to bring to book all relevant impact factors, their consequences and to chart a business continuity plan commensurate to the size and complexity of the business. Reference can be made here of a concept called *PESTLE analysis*.

PESTLE Analysis for BIA

PESTLE analysis, which is sometimes referred as *PEST analysis*, is a concept used as a tool by companies to track the environment they are operating in or are planning to launch a new project/product/service, and so on. It is a useful tool for analyzing the macro environment for business impact analysis.

PESTLE is a mnemonic, which in its expanded form denotes P for political, E for economic, S for social, T for technological, L for legal, and E for environmental. It gives an overview of the environment in which a business exists and enables the BCM team to view business environment from different angles. It is useful in pointing at market trends in order to forecast economic trends such as a slowdown.

P for political factors: These factors consider political leadership and its impact on the business environment. It includes taxes, tariffs, and trade laws.

E for economic factors: Economic factors include the inflation rate, the interest rates, the monetary and fiscal policies, and forex rate fluctuations, which predetermines economic trends and will prove useful in the BIA analysis.

S for social factors: Every country is different, and every country has a unique culture and way of thinking. This impacts business, hence companies consider these factors such as demographics, social lifestyles, and so on to understand markets and consumer behavior.

T for technological factors: Technology greatly influences a *business*; therefore, PESTLE analysis is conducted upon these factors too. Technology is all pervasive, it is changing every minute, and therefore companies need to integrate technology and align it into business processes to get a more effective infrastructure. Technology is important as it is a department within organizations as well as a service provider for carrying out the ITDR function.

L for legal factors: Business is impacted by changes in laws as well as delayed compliance due to disaster. Regulatory bodies regulate business direction. For instance, the Reserve Bank of India (Central Bank) regulates banking operations and compliance.

E for Environmental factors: The location of countries influences on the trades that businesses do. Certain areas are in high earthquake seismic zones; some areas are prone to floods, and some other to some natural disaster or the other. Geography and the inherent features make them vulnerable, and these factors need to be considered while doing a BIA.

PESTLE analysis can be used in the first section to know about the organizational context and also as a tool for analysis to gauge the nature of impact from the above factors.

Impacts can be classified into:

1. Impact from Economic Downturn
   Economic downturn affects business sentiment all around and has manifold impacts including fall in revenue, low employee morale, and slow growth. It has to be understood that when business as a whole is down and the organization is striving to keep the business up and running as usual, an organization will be inclined toward the following goals:
   a. Retaining existing customers
   b. Consolidating customer base

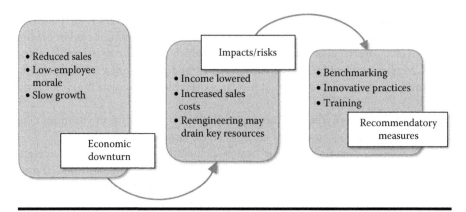

Figure 2.12 Impact from economic downturn.

    c. Keeping costs in control and adopting alternative means of marketing by use of social media and incentives for word of mouth advertising

    d. Adapting product design to customer requirements

    e. Business uncertainties

    f. Stay abreast of economic indicators

Benchmarking: One of the best methods of surviving an economic downturn is benchmarking (Figure 2.12). This can be effected by

    – Attending trade shows.

    – Trade publications.

    – Extended learning programs.

    – Knowing your customers program.

    – Optimum location.

    – Defined markets.

    – Kaizen or employee suggestion box.

2. Financial Impact

Finance is critical to run every business. Any impact that causes hit to the bottom line or leads to payment of fines and penalties, and pressures on the cash flow leading to severe operational and people-related problems may be categorized under financial impact (Figure 2.13). Fiscal discipline, benchmarking, and constant calculation of ROI will help balance financial impact.

    Examples of financial impacts at the university include, but are not limited to, the following:

    – Reduced productivity

    – Increased expenses

    – Delayed collection of funds

    – Reduced income/revenues

    – Breach of contract

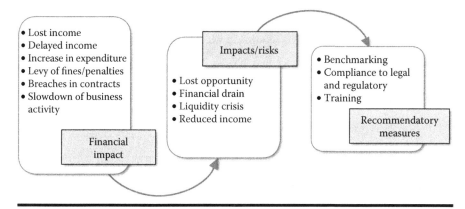

Figure 2.13   Financial impact.

- Lateness penalties
- Loss of future business
- Payment deadlines unmet
- Loss of sales

3. Impact from Operational Impact

There is a suite of operational issues that need to be considered while planning the business continuity management (Figure 2.14). Such issues include the following:

a. Regulatory/compliance issues
b. Increase in liability
c. Vendor relations
d. Customer services
e. Regulatory compliance
f. Brand image

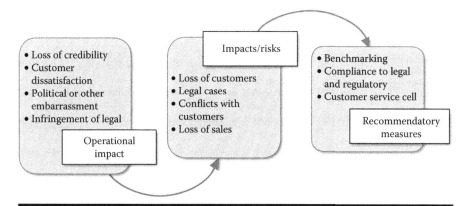

Figure 2.14   Operational impact.

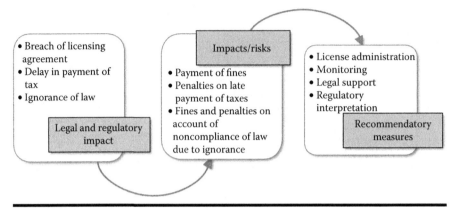

Figure 2.15   Legal and regulatory impact.

     g. Employee morale

     h. Shareholder's confidence

     i. Competitive advantage

     j. Financial reporting and cash flow

4. Impact from legal and regulatory

    Interplay of the internal, external, environmental, and regulatory factors is seamless, and it puts forth several risks that can impact, impair, and cause disruption to business functions (Figure 2.15).

5. Impact from Reputational impact

    Impact from reputational impact and its severity in qualitative terms need to be ascertained. For performing the analysis, we need to combine all of the data into an organization-wide basis (Figure 2.16). It is not right to carry out any analysis at an individual department level since there

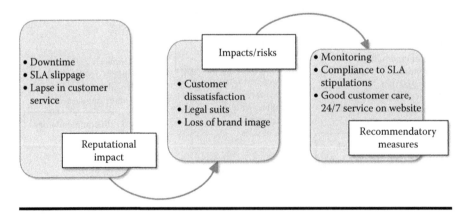

Figure 2.16   Reputational impact.

is connectivity between departments and interdependencies with internal and external entities.

As seen earlier, there are mainly four main impacts that organizations consider in their BIA:

1. Damage to reputation
2. Embarrassment
3. Legal and regulatory impact

The loss causes can be different for different businesses. Let us consider some tangible impacts for a variety of businesses.

1. Quantifiable impact for a manufacturing company might include the following:
   a. *Inability to order materials*: Continuity in production is critical for a manufacturing company. When systems are down and online order system is on, it becomes difficult to procure the raw materials.
   b. *Inability to receive materials*: In case of a transport strike, it is not possible to get the materials on time.
   c. *Inability to assemble materials*: Inability to access the manufacturing facility due to a major disaster suspends the organization's ability to assemble the products till alternative facility is arranged.
   d. Inability to advertise products.
   e. Inability to process orders; when systems are down, processing of transactions becomes difficult.
   f. Inability to ship products.
   g. *Inability to collect payment*: This can cause an imbalance in cash flows and cause liquidity problems.
2. Quantifiable impact for a finance company includes the following:
   a. *Inability to collect payment*: Creates financial impact, which directly affects the cash flow of the enterprise.
   b. Inability to record or process payments.
   c. *Inability to invest funds*: Leads to a lot of revenue impact.
   d. Inability to get in new customers.
   e. Inability to make changes to price structure or rate changes.
   f. *Regulatory or contractual impact*: Leads to fines, penalties, or other disruption.
   g. Delay in tax filings.
3. Quantifiable impact for a retail business includes the following:
   a. *Inability to record sales*: POS systems are critical for the working of retail stores. If systems are down, it will lead to a halt in sales.
   b. Inability to accept returns.

    c. Inability to process credit cards, cheques, gift cards, and cash certificates.

    d. *Inability to replenish merchandise between locations*: If inventory management and reorder levels have not been defined; then unavailability of goods in stock can cause loss of customers and hence loss of revenue for the business.

    e. *Inability to respond to customer complaints/queries*: This is of highest priority. This is sensitive, and businesses strive to achieve a 24/7 service for their customers.

    f. *Inability to advertise their goods*: At the time of a BIA analysis, it is equally important that we understand the nuances of the client's business and give our criticality findings and document our results. It is important to note here that business impact analysis does not have a set methodology or a set of rules that must be followed. In business, every industry is typical, with its own set of regulations, trade practices, compliance requirement, and so on, and within same industry also, there are variations in style of management, size, technology used, and many other variations, which are typical to the organization.

Workaround procedures: It is important to note here that there can be multiple workaround procedures for processes, and workaround procedures should be mapped for recovery alternatives. Information about workaround should be provided and may include the following:

- Workaround name.
- How it is to be performed?
- Date last tested or used.
- IT resources (Hardware, software, database) needed to perform.
- Additional staff to be deployed.
- Time to implement the workaround.
- Maximum time for which it can be used.
- Whether it would be time and cost effective to use?

Interpreting and documenting results:

- It is preferable to start documenting immediately. Otherwise you may miss out or forget to document some vital point.
- Develop individual summary top sheets for every department for which BIA was conducted.
- List down all mission-critical processes along with the financial, operational, and reputational impacts associated with them (Tables 2.18 and 2.19).

Table 2.18   Tabulating Business Process Criticality

Name of Department	Critical Business Processes	Criticality Ranking	Application that Runs Process
Finance and Accounts	Filing returns MIS Regulator report	5 Compliance to legal and regulatory obligations	Oracle Financials
Human Resources	Sourcing Appointing contract personnel	6 Proactive filling of vacancies 7 Background checking of selected candidates	PeopleSoft
Admin. Department	Facilities management	8 Contracts management	Admin One
Investment	Investing of funds Sale of securities	1 Purchase of securities 2 Sale of securities	Credence
Operations	Procurement	3 Customer service 4 Receipting of applications	SAP R3

Note: Please note that all tables are mere illustrations to give you an idea to customize tables, questionnaire, and checklists.

Table 2.19   Classifying Impacts based on Criticality

Criteria	Mission Critical (High Impact)	Important (Medium Impact)	Minor (Low Impact)
Impact on revenue (Financial)	Long term	Medium	
Impact on legal and regulatory	Noncompliance penalties/fines	Noncompliance	Noncompliance
Impact on contracts	Breached penalties	Breached	
Impact on competitive advantage	Immediate loss	Loss over a period of time	
Impact on goodwill and customer confidence	Loss of customer confidence	Loss of goodwill	
Impact on employee morale			

Table 2.20 RTO per Category of Process

- **Category 1**: Mission-Critical—0–12 hours
- **Category 2**: Vital—13–24 hours
- **Category 3**: Important—1–3 days
- **Category 4**: Minor—more than 3 days

A loss impact analysis to determine the loss quantitatively or qualitatively. As seen in Table 2.20, there is commonality of objectives, and BIA is the base tool to meet these objectives.

We have considered criticality domains in the previous subsection. Let us recapitulate the following:

a. *Mission-critical processes* are those processes that are the baseline to be performed in any condition to keep the business going.

b. *Vital* functions are functions that have to be performed immediately after the mission-critical functions are recovered.

c. *Important* functions and processes will not affect business operations in the short term but will have a long-term impact if they are missing or disabled.

d. *Minor* business processes are often those that have been developed over time to deal with small, recurring issues or functions. They are not necessary for recovery and will have to be recovered only in the long term (Table 2.20).

Application Impact Analysis

The responses should identify the most critical applications that are required by the business units to keep the business functioning. During the definition of recovery strategies, IT will have the opportunity to implement supporting protective measures and recovery strategies to ensure that the business unit's critical applications will be available in a timely and cost-effective manner during an actual recovery effort.

- Inventory of all desktop applications and local databases used within the enterprise.
- Include standalone critical systems (Table 2.21).

Evaluate downtime procedures associated with an application, ask questions like

a. Have these procedures been used in the past?
b. How long the operations will work by using them?
c. How have these procedures worked in the past?

Business mission will make customers a first priority and all efforts toward providing existing customers with a very good after sales service. In the light of these

Table 2.21   Mission-Critical Applications Worksheet

Company Name:			Date:	
Location	Application Name	Application Priority	Maximum Outage (days/hours)	Maximum Data Loss (days/hours)

circumstances, it would be obvious that customer-facing applications and communication channels would be mission critical and would have low RTOs and would have to be made available on a continuous basis.

The main objective is to identify time-critical functions, the recovery priority or the time within which they need to be up and about their interdependencies on both internal and external parties so that the time criticality can be calculated keeping in mind these interdependencies. Mission-critical business applications include all information, processes, activities, equipment, and personnel required if system becomes unavailable. It would be better to include secondary applications such as e-mail and EDI.

Evaluate any legal, regulatory financial, customer service, goodwill, and other impact due to nonavailability of applications through different time thresholds. BIA supplies inputs to quantify the costs of downtime. It helps to prioritize high availability investment and choose high availability technology needed to minimize downtime risk.

The Internet can connect the business directly to millions of customers. Application downtime can disrupt this connection, cutting off a business from its customers. In addition to lost revenue, downtime can have an equally negative effect on other critical and interdependent business issues such as customer relationships, competitive advantages, legal obligations, industry reputation, and shareholder confidence (Figure 2.17).

a. You can ask what would be the loss if system cannot accept orders?
b. What can be the cost of lost productivity?
c. How much would be the fines and penalties for nonperformance?

Corporate information assets: If there is a list of known and approved proprietary trade secrets or sensitive information, review it with the perspective that everything on the list must have value to the organization and must have some measures in place to reduce the potential risks derived from loss, modification, or destruction.

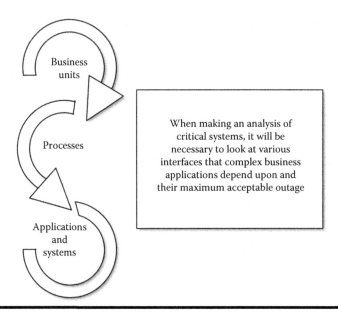

Figure 2.17 Application interfaces.

Identify Mission-Critical Records

In a BIA, we collect information of all "mission-critical records" items protected in your business function (list magnetic media first, then hard copy, and then any mission-critical records on local drives). A mission-critical or vital record is an item of information that is required for the resumption of a business process but is not necessarily delivered by a recovered system or application. Examples are operational procedures, printed reference material or documentation, legal documents, and so on (Table 2.22).

Table 2.22 Criticality of Storage and Backups

Record Type	Type of Storage	Backup Frequency	Restores Stored at (Location)	Criticality
Legal documents	Magnetic media	Daily	Data center	Minor
Client contracts	Hard copy	Weekly	Service provider for storage	Mission critical
Personnel records	Local drive	Monthly	Data center	Mission critical
Sales contracts	Local drive	Weekly	Data center	Important

Recovery of Documents

- Develop, maintain, and implement an effective storage and recovery plan for the enterprise original documents and vital records.
- Recovering business operations after a disaster often requires the use of original documents and vital records not stored as electronic data. The contingency plan should include plans for the consolidation and storage of appropriate original documents and vital records in a central fireproofed location, including the following:
  - Contracts
  - Insurance policies
  - Corporate papers
  - An inventory list of stored items, stored in two locations
  - Annual review for applicability, currency, and legality

The BIA mainly focuses on identifying resource requirements; the base minimum resources needed to resume mission-critical business processes, and related interdependencies as quickly as possible. For example, during an outage, there will be need for key personnel, facilities, equipment, software, data files, system components, and vital records. Prioritizing system resources to meet critical processing needs is one of the business continuity objectives.

Minimum Business Continuity Objectives (MBCOs)

As defined by ISO 22301, "minimum business continuity objective is the lowest acceptable level of product or service that can be tolerated during a disruption. Below this minimum level, the organization is no longer able to provide an acceptable level of product/service to achieve its business objectives."

In the BIA process, asking the business process owners, what is the minimum level of activity needed to meet their suggested RPOs at say 25% or 50% level of service? They will give a much realistic picture than later on randomly fixing the resource level.

When a disruption occurs, there are three steps to resumption:

1. Emergency response (minute/hour)
2. Recovery resume (hours/days)
3. Restore and retain (days/weeks)

The minimum MBCO helps to map requirements in terms of

a. Staffing
b. Location of activity
c. Technology resources
d. Equipment
e. Key dependencies (departments, suppliers, customers)
f. Data backup

Table 2.23   Mission Critical Resource Table Per Critical Business Process

S. No.	Mission-Critical Business Process	People	Vital Records	Applications	Equipment	Others-Specify

As observed from Table 2.23 above, we have complete mapping of critical resources and critical processes. Enterprise can go for part implementation of high availability solution and other standard product where the time criticality is low. In this contest, let us view the manageability goal above.

It will be necessary to run only critical processes from a designated location (if primary facility is unavailable) and the different components of business needed to sustain business activity at that level till the recovery phase is completed and operations can be run in a business as usual mode. During this effort, impact on stakeholders, critical operations/services, and recovery time objectives need to be monitored carefully.

It is assumed that all identified resources support the mission/business processes unless otherwise stated (Table 2.24).

Technology Impact

BIA provides a means of combining business and IT initiatives in aligning business needs with technological capabilities to deliver a cost-effective BCM solution for the enterprise. The review will focus on the IT continuity plan (ITDR) and its alignment with the enterprise BCP, policies, standards, guidelines, procedures, laws, and regulations that addresses maintaining continuous IT services.

This will include the following activities:

■ Identifies which business processes and assets require the highest level of protection.
■ Includes recommendations on possible recovery strategies and alternatives.
■ Development, maintenance, and testing of the IT continuity plan.
■ Ability to provide interim IT services and the restoration of same.

Table 2.24   Prioritizing Resources over RTO

System Resource/Component	Priority	Recovery Time Objective
x	2	2 hours
y	3	24 hours
z	1	0 hours

- Risk management and costs related to the IT continuity plan.
- Provides financial data to help you select the appropriate levels of investment for business protection.
- Understanding how your business works—which processes must interlock and be continuously available to sell, produce, and support your clients—is the foremost goal of a business impact analysis.

Objectives of Continuity High Availability

Any business impact analysis and impact mapping have to be coupled with technology as a major internal dependency for setting recovery strategy and for enabling enterprise to provide recover processes as per minimum business continuity objectives (Figure 2.18).

Enterprises aiming at a high availability strategy have to focus on the drivers who require high availability. BIA can help identify those processes that are redundant and need redesign. Training of personnel needs to be planned, and investment in more efficient and effective systems needs to be arranged for continued availability of products and services.

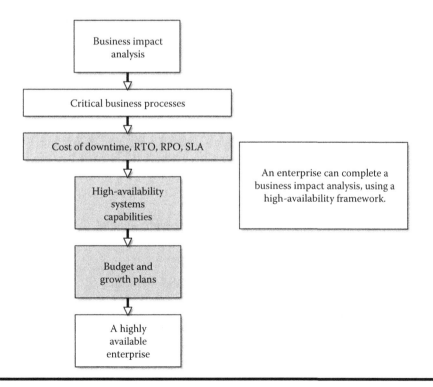

Figure 2.18   Analysis of time criticality and high availability.

Many enterprises especially in the financial services sector require a 24/7 operations

24/7 availability implies

1. 24/7 Customer service and support.
2. 24/7 e-commerce activities.
3. 24/7 SLA.
4. 24/7 Manufacturing.
5. 24/7 Expanded Internet dependency.
6. 24/7 supporting a mobile workforce.

Note: Peak period revenue is to be taken to calculate lost revenue and in planning availability.

An overall redesign of IT infrastructure may be necessary to accommodate high availability requirements. For doing this, we have to identify to categorize critical business processes that have high degree of availability requirements and calculate the cost of downtime. Also return on investment on spending for high availability also needs to be established.

This framework enables the business to define service level agreements (SLAs) in terms of high availability for critical aspects of its business.

For example, it can categorize its business processes into several high availability tiers:

- *Mission-critical processes* have maximum business impact. They have the most stringent high availability requirements, with RTO and RPO close to zero, and the systems supporting it need to be available on a continuous basis. For instance, data for a National Stock Exchange have near to zero RPO.
- *Important processes* that have slightly relaxed high availability and RTO/RPO requirements. For example, these systems do not need to maintain extremely high degrees of availability and may have nonzero RTO/RPO values. These two categories of processes will have to be treated as high availability processes.
- *Minor processes* may be related to internal development and quality assurance processes. Systems supporting these processes can be excluded from high availability categorization and treated differently.

Using the high availability analysis framework, a business can

- Complete a business impact analysis.
- Identify and categorize the critical business processes that have the high availability requirements.
- Formulate the cost of downtime.
- Establish utilization, RTO, and RPO goals for these various business processes.
- Understand your goals for manageability, TCO, and ROI.

Recovery can be phased: There is an onerous task on the IT head to plan recovery strategies. Most of the times, budget is limited, and cost of recovery is high. In these circumstances, optimizing the process by phasing resource requirement within a single process or splitting process into two or more phased activities makes sense.

Failover and Failback Systems

Failover is a backup operational mode in which the functions of a system component such as server, processor, or other component are assumed by secondary components when primary component is unavailable. RAID servers are generally maintained to keep redundancy, and have fault tolerant systems, and help recover mission-critical systems quickly during downtime. It can apply to a connection path, a Web server, or any other device.

Failback is the process of restoring operations to a primary machine or facility after they have been shifted to a secondary machine or facility during failover. During a site-wide failover, I/O (input/output) and its processes are shifted from a primary location to a temporary disaster recovery (DR) location. The process temporarily halts I/O and restarts it from a remote location. During the actual failback, we are moving toward our *recovery point* after which business will be restored to business as usual mode.

The next step for the business is to evaluate the capabilities of the enterprise under its existing infrastructure to meet the high availability (low/no RTO & RPO) demands as per the BIA analysis. Management has to give final signoff with upper limit of spending on high availability technologies predetermined. Enterprise stipulations on SLA must be met.

With an increase in the sophistication and scope of high availability systems, it leads to more of technology infrastructure such as data storage, server, network, applications, and facilities. They can reduce RTO and RPO from days to hours, or even to minutes and seconds. It is up to the enterprise policy that how much they can afford to have at the same time to maintain their critical processes RTO/RPO.

Consider the business of an e-commerce business "Amazon.com." For this business, customer applications, the core e-commerce engine must be resilient and tamper proof. The enterprise may choose clustering for web servers, application servers, and database servers. With built-in redundancy, clustered solutions eliminate single points of failure. Another advantage of clustering is that it provides load balancing to handle peak times and scalability to accommodate volume increase and hence used for capacity planning as well.

Data security is one of the critical points in e-commerce transactions as it is for any other application. Data should be backed up at regular intervals in line with the RPO requirement frozen in the BIA presentation. Backup should be stored locally and also be sent to remote data centre connected over a high-speed redundant network.

The remote data center should have secondary servers, databases should be readily available, and should be synchronized with the primary servers/databases. In this way, enterprises can switch to remote servers at minimal time thus controlling downtime and maintaining assured service levels. But remote data centers are costly to maintain, and the ROI should be considered in planning for BIA.

Data Protection in Cloud: The perpetual question always asked is "where does enterprise data lie?" One economic and viable solution nowadays is to consider cloud storage for data. Where the electronic information in the form of documents, images, e-mails, videos, pictures is increasing, storing everything in data center is going to be very expensive. Cloud storage comes at fraction of the cost of storing data in a data center. Hence segregating your data into layers makes it easy to choose the storage options based on security, accessibility, and availability as follows:

1. Business data
2. Analytical data
3. Regulatory data

RTO projections will help determine the business data that are critical to recover, and how fast it has to be recovered. Also IT has to ensure the security of data stored on cloud and has to suggest encryption of sensitive data.

IT department has the difficult task in matching the sensitive RTOs with high availability technology. But care should be taken to see that such ad hoc investment of enterprise finances does not backfire the following:

▪ New application may not integrate with existing infrastructure.
▪ Maintenance and integration costs become excessive.
▪ Forces a vendor lock-in.

Hence high availability solutions should always be based on financial considerations and future growth estimates.

Threat Impact Analysis: Once you have completed the identification and prioritization of the business functions, it is time to outline your planning objective, or basically what gets fixed, how quickly and to what level of service. It may help to structure this in the form of a table such as that shown in Table 2.25.

Table 2.25 Resumption Objectives

Essential Function	Resumption Objective	Resumption Alternative
Telephone service	0 (immediately)	Mobile phones
Customer service application	2 hours	Alternate site

BIA identifies and quantifies the direct and indirect quantitative and qualitative impacts on critical and essential services caused by disruption/disaster. It is necessary to set the classification criteria for processes in advance, which will then be used to present critical processes from every department. This has to be done by collaborative efforts. Like we always like to hold risk workshops for different functional groups.

But please note that a Risk Assessment has to be concluded just before the final findings of the BIA are presented to the management. A risk assessment deals with a threat analysis in detail to identify inherent risks, operational risks, financial risks, reputation risks, and other risks to business and its impact on materializing. (Please refer to Chapter 3 on risk assessment. Section "Business Impact Analysis" has to be read along with Chapter 3).

It is prescribed to integrate the risk assessment of the organization with the business continuity management exercise. BIA findings are incomplete without understanding threats affecting the enterprise, categories, and levels of risk and ranking of these risks for prioritizing the risks. The purpose of a vulnerability analysis is to study the potential impact of disruption/disaster on the business of the organization.

Efforts must include consideration of internal and external environments and risks that impact financial position and goodwill of the organization. A business impact analysis takes into consideration the business context listing critical processes critical functions, critical people, and critical applications which are keys to the continued running of key business processes in case of a disruption/outage/disaster.

This process interlinked to the risk assessment process where these critical elements are parsed on a timeline, and the impact/loss is ascertained either on a quantitative basis or a qualitative basis so as to put a BIA report; a business case in front of top management to sanction necessary resources to frame recovery strategy to minimize, reduce, and control risks.

Vendor Dependency Evaluation: External vendor dependencies (upstream) refer to the *supply chain continuity*: The need for establishing the business continuity capability of key suppliers, and how they can contribute to the organization's business continuity capability. Factors to be considered for third-party vendors/suppliers are

- Good relationship.
- Inventory delivery/turnaround time (TAT).
- Quality stipulations.
- Payment terms specified.
- Regular communication.
- Third-party audit reports/right to audit clause in SLA.
- Good inventory control.

- Routine maintenance/improvement programme.
- List threats, vulnerabilities, and brainstorm on probability of occurrence based on precedents and vulnerabilities.
- Controls and documentation requirements mapping.
- List of gaps identified in BIA.
- Documentation/amendment in policies and procedures to include new controls.
- Implementation of controls and finalization of all mandatory documentation.
- Segregation of business and IT controls.
- Make a risk matrix projecting qualitative or quantitative projections on risks faced by the enterprise.

Note: Annexure A in the Section "Data Gathering for the Business Impact Analysis" discusses about a dependencies workshop. (It can be used as a tool to analyze requirement for critical vendors during crisis.)

Sometimes for multinational organizations, some applications are controlled from overseas office. In one such business impact analysis, we found that an application X which was a mission-critical and customer-facing application was controlled from their overseas office (Table 2.26).

There was a reverse risk here since the application was supporting a mission-critical process in home country, but that application had no provision for disaster recovery. This produced a reverse risk; although the application would not be affected by disaster in-home country, the operations in home country could get paralyzed due to an outage in the overseas office. Thus we see that tabulation of single point of failure and such overseas dependency and lacuna should be projected in the BIA report.

Impact increases with time so also the cost to recover becomes more:
Consider Table 2.27. Just assume that statutory dues were due to be paid on the eighth, and a massive fire breaks in the premises on seventh evening. Fine for late payment is $500 per day and $1,000 after the eighth day.

Table 2.26   Single Point of Failure

S. No.	Name of Vendor/Person	Single Vendor Dependency	Single Location Vendor	Single Person with know how to Operate
1	XYZ	Single courier service vendor		
	ONM Software		Operates from the United States	Only Mr. P is trained in ONM s/w

Table 2.27   Impact Increases with Time

Impact:	Fines levied because of nonpayment of statutory dues to authorities		
Authorities to charge $500 per day of default			
Time:	1 day	**Severity Level:**	Moderate
We will be charged $500 per day of default			
Time:	4 days	**Severity Level:**	Severe
Fines amount will be $2,000 for 4 days			
Time:	7 days	**Severity Level:**	Severe
Fines amount will be $3,500 for 7 days			
Time:	12 days	**Severity Level:**	Catastrophic
Fines amount to $8,500 for 12 days. There is an inquiry from authorities for default.			

Outage Impacts: Value of impact also needs to be considered for a proper comparative analysis. Let us view some severity levels based on cost (Tables 2.28 and 2.29). Let us consider some impact severities.

Table 2.29 summarizes the impact on each mission/business process if systems are not available based on cost impact. The trade-off is normally between the cost of recovery and the cost of impact that is continuously increasing over time.

Table 2.28   Impact Categories/Cost

Example impact category = Cost
• **Severe**—Costs exceeding $1 million
• **Moderate**—Fines, penalties, liabilities potential $550k
• **Minimal**—Costs amounting to upto $75k

Note: Every organization can set their benchmarks for severity depending upon the size and complexity of business.

Table 2.29   Quantitative Benchmarks for Severity

Mission/Business Process	*(Severe) $*	*(Moderate) $*	*(Minimal) $*	*Impact*
Pay supplier invoice				

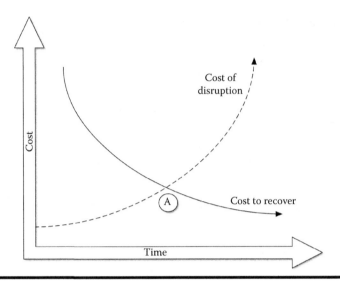

Figure 2.19   Balancing cost of disruption versus cost of recovery.

Total Cost of Ownership and Return on investment: TCO includes all costs such as acquisition, implementation, systems, networks, facilities, staff, training, and support over the useful life of the solution chosen.

As seen in Figure 2.19, the cost of disruption is steadily increasing. Along with it, the cost to recover is on the slide. At point A which is the point of interception, cost is optimized. Through effective business impact analysis, the inventorying of risks and exposures with a fair idea as to the loss that can result on materializing of threats can be done. Under this approach, a risk assessment can be done to project to the BOD, the risks, and financial impact resulting from disruptions, incidents, and disasters. This can smoothen the process of having resource commitment for imposing appropriate controls for risk reduction.

In our analysis, we can use different analysis techniques:

- *Trend analysis*—the examination of a trend to identify its nature, causes, speed of development, and potential impacts.
- *Trend monitoring*—trends viewed as particularly important in a specific community, industry, or sector are carefully monitored, watched, and reported to key decision makers.
- *Trend projection*—when numerical data are available, a trend can be plotted on graph paper to display changes through time and into the future.
- *Computer simulation*—complex systems can be modeled by means of mathematical equations, and different scenarios can be run against the model to determine "what-if" analysis.
- *Historical analysis*—the study of historical events in order to anticipate the outcome of current developments.

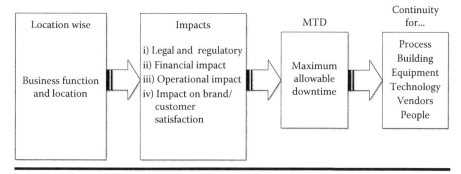

Figure 2.20   Content of the BIA workbook per business unit.

A business impact analysis (BIA) measures the potential impacts to a business function if it was unable to operate following a disruption. This measurement establishes a "prioritization" of business functions and application recovery requirements, which are then used as a baseline to develop business continuity and disaster recovery plans and strategies (Figure 2.20).

Content of the BIA Workbook per Business Unit

For each business unit, include the business unit name. Next, for each business unit entry, include the following information in the appropriate columns. The site's IT organization will be able to gain an early understanding of the critical business units' application requirements:

■ The business unit's operational priority.
■ The business impacts of an extended interruption to the business unit's processes.
■ The maximum length of the outage that a business unit can sustain before it has a significant negative operational impact on the company (MTPD).
■ The vulnerability and recovery complexity of the business unit's critical processes (MBCO).
■ The recovery time frame requirements of the business unit (RTOs/RPOs).
■ The business unit's recovery strategy and plan development priorities (recommended recovery options).

You can incorporate a signoff section to the tail of the BIA workbook Every Business Unit to sign off the BIA Workbook in suggested format given in Table 2.30.

Business Impact Analysis (BIA) Signoff Document

The undersigned acknowledges that he or she has reviewed the business impact analysis (BIA) document for .... Department/Function/Project.

I hereby agree with the BIA approach and the resultant report. Any change to the document shall be coordinated and approved by the undersigned or their designated representatives.

Table 2.30 Signoff Template for BIA

Signature			
Date			
Name			
Title			
Role			

Facilitator receives BIA workbooks from all divisions duly filled and duly signed by HODs. When all of the questionnaires have been returned, all of the questions have been answered completely, and the answers make sense; it is time to consolidate the responses and prepare a summary of the critical IT applications. This should be prepared using the "Mission-Critical IT Applications Worksheet" discussed earlier.

Consolidate BIA Responses

By the time the workbooks are signed and ready, we have all relevant data from the business units that identify their critical processes, their RTOs, RPOs, MTPDs, vital records, IT applications used, upstream dependencies, downstream dependencies, people dependencies, and so on. Now is the time to collate them, sit along with the IT professionals in the enterprise, and consider what recovery strategies can be recommended within the infrastructure or after acquisition of high availability technological solutions.

Aggregating all critical processes and also taking with them their internal dependencies that may not be critical as a standalone but considered along with its dependency by the critical process has to be categorized as critical with them and considered for recovery during a disruption. For instance, if Department A has maximum critical processes but many of these processes are dependent on Department B for completion, it makes both A and B as critical.

Secondly IT may like to segregate priorities into

Type A: 0 RTOs.
Type B: 24 hours.
Type C: 1 week.

Every reduction in RTO costs a substantial sum of money to be invested in high availability technology, and over the years we have witnessed, it is by far the toughest decision/trade-off that IT managers have to make in order to get at an optimum recovery mix.

Complexity is increased when they have to consider scenarios of

1. Facilities not available (fire, structural damage).
2. City outage (terrorism, strikes).
3. Country outage (war, severe disturbances).

In these situations, planning for data centers and disaster recovery sites to ensure that in all circumstances, data are available, is itself a challenge. If data center is in the same city, there is problem; if recovery site is in a high earthquake zone, there is problem; if recovery site is in a contracted DR and they have clients from same location, there is problem; and if there is a global geographical disaster, the capacity of service provider to serve all their clients becomes questionable.

Again, in a highly-dispersed organization, having a plan for each location and educating employees in the practicing of the plan are challenging.

If recoverability time is the criteria that IT follows, then it can recommend options at the time, of management presentation. Many times redundancies are there within the organization such as alternate locations, which can be used to carry on critical functions during an outage.

Also practically, every organization equipped with laptops and the option of work-from-home is the most economical option. Only speed limitations due to USB devices/WIFI dongles are a drawback as it slows down recovery process.

Working from nearest branches is a second option, which is nowadays configured into recovery options.

Having one data center in city and one at remote location is generally preferred. Assembling data and identifying essential components and extended dependency make choice of recovery options more realistic and cost effective.

Hence analyzing BIA data and defining recovery priorities consist of the following activities:

1. Define process/component criticalities
2. Define MAO for process/components
3. Define recovery sequences
4. Define RTO and RPO
5. Define workaround/recovery/restoration procedures and resources
6. Draft, socialize, and validate analysis results

Note: A BIA does not assess the risks that could negatively impact the business functions; a risk assessment (RA) needs to be conducted before completing a BIA.

The RA determines specific risks that could impact the business and proposes mitigating controls and refines strategies.

Let us consider that a recovery strategy is formulated without a formal and effective BIA. What can be its effects?

- *Underestimation* of the resources required to meet the plan.
- *Overestimation* of resource requirement leading to a wastage and inefficiency in operations and hence a low return on investment on BCM. BIA may be used during relocation or reorganization to identify which configurations provide required resilience.

BIA when done in a conventional way serves two critical objectives:

1. Identify the processes that support primary products/services and determine what areas require augmenting of the organization's resiliency strategies (the redundancies or backup infrastructures that the organization has in place):
   - IT resiliency/recovery strategy
   - Facility recovery strategy
   - Strategy to manage a limited workforce
   - Vendor/supplier resiliency strategy
2. Identify the components that will be the foundation for the organization's business continuity plans (processes, dependencies, RTOs). In order to ensure we get the value we are looking for, let us take the two objectives above one at a time. Business impact analysis examines both financial and intangible losses that could result if the systems, assets, and data were not available due to an outage emergency.

   Having seen the manifold angles of performing a BIA exercise, let us see some well-known *myths surrounding BIA*:
   a. *Considering the impact of individual business functions*: The objective of a BIA is to evaluate integrated applications with main focus on business as a whole. Hence processes that would have serious impact on business and applications that support these businesses should be included in mission-critical list. But many times, individual functional department put their issues in the forefront, and it creates silos. The main driver of BIA is the business, and a BIA facilitator needs to keep that in mind and view the process globally rather than in parts.
   b. *Considering individual applications*: While business users may use different applications in different processes, the business impact analyst concentrates only on individual functional applications without considering IT environment including servers, databases, network infrastructure, and other applications in the organization.

c. *Underestimating the financial impact*: Everything in business has an economic impact and if a facilitator tries to calculate individual financial impacts without collating the enterprise-wide impact in terms of losses, payout, and missed sales, then the BIA is incomplete.

d. *Paying too much attention to financial impact*: On the other hand, focussing only on financial impact may be erroneous since there are impacts other than financial loss that may be more important to senior management. The effect on reputation and customer retention may weigh more heavily and have a lasting impact on business.

e. *Failing to distinguish enterprise applications*: Some applications are more evident on account of the fact that they are enterprise wide. For instance, ERP systems such as SAP, Oracle Financials, and so on. There are others that may serve limited sector yet are equally important. Facilitators tend to concentrate on big applications and fail to consider the suite of applications used by the enterprise.

f. *Failing to recognize data center applications*: Some applications do not have business users. These applications include the operating systems. Since BIA covers business processes and users, this part may be missed out. Hence a good BIA considers Information Technology also as a business department and prepares a separate BIA workbook for IT.

g. *Going beyond the rule book*: Sometimes the rule book gives a different picture. If policy requires that infrastructure is to be recovered before all applications, question arises whether an operating system that is run on an isolated server be given priority over enterprise live systems such as inventory or credit and trading?

h. *Confusing a risk assessment with a business impact analysis*: Clarity between risk assessment and business impact analysis is missing with many people. While risk assessment determines, the threat causes, a BIA will determine the effects if the threat materializes. Both processes need to be performed before drawing a conclusion on the findings and making a presentation to the management.

i. *Confusing risk acceptance with a business impact analysis*: Business managers are governed by many factors in their decision on accepting risk. Main being the cost factor.

    They may be ready to take the risk of unavailability due to cost considerations, but it has to be brought out in a BIA since the business process involved may be mission critical, and the BIA exercise is not just for one division but for the entire enterprise.

j. *Backing into a BIA result*: It is possible that a business manager may understate the financial, operational, or reputational impacts of his/her applications being unavailable because of the perceived cost of recoverability.

k. *Conclusion*: The BIA process is probably the longest running and also the most critical among all business continuity activities. At its core, a BIA is a time-tested method for identifying vital business functions, processes, applications, and dependencies to better understand the potential impacts that a business will suffer should they become unavailable.

When these impacts are taken into consideration in the business continuity planning process, they help to define adverse effects on staff, regulatory requirements, corporate reputation, and service quality deterioration. The information uncovered during a BIA engagement will pinpoint what is most important to your business from operational and financial perspectives, as well as to increase awareness pertaining to application.

The major benefits of BIA can be listed as follows:

- Reduce legal liability.
- Minimize the potential revenue loss.
- Decrease exposures.
- Minimize the loss of data.
- Minimize the length of the outage.
- Reduce the probability of any disaster occurrence.
- Ensure an organized recovery of critical applications.
- Reduce the reliance on specific personnel.
- Ensure legal, statutory, and regulatory compliances.

An enterprise plans for its business continuity for continuing to be in business. Hence BIA is not a one-time exercise. Ideally if there are no significant changes in business environment, it can be performed annually. It enables organizations to

1. Present results with implementation priorities.
2. Leverage BIA above business continuity.
3. Ongoing change management to controls risks and pitfalls.

Management Approval of BIA: Business units and executive sponsor agree on the following:

1. Prioritized list of Business units, business processes, and associated activities
2. Approve the list of vital assets/records
3. Approve on action items to be undertaken and fixation of time within which it will be fixed
4. Proposed dates for strategy development and final BCM team fixation

Note: Department-level signoff and management signoff both are vital to give justification to the findings and make a business case for business continuity management system. It will remove *analysis paralysis*, which means any bias that the facilitator may have and self-validate findings achieving a consensus from people directly associated with processes. Also, collaborative sharing of experiences will throw more light on what could happen, what could be the impacts and action items that can reduce impact.

Annexure A

Case Study of Ambiguous Bank Inc. Disaster Recovery and Business Continuity Planning

Valsec Solutions Ltd was engaged by Ambiguous Bank to assess the organization's current ability to maintain business continuity in the event of major and minor disruptions to the technology, facilities, and business of the bank.

Valsec undertook the project and adopted methodology to perform a business impact assessment together with an enterprise risk assessment, which included a gap analysis report. Objective was to provide information to base the BCM strategy and formulate the business continuity plan.

Valsec Solutions had two rounds of meeting with the Head of risk to understand the present level of awareness to BCM and expectations that management had in respect of the following:

1. Number of divisions to be covered.
2. Selection of single point of contact at each location under scope to coordinate with the Valsec team and facilitate their movement and data collection.
3. Management also identified their list of mission-critical divisions, which needed first priority in the BIA exercise.

Kickoff meeting involved Heads from various sections of the bank to whom via a PowerPoint presentation, the Valsec TL explained what has to be done, how the BIA would be conducted, and what would be the inputs necessary to complete the data gathering process.

Train the trainer: Ambiguous gave Valsec a list of personnel who would be on the BCM team (SPOCs). These people had to be trained in BCM procedures to take the responsibility of maintaining, exercising, and reviewing the plan periodically. Tentative schedules for weekly training for these SPOCs were also discussed.

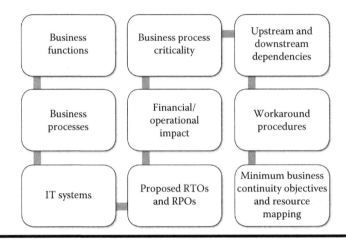

Figure 2.21   Business impact analysis.

Implementing methodology: From every business division, data about business functions, their business processes, and the IT infrastructure were obtained. Not only the core banking system, but other systems in other functions, their interfaces, and interdependencies were examined. The consulting firm identified existing mission-critical systems including telephony equipment, front-office systems, back-office systems, enterprise systems, and operational support infrastructure and established benchmarks for maximum allowable outage (MAO).

The criticality of mission-critical functions and the proposed maximum acceptable outage period were mapped and documented. Workaround procedures for processes were discussed, and recovery options were contemplated upon. For mission-critical systems, review the existing operational infrastructure, implementations, and processes (Figure 2.21).

A few scenario-based study was undertaken, the maximum tolerable period of disruption for mission-critical systems was determined, and the minimum resources required for resuming mission-critical systems in the period of disruption was ascertained.

Completed a research and analysis of best practices for Operational Recovery within the financial services industry and more specifically within the banking sector. Further, and most importantly, this assessment led to aid the organization to develop a robust plan to be resilient and recover from disaster in order to resume normal operations within a defined time frame.

Ambiguous Bank could develop a live plan, plan a schedule for testing and exercising the plan, and had the handholding and external support from Valsec for the first three quarters till all the BCM personnel were trained and confident in handling the *business continuity management system* (*BCMS*) for Ambiguous Bank. The following criticality criteria were set by them (Table 2.31).

Table 2.31 Levels of Severity of Impact Set by Ambiguous Bank

Impact Level	Description	Customer Dissatisfaction	Financial Cost	Adverse Publicity Reputation Loss	Performance of Business Objectives (Operations)
0	None	No complaints on service	No loss	No impact	No impact
1	Insignificant	Unsatisfactory customer experience not directly related to service rendered	Small loss	Rumors	Minor delay in delivering some noncore business objectives
2	Minor	Unsatisfactory customer experience–easily resolved	Loss up to 0.1% of budget	Local media – short term. Minor effect on staff morale.	Inability to operate some noncore business objectives
3	Moderate	Mismanagement of customer care, short-term effects (less than a week)	Loss up to 0.25% of budget	Local media – long term. Significant effect on staff morale.	Ability to operate/ provide core business objectives only
4	Major	Serious mismanagement of customer care, long-term effects (more than a week)	Loss up to 1% of budget	National media < 3 days	Inability to operate/ provide some core business objectives
5	Catastrophic	Totally unsatisfactory customer experience	Loss exceeding 5% of the budget	National media > 3 days	Inability to operate/ provide any core business objectives

Valsec solutions had the following goals to conduct an effective BIA:

- Identify weaknesses and recommend a disaster prevention program.
- Map down the gaps, the mission-critical processes, suggested RTOs and RPOs, and mapping resources required for resumption of processes after a disaster.
- Build a business case for BCM strategy and recovery planning.

The BIA objectives were met, and a business continuity strategy for the bank was proposed within one month of the management presentation as had been declared, and a fully trained BCM team was prepared who were taking an active interest in the BCM implementation.

Chapter 3

Risk Assessment and Reporting

Introduction

Business has undergone a paradigm shift with global markets predominantly capturing a chunk of the market share. Technology is used as an enabler of business and continuously provides infrastructure, applications, and networks to facilitate business processes.

A constant factor in the business landscape is "uncertainty." Uncertainty may be defined as a state or condition that involves a deficiency of information, event, or the likelihood of event, and leads to inadequate or incomplete knowledge or understanding. It is this uncertainty that is the origin of risk.

> *ISO 31000 defines risk* as the "effect of uncertainty on objectives," and an effect is a positive or negative deviation from what is expected. It is apparent from the definition that risk can be positive or negative and requires different treatments depending on its nature.
>
> *Positive risk* is the chance that your objectives will produce too much of a good thing. In the context of positive risks, risk management normally deals with opportunity. Let us see some examples of positive risk:
>
> 1. Organization is faced with a higher level of taxation if its profits exceed by a certain stated limit.
> 2. A project management office that handles a portfolio of projects runs the risk that one or many projects will run late, but the positive risk is that they will be finished before their scheduled time.

3. An ambitious head of department works hard, takes on multitasking, and manages the positive risk that he or she wins the trust of his bosses, and they overburden him or her with so much work that he or she finds difficult to handle.

4. A nightclub in a small town, which is popular on weekends, introduces Thursdays as happy hour day and cuts prices on that day. Here marketing division runs the positive risk of popularizing Thursdays and risking fall in sales on week days.

Managing positive risk: As we observe, positive risks offer an opportunity, and business gets lured by such positive risks. They can often be managed as opportunities when they occur. When income is rising, the positive risk is of a higher slab of tax, and one can manage by donating to charity in order to reduce the taxable income.

Negative risks: On the other hand, negative risks have dire consequences and hence call for a proper risk management methodology to manage them. *The Economic Times* has defined such risks as, "Risk implies future uncertainty about a deviation from expected earnings or expected outcome. Risk measures the uncertainty that an investor is willing to take to realize a gain from an investment."*

Risk: It is the chance or probability to incur a loss or damage if exposed to a hazard.

Hazard: It is any source of potential damage, harm, or adverse health effects on something or someone under certain conditions at work. Hazard is a source that may result in a risk condition, as shown in Table 3.1. So, we see that hazards lead to risk conditions as shown in the table.

Table 3.1   Risk Conditions

Some Hazards and Their Effects		
Description	*Hazard*	*Example of Harm Caused*
Thing	Dagger	Injury
Substance	Kerosene	Burns
Material	Cooking gas	Fire
Source of energy	Electricity	Shock
Condition	Rain	Flooding
Process	Welding	Metal fume fever
Practice	Rigid management	Employee dissatisfaction

---

* http://economictimes.indiatimes.com/definition/risk.

Likewise, we can look at some more sources of risk:

1. Technological innovation and its implementation
2. Changes in economic environment
3. Compliance to laws and regulations
4. Obligations from commercial contracts and obligations therefrom
5. Changes in political environment and trends
6. Shortcomings in managerial decision-making
7. Terrorist activities
8. Human errors and weaknesses
9. Lack of integrity in employees

Hazards are all around. For example, you are walking on the road, and somebody throws some heavy object that hits you; you are standing near the pedestal fan, suddenly it catches your scarf unwittingly, and you get suffocated at the neck; you are working in office, a sudden bout of heavy rains causes local transport to get still, and you find yourself spending the night in office on an empty stomach.

If you travel to office without an umbrella in spite of a rain forecast, you do so at your own risk. If there is a hazard of a whirlpool, there is a board set by authorities asking visitors to the beach to refrain from swimming there; in spite of that if you swim on the forbidden patch, you do so at your own risk. Hence we see that risk is nothing but what we willingly undertake knowing the existence of the hazard. Originating from hazards, threats hover over the business landscape, and when threats exploit existing vulnerabilities, risk consequences occur.

The next question is what is it that we are trying to protect? Every organization has its assets; people, processes, facilities, information assets, customers, contractors, and third parties are all assets that we want to protect.

What is it that we are protecting our assets against? We are trying to protect our assets against threats. *Threats* are surrounding the business environment and are defined as "anything that can exploit a vulnerability and obtain, damage, or destroy an asset whether intentionally or unintentionally." Hence, we now turn to what is vulnerability in the context of risk? ISO 27000 defines *vulnerability* as the weakness of an asset or control that can be exploited by a threat. Vulnerabilities can further be classified as follows:

■ *Intrinsic vulnerability*: It is an intrinsic character of an asset that can be exploited by a threat, and many times it is an inherent quality of the asset. For instance, anything made of glass is intrinsically fragile and hence vulnerable to breaking.
■ *Contextual vulnerability*: It is a weakness in control or security that can be exploited by a threat. For instance, weak password syntax or weak perimeter

control that makes an organization vulnerable to unauthorized intrusion. The risk identification process must focus on intrinsic vulnerabilities as they pose a larger element of risk.

Risk may be a sum of assets, threats, and vulnerabilities. It is the potential for loss if a threat exploits a vulnerability. While doing a risk assessment, the following formula can be used for determining risk:

$$\text{Risk} = \text{Assets} + \text{Threats} + \text{Vulnerabilitie}$$

Note: Risk materializes if there are vulnerabilities, that is, a gap in control systems exists. If the business environment is adequately protected, there may be threats, but in the absence of vulnerabilities, they cannot pose risks since the environment is controlled. So, if there are no vulnerabilities, there is low or no risk.

Risk is at the core of every business, risk may exist in different forms.

- *Inherent risks*: Some risks are by the very nature of the business. For instance, a dealer who deals in perishable goods runs the risk of goods deteriorating at the end of the day.

  Further, there are several risk factors that might be proprietary to a particular organization. The following are the more common risk factors:
  - Resources to conduct IT repairs and mitigation activities.
  - Costs associated with protecting PII of customers.
  - Loss of public image and relations.
- *Demographic risks*: This refers to the place of business; risk exists if that place becomes unavailable or that country is barred to deal in certain specific good.
- *Legal and regulatory risk*: Refers to the law of the land and associated compliances.
- *Operational risk*: Refers to risk in the way business processes are run.
- *People risks*: Are those associated with the people working for the organization. For instance, the risk of not getting people proficient in a specialized skill at alternate location, risk of bad management, risk of disgruntled employees, and so on.
- *Financial risks*: Refer to anything that affects profitability of the organization for instance, liabilities arising from lawsuits, penalties for noncompliance, and so on.
- *Technology risk*: Refers to risk arising from use of technology. For instance, the risk of computer network failures and problems associated with using outdated equipment, changes in business that renders the current technology redundant, and so on.
- *Sourcing risk*: Such as issues within the business or industry resulting in failure or interruptions to the supply chain of raw materials and products.

- *Market risk*: Such as changes in consumer taste and increased competition.
- *Pandemic*: Such as human influenza, swine flu, or bird flu.
- *Workplace safety risks*: Such as accidents caused by materials, equipment, or location of work. For instance, a workshop for jewelry situated in the basement of an industrial center is having an outlet as a narrow space due to security, and this can be a risk during a crisis when evacuation may take exceptionally long time.
- *Information security risks*: Such as theft, fraud, loss of intellectual property, terrorism, extortion, and online breach of security/fraud.
- *Risk from suppliers of utility services*: Such as failures or interruptions in power supply, water, transport, and telecommunications.

Risk Breakdown Structure

The Risk Breakdown Structure (RBS) lists categories and subcategories of risk. It also includes the identification of possible causes and potential consequences. You can use historical data, theoretical analysis, informed opinions, expert advice, and stakeholder input to identify organization's risks. As you describe the issue/risk, consider threats, vulnerabilities, and impact if the risk is not managed. Place this information in the column called *"Risk Description"* (Figure 3.1).

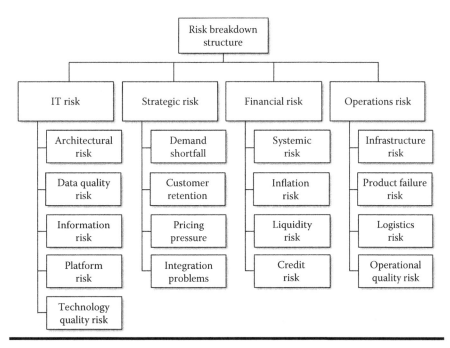

Figure 3.1   Risk breakdown structure (illustration).

Instead of going through big spreadsheet with hundreds of verbose entries about risks, RBS provides—a pictorial representation of related items through tree structure as an excellent way of getting the whole picture in a single place for effective communication, management, and governance.

In the last section, we saw how business impact analysis is performed. Before we delve into the finer aspects of risk management, it is better to see the connection between BIA and RA since it is a much-discussed issue.

Risk Assessment and Business Impact Analysis

Although there is no doubt that risk management and business impact analysis are both vital to business continuity, there is a lot of disagreement on the order of execution of both about whether it is better to perform the risk assessment before, during, or after the BIA. Although many professionals argue that it is best to perform the risk assessment before the BIA to establish the risk landscape in which the organization operates, it would be better to look at the outcome of BIA as listed below:

1. The output from BIA is
   a. The identification of key processes and key dependencies on which the business operates.
   b. The identification of resources needed to perform business activities.
   c. The understanding/estimation of impact of downtime, that is, the RTO and RPO and the impact of nonfunctioning of core processes on business reputation and customers.
2. The inputs into the risk assessment are
   a. The identification of key assets/resources that may be impacted on materialization of a threat.
   b. An understanding of business impact in order to prioritize on risks and plan risk mitigation strategies.

Considering the above, business impact analysis studies the organizational context, its business, the people, process, technology model, the chart of dependencies and maps on a time scale the organization's ability to do without its key processes or vital data. Hence identification of key assets/resources is available for performing a RA.

Ideally the BIA exercise of data gathering and compiling should be over, and just before final analysis and reporting for BIA, the risk assessment can be conducted. Both work in concentric circles, and the commonality is that asset/resource identification and identification of key business risks such as single point of failure due to dependency on single vendor, IT risks, and so on, which is applying to both. Sometimes it is the call of standards that prescribe the order. Although

American standard promotes RA in precedence of BIA, the UK standard promotes BIA before RA. But in any case, both advocate that BIA and RA are important for mapping and mitigating business risks and preparing the business resilience plan. A third school of thought is to run both simultaneously; it will help to crash on time of evaluation.

Risk Management

In the previous section, we saw that risk is the sum of assets, threats, and vulnerabilities. Organizations aim at safeguarding assets and maintaining data integrity. Hence, they establish a risk management system to manage their risks.

Risk management: Comprises of a coordinated set of activities and methods used to direct the organization and to control the risks that can adversely impact the activities and obstruct organization's ability to achieve objectives. The management of risk requires the identification of risk, and this process is facilitated by the creation of a base of risk scenarios or risk situations.

FISMA 3544: Prescribes annual evaluation of InfoSec security policies, procedures, and practices.

ISO 27001: Lays down that organizations to assess risks against risk criteria and organizational objectives.

NIST SP 800-30: Defines risk assessment as an analysis of threats in conjunction with vulnerabilities and existing controls.

OCTAVE: Provides that risk assessment will be needed to make risk management decisions regarding the degree of security remediation.

ISO 27005: Defines risk assessment as a sum of risk identification, risk estimation, and risk evaluation.

ISO 31000: Lays down "a risk management process is one that systematically applies management policies, procedures and practices to a set of activities intended to establish the context, communicate the context and consult with stakeholders and identify, analyze, evaluate, treat, monitor and review risk." In this context, it is desirable to understand that every management has its own perception of risk.

Management commitment plays an important role in management of risks

■ To set accountabilities.
■ To commit resources.
■ To provide a rationale or criteria for dealing with risk.
■ To set risk management matrix.

■ To arrange for periodic reviews.
■ To democratize risk management.
■ To communicate risk policy within the organization.
■ To build an incident response system and provide for change management corresponding to change in risks.

Management represents the tone at top and determine the risk attitude. An organization's *risk attitude* reflects the organization's perception and approach to risk. It describes the way risks will be assessed and addressed according to *risk criteria* and in line with the risk attitude adopted by the organization.

Risk attitude: Generally, it determines risk treatment, whether risks are to be tolerated, shared, avoided, retained, or transferred and also whether these treatments are to be implemented or postponed to some future date. Like business continuity, a risk assessment process is also driven by the top management.

Risk appetite: In the context of ISO 22301 standard, *risk appetite* refers to the amount and type of risk that an organization is prepared to accept, tolerate, or pursue.

Risk policy: Defines a general commitment direction or intention and expresses an organization's top-level commitment to risk management and gives it general direction or intention.

It will be beneficial to assess management approach to risk as it will help do the risk assessment walkthrough. The objective of risk management is not to prohibit or prevent risk-taking activity, but to ensure that the risks are consciously taken with full knowledge, clear purpose, and understanding so that it can be measured and mitigated. Basic tenets of risk do not change. This is apparent in the different models of risk that we will see shortly.

Risk Management Framework

A risk management framework is a set of components that support and sustain risk management throughout an organization. There are two types of components:

1. Foundations include risk management policy objectives, mandate, and commitment.
2. Organizational arrangements include plans, relationships, accountabilities, resources processes, and activities used to manage organizational risk.

When a practitioner enters the organization, he or she has to grasp two things:

1. Level of awareness and understanding of risks faced by the organization.
2. Management's acceptance to a certain risk level, its consensus to live with those risks.

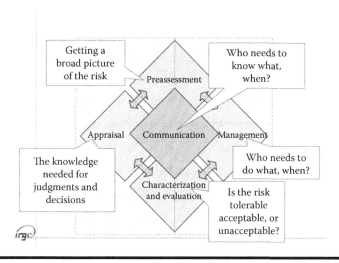

Figure 3.2   IRGC risk governance framework.

Risk Management Framework Development

An organization's ability, willingness, and capacity to manage risks are usually reflected in the risk management framework defined by the organization. It is an essential part of the risk governance framework. The risk management framework should adopt best practices so that the adopted risk framework is reliable, robust, and consistent.

Let us discuss some established risk frameworks.

In the previous section, we saw that risk is the sum of assets, threats, and vulnerabilities. Organizations aim at safeguarding assets and maintaining data integrity. Hence, they establish a risk management system to manage their risks (Figure 3.2).

In this model, communicating effectively is at the heart of the model and a role and need based evaluation of risk is made for management to appraise and deal with risk. This enables taking a holistic picture of risk environment that helps determine risk treatment.

PPRR Risk Model

The prevention, preparedness, response, and recovery (PPRR) model is a comprehensive approach to risk management. This model has been used by Australian emergency management agencies for decades and can save time and money when responding to an incident or disaster. PPRR will help to anticipate possible direct impacts to business and impacts on your suppliers and customers, which may flow on to your business (Figure 3.3).

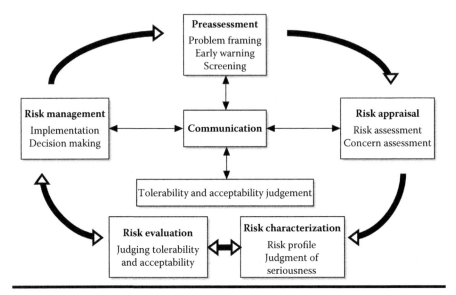

Figure 3.3   PPRR risk model. (From Government of Queensland, www.business. qld.gov.au/business.)

PPRR Steps

- *Prevention*: Take actions to reduce or eliminate the likelihood or effects of an incident.
- *Preparedness*: Take steps before an incident to ensure effective response and recovery.
- *Response*: Contain, control, or minimize the impacts of an incident.
- *Recovery*: Take steps to minimize disruption and recovery times.

Risk IT Framework (ISACA)

Risk IT is a framework based on a set of guiding principles for effective management of IT risk. The framework complements COBIT, a comprehensive framework for the governance and control of business-driven, IT-based solutions and services. While COBIT provides a set of controls to mitigate IT risk, Risk IT provides a framework for enterprises to identify, govern, and manage IT risk. Simply put, COBIT provides the means of risk management; Risk IT provides the ends. Enterprises who have adopted (or are planning to adopt) COBIT as their IT governance framework can use Risk IT to enhance risk management (Figure 3.4).

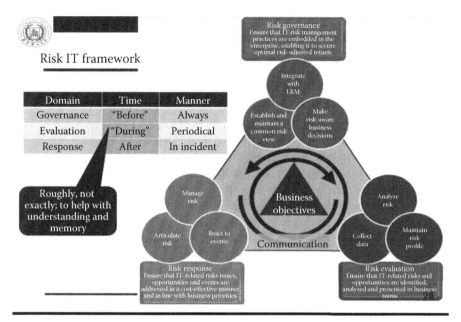

Figure 3.4   Risk IT framework (ISACA).

The Risk IT Principles

The Risk IT framework is about IT risk—business risk related to the use of IT.

The connection to business is founded in the principles on which the framework is built. Effective enterprise governance and management of IT risk are as follows:

- Always connects to business objectives
- Aligns the management of IT-related business risk with overall enterprise risk management (ERM)—if applicable, that is, if ERM is implemented in the enterprise
- Balances the costs and benefits of managing IT risk
- Promotes fair and open communication of IT risk
- Is a continuous process and part of daily activities
- Establishes the right tone from the top while defining and enforcing personal accountability for operating within acceptable and well-defined tolerance levels

The Risk IT framework explains IT risk, allows the enterprise to make appropriate risk-aware decisions, and will enable users to

- Integrate the management of IT risk into the overall ERM of the organization.
- Make well-informed decisions about the extent of the risk, the risk appetite, and the risk tolerance of the enterprise.
- Understand how to respond to the risk.

The Risk IT framework provides

- A set of governance practices for risk management.
- An end-to-end process framework for successful IT risk management.
- A generic list of common, potentially adverse, IT-related risk scenarios that could impact the realization of business objectives.
- Tools and techniques to understand concrete risks to business operations, as opposed to generic checklists of controls or compliance requirements.

The model is divided into three domains:

- Risk governance
    - Establish and maintain a common risk view
    - Integrate with ERM
    - Make risk-aware business decisions
- Risk evaluation
    - Collect data
    - Analyze risk
    - Maintain risk profile
- Risk response
    - Articulate risk
    - Manage risk
    - React to events

The Risk IT Practitioner Guide is a support document for the Risk IT framework that provides examples of possible techniques to address IT-related risk issues more detailed guidance on how to approach the concepts covered in the process model.

What Are the Benefits of Using Risk IT?

The benefits of using Risk IT include the following:

- A common language to help communication among business, IT, risk, and audit management
- End-to-end guidance on how to manage IT-related risks

- A complete risk profile to better understand risk, so as to better utilize enterprise resources
- A better understanding of the roles and responsibilities with regard to IT risk management
- Alignment with ERM
- A better view of IT-related risk and its financial implications
- Fewer operational surprises and failures
- Increased information quality
- Greater stakeholder confidence and reduced regulatory concerns
- Innovative applications supporting new business initiatives

Business Rationale for Risk Management Framework

Return on investment: Structured risk assessment methodology follows a systematic, predefined approach, which is more process driven and hence less susceptible to errors. This makes the risk management more cost effective, and it gives an optimum ROI (Figure 3.5).

- *Efficient use of resources*: It facilitates a more efficient and effective use of resources.
- *Controlled risk environment*: It promotes a more controlled risk environment, which is more resilient.
- *Budgets*: It enables budgeting for the risk management to be more accurate and flexible.

As seen above, risk management is all about planning risk identification, analyzing risks using qualitative and quantitative methods, and then planning mitigation strategies. Continuous risk monitoring is imperative in a dynamic constantly changing risk environment.

Figure 3.6 lists down processes used in risk management. In the above model, the main processes laid down are risk identification, risk impact analysis, risk ranking, and risk mitigation while risk tracking or monitoring has been shown as a constant activity (Figure 3.7).

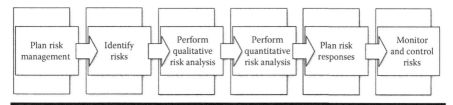

Figure 3.5 Phases of risk management.

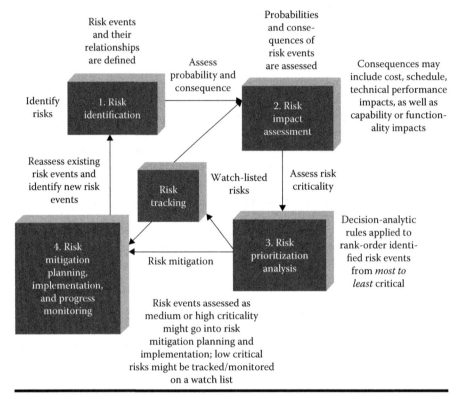

Figure 3.6   Processes in risk management.

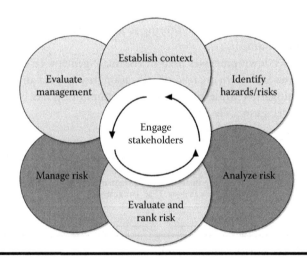

Figure 3.7   Risk assessment process.

The differentiating factor here is the presence of stakeholders at the center and evaluating management intent in terms of setting the risk criteria and risk appetite of the enterprise.

Stakeholder is a person or an organization that can affect or be affected by a decision or an activity. Stakeholders also include those who have the perception that a decision or an activity can affect them. ISO 31000 further distinguishes between external and internal stakeholders.

ISO 27005 gives a more practical model of risk management and planning. It distinctly defines the phases of risk management and is self-explanatory. It mentions establishment of a risk context before assessment, and it also stresses on stakeholder communication (Figure 3.8).

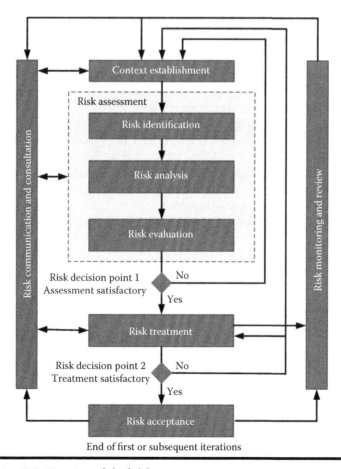

Figure 3.8   ISO 27005 model of risk management.

1. *Risk context to be established*: In the first step, the organizational context has to be considered; it means to define the external and internal risk parameters to be considered by organizations while planning their risk management approach. Context can be of two types:
   a. *External context* that includes its organization's stakeholders, contractual relationships with suppliers and service providers, organizational ethics, culture and capabilities, and standards being implemented. It represents stakeholder values, perceptions, and relationships, as well as its social, cultural, political, legal, regulatory, financial, technological, economic, natural, and competitive environment.
   b. *Internal context* that includes internal stakeholders, its approach to governance, its contractual relationships, its capabilities, culture, and standards. It is a sum of internal environmental parameters that govern how an organization manages risk and tries to fulfill its business objectives.

   ISO 31000 also advocates organization's context when you define the scope of the risk management program in determining its risk criteria and while formulating its risk management policy.
2. *Communication and consultation*: Is an integral part of risk assessment. It is an umbrella activity that goes on throughout the risk assessment process. It stands for a continual and iterative dialog between an organization and its stakeholders. Communication is a two-way process that involves both sharing and receiving information about the management of risk. These include discussions on existence of risk, forms of risk likelihood of risks, probable ways of treating risks, and what the acceptable risks should be.

   But a point to note is that the ultimate risk decisions are that of the organization and not the key stakeholders.
3. *Risk assessment* consists of three distinct processes, which are described as follows (Figure 3.9).

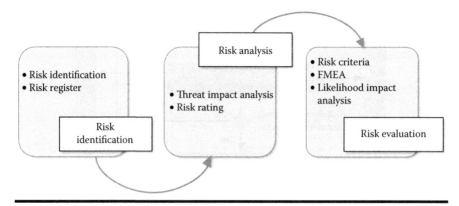

Figure 3.9   Phases of risk assessment.

Risk Identification (Risk Identification, Risk Register)

Risk identification: Risk identification is a process that is used to find, recognize, and describe the risks that could affect the achievement of objectives. It consists of the identification of hazards, and the analysis and evaluation of risks associated with exposure to those hazards.

Quality risk assessments begin with a well-defined problem description or risk question. Some questions relevant to risk assessment are:

1. What, when, where, why, and how are risks likely to happen in your business?
2. What is the likelihood (probability) it will go wrong?
3. Are the risks internal or external?
4. Who may be affected if an incident happens?

Identifying risks involves identification of risk assets, threats, vulnerabilities, and their relationships. ISO 27005 provides for identification of the following:

Assets: Anything of value consisting of people, process, technology, information, data, supporting infrastructure, and business processes are all organizational assets. The primary identification of assets will come with identification of three types of needs within the organization:
- – Need of services
- – Need for information and data
- – Need for compliance to processes and policies

Secondary assets usually comprise of media and dependencies that form part of the assets of the organization. Organizations have to identify their secondary assets for each type of primary asset. This is a process in identification of the organizational context including its dependencies.

Risk assessment envisages inventory of assets, documenting owners, location of assets, and function of these assets. The list of associated business processes that use these assets must also be compiled.

NIST SP 800-30 defines risk assessment as an analysis of threats in conjunction with vulnerabilities and existing controls. In this context, it must be remembered that threat effects cannot be controlled but threats need to be identified. Vulnerability can be treated, and risks have to be managed or balanced (Table 3.2).

Threat Identification and Assessment: The term "threat" refers to the source and means of a particular type of attack. A threat assessment is performed to determine the best approaches to securing a system against a specific threat or class of threat. Threats comprise of the main act or trigger the circumstances attached to the event. There is a major difference between a risk assessment and a threat assessment.

Table 3.2 Vulnerability/Threat Analysis (Illustration)

S. No.	Vulnerability	Threat Source	Threat Action
1	Antivirus is not installed at network level	External	Can attack on machine not updated manually with latest patches
2	Disgruntled employee	Dismissed employee not immediately relieved	Unauthorized modification to system
3	Biometric attendance machine not repaired	Employees	Not attending regularly

A threat assessment is typically an inventory of all threats that may impact the organization. The conclusions drawn from a threat assessment may be helpful in planning where threat-specific response and recovery procedures are to be placed. Based on feedback, executive managers normally assess the potential threats that could impact them and their organizations, or they recognize that they cannot predict all threats.

Ways of Identifying Risk: Prior to identifying what risks matter to you, it would do good to review the business plan and think about what you could not do without, and what type of incidents could impact on these areas.

Techniques for Risk Identification

1. *Ask "what-if?" questions*: A useful technique is to review your business plan and ask "what-if" questions such as
   a. What if there is no power supply?
   b. What if there is no Internet?
   c. What if key documents are destroyed?
   d. What if premises were destroyed or not available?
   e. What if key personnel quit the job?
   f. What if key suppliers went out of business?
   g. What if a natural disaster strikes your primary place of business?
   h. What if essential services such as roads or communication facilities are unavailable?
2. *Brainstorm*: Brainstorming with different people, such as your accountant, financial adviser, staff, suppliers, and other interested parties, will help you get many different perspectives on risks to your business.
3. *Analyze other events*: Think about past events that have, or could have, affected your business. What were the outcomes of those events? Could they happen again? Think about what possible future events could affect your

business. Analyze the scenarios that might lead to an event and what the outcome could be. This will help you identify risks that might be external to your business.

4. *Assess your processes*: Use flowcharts, checklists, and inspections to assess your work processes. Identify each step in your processes, and think about the associated risks. Ask yourself what could prevent each step from happening, and how that would affect the rest of the process.

5. *Consider the worst-case scenario*: The safest underlying assumption in risk management is assumed worst-case scenario. For example, someone running a restaurant could lose power, which could then cause the food to spoil. If the restaurant owner was unaware of the power outage or the chef decided to serve the food anyway, customers could get food poisoning, and the restaurant could be liable and could suffer from financial losses and negative publicity. Once you have identified risks, you will need to analyze their likelihood and consequences and then come up with options for managing them.

6. *Analyze and evaluate the impact of risks*: It can be possible to assess impacts from collecting information, past reports, and so on. Task now is to segregate the less important risks from the more significant risks. Risk rating is an integral part of risk management.

7. *Effect of Risk on Net Worth*: Business risks negatively affect net worth of the company. A business more exposed to risk is worth less than an identical business exposed to less risk. Reducing risk is therefore important not only in helping your business to succeed but also in maximizing its value (Figure 3.10).

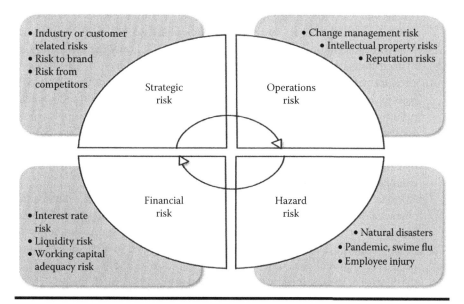

Figure 3.10   Four quadrants of business risks.

Risks That Affect Business

Identifying Business Risk

Business risk is the possibility that a company will have lower than anticipated profits, or that it will experience a loss rather than a profit. Business risk is affected by factors such as volume of sales, price competitiveness, input costs, economic conditions, and legal and regulatory framework. Business risks are those risks internal or external that can affect directly or indirectly a business' ability to operate. Business risk refers to the probability of a business not able to meet its operating expenses that enables continuity of production of goods or delivery of services. There are two types of business risks: systematic risk and unsystematic risk.

Systematic risk: It refers to business operating in a general economic slow-down, war, or some natural disaster. Any business operating in the market is exposed to this risk, and small businesses will be most affected in this situation.

Unsystematic risk: Describes the downturn of individual business caused by investment decisions or management attitude. Hence investors divest from single industry investments and diversify their portfolio.

Strategic risk: Every organization works on a business plan. But we live in a dynamic world and business environment changes. Risks due to such changes are called strategic risks. It represents the decrease in effectiveness and organization's ability to achieve its goals. Changes occur due to new competitors, technology change, and so on. Organizations need to adapt to changing conditions and learn to be in competition. A classic example is Kodak, which had such a dominant position in the film photography market that when one of its own engineers invented a digital camera in 1975, it saw the innovation as a threat to its core business model and failed to develop it.

Compliance risk: Laws change continuously, and risk is that organization will have to face additional regulations in the future. For instance, a food supplier running his business in Asia decides to market his goods in Europe. There are significant food safety regulations in addition to the ones in Asia that the organization must follow, which creates compliance risk. Compliance risk may increase by adding a new product line, which requires a lot of regulatory compliance.

Operational risk refers to an unexpected failure in the organization's day-to-day operations. It could be a technical failure, such as a server outage, or it could be caused by your people or processes. People, process, and technology are three components of business and any risk arising due to any these components is operational risk. Operational risk may also arise due to events not in the control of the organization. It could be power outage, earthquake, website being down, and so on.

Financial risk: Most categories of risk have a financial impact, in terms of extra costs or lost revenue. But the category of financial risk refers specifically to the money flowing in and out of your business and the possibility of a sudden financial loss. Say more than 50% of an organizations' profits are coming from a single client; organization is facing a significant finance risk as loss of that client may lead to a substantial loss.

Reputational risk is the risk of damage to reputation/goodwill resulting in immediate loss of customers, revenue, and customer dissatisfaction. There are many kinds of business, but every business values its reputation and its customers. Due to decline in goodwill, organization may not be able to hire the best hands in industry or lose on advertisers, sponsors, or other partners who may not want to associate with the organization. Consequences of reputation risk are major lawsuits, product recall, embarrassment, and so on.

Risk Inventory and Risk Register

It is mandatory for many organizations to maintain an inventory of assets and document applicable risks in a risk register. It will contain all identified risks, potential responses, and documents root causes of identified risks (Table 3.3).

Optionally, organizations may choose to preserve the updated risk categories to have audit traceability.

Risk Analysis (Threats, Vulnerabilities, Analysis, Business Impact from Risk and Recommendations for Risk Treatment Strategies)

Risk analysis is a process used to understand the nature, source, and causes of the risks that have been identified and to estimate the level of risk. It is also used to study impacts and consequences and to examine the controls that currently exist. The depth of risk analysis depends upon the risk, the purpose of the analysis, the information that exists, and the resources available.

Table 3.3 Probable Format for Risk Register

Threat	Predisposing Condition	Vulnerable Entities	Loss	Probability	Impact	Priority Ranking

The chief functions in risk analysis are as follows:

1. Ascertain level of risk
2. Study the risk impact and perform analysis
3. Assess the adequacy of existing controls
4. Achieve at a risk priority for identified risks
5. Make a risk estimation by use of qualitative and quantitative methods
6. Make final recommendations for risk treatment

Risk analysis = Risk identification + Risk estimation

Hence, we see that risk analysis comprises of risk identification (already dealt with in earlier section) and risk estimation. While risk identification deals with identification of assets, threats, controls, vulnerabilities, and consequences, risk estimation is the qualitative and quantitative assessments of risk. To estimate risk, we need to determine the level of risk for the organization.

Level of risk is its magnitude and is represented by combination of likelihood and consequences. Risk levels can be assigned to individual risks or to a combination of risks. Level of risk is often described as low, medium, high, or very high. It should be analyzed in relation to what you are currently doing to control it. It must be borne in mind that control measures can lower the level of risk, but it cannot eliminate risks completely. To analyze risks, you need to work out the likelihood of it happening (frequency or probability) and the consequences it would have (the impact) of the risks you have identified.

Likelihood of an event is the chance (probability) that something might happen, whereas a consequence is the outcome of an event and has adverse effect on organizational objectives (Table 3.4). This is referred to as the level of risk and can be calculated using this formula.

Level of risk = consequences * likelihood

Note: Ratings vary for different types of businesses. The scales above use four different levels; however, you can use as many levels as you need. Also, use descriptors that suit your purpose (e.g., you might measure consequences in terms of human health, rather than dollar value Table 3.5).

Refer to Figure 3.11 for XYZ Corporation, the threat-risk analysis chart is depicted.

As one can see, the rating is given on the *x*-axis, and threats are plotted on the *y*-axis. As can be noticed, the highest risk is from earthquake which is rated at 8.25, the second is from fire which has a rating of 7, and so on. The rating scale

Table 3.4   Likelihood Scale Example

Level	Likelihood	Description
4	Very likely	Happens more than once a year in this industry
3	Likely	Happens about once a year in this industry
2	Unlikely	Happens every 10 years or more in this industry
1	Very unlikely	Has only happened once in this industry

Table 3.5   Consequences Scale Example

Level	Consequence	Description
4	Severe	Financial losses greater than $50,000
3	High	Financial losses between $10,000 and $50,000
2	Moderate	Financial losses between $1,000 and $10,000
1	Low	Financial losses less than $1,000

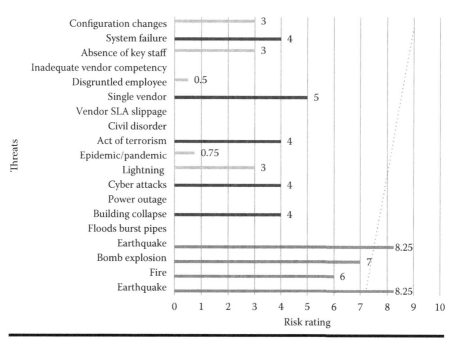

Figure 3.11   Threat-risk analysis chart.

Table 3.6   Risk Rating Table Example

Risk Rating	Description	Action
1–4	Low	Does not need corrective action
4–8	Moderate	Requires corrective action within three months
8–12	High	Requires corrective action within one month
12–16	Severe	Requires immediate corrective action

differs from organization to organization depending on the risk acceptance and risk criteria adopted by the organization.

Once you have identified, analyzed, and evaluated your risks, you need to rank them in order of priority and bifurcate between acceptable risks and unacceptable risks to the organization (Table 3.6).

Risk Evaluation Techniques

Risk evaluation is a process that is used to compare risk analysis results with risk criteria in order to determine whether or not a specified level of risk is acceptable or tolerable.

Organizations have to set the following criteria for risk:

1. Risk evaluation criteria
2. Impact criteria
3. Risk acceptance criteria

Selection of criteria depends upon the following factors:

1. Strategic value of business assets
2. Criticality of business processes
3. Legal and regulatory impact
4. Operational impact
5. Expectation of stakeholders

Results of risk analysis are matched against risk criteria in order to determine whether a particular risk should be acceptable or not acceptable.

Risk decision flow:

1. The decision you are asking the managers to make
2. The background on what you did and why
3. The results of your assessment, focusing on business impact

4. Your recommendations for mitigating risk and cost/benefit analysis (include recommendation with an action plan with expected completion dates, required resources, etc.)

Risk evaluation is performed on a backdrop of existing controls. A risk control is any measure or action that modifies risk. Controls include any policy, procedure, practice, process, technology, technique, method, or device that manages risk.

Risk impact assessment is the process of assessing the probabilities and consequences of risk events if they are realized. The results of this assessment are then used to prioritize risks to establish a most-to-least-critical importance ranking.

Ranking risks in terms of their criticality or importance provides insights into the resource requirements to manage or mitigate the realization of high probability/high consequence risk events.

Evaluating risks is to compare and prioritize risk levels based on risk evaluation criteria and risk acceptance criteria. Once you have established the level of risk, you then need to create a rating table for evaluating the risk. Evaluating a risk means taking a decision about its severity and ways to manage it. For example, you may decide the likelihood of a fire is "unlikely" (a score of 2), but the consequences are "severe" (a score of 4). Using the tables and formula given in this chapter, a fire therefore has a risk rating of 8 (i.e., $2 \times 4 = 8$).

When the level of risk is established, a risk rating table can be developed. Risk rating is fixing risk severity and determining ways to manage it. For instance, if the likelihood of earthquake is 5 but consequences from earthquake are severe, and scale is 4, then the risk rating for earthquake shall be 20.

Risk evaluation should consider

- The significance of the activity for the organization.
- The amount of control organization has over the risk.
- Potential losses to your business.
- Any benefits or opportunities presented by the risk.

Once you have identified, analyzed, and evaluated your risks, you need to rank them in order of priority. You can then decide which methods you will use to treat unacceptable risks in your organization.

Risk Evaluation Techniques:

Preliminary Hazard Analysis (PHA)

PHA is a tool of analysis based on applying prior experience or knowledge of a hazard or failure to identify future hazards, hazardous situations, and events that might cause harm, as well as to estimate their probability of occurrence for a given activity, facility, product, or system.

Table 3.7   Risk Rating Table

		Minor	Moderate	Major
Likelihood	Very likely	Acceptable risk Medium 2	Unacceptable risk High 3	Unacceptable risk Extreme 5
	Likely	Acceptable risk Low 1	Acceptable risk Medium 2	Unacceptable risk High 3
	Unlikely	Acceptable risk Low 1	Acceptable risk Low 1	Acceptable risk Medium 2
	What is the chance it will happen?	Minor	Moderate	Major

Impact
How serious is the risk?

The tool consists of (i) the identification of the possibilities that the risk event happens, (ii) a relative ranking of the hazard using a combination of severity, and (iii) likelihood of occurrence and the identification of possible remedial measures (Table 3.7).

Risk Ranking and Filtering

Risk ranking of complex systems involves evaluation of multiple diverse quantitative and qualitative factors for each risk. The tool involves breaking down a basic risk question into as many components as needed to capture factors involved in the risk. These factors are combined into a single relative risk score that can then be used for ranking risks.

"Filters," in the form of weighting factors or cut-offs for risk scores can be used to scale or fit the risk ranking to management or policy objectives. Risk ranking is useful for management to evaluate both quantitatively assessed and qualitatively assessed risks within the same organizational framework.

Supporting Statistical Tools

Statistical tools can support and facilitate quality risk management. They can enable effective data assessment, aid in determining the significance of the data set(s), and facilitate more reliable decision-making.

A listing of some of the principal statistical tools commonly used are

- Control charts.
- Histograms.

■ Pareto charts.
■ Process capability analysis.

Basic Risk Management Facilitation Methods

Some of the simple techniques that are commonly used to structure risk management by organizing data and facilitating decision-making are

■ Flowcharts.
■ Check sheets.
■ Process mapping.
■ Cause and effect diagrams (also called an Ishikawa diagram or fishbone diagram, Figure 3.12).

As seen in the below diagram, there is one effect, which is growth in attrition rate. In order to analyze the problem using fishbone, we could point out the various causes of this attrition. The style of management is autocratic, and people work in silos. There is lack of effective coordination. There is a tall hierarchy, and management does not plan for the career progression of its employees.

Globalization has led to employees opting for international certifications, which gives them new international opportunities. Other factor like climate and location also contribute toward nonretention of employees. Lack of incentives and low retirement benefits to employees further contribute to attrition. Likewise, there can be a brainstorming exercise to discuss the factors and suggest recommendation for this situation (Table 3.8).

In the matrix above, we see differential zones of values 1–2, which represents low risk. Such risks can be accepted by the enterprise. Values between 3 and 5 are in the middle belt, and they can be treated by controls. Values above 5 would fall

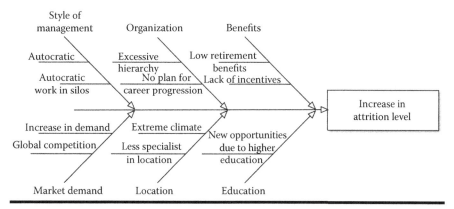

Figure 3.12 Fishbone cause-effect diagram.

Table 3.8   Probability Impact Matrix

		Likelihood of incident scenario				
		Very low	Low	Medium	High	Very high
Business impact	Very low	0	1	2	3	4
	Low	1	2	3	4	5
	Medium	2	3	4	5	6
	High	3	4	5	6	7
	Very high	4	5	6	7	8

in high alert zone since their impact would be highest, and such risks should be controlled immediately.

Failure mode and effects analysis (FMEA) illustration: It is a systematic, proactive method for evaluating a process to identify where and how it might fail and to assess the relative impact of different failures, to identify areas that need to be rectified.

FMEA provides an evaluation of potential failure modes for processes and their likely effect on outcomes and/or product performance. Once failure modes are established, risk reduction can be used to eliminate, contain, reduce, or control the potential failures. FMEA relies on product and process understanding.

FMEA methodically breaks down the analysis of complex processes into manageable steps. It is a powerful tool for summarizing the important modes of failure, factors causing these failures, and the likely effects of these failures. FMEA can be used to prioritize risks and monitor the effectiveness of risk control activities (Table 3.9).

Risk mapping: Risk mapping and monitoring is important for keeping risk levels to acceptable levels (Figure 3.13).

Red and amber green are risk benchmarks based on a proper business impact analysis and qualitative and quantitative risk evaluation. After that risk treatment measures such as risk avoidance, mitigation, sharing, or transfer is done. Since risk treatment involves a cost and risk loss can be ascertained, a cost benefit should be the right indicator of an organization's willingness; to accept risk is not an ad hoc decision.

Organizations would like to mitigate risks in the red belt; amber would be medium risks and would not require such a vigilant risk treatment. Risks under green would be those that can come under acceptable level.

Taken on a dashboard during risk monitoring, the same red would indicate high risks blinking for immediate attention. Amber would indicate medium risks that will be prioritized after the red belt risks. Green stands for full mitigation and control over risks that need no attention. Organizations can configure and prioritize as per risk policy.

Identification of existing controls, and potential control enhancements or new strategies to mitigate business risk by protecting resources (as to decrease the likelihood or severity associated with a disruptive incident).

Table 3.9 FMEA

Dept.	Potential Failure Mode	Potential Effect of Failure	Severity Level	Cause of Failure	Occurrence Rating	Detection Rating	Risk Priority Number
IT	Weak passwords	Unauthorized intrusion	5	No password policy	2	3	30
Ops	Single point of failure	Disruption of ops	.3	Single vendor	1	2	6
Finance	Debtors do not pay on time	Bad liquidity position	4	Ineffective credit policy	2	1	

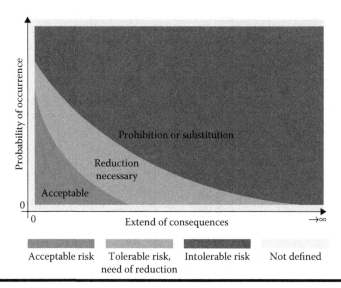

Figure 3.13 Risk mapping: Acceptable, tolerable, and intolerable risks (traffic light model).

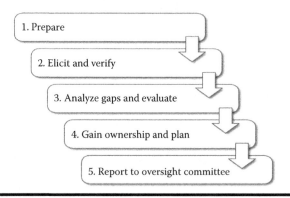

Figure 3.14 Phased approach to evaluate effectiveness of controls.

It is advisable to use a phased approach to evaluate effectiveness of current controls for mitigating risks (Figure 3.14). The risk proportions attached with a widespread deployment of information technologies increase with growth in customers, business partners, and outsourced operations (Figure 3.15).

Risk scenarios are very useful in assessing different categories of risk. The Figure 3.16 lays down risk scenario categories. It may be loss of data, or loss of IT services, or loss of key skills, or nonavailability of premises.

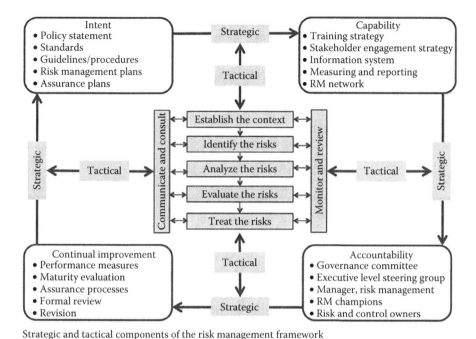

Strategic and tactical components of the risk management framework

Figure 3.15   Evaluation of the risk management effectiveness.

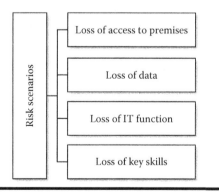

Figure 3.16   Risk scenarios.

Considering the above scenarios, risk assessments focus on the following:

Facilities not available: A scenario analysis can be made of this situation, and a risk program can be tailored to suit your organization. A workshop mode can be arranged, and there can be a brainstorming session. It can be due to fire or bomb blast where the authorities have blocked access to offices and nothing is available. In that scenario, resumption of even critical business operations needs to be planned

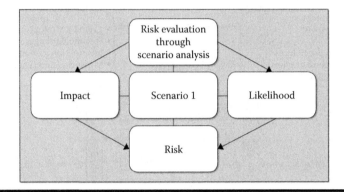

Figure 3.17   Scenario analysis.

Table 3.10   Risk Score

Risk Score	Risk Category	Description
40–50	High	Potential for serious damage to business assets, finances, reputation, employees, or customers. There is a need to plan mitigation immediately.
20–39	Medium	Potential for moderate damage to business assets, finances, reputation, employees, or customers. Mitigate risks within reasonable time after considering other security challenges if any.
1–19	Low	Organizations choose to accept such risks.

carefully, and RTOs will have to be net. Business impacts have to be considered and in the end have to preserve results for future repeatability or reference (Figure 3.17).

Risk scenario analysis focuses on existing and emerging risks, risk consequences, and risk plans. It can lead to understanding stakeholder activities and communication before, during, and after a risk issue occurs. Risk scenario analysis typically gets incorporated into more effective responses and programs that fetch a higher value to the enterprise (Table 3.10).

Residual risk is the risk left over after you have implemented a risk treatment plan. It is the risk remaining after you have reduced the risk, removed the source of the risk, modified the consequences, changed the probabilities, transferred the risk, or retained the risk.

While performing risk evaluation, decision-makers should

■ Take responsibility for coordinating quality risk management across various functions and departments of their organization.
■ Ensure that a quality risk management process is defined, deployed, and reviewed and that adequate resources are available.

Initiating a Quality Risk Management Process

Quality risk management should include systematic processes designed to coordinate, facilitate, and improve science-based decision-making with respect to risk. Possible steps used to initiate and plan a quality risk management process might include the following:

- Define the problem and/or risk question, including pertinent assumptions identifying the potential for risk.
- Assemble background information and/or data on the potential hazard, harm, or other impact relevant to the risk assessment.
- Identify critical resources.
- Specify a timeline, deliverables, and appropriate level of decision-making for the risk management process (Figure 3.18).

Risk Assessment Methodologies (Qualitative Assessment, Quantitative Assessment)

Risk Estimation Techniques

The output of a risk assessment is either a quantitative estimate of risk or a qualitative description of a range of risk. When risk is expressed quantitatively, a numerical probability is used. Alternatively, risk can be expressed using qualitative descriptors, such as "high," "medium," or "low," which should be defined in as much detail as possible.

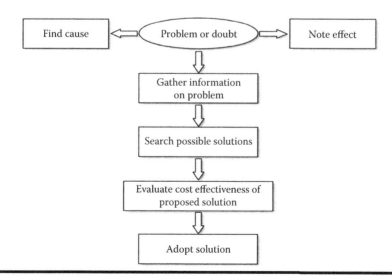

Figure 3.18   Modeling of risk problems.

Risk estimation can be done by adopting any of the following methods:

1. Qualitative assessment
2. Quantitative assessment
3. Mixed assessment

Tools and techniques for qualitative analysis include surveys or questionnaires, interviews, and group sessions to determine the threat level and annualized loss expectancy. Qualitative risk assessments are usually well received because they involve many people at different levels of the organization. Those involved with a qualitative risk assessment can feel a sense of ownership of the process.

Qualitative Risk Analysis

Qualitative assessment is a scenario-driven assessment that ranks the seriousness of threats and sensitivity of assets by grade or class, such as low, medium, or high. A rating of low, medium, or high is subjective. In this example, the following categories are defined:

- *Low*—Minor inconvenience; can be tolerated for a short period of time but will not result in financial loss.
- *Medium*—Can result in damage to the organization, can cost a moderate amount of money to repair, and can result in negative publicity.
- *High*—Will result in a loss of goodwill between the company, client, or employee, may result in a large legal action or fine, or cause the company to significantly lose revenue or earnings.

Qualitative risk estimation relies on employee knowledge and experience. This type of assessments involves studying assets in the light of known vulnerabilities against a database of potential vulnerabilities. Risks thus identified are measured against probability of occurrence and threat impact.

Since risk is subjective, two experts evaluating the same risks can come to different conclusions. Sometimes employees do not have the level to arrive at quantitative assessments. To save time and cost, a qualitative risk assessment is preferred. Also qualitative risk assessment is very useful when it is too difficult to assign a dollar value to a specific risk, for instance, loss of goodwill, customer dissatisfaction, and loss of reputation. Other types of qualitative assessment techniques include the following:

1. *The Delphi technique*—A group assessment process that allows individuals to contribute anonymous opinions. Identifying and assessing the potential impact and likelihood of future events, which might evolve into risks, are a

prerequisite to identify future security challenges. In particular, risks associated with global supply chains are special since they involve a multitude of international stakeholders with different perspectives on security needs and measures. Therefore, it is essential to determine which techniques and instruments are best suited for risk assessment in complex and multiorganizational environments.

Delphi technique makes a fivefold contribution to risk analysis as follows:
1. Identification and quantification of risks
2. Analyzing stakeholder perceptions and views
3. Stimulating a global communication process
4. Identifying weak signals, outlier opinions, and wildcards
5. Facilitating risk scenario development

2. *Facilitated risk assessment process (FRAP)*—FRAP or facilitated risk assessment process was created by Thomas Peltier, a prolific and respected author and educator in the area of information security. FRAP is designed to enable an organization to use its own people to facilitate the main steps involved in risk assessment much as the others are. FRAP fully situates itself in the qualitative camp and basically conforms to the standard pattern of risk assessment for qualitative risk. It is a subjective process that obtains results by asking a series of questions. It places risks into one of 26 categories. FRAP is designed to be completed in a matter of hours, making it a quick process to perform.

3. *OCTAVE (operationally critical, threat, asset and vulnerability evaluation)*—It was created at the Software Engineering Institute (SEI) at Carnegie Mellon University, a federally funded (DoD) research and development center.

OCTAVE is a set of criteria that can be used as the basis of a methodology. The criteria specify that a skilled analysis team, made up of people within an organization, gather input from the organization, analyze the results, and act upon them in a structured and methodical manner.

The process flow is as follows:

Phase 1: Build asset-based threat profiles
Phase 2: Identify infrastructure vulnerabilities
Phase 3: Develop security strategy and plans

Build asset-based threat profiles: The analysis team meets with members of the organization from the top to the bottom to identify assets, vulnerabilities, threats, and current controls. After that, identify infrastructure vulnerabilities. The analysis team expands on phase 1 by analyzing the key infrastructure associated with the assets identified and searching for vulnerabilities. In phase 3, the security strategy and plan are drafted and finalized.

Table 3.11 Qualitative Risk Assessment

Asset	Loss of Availability	Loss of Integrity	Loss of Confidentiality
Customer credit card and billing information	M	H	H
SLA documents	L	M	M
Advertising brochures	L	L	L

Steps to perform a qualitative risk assessment: The following steps calculate annualized loss expectancy (ALE) for a threat/vulnerability pair identified for a specific business process or technical component of a process.

1. Calculate the aggregate value of assets and the processes they support.
2. Calculate the expected loss related to a single incident, the single loss expectancy (SLE). SLE is affected by the presence of a documented and practiced incident response plan.
3. Calculate the annualized rate of occurrence (ARO). We do not usually expect an incident to occur each year. Rather, a specific event is likely to repeat on a multiyear cycle. For example, if an incident occurs one time in a year, the ARO is taken as 1. If an incident occurs once in two years, ARO is taken as 0.5. Loss suffered during one occurrence is SLE and when ARO is multiplied by SLE we get ALE for that incident. For example, if the SLE of an incident is $100,000 and the ARO is 0.20, the ALE is $2,000. In other words, the SLE is the annual cost of a single incident when total cost is spread over five years or the expected repetition cycle of the incident.

Please note that *NIST 800-26* has to document that uses confidentiality, integrity, and availability as categories for a loss. It then rates each as high medium or low (Table 3.11).

Quantitative risk assessment utilizes mathematical formulas to get the risk exposure factor and SLE. Peter Drucker's famous quote on risk is "if you can't measure it, you can't manage it."

$$R(E) \text{ (Risk exposure)} = P(L)(\text{Potential Loss})$$

$$\times S(L)(\text{Severity of potential loss})$$

1. *Risk exposure factor*: The first step is to find the exposure factor. Risk exposure is defined as a subjective potential percentage of loss to a specific asset if a specific threat is realized. This is usually expressed as a percentage. For instance, if the risk exposure to total assets is 10% and if value of total assets is $100,000, then the risk exposure is $10,000.

2. *Calculate the single loss expectancy (SLE)*: The SLE value is a dollar figure that represents the organization's loss from a single loss or the loss of this particular information asset. SLE is calculated as follows:

$$\text{Single Loss Expectancy} = \text{Asset Value} \times \text{Exposure Factor}$$

For instance, if the goodwill is valued at $200,000, then SLE = 200,000 * 10% as described above = $20,000. Items to consider when calculating the SLE include the physical destruction or theft of assets, loss of data, theft of information, and threats that might delay processing.

ARO: The probability of a threat being realized is called the ARO. The ARO represents the estimated frequency at which a given threat is expected to occur, say in a year. Suppose a threat materializes once in two years, then the ARO is ½ = 0.5.

3. *ALE*: The ALE is an annual expected financial loss to an organization's information asset because of a particular threat occurring within that same calendar year.

Annualized Loss Expectancy (ALE)

$$= \text{Single Loss Expectancy (SLE)} \times \text{Annualized Rate of Occurrence (ARO)}$$

In the calculations done above, we can calculate the ALE now. It will be SLE $20,000 * ARO 0.5 = $10,000. Prioritization of risk and risk rating is based on the ALE calculation. Senior management needs to assess to prioritize resources and determine what threats should receive the most attention.

4. *Analyze the risk to the organization*—The final step is to evaluate the data and decide to accept, reduce, or transfer the risk (risk treatment).

The following is a step-by-step breakdown of the quantitative risk analysis:

1. Conduct a risk assessment and vulnerability study to determine the risk factors.
2. Determine the historical attitude of the company under assessment in regard to their security practice for reporting loss incidents.

A simple risk calculator works on Table 3.12:

$$\text{Risk} = \text{Probability of Occurrence} * \text{Business Impact}$$

As can be seen from the table, once all risks are categorized, a table plotting the assets, risks, and the probabilities can be made, and impact can be calculated by a simple formula as mentioned above.

Table 3.12 Risk Ranking Table

Assets	Threat	Likelihood	Expected Loss	Impact	Risk Ranking
Key people	Attrition	0.75	$1,000	$750	3
Laptop	Stealing	0.5	$500	$250	4
Network	Intrusion	0.2	$7,000	$1,400	2
Building	Earthquake	0.4	$10,000	$4,000	1

Risk Calculator

A useful guide for ranking risks is the risk calculator. Before we delve into a practical working of risk, let us see Table 3.13.

The risk calculator enables organizations to attribute risk value to identified risks. Refer to illustration in Table 3.14.

When we use the risk calculator in Table 3.12, we can translate all our work from this and previous steps into an overall risk value. Risk (8) = (3 + 4) * (5 + 6 + 7), that is, (3 + 2) * (2 + 2 + 2) = 30 as per Table 3.14.

$$\text{Risk} = (\text{Reproducibility} + \text{Exploitability}) *$$

$$(\text{Damage Potential} + \text{Affected Users} + \text{Discoverability})$$

Mixed Risk Assessment

A third approach, termed mixed or hybrid, combines elements of the qualitative and quantitative approaches. Let us take a practical example to study the concepts. A mixed approach to risk assessment combines some elements of both the quantitative and qualitative assessments. Sometimes quantitative data are used as one input among many to assess the value of assets and loss expectancy. This approach gives

Table 3.13 Risk Calculator

Threats Source (1)	Threat (2)	Probability Reprod (3)	Probability Exploit-ability (4)	Damage Potential (5)	Affected Users (6)	Discover-ability (7)	Risk (8)
Hacker	Unauthorized access	3	2	2	2	2	30

Table 3.14 Dread Table

Rating	High	Medium	Low
Reproducibility	The perpetrator can break the control every time to advance toward its target	The perpetrator can break the control only when special circumstances exist	It is very difficult to pass through the controls
Exploitability	Requires little skill novice	Requires moderate skill	Requires expert skill
Damage Potential	Perpetrator can gain full access, operate in a privileged mode, or upload malicious content. Full breach of security is possible	Sensitive information leakage. Full breach is possible	Little or no sensitive information loss
Affected Users	Users, key customers, and critical processes relating to them are affected	Some users affected. Critical processes are hindered	Very little impact on users or critical processes
Discoverability	Adequate detection controls are missing	Inadequate log management and other controls cannot detect an intrusion easily, and manual controls must be set	Existing log management and other controls can easily detect an intrusion

the assessment more credibility, but it also involves people within the organization to gain their individual insight. The disadvantage of this approach is that it may take longer to complete. However, a mixed approach can result in better data than what the two methods can yield alone.

Features of quantitative risk analysis are:

■ Gives measurable results in the form of financial impact. All findings are expressed in monetary values, percentages, and probabilities.
■ It suggests remediation based on risk loss and cost of remediation.
■ Allows for more control and understanding regarding procurement and budgeting.

Table 3.15 Expected Monetary Value (EMV)

Situation Status	Likely Spend in Crisis	Probability that Spend will be Done	Monetary Impact
Optimistic outcome	$150k	0.2	$30k
Likely outcome	$220k	0.5	$110k
Pessimistic outcome	$558k	0.3	$167.4k

- Requires larger organizational cooperation.
- Very time intensive (Table 3.15).

$$Risk = Threat * Vulnerability * Impact$$

Based on the above analysis, determine the return on investment using Internal Rate of Return (IRR).

A cost-benefit analysis is used to measure the economic benefit of asset over its useful life. When the economic conditions are not favorable, the income approach leads to a relative low valuation of assets. This approach is best suited for the valuations of patents, trademarks, computer software, and copyrights.

Controls Recommendations

Based on our risk calculation, we must begin immediately to plan for remediation. Every organization has its own perception of risk, and hence capacity of an organization to tolerate risk determines the risk appetite for the organization.

Recommend Recovery Strategies

In general, ISO 31000 expects you to review your risk management framework and your risk management process. It specifically expects you to review your risk management policy and plans as well as your risks, risk criteria, risk treatments, controls, residual risks, and risk assessment process.

- *Prioritize critical systems*: It is necessary to identify which business processes and assets should be recovered first.
- *Highlight interdependencies*: It is important to map connections to understand how an outage of one system can affect others.
- *Recommend recovery options*: Determine primary and alternative strategies for getting up and running.
- *Detail recovery requirements*: Document estimated recovery times and processes.

- *Assess risk*: Estimate the financial, productivity, and personal impact of a business disruption.
- *Build a business case*: Once problem is identified, provide management with financial data and a business case to help justify business continuity investment.

Risk Treatment (Accept, Avoid, Share, Transfer, Insure)

In section "Risk Management", we have dealt with risk assessment methods and risk rating. We have studied existing controls and arrived at some recommendations for improvement in risk profile. Now we move to risk treatment (Figure 3.19).

Plan risk response strategies:

1. Strategies for positive risks
2. Strategies for negative risks
3. Plan for contingent response strategies
4. Expert judgment

Risk treatment is a risk modification process. It involves selecting and implementing one or more treatment options. Once a treatment has been implemented, it becomes a *control* or it modifies existing controls. Risk treatment is in accordance to the risk attitude of the organization (Figure 3.20).

An organization's risk attitude reflects the organization's perception and approach to risk. Risks will be assessed and addressed according to risk criteria and in line with the risk attitude adopted by the organization. Risk perception differs from organization to organization. It is a subjective process, and some organizations have a bigger appetite to live with risks.

As seen in Figure 3.21, risk appetite has been defined in the area earmarked. This dark area can be made wider or more narrow depending on the risk attitude of the organization.

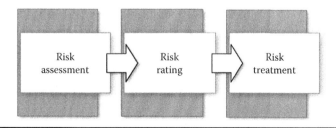

Figure 3.19   Risk assessment process.

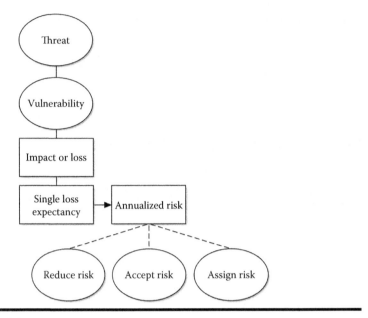

Figure 3.20 Risk treatment process.

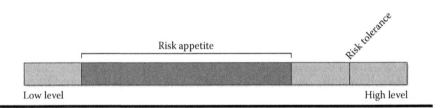

Figure 3.21 Risk appetite.

Risk attitude generally determines risk treatment, whether or not risks are to be tolerated, shared, avoided, retained, or transferred and also whether these treatments are to be implemented or postponed to some future date.

Risk treatment is working through options to deal with risks that are unacceptable to the organization. Unacceptable risks range in severity; some risks will require immediate treatment, while others can be monitored and treated later. Before developing the plan for risk treatment, the following points should be considered:

■ Method of treatment
■ People responsible for treatment
■ Costs involved and benefits of treatment
■ Likelihood of success and ways to measure the success of treatments

While considering controls for risk, it will be necessary to note the following factors:

■ Risk mitigation through control techniques
■ Deputation of competent officers to deal with the risks
■ Risk monitoring
■ Supervise the risks
■ Reporting on progress
■ Compliance with regulations follow-up
■ Risk-return trade-off
■ Balancing of risk against return

Treating risks involves working through options to deal with unacceptable risks to your business. One must understand that risks are categorized into positive risks and negative risks, and the means for treating each one may differ.

Positive risks represent an opportunity for the organization. Treatment of positive risks can be through

■ Exploiting opportunity.
■ Sharing.
■ Enhancing the risk.
■ Accepting the risk.

Negative risks are the real concern of the organization since it can lead to a tangible or intangible loss to the organization. Unacceptable risks range in severity; some risks will require immediate treatment, whereas others can be monitored and treated later.

The following are different options for treating risks:

Avoid the Risk

If it is possible, you may decide not to proceed with an activity that is likely to generate risk. Alternatively, you may think of another way to reach the same outcome that does not involve the same risks. This could involve changing your processes, equipment, or materials. For instance, if you find that a particular product is risky to launch, due to market conditions you may decide to drop the launch or delay it by a few months till the market improves.

Reduce the Risk

You can reduce a risk by reducing the likelihood of the risk happening—for example, through quality control processes, auditing, compliance with legislation, staff training, regular maintenance or a change in procedures reducing the impact if the risk occurs—for example, through emergency procedures, off-site data backup, minimizing exposure to sources of risk, or using public relations. Thus, we see that risk control is an effective means to reduce risk.

Risk reduction is also possible by sharing risks with business partners, coinsurers, and stakeholders by prior arrangement or contract. For instance, a big insurance company may choose to hedge its risks by sharing its risks with another insurance company through reinsurance.

Risk Control

Risk control includes decision-making to reduce and/or accept risks and reduce risk to an acceptable level. The amount of effort used for risk control should be proportional to the significance of the risk. Decision-makers might use different processes, including cost-benefit analysis, for understanding the optimal level of risk control.

Risk control might focus on the following questions:

- Is the risk above an acceptable level?
- What can be done to reduce or eliminate risks?
- What is the appropriate balance among benefits, risks, and resources?
- Are new risks introduced as a result of the identified risks being controlled?

Risk reduction aims at risk mitigation above the accepted level of risk. Risk reduction might include actions taken to mitigate the severity and probability of harm. Processes that improve the detectability of hazards and quality risks might also be used as part of a risk control strategy.

The implementation of risk reduction measures can introduce new risks into the system or increase the significance of other existing risks. Hence, it is advisable to revisit risk assessment to check out that the risk control and reduction have not introduced fresh risks.

Transfer the Risk

It is possible to shift some or all of the responsibility for the risk to another party through insurance, outsourcing, joint ventures, or partnerships.

Risk may be transferred by:

- Cross-training staff so that more than one person knows how to do a certain task, and you do not risk losing essential skills or knowledge if something happens to one of your staff members.
- Identifying alternative suppliers in case your usual supplier is unable to deliver and hence avoiding a single point of failure.
- Keeping old equipment (after it is replaced) and practicing doing things manually in case your computer networks or other equipment cannot be used.

Adequacy of insurance for all assets is important, otherwise in times of disaster, insurance companies shall not pay the full insured amount. Take advice from insurer as to appropriateness of insurance cover chosen to suit the business. Ideally, all risks that have been identified in the risk management plan must be insured.

Some **illustrations** on what is to be insured are given below:

- Loss of income if customers are affected by the crisis, and they stop ordering your product or service.
- Pilferage of goods or cash.
- Fidelity insurance for key employees.
- Insurance for on-site injuries to staff or visitors.
- Supplier insurance to cover inability of supplier to provide services during crisis.
- Meeting your worker's compensation obligations in case any of your staff are injured in a crisis.

No matter how much it is easy to transfer risk, the point to be remembered is that it is your risk and consequences are yours. There can be reimbursement of loss or monetary value, but the intangible losses like loss of customer confidence and goodwill are only yours. So, it is better to have a risk management program to control and mitigate risks in time to avoid extreme consequences and provide for resilience and continuity.

Accept the Risk

Risk acceptance is a managerial decision. You may accept a risk if it cannot be avoided, reduced, or transferred. Sometimes the cost of a risk control far exceeds the business impact if the loss materializes. It is through a proper risk management plan for the organization that criteria for risk acceptance may be specified. However, an incident response plan and a disaster recovery plan have to be developed to deal with accepted risks if and when they occur.

Risk acceptance can be a formal decision to accept the residual risk, or it can be a passive decision in which residual risks are not specified. Residual risk is the risk left over after all controls are applied. Risk is dynamic, and risk assessment is a subjective process.

Risk attitude determines risk levels that are acceptable and risks that are not acceptable. It is very important to have a risk awareness program to inculcate a risk culture within the organization. This will serve as a preventive control and will lead to risk reduction.

Risk Management Plan, Risk Review, and Risk Monitoring

Risk management should be an ongoing part of the quality management process. A mechanism to review or monitor events should be implemented. The output/results of the risk management process should be reviewed to consider new knowledge and experience.

Once a quality risk management process has been initiated, that process should continue to be utilized for events that might impact the original quality risk management decision, whether these events are planned (e.g., results of product review, inspections, audits, change control) or unplanned (e.g., root cause from failure investigations, recall). The frequency of any review should be based upon the level of risk. Risk review might include reconsideration of risk acceptance decisions.

Risk Treatment Plan

Your risk evaluation will help you prioritize the risks that need to be treated. When you are developing a plan for treating the risks, consider the

- Method of treatment.
- People responsible for treatment.
- Costs involved.
- Benefits of treatment.
- Likelihood of success.
- Ways to measure the success of treatments.

Risk monitoring means to continuously observe, check, and supervise. It is the tracking and monitoring and reporting of risk to external stakeholders. It means to determine the updated status and to assess whether required or expected performance levels are actually being achieved.

Risk monitoring is an important element of risk management. The process involves organizing and planning for risks in the same way as strategic, financial, marketing, and human resources planning. Once your basic risk management plan is in place, monitoring risk means to review it and update it continuously.

As seen in Figure 3.22, the starting premise is the risk management objectives and the IT portfolio. Existing resources may include a knowledge repository of identified risks and past precedents that will feed into the risk assessment processes of risk identification, analysis, evaluation, and estimation.

In this process, the existing risk controls will be assessed, and a gap analysis exercise may be conducted to identify gaps in controls that have created vulnerabilities. The cost of control as against the annualized loss if the risk exploits vulnerabilities can be done, and recommended controls can be implemented.

Again, the risk environment has to be continuously monitored, and all learnings from lapses and incidents will be stored in the risk repository. Lessons learned will be used when the next assessment takes place, and this is an iterative process.

The main objectives of risk monitoring are

- Identifying new risks at the earliest.
- Continuously identifying risk reduction avenues that will give cost-benefit effect.

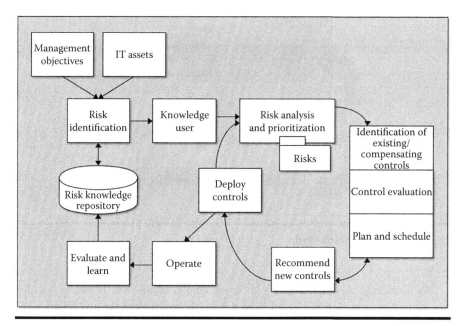

Figure 3.22 Risk monitoring process.

■ Ensuring that change in risks due to change in business volumes or any other factor are identified, assessed, and treated appropriately.
■ Deciding where and how to handle that risk.
■ Risk monitoring that aims at continuous improvisation.

Point to be noted here is that varied organizations will have varied risks, and some risk factors might just be proprietary to a organization.

Resources to conduct IT repairs, mitigation activities

■ Costs associated with protecting personal identification information of customers
■ Loss of public image and relations

Tools and Techniques used in risk monitoring are described as follows.

Use of Dashboards for Risk Monitoring

Business has become diverse and is spread across geographical locations. Risk is a specialized function and mostly is a part of the centralized corporate function. Hence it is necessary to have a monitoring system that gives a dashboard to give early warning signals of impending risks so that prompt response is given (Figure 3.23).

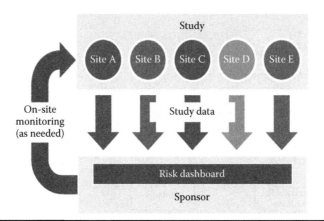

Figure 3.23 Risk dashboard.

As illustrated above, risk-oriented monitoring program will typically contain the following activities, which all flow through a comprehensive risk dashboard. In this process, data from different sites are falling into a centralized system that alerts the sponsor to situations that need further investigations:

- *Data collection and submission*: A centralized approach requires a steady and reliable flow of data from each site to the central monitoring system. This may occur either through manual entry and transfer of relevant data, or through an automated or online connection between the data entry system and the central dashboard.
- *Dashboard monitoring*: The function of the dashboard is to provide, at a glance, existing status of each site may be in a visual form based on pre-defined criteria that will show red, amber, or green depending upon the severity of risk level. These indicators help in deciding risk mitigation strategies.
- *Statistical analysis*: The system can be configured to perform some supplementary statistical analyses to help identify problems. Simple histograms and box plots can be extremely useful for spotting outliers between sites or countries for various risk indicators. More advanced techniques like clustering can also help identify problematic sites or even fraud.

Benefits of Risk-Based Monitoring

- *Fewer errors*: As compared to on-site monitoring manual methods, which are limited in scope and prone to error, risk-based, centralized monitoring uses more automated reviews to determine the need for manual intervention and is more accurate and more likely to uncover errors.

- *Lower cost*: With centralized monitoring, it will help risk department to focus on sites that are giving trouble and save time and money on conducting on-site audits for all sites.
- *Better analysis*: Collection of all relevant data into one central dashboard facilitates statistical and graphical checks, and it is easier to do data modeling and to identify useful correlations and trends.
- *Cross-site comparison*: Centralized monitoring enables multisite comparison and categorizing them into risk zones.
- *More timely results*: A dashboard also makes it possible to identify and resolve issues on a timely basis and leads to more proactive monitoring.

Risk Heat Map

Risk heat map is a tool used to present the results of a risk assessment process visually and in a meaningful and concise way. A well-designed heat map will help to understand the multiple variables that combine to threaten a company. Enterprise risk teams use heat maps to represent pictorially the state of risks faced by the organization (Figure 3.24).

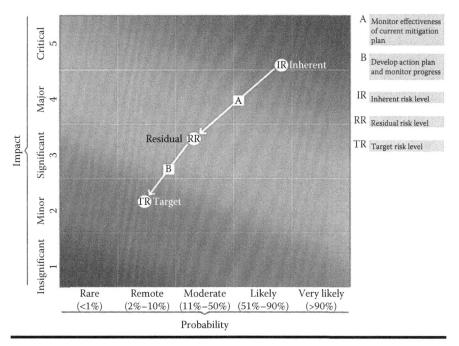

Figure 3.24   Risk heat map (1).

Some Hints for Use of Heat Maps

1. Separate the "impact ratings" for different kinds of risk (e.g., financial, operational, and strategic).
2. You can add to traditional displays by displaying more variables such as risk velocity and effectiveness of controls.
3. Demonstrate the effectiveness of risk mitigation plans by including inherent and residual risks. Illustrate reductions in risk exposure based on mitigation/internal controls.
4. Differentiate zones of acceptable and unacceptable risk exposures on the heat map.
5. Display changes over time by demonstrating movements in risk exposure value.
6. If possible, filter the risk assessment data to show different perspectives across the organization.

The heat map shown below provides an illustration of how organizations can map probability ranges to common qualitative characterizations of risk event likelihood and a ranking scheme for potential impacts. They can also rank impacts based on what is material in financial terms or in relation to the achievement of strategic objectives. In this example, risks are prioritized using a simple multiplication formula.

Organizations generally map risks on a heat map using a "residual risk" basis that considers the extent to which risks are mitigated or reduced by internal controls or other risk response strategies (Figure 3.25).

What Benefits do Risk Heat Maps Provide?

- A visual, big picture, holistic view to share while making strategic decisions
- Improved management of risks and governance of the risk management process
- Increased focus on the risk appetite and risk tolerance of the company
- More precision in the risk assessment process
- Identification of gaps in the risk management and control process
- Greater integration of risk management across the enterprise and embedding of risk management in operations

Sensitivity Analysis

It is very useful when attempting to determine the impact that the actual outcome of a particular variable will have if it differs from what was previously assumed. By creating a given set of scenarios, the analyst can determine how changes in one variable(s) will impact the target variable.

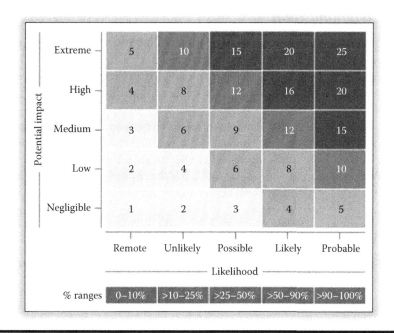

Figure 3.25   Risk heat map (2). (From McKay, S., *Risk Assessment for Mid-sized Companies: Tools for Developing a Tailored Approach to Risk Management,* **AICPA, 2011.)**

Internal Rating System

An internal rating system helps financial institutions manage and control credit risks that they face through lending and other operations by grouping and managing the credit worthiness of borrowers and the quality of credit transactions. This is done on periodic basis so that results documented are current and latest.

Risk governance includes the organization's structure, policies, objectives, roles, accountabilities, and decision-making process; and capabilities include its knowledge and human, technological, capital, and systemic resources.

Risk management should be an ongoing part of the quality management process. A mechanism to review or monitor events should be implemented. The output/results of the risk management process should be reviewed to consider new knowledge and experience.

Once a quality risk management process has been initiated, that process should continue to be utilized for events that might impact the original quality risk management decision, whether these events are planned (e.g., results of product review, inspections, audits, change control) or unplanned (e.g., root cause from failure investigations, recall). The frequency of any review should be based upon the level of risk. Risk review might include reconsideration of risk acceptance decisions.

Risk Communication

Risk communication is the sharing of information about risk and risk management between the decision-makers, employees, and other stakeholders. This is a background activity that can go on at any stage of risk management process. It is necessary to document the results of the quality risk management process to interested parties.

The included information might relate to the existence, nature, form, probability, severity, acceptability, control, treatment, detectability, or other aspects of risks to quality. Communication need not be carried out for each risk acceptance. Organization has to provide regulatory bodies the requisite risk information in the form or formats specified by them at predetermined intervals.

Review and Update Your Risk Management Plan

ISO 31000 provides organizational review of their risk management process on a periodic basis. This review must include

- Risk policy
- Risk assessment process
- Risk criteria
- Risk plan
- Risk treatment
- Risk mitigating controls Residual risks

You will need to test, evaluate, and update your risk management plan regularly as risks can change as your business, your industry, and the environment you operate in change. Regularly reviewing your risk management plan is essential for identifying new risks and monitoring the effectiveness of your risk treatment strategies.

Justification for risk treatment plan must be outlined in the risk management plan. How and why you have chosen to treat risks should be outlined in your risk management plan. It is important to review your plan regularly to take into account any new risks associated with changes in your business or improvements in techniques for treating risks.

Risk profile includes a portfolio of acceptable and nonacceptable risks, organizational perception of these risks (risk attitude), and chosen methods of risk response or treatment.

Customize a Risk Management Plan for Your Organization

Based on the risk appetite and risk attitude, an organization prepares its risk management plan in line with type of industry, industry best practices, and changing risk conditions. The following steps should be taken:

1. *Identify risks*: What are your risks and how likely are they to occur? Some will cause major disruption while others will be a minor irritation. You must make an educated assessment of both the likelihood and potential severity of each risk to prioritize your planning efforts.
2. *Minimize or eliminate risks*: Once risks have been identified, you need to either eliminate or reduce those risks.
3. *Identify who has to do what should a disaster occur*: One of the simplest and most powerful tools for a speedy recovery from a disaster is a clear plan as to the steps to be undertaken for recovery. This plan has to be tested and kept operational.
4. *Determine and plan your recovery contingencies*: Recovery contingencies should be determined by the type, style, and size of your business and by the extent of the damage.
5. *Communicate the plan to all the people it refers to*: This stage of planning is all about ensuring that all people within your business sphere (staff, suppliers, contractors, service providers) are made aware of the strategies you have put in place to either mitigate or recover from a disaster situation. Make decisions about whether the physical communication will be done by phone, e-mail, text, or other means.
6. *Controls recommendations and deployment*: Based on risk assessment, estimation, and calculations, a remediation plan has to be formulated. Many times, controls to be implemented do not involve a cost but only take time of employees. Simple in nature, they form the first step in risk mitigation.

Conclusion

Risk assessment process substantiates the BIA by putting values and risk priorities to identified business risks. In present times, they are becoming more data centric in nature. Understanding the impact of failing to protect the confidentiality, integrity, and availability of target data directly affects both attacker motive and business impact components of the risk formula. Accuracy of data classification and persons who do the criteria setting are important. Data owners have to prescribe data classification schemes.

Risk is the effect of uncertainty on business objectives. Modern business is full of both positive and negative risks. Positive risks also need treatment, and they generally get converted into opportunities.

Risks can be categorized into strategic, HR, financial, operational, information, outsourcing risks, and so on. Some risks are inherent to the business. Risks are associated with threats from internal and external sources. They hover around vulnerabilities, which appear as control lacuna and where these vulnerabilities exist, threats can exploit them and reach their target wiz organizational assets.

Risk assessment begins with risk identification, analysis, and evaluation; and risks so arrived at have to be quantified; and risk criteria have to be applied in order to set priority to each of the risks. Risk policy lays down the basis for preparation of the risk management plan.

Risk register notes all identified risks and additional risks identified by the process of risk monitoring. Quantitative, qualitative, or mixed methods of risk estimation can be used to calculate risks and determine risk mitigation measures.

Organizations may adopt risk frameworks established by various organizations such as risk IT framework from isaca on which they can fit their organization's risk profile. With the successful completion of BIA and risk assessment, the entire business, its processes, time criticality of processes, the recovery point objective for data, the different risks, their categorization and ranking, and recommended mitigation for identified risks have been evaluated.

The next step is presenting reports to the appropriate levels of management and building a business case for setting a resilience system.

Risk References

Isaca	COBIT
AS/NZS 4360	OCTAVE
NIST SP 800–30	FRAP
FTA	ISO 27005
MEHARI	COSO
ISO 31000	

Risk Glossary

- *Risk* is the chance or probability to incur loss or damage if exposed to a hazard.
- *Hazard* is any source of potential damage, harm, or adverse health effects on something or someone under certain conditions at work. Hazard is a source that may result in a risk condition.
- *Threat* is anything that can exploit a vulnerability and obtain, damage, or destroy an asset whether intentionally or unintentionally.
- *Vulnerability* is a weakness or gap in security or controls that can be exploited by threats to gain unauthorized access. Hence vulnerability is a gap in our security program.
- *Risk evaluation* is a process that is used to compare risk analysis results with risk criteria to determine whether or not a specified level of risk is acceptable or tolerable.

- *Risk treatment* is a risk modification process. It involves selecting and implementing one or more treatment options. Once a treatment has been implemented, it becomes a *control*, or it modifies existing controls. (You have many treatment options. You can avoid the risk, you can reduce the risk, you can remove the source of the risk, you can modify the consequences, you can change the probabilities, you can share the risk with others, you can simply retain the risk, or you can even increase the risk in order to pursue an opportunity.)
- *Risk monitoring* means to supervise and to continually check and critically observe. It means to determine the current status and to assess whether or not required or expected performance levels are actually being achieved.
- *A risk control* is any measure or action that modifies risk. Controls include any policy, procedure, practice, process technology, technique, or method that modifies or manages risk. Risk treatments become controls or modify existing controls, once they have been implemented.
- *Residual risk* is the risk left over after you have implemented a risk treatment option. It is the risk remaining after you have reduced the risk, removed the source of the risk, modified the consequences, changed the probabilities, transferred the risk, or retained the risk.
- *Risk profile* is a documentation of the set of risks faced by the organization. A *risk profile* can include the risks that the entire organization must manage or only those that a particular function or part of the organization must address.
- *Risk review* is an activity carried out in order to determine whether something is a suitable, adequate, and effective way of achieving established objectives.
- *Risk identification* is a process that involves finding, recognizing, and describing the risks that could affect the achievement of an organization's objectives. It is used to identify possible sources of risk in addition to the events and circumstances that could affect the achievement of objectives. It also includes the identification of possible causes and potential consequences.
- *Risk management plan*: an organization's *risk management plan* lays down management intent and methodology to manage its risks. It describes the management components, the approach, and the resources that will be used to manage risk.
- *Risk attitude*: an organization's *risk attitude* reflects the organization's perception and approach to risk. It describes the way risks will be assessed and addressed according to risk criteria in accordance to the risk attitude adopted by the organization.
- *Risk policy* defines a general commitment direction or intention and expresses an organization's top level commitment to risk management and gives it general direction or intention.
- *A risk owner* is a person or entity authorized to manage a specific risk and is accountable for doing so.

Table 3.16 Risk Formulas

RISK	Risk = Assets + Threats + Vulnerabilities
	Risk = Threat * Vulnerability * Impact
RISK ANALYSIS	Risk Analysis = Risk identification + Risk estimation
LEVEL OF RISK	Level of risk = Consequences * Likelihood
RISK EXPOSURE (RE)	Probability of loss * Severity of loss
SINGLE LOSS EXPECTANCY (SLE)	Asset Value * Risk Exposure (RE)
ANNUALIZED LOSS EXPECTANCY (ALE)	SLE * ARO
	Single Loss Expectancy * Annualized Rate of occurrence

- *Level of risk* is its magnitude; generally, it is estimated by considering and combining consequences and likelihoods. Risk level can be accorded to a single risk or a combination of risks.
- *Risk analysis* is a process used to understand the nature, source, and causes of the risks that have been identified and to estimate the level of risk. It is also used to study impacts and consequences and to examine the controls that currently exist.
- *Risk impact assessment* is the process of assessing the probabilities and consequences of risk events if they are realized.
- *Risk governance* includes the organization's structure, policies, objectives, roles, accountabilities, and decision-making process, and capabilities including its knowledge and people.
- *Risk context*: to *establish the context* means to define the external and internal risk parameters to be considered by organizations while planning their risk management approach.
- *Counter party risk* is the risk that other firms will break their contractual obligations to you (Table 3.16).

Chapter 4

Business Impact Analysis Reporting and Commitment of Resources

On successful completion of business impact analysis (BIA) and risk assessment (RA), we are now ready to set the stage, tabulate, and present our findings and results to the management. At this level, we can weave IT department into the loop and discuss the requirements of the different departments/functions in respect of real-time operating systems (RTOs), recovery point objectives (RPOs), alternate processing arrangements, and so on, so as to build a business case for the IT DR activity and base the business continuity management (BCM) strategy.

Report to management has to be based on BIA and RA (Figure 4.1).

As shown in the figure, the input and output vary slightly between BIA and RA. Business impact analysis focuses on the examination of business processes, the interdependencies of both upstream and downstream and the criticality of these processes on the yardstick of time and data loss. Risk assessment covered threats, vulnerabilities, and the loss suffered if they materialize. It also covers countermeasures to be adopted to contain the loss.

The RA is conducted ideally just before finalizing the BIA, and hence it would make sense to give an integrated report showing findings from both these assessments. We optionally provide a separate BIA report and Risk Assessment

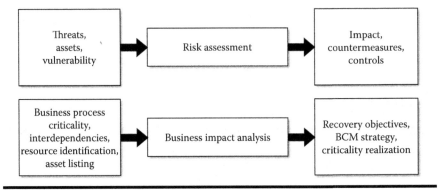

Figure 4.1 I/O for BIA/RA.

report depending on agreement with the client organization. A useful method for validating BIA/RA findings is to

1. Prepare a draft report containing initial findings and issues.
2. Issue the draft report to participants and request feedback.
3. Review feedback and revise findings accordingly.

The report must give a holistic picture of business impact and risks faced by the business, and to build a successful business case to be presented to the top management. Business resilience is built on a recovery infrastructure and an organized data-recovery system and for establishing these requirements, a financial outlay or budget is necessary. Buy-in is critical in order to set the system for management oversight and allocate resources to make and implement a resilience system. Effectiveness of the business impact analysis is reflected by the management's commitment of people and technological resources to mitigate risks of business continuity projected by the findings.

Format for Management Report

There is no standardized format for a business impact analysis report, but every organization has some standard reporting formats and the management may want you to prepare the report in that format. Generally, a PowerPoint presentation to top management is the order of the day. Wherever possible, the insertion of graphs to represent relations, single point of failure, risk bifurcation, and so on would be visually understandable. A detailed report to the functional management prior to that to deliberate on risks, controls, IT agreement on RTO and RPO, and other factors can be distributed for getting sign off on findings, observations, and recommended controls.

Contents of the Report

A BIA report must consider the internal and external environments that impact the business as also the risks affecting the financial viability and market standing of the organization. The format and style of reporting and the level of detail portrayed depend on the level of management interest, comprehensibility, and time allotment to the project. The integrated BIA/RA report should include the following:

Business Units, Business Processes, Criticality Benchmarks

When we started with the BIA, we studied the organizational context and through data-gathering techniques such as interviews, surveys, questionnaire, workshops, we gathered an understanding of the business processes, and with the help of process owners, we identified critical processes.

When we put forth the critical business processes in the report, we have to portray internal and external dependencies of these processes and the criticality criteria on which to rank the criticality.

Figure 4.2 depicts critical functions and their ranking. A point to note here is that for all dependent processes in critical departments, the corresponding noncritical department would be equally ranked if processes are interlinked.

Business units have to give sign off on the risk assessment and BIA, and it should be one with the forthcoming recommendations to be given to management. First cut-off prioritization has to be discussed with BU owners.

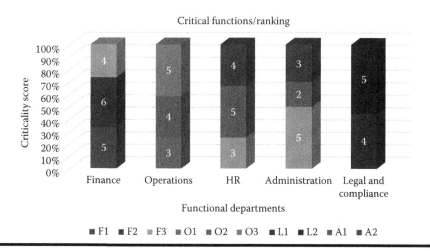

Figure 4.2   Critical functions with ranking.

Depiction of Critical Functions/Departments and Criticality Scores

Illustration: ABC Corporation has five main functional departments: finance, operations, administration, HR, and legal and compliance. Within finance, accounts receivable, investment, and statutory payments are critical processes. Likewise, operations have three critical processes: customer service, production control, and procurement of raw materials. The administration department is not having any critical process as a stand-alone, but, if we take into consideration the dependency that other departments have in times of crisis, it is deemed to be a critical department.

Further operations may be dependent on HR for getting the key people for the critical jobs to be performed. Again during a crisis, communication with stakeholders, employees, and outsiders is very important, search operations for missing personnel and intimating the next in kin in cases of emergency is also handled by the Admin/HR, and hence they are taken under critical functions. The administration department has to arrange for logistics and procurement of materials and equipment at a recovery site.

Criticality Benchmarks

Organizations may set their criticality criteria so long as they are consistently applied across the enterprise. Figure 4.3 shows IT resources including applications, hardware, telecom facilities, vital records, services internal and external, and some key people on whom the business is dependent are useful benchmarks for drawing the recovery strategy.

1. *IT dependencies*: Disruption of business processes may not impact IT, but the disruption of IT systems, either primary or secondary, can impact key business processes. These interdependencies must be clearly documented and projected in the BIA report.

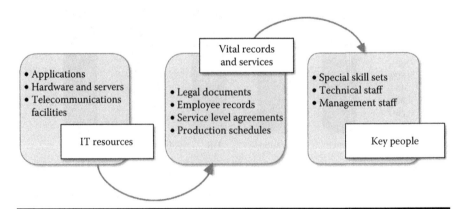

Figure 4.3   Criticality benchmarks.

2. *Vital records*: *Business processes may be depending on some vital records* that have to be at hand for the business process to function, including:
   - *Hard copies* of contracts, employee data, insurance records, legal documents, notification diaries, process manuals, and so forth. For manufacturing units, customer orders, supply schedules, and product content are vital records. For a research and development unit, research notes are vital records because they signify days of research work, which would be lost if the records became inaccessible.
   - *Soft copies* such as magnetic tapes, microfilm, microfiche, photos, and so forth. It is important to ensure that these records are backed up and stored off-site and are available at the time of outage to enable business processes to access these for their operations.
3. *Key people*: Certain processes require specialized skills, and hence key personnel become a vital factor in the mapping of critical resources. Often sole dependency on a single person becomes the cause of a single point of failure. These dependencies must be identified and presented in the BIA report so that corrective actions can be implemented.

Business Interdependencies

1. In cases of process dependencies, the following charts help to depict the dependencies along with time criticalities (Table 4.1):
   - *Business department/function*: Self-explanatory
   - *Head count*: Number of full-time staff in the business unit
   - *Parent process*: A brief description of the principal activities the unit performs, for example, sales, contractor interface, or investor relationship management
   - *Priority ranking*: Subjective ranking of parent process(es) according to criticality to the business unit
   - *Recovery time objective*: The time needed to recover the parent process to business almost as usual following a disruption
   - *Recovery point objective*: The point in time to which the parent process work should be restored following a disruption
   - *Upstream dependency of parent process*: Names of organizations and/or processes that the parent process needs for normal operations

Table 4.1 Maximum Downtime for Parent Processes

Function or Department	Head Count	Parent Process (PP)	PP Upstream Dependency	PP Downstream Dependency	RTO	RPO	Priority Ranking	MAD

  — *Downstream dependency*: Names of organizations and/or processes that need the parent process for normal operations
  MAD is maximum allowable downtime.
  Note-maximum allowable/tolerable downtime/maximum tolerable outage denotes the total time to recover from a business disruption and includes the recovery point objective, which is the lag between the time of the last good backup and the business disruption, the time it takes to recover systems, the time it takes to recover data, and the testing and verification of repaired systems.
  For subprocesses, refer to Table 4.2.
 — *Subprocess*: Self-explanatory
 — *Priority ranking*: Subjective ranking of parent process(es) according to the criticality to the business unit
 — *Recovery time objective*: The time needed to recover the parent process to business almost as usual following a disruption
 — *Recovery point objective*: The point in time to which the parent process work should be restored following a disruption
 — *Upstream dependency of subprocess*: Names of organizations and/or processes that the parent process needs for normal operations
 — *Downstream dependency of subprocess*: Names of organizations and/or processes that the parent process need for normal operations
 — *MAD* is maximum allowable downtime
  Criticality levels on processes and subprocesses are dependent on people and the technology that drive these processes. Hence it is necessary to enlist technology and identify key people who drive business.
  This can be represented in the report in the following manner (Table 4.3).

Table 4.2 Priority Ranking for Subprocesses

Subprocess	Priority Ranking	RTO	RPO	SP Upstream Dependency	SP Downstream Dependency	MAD

Table 4.3 Format for BIA Report

Business Function	Critical Process	RTO	RPO	Vital Records	Key Personnel	IT Resources

Process and resource interdependencies: The people–process–technology model of business is interlinked. Interdependencies exist between departments or business units and also on those factors or components that help to run the business. These interdepency have to be mapped in the report so that it is considered for remedial action and is influencing the strategy for business resilience.

2. *Vital applications* run business processes and key people manage these operations. External elements such as regulatory compliance and reporting must also appear in the management report. Vendor dependency/supply chain dependency is to be factored in the report as it can lead to a single point of failure if vendor is only one for the entire operations.

3. *External dependencies* such as suppliers, vendors, or outsourced service providers also need to factor in the BIA, as the critical processes may be dependent on their services. Therefore, business continuity arrangements on the vendor's installation need to be assessed.

Single Point of Failure

Consider the following table for identifying "single point of failure" (Figure 4.4).

Dependency on one vendor can lead to a single point of failure. Such cases have to be projected for corrective action. Corrective action is generally in the form of mitigating the single dependency risk by introducing a second vendor, cross training of employees, spreading risk across business locations, and so on.

Illustration: While planning for business continuity of an insurance company, we discovered that printing of policies was being done by only one vendor across different locations. Further on visit to the vendor, it was discovered that vendor was using an application for the job that was not supported by the vendor. We assessed that if vendor has a breakdown of system, services can be disrupted at all locations leading to a single point of failure.

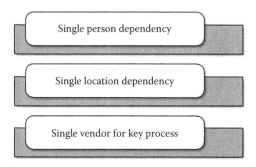

Single person dependency

Single location dependency

Single vendor for key process

Figure 4.4 Sources of single point of failure.

Criticality Can Be Defined across Timelines

The listing of critical processes and their criticality ranking in graphical form provides clear picture of what processes needs to be prioritized (Table 4.4, Figure 4.5).

Table 4.4 Criticality Timelines

Levels	Description	RTO	RPO	Number of Processes
Level 1	Business processes must be available during all business hours	0–2 hours	24 hours	14
Level 2	Business processes can be run without normal processes for a limited amount of time	2–24 hours	24 hours	26
Level 3	Business can survive for a longer period	24–72 hours	24 hours	46
Level 4	Business can survive for an extended period	More than 72 hours	48 hours	20

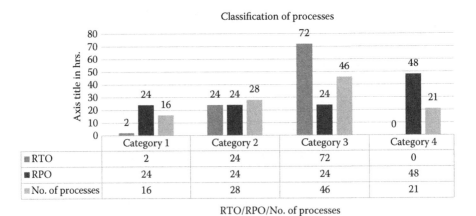

Figure 4.5 Criticality ranking graph.

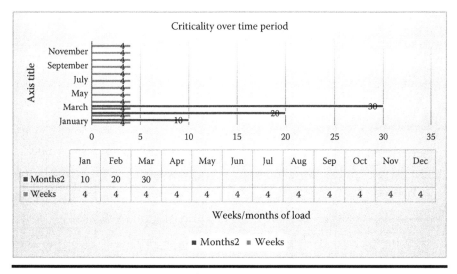

Figure 4.6 Time criticality for processes.

Load Analysis Chart

In our analysis, we always assume a worst-case scenario. In business, there are peak times such as in insurance business, the months from December to March are critical, and past week of the month is also critical. It would do good to portray this in the form of a graph for emphasizing to management the criticality of controls in this period.

In Figure 4.6, we see that week 4 of every month is heavy business time and the months of January, February, and March are critical to business. We have given them weights 10, 20, and 30 for clarity. When we project a business case, we shall always project a worst-case scenario and base our planning on this premise.

Recovery Objectives and Workaround Procedures

The management report must contain workaround procedures available for critical processes that have been identified by business units for further discussion during the final meeting.

Figure 4.7 sums up our BIA exercise. Along with criticality yardsticks, we must have gathered information about workaround procedures to be followed in case of outage for critical processes.

Workaround procedures are alternate procedures that may be used by business units to perform critical business processes during temporary nonavailability of specific applications, data, equipment office facilities, and personnel or external services. For instance, if office facility is not available, a workaround can be work from home with VPN and use of laptop. Such procedures require mention in the proposed mitigation measures presented in the report.

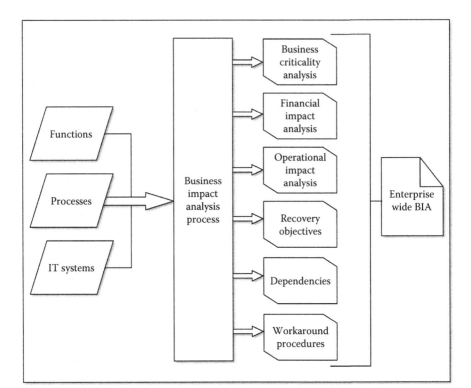

Figure 4.7   Process diagram for enterprise wide BIA.

Turnaround Time (TAT)

It is worth mentioning that some critical processes may be contractually bound by a turnaround time to fulfill the process failing which it will lead to penalties, fines, or loss of customer confidence. Our management report should highlight such processes along with their impacts.

Recovery Objectives

During our reporting exercise we must bear in mind the main recovery objectives of the enterprise:

1. *Reduce overall risk*: In this context, we need to ask the question; "Is there anything which we have missed out which has bearing on the continued operations of business?" The baseline we portray must be based on actual findings, only then it will give us a robust strategy.

2. *Restoration of business operations*: The next objective is to restore business operations within an agreed timeline (RTO) and restore data on an agreed RPO. This fixation will be done in the management presentation day and will be the accepted standard for the enterprise.
3. *Compliance to legal and regulatory norms*: Every industry has a regulatory body that lays down protocols, norms to be followed failing which there is penalty, fine, or expulsion.

It will now be possible at this stage, to add the results of our Risk Assessment, to give a more realistic dimension to our integrated report.

Integrating Risk Assessment Findings into the Management Report

Risk is an integral factor for considering the impact. Risk is all about assets, threats, and vulnerabilities. Every organization sets its own criteria or definitions to define severity. We must put these in our report for better understanding.

1. *Define severity levels*:
   a. Vulnerabilities (Table 4.5)
   b. Probabilities matrix (Table 4.6)

Table 4.5   Vulnerability Matrix

Vulnerability Level	Description	Vulnerability Score
A	Effects of vulnerability tightly contained. Does not increase the probability of additional vulnerabilities being exploited.	Low
B	Vulnerability can be expected to affect more than one system element or component. Exploitation increases the probability of additional vulnerabilities being exploited.	Medium
C	Vulnerability affects a majority of system components. Exploitation significantly increases the probability of additional vulnerabilities being introduced.	High

Table 4.6 Probability Matrix

Probability Ranking	Description	Definition of Periodicity
1	Rare	Likelihood of occurrence is more than five years
2	Occasional	Likelihood of occurrence is once every three years
3	Frequent	Likelihood of occurrence is once every one year
4	Very frequent	Likelihood of occurrence is once every six months

2. *Threats impact analysis report*:

   Threats are on assets, so impact of threats on assets needs to be documented in the management report.

   a. *Impact criteria*: The report must mention impact criteria on which the report is based (Table 4.7).

   Note: Please note that this criterion is only suggestive. Enterprise may define their own set of criteria for the above categories.

   Along with risk impact, it would be good to view the impact categories that affect our risk structure.

   b. *Impact categories*: Whereas some risks can be represented in tangible dollar value, some risks are more significant to the enterprise, may be presented in intangible form. Let us see the instances of both as given in Table 4.8.

3. *Risk criteria for tangible loss* (Table 4.9).

   Tangible impacts include the following:
   − Accounts receivable systems.
   − Property damage.
   − Loss of revenue collection facilities (e.g., recently it was found that for a reputed insurance company, they were not able to accept intercity premiums because their network connectivity was down).
   − Any failure of process that causes business to disrupt for a certain period of time.
   − Penalties, fines, and lawsuits (Figure 4.8).

4. *Nontangible impact is based on qualitative evaluation and is a subjective analysis. It includes the following*:
   − Loss of credibility and customer goodwill.
   − Leading to noncompliance with certain regulatory requirement.
   − Environmental damage.

Intangible qualitative impacts can be given ranking as per agreed criteria as there is no value associated with them (Figure 4.9).

Table 4.7 Impact Criteria for Assets

Asset	Negligible	Moderate	Severe	Catastrophe
People	Minor or no effect on people or business	Temporary unavailability of 25% of current manpower up to 24 hours	Extended unavailability of 50%–60% of current manpower up to three days	Permanent unavailability of more than 75% of the current manpower for one week or more
Facilities	Minor or no effect on building facilities	Premises become unavailable for 24 hours	Premises become unavailable for three days	Premises unavailable for more than seven days
Technology	Minor or no effect on technology	Temporary unavailability of technology up to six hours	Unavailability of technology for more than one day	Unavailability of technology for more than three days
Information	Minor or no effect on information	Unavailable for six hours	Unavailable for more than one day	Effect is high, unavailability of information for more than three weeks

Table 4.8   Impact Categories

Impact Category	Definition
Loss of revenue	Loss of income received from selling goods or services
Additional expenses	Temporary staffing, overtime, equipment, and services
Regulatory and legal	Fines, penalties, compliance issues, contractual obligations, and financial liabilities
Customer service	Termination or reduction of service level (internal of external), live operators versus automated response
Goodwill	Public image, shareholder relations, and market share

Table 4.9   Tangible Impacts

Score	Loss Range
0	none
1	< $1,000
2	≥ $1,000 < $5,000
3	≥ $5,000 < $10,000
4	≥ $10,000 < $25,000
5	≥ $25,000 < $50,000
6	≥ $50,000 < $100,000
7	≥ $100,000 < $150,000
8	≥ $150, 000 < $250,000
9	≥ $250,000 < $500,000
10	≥ $500,000

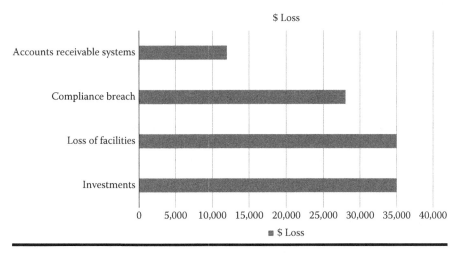

Figure 4.8   Tangible loss expressed in dollar value.

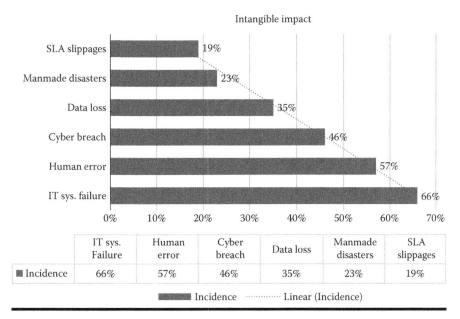

Figure 4.9   Intangible impact.

Customer Service and Goodwill Loss Ranges (Intangible)(Suggestive)
Let us take the following example. The incidence of intangible impacts has been plotted in the diagram. Plotting it in graphical form gives a quick review of the nature of events that are frequent and to plan strategy to remediate the risk of these events (Table 4.10).

Table 4.10 Intangible Loss Ranking

Score	Effect
0	None
2	Minimal
4	Moderate
6	Moderately heavy
8	Heavy
10	Severe

Losses on Past Incidents

Depiction of past incidents and their loss value can be graphically depicted to underline the vulnerabilities to such incidents and remediation controls to be recommended for prevention of the same.

Please consider the financial impact of losses suffered in prior two years. This will throw light on repetitive incidents and help identify high risk areas and gaps and vulnerabilities in the current environment (Figures 4.10 and 4.11).

Note: Past occurrence and frequency of incidents need to be highlighted to emphasize need for countermeasures to contain the incidents and prevent them from occurring.

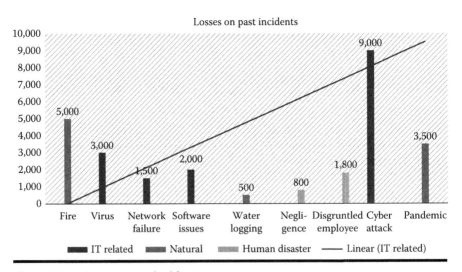

Figure 4.10 Loss on past incidents.

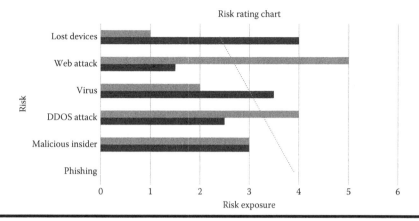

Figure 4.11   Risk rating for IT related incidents.

Dollar Loss by Downtime

As availability is critical for every business, the main disruption in every organization is caused by nonavailability of information systems or downtime. Hence it would be helpful to put your analysis of the loss caused by downtime in the organization based on the statistics gathered from different business units during the data gathering phase of BIA.

It would be necessary to present an estimate on the dollar loss by downtime (Figure 4.12).

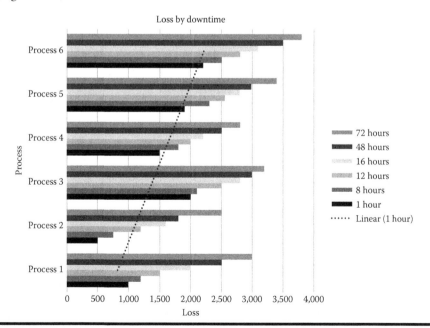

Figure 4.12   Loss by downtime.

Once we have the loss per process per hour of downtime, it can be used in the report to build a good business case. So you see we parse our findings of BIA and RA in different ways, trying to project to the management, different repercussions of disruption, whether it is of machine, external attack, dependency failure, or any other factor that causes nonavailability of manpower, technology, or process for a certain time period. Also it has to highlight the loss value due to such incidents.

Formalizing Management Report and Presentation

In Figure 4.13, we observe that BIA is a turning point. From this exercise, the recovery time objectives for critical processes are identified. At the same time in a dependency analysis, the single point of failures may be listed. In a technical dependency that can be on any one of the following component namely,

1. IT platform
2. Network
3. Data center facility
4. Hardware
5. Applications
6. Information security (confidentiality, integrity, and availability)
7. Data

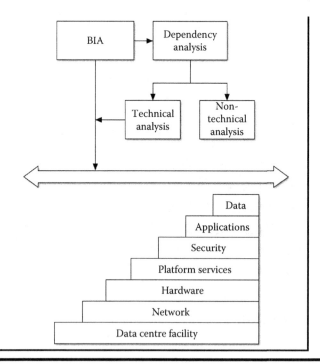

Figure 4.13   Recovery baseline diagram.

IT serves both as a service department and as a provider of IT disaster recovery at the time of disaster. Planning for meeting technical aspects in the recovery of business processes as per defined RTOs and especially RPOs. As commitment to the RTO and RPO presupposes a certain technical infrastructure, proper data center facilities and application support, IT is a critical function during the outage and during the recovery process.

By this time our requirements mapping is documented in terms of resource requirements for

1. Number of personnel required during the outage to work for critical processes from each business unit and the support departments.
2. Vital records that will be required to carry on critical processes.
3. Minimum IT facilities, equipment, and data required to run critical processes.

Essential Features of BIA/RA Report to Management

The management report can be in the form of a visual slide presentation or a word format. But it has to build the case for business resilience. Consider the following inclusions:

1. *Legal and Regulatory Compliance*: Certain mandatory requirements and norms from legal, regulators make time-critical demands that fall in the list of critical activities whether by operations or finance and here the financial impact from noncompliance can be highlighted.
2. *Customer-centric processes*: All those processes or subprocesses that relate to customer service or customer inquiry have to have highest precedence. When these processes are projected to management, the interest of management starts building.
3. *Customer-facing applications*: Continuous availability of customer facing applications is critical to business and RTOs relating to those to be underlined, so that the recovery options contain these requirements.
4. *Past incidents*: The loss figures on security incidents in the prior two years can give a realistic threat realization in the risk projections for the enterprise.
5. *Classification of assets*: The classification criteria and categorizing assets into negligible, moderate, severe, or catastrophe.
6. *Risk impact analysis report*: Losses on account of tangible and intangible impacts on risk materialization.
7. *RPO projections and data backups and restoration*: Considerations of backups, data center and DR site, and transfer of data with defined latency so as to finalize the recovery point objective after collaborative deliberation.
8. *Single point of failure*: Graphically project single point of failure and rank them in accordance to the dollar loss to be sustained if failure occurs.
9. *Dollar loss by downtime*: This indicator is useful in justifying the RTOs of critical processes.

10. *ROI calculation for proposed recovery strategy*: Based on the estimated cost of countermeasures and the annual loss expectancy (ALE), the ROI is calculated, and when the management sees the ROI and benefits from remediation in the form of reduction in incidents, reduction in costs due to increased controls and an improved bottom line.

Recovery alternatives may involve additional outlay and it would be good to present this cost sheet during the presentation to be deliberated on so that faster approval of budgets is possible. This cost sheet should be prepared after due interactions with IT, HR, Admin, and all people related to recovery of critical processes during a disaster.

The suggestive cost sheet shown in Table 4.11 gives a component wise breakup of the additional costs to be incurred. Recovery is always tailored to meet the

Table 4.11   Estimated Cost Sheet for BCM Outlay

S. No.	Component	Estimated Cost	Budget Approved in Meeting
1	Full time internal staff	$ 49,000	
2	Consultants/contractors (business focus)	$ 76,000	
3	Consultants/contractors (IT focus)	$ 50,000	
4	Emergency operations center (EOC)	$ 175,000	
5	Emergency supplies	$ 30,000	
6	Hardware	$ 55,000	
7	Hot-site/outsourced alternate site	$ 98,000	
8	Internal recovery site	$ 63,000	
9	Software	$ 100,000	
10	Notification/alerts	$ 18,000	
11	Mobile recovery	$ 40,000	
12	DR technology	$ 3,000,000	
13	Exercises	$ 55,000	
14	Training/awareness	$ 25,000	
15	Travel	$ 60,000	
16	Other	$ 10,000	
	Average total	$ 1,204,000	

requirements of the business units in the most appropriate or optimal manner. There is an optimal point between the cost of downtime and the cost of recovery. The longer systems are down, the more expensive it is for the enterprise. The shorter the required recovery time, the more expensive it is for the enterprise. Therefore, the intersection of the cost of downtime and the cost of recovery is the optimal point.

Note: Please note that the above figures are arbitrary and have been stated for carrying out the ROI exercise. In a management presentation, management will probe into the subcomponents, the decision to buy or hire, workarounds, and many other aspects connected to each of the components given earlier. The best option is that which is justifiable in terms of benefits realized from the spend. Cost benefit evaluation is by far the best methodology for choice of budget and its justification.

Calculation of ROI on Investment in BCM

We will base our ROI calculations on direct financial loss prevention: if by spending $1 you can prevent a highly probable annual loss of $10, then management will be happy to spend the $1. This is based on the principle of benefit realization. For calculating the ROI, we have to calculate the ALE as discussed in the earlier section. The ALE is calculated by the formula

ALE = (Number of Incidents per Year) × (Potential Loss per Incident).

It will be prudent to note that the number of incidents portrayed in the report should be a realistic expectation based on empirical research and past precedents. Management is always skeptical on the amount of spend especially if it is not going to generate a return, so overstatements should be avoided.

One has to use benchmarking for ascertaining the cost of a breach. Costs related to third-party consultants are also simple to calculate, estimating that they will have to spend at least one week investigating the incident—you already have at least $10,000. The common breaches on account of third parties may include the following:

- Cost of customer database and other sensitive information theft and exposure
- Cost of e-commerce portal unavailability during forensics and recovery
- Cost of third-party experts allocated to investigate and remediate breach
- Cost of legal and compliance fines

Another determinant based on empirical research gives a thumb rule; it states that every £1 spent on a quality management system can

- Increase revenue by £6.
- Reduce costs by £16.
- Increase profits by £3.

Going by this, the decision to spend on controls and countermeasures makes sense. The Information Security Breaches Survey published by UK government and PwC, conducted in 2015, estimates the average cost of data breach for SMEs to be between £75,000 and £310,800 that is cost per incident.

$$ALE = (Number\ of\ Incidents\ per\ Year) \times (Potential\ Loss\ per\ Incident)$$

$$ALE = 12 \times £75,000$$

$$ALE = £\,900,000\,(\$1,170,000)$$

This is the amount a company should expect to lose per year if nothing is done to protect its occurrence. Countermeasures need to be taken to cover identified control gaps, so that vulnerabilities and for that the costs for control need to be justified. The easiest way to do so is to provide management with the most efficient and effective solutions and products, carefully selected by the price/quality ratio, in order to protect the assets.

For example:

- Continuous vulnerability scanning and security monitoring solution.
- Regular manual or hybrid assessments involving third-party experts.

In our present example, say the cost of countermeasures is $1,104,000 from the cost estimation sheet,

$$ROI = \left(\frac{ALE}{Cost\ of\ Countermeasures} \right) \times 100\%$$

$$ROI = \left(\frac{\$1,170,000}{\$1,204,000} \right) \times 100\%$$

$$ROI = 97\%$$

There are two main concepts that can enable management to gauge whether BCM spend will give value to business:

- *Measuring IT spend against two factors*: Operating expense and net revenue—is a more accurate gauge of IT effectiveness than the traditional metric of measuring solely against net revenue. This is known as a method of optimal IT intensity and it compares IT spend with operating expenses as well as net revenue.
- *Active analysis techniques* are used in BIA to facilitate the alignment of three key executive spheres.
  - *Interest*: Where the assets and capabilities of others can affect an organization's action.
  - *Influence*: Where organizational assets and capabilities can affect the courses of action of others.

– *Responsibility*: To respect and uphold organization's mission, vision, and values.

Note: IT intensity curves help decision makers to determine whether they are optimally investing and prevents over investments.

Recommendations to Management

There are certain points that are foremost in running an organization. Every business is governed by the "going concern" concept. Policies and procedures are directive controls and it helps in proper governance of the entity.

While we perform the BIA/RA, we come across gaps in the control infrastructure that brings in risks that may prove to be impactful. A byproduct of this exercise is identification of some simple countermeasures that may not involve cost. Let us look at these countermeasures.

Segregation of Duties

Segregation of duties (SOD) based on shared responsibilities is a basic control for sustainable risk management and internal controls for a business. The basic idea underlying segregation of duties is that no employee or group should be in a position both to perpetrate and to conceal errors or fraud in the normal course of their duties. In general, the principal incompatible duties to be segregated are

- Custody of assets.
- Authorization or approval of related transactions affecting those assets.
- Recording or reporting of related transactions.
- Execution of the transaction or transaction activity.

In addition, a control over the processing of a transaction generally should not be performed by the same individual responsible for recording or reporting the transaction. In the absence of segregation between noncompatible duties, chances of fraud and error risks increase. For example, access rights given to a software engineer in the development environment has authority to move code in the live production environment.

Or consider that access to proprietary engineering drawings be given to finance; there is an exposure of unauthorized sharing or selling of the designs. Every organization has a certain tolerance for risk. Risks for successful ventures, risks of losses from fraud or error, market risks and legal risks all have different "preference curves" in any given organization.

But concept of SOD helps reduce risk by providing a management tool for allocating resources and managing to budgets. If roles and responsibilities are not followed, the opportunity for collusion cannot be controlled within an organization's risk preferences or within any acceptable framework. Hence the integrated report must list down all unnecessary access and include them in findings and subsequently the recommendations to management.

Managing Change

Change management in software development life cycles, network operations, and IT security departments use the concepts of SOD to ensure proper approvals and release to production processes. There are five basic steps to all change management that need segregated management and process steps to maintain a proper risk management model:

1. Initiation of change with appropriate authorization.
2. Project management oversight of the change process.
3. Tracking of changes to key process steps.
4. Corresponding management and risk controls must be developed and documented.
5. Management oversight and approval for implementation of changes into "production."

In short, segregation of production and test environment and change controls also contribute toward reduction of security incidents.

Case Study

A very techno-savvy sales representative for an advertising firm built an advertising revenue model that only he understood. The revenue was based on selling access to a large customer base to potential advertisers, and then broadcasting advertising messages to those customers. The sales rep would sell the deals, write the insertion orders for the broadcasted content, and report to accounting on the closed and delivered deals. Many times, these deals were structured with a barter component. Clearly, the sales rep had too much control over too many of the components of revenue recognition—he created fraudulent insertion orders that he would have his trading partners sign to complete the barter transaction. However, the trading partners never delivered their commitments to the insertion orders, and the sales rep was the only one who understood the broadcast e-mail system, including how to access log files.

This fraudulent activity went undetected until the trading partner was sold to another corporation. The new management of the trading partner was presented with insertion orders that did not have proper supporting documentation. In turn, management decided to call the sales rep's company to discuss the matter. It was only at this time that this $900,000-dollar scheme was uncovered!

Lessons learnt: Proper SOD should exist between revenue and technical operations.

Continuous Monitoring of BIA/RA Results

A well written and presented BIA report can significantly increase senior management's interest in and awareness about, disaster recovery; this, in turn, increases the likelihood that management will approve the next stage of the project.

Keeping the BIA Alive

BIAs should be performed again when changes or expansion of business occurs. An annual BIA can take care and be refreshed as your business expands and new systems are added. We recommend conducting a new BIA at least once every three years or whenever you have a significant product or service expansion.

Conclusion

On successful completion of BIA and RA exercise, practitioners gather enough information on the business, its processes, the internal and external dependencies, the infrastructure, geographical spread, locations, data center, and so on.

Main area of interest to business is to safeguard against intangible impacts such as loss of goodwill and loss of customer confidence that has direct bearing on the profits of the organization. Countermeasures in the form of SOD, change controls, removal of dependency on single vendor, single location or single person by introducing cross training, new vendors, and spreading of functions at different locations, must be projected effectively.

The deliverable from this phase is the conscious realization by management of the risks and impacts that are being faced by the business. This leads to prioritization of customer-centric processes and applications that has to be given highest priority. After due deliberation with all the business heads and the IT, fixation of final RTOs and RPOs, and projecting a cost sheet of expected expenses for carrying out infrastructure changes and control countermeasures, management will weigh the cost against benefit and agree to give a BCM sponsor who will commit a dollar value to the BCM project and fund its implantation. Management shall provide DR budget, resources, and manpower to implement the BCM program. This is the deliverable out of the management presentation of the report and findings. It will feed into the next phase of preparing the strategy for business continuity and resilience.

Chapter 5

BCM Strategy and Plans

Introduction

Business continuity strategy is based on management sponsorship, fixation of BCM budget, coordination with IT section for alignment of BCM requirements to business requirements, documenting the most cost-effective strategy for implementation, and maintenance. As seen in Figure 5.1, all recovery strategies should be based on MTPDs documented in BIA stage and must have continuous improvement as its main business continuity objective.

Formulation of Business Continuity Strategy

BCM strategy should be aligned with business and IT strategies to ensure that regulatory and legal requirements are met. BCM policies and procedures should incorporate the necessary controls to ensure that data integrity and privacy are not compromised during recovery efforts. While developing business continuity strategy, practitioners should focus around:

1. Business processes and operations
2. Users
3. Data center
4. Networks
5. Facilities
6. Supplies
7. Data (off-site storage of backup data and applications)

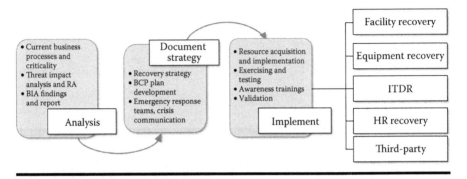

Figure 5.1 Recovery strategy to be developed for continuous improvement.

The following factors pose a large challenge in the choice of appropriate BCM strategies:

1. Presence in multiple locations
2. Availability of recovery options such as owned, leased, shared or mobile facilities
3. Increasing number of threats, risks and vulnerabilities
4. Complexity of external dependencies on supply chain channels

BCM strategy is based on *worst-case scenarios*, and BCM team will help build these scenarios based on past incidents and future predictions. Some businesses propose business recovery strategies that are different from the rest of the organization. There is a budget for BCM, and there will be a constant tussle between business requirements and the available budget for implementation.

Some organizations follow the *Y-model for planning BCM strategy* (Figure 5.2).

This involves an assessment or stock taking of our requirements and our business continuity objectives. It is important to ascertain where we are and where we want to go. This involves taking stock of basic BCM awareness, existing potential for meeting continuity objectives, and on that basis, prepare the planning for the organizational business continuity management system (BCMS).

Up to this stage, the risk-based evaluation is done, and the risk is prioritized. A practitioner conducts his BIA/RA and presents his findings in a management report. Management has reviewed findings and have arrived at an amicable level of RTOs and RPOs and have sanctioned a dollar amount as BCM budget to carry out the BCM implementation, testing, and oversight.

On the basis of BIA/RA reports, the risk strategy is documented. Risk treatment to be determined, all known risks to be entered in risk register, and residual risk impact have to be documented.

Once the preliminaries are done, the next question is how far spread is the organization? Which type of incidents has been identified as probable? How do you define incidents? A practitioner should have working knowledge how to bifurcate scenarios between:

Figure 5.2   BCM strategy on the "Y-model."

1. Facilities outage where primary facility is not available for a few days or for an extended period.
2. Technological outage where IT systems are unavailable disrupting normal operations.
3. Where any branch office is not working due to riots, fire, or any other outage?
4. A city outage.
5. A country outage.

As can be seen from Figure 5.3, a risk-based strategy for BCM is advisable since it lists down all threats, risks, and the residual risks and on this basis, the BCM strategy is developed. BCM strategies are based on the MTDs that were fixed in the BIA and which have been signed off by the operations management as well as the

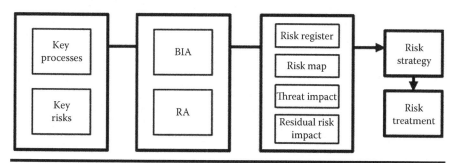

Figure 5.3   BCM risk-based strategy.

executive management at the time of presentation and commitment of resources. Risk treatment or mitigation controls can help reduce the occurrence of security incidents. Strategy planners can focus more on residual risks as well as monitor them to guard against any new risks or vulnerabilities entering the organization.

Mitigation measures denote what needs to change, and the practitioner has to focus the BCM strategy on a post remediation state. Consider the budget is a constant factor, we need to see what recovery options are available, and what options are affordable? Hence BCM teams have to work in close association with IT to interweave recovery options into the existing and to be set infrastructure. Alignment is not a choice; it is a compulsory step for effective BCM strategy.

Once we have fixed the strategy, we can match it with plans to execute them. The BCM strategy of an organization denotes its fundamental approach to business management.

It includes the building up of the BCM infrastructure and the BCM teams delineating roles and responsibilities and the scope of the BCM.

Corporate Sponsorship

An important part of the BCM strategy is corporate sponsorship. The steps in this direction are as follows:

1. Develop BCM plans and policies in line with management approval.
2. Develop and utilize a suitable reporting structure to provide periodic status reports to the management throughout the process of strategy development.
3. Senior management vetting of proposed plan against risk exposure faced by the organization.
4. Approval for selected strategies to be given by senior management.
5. Periodic evaluation and review to maintain effectiveness.

The following are critical areas to focus on while developing a business continuity strategy:

1. Secure stable information-processing facilities and office locations with adequate physical and environmental safeguards.
2. Redundancy in communications and critical systems.
3. Data-protection procedures and regular backups of critical applications, platforms, configurations, and off-site storage of backups.
4. Diverse vendors for critical services in order to limit a single point of failure in the event of disaster and regular vendor review.
5. Contact information to contact local, state, and other related authorities during disruption.

6. Emergency incident response measures such as maintaining adequate reserves of food, water, medical supplies, and batteries.
7. Regional diversity for alternate recovery sites for all critical business processes, including service providers, telecommuting, and alternative workforce.
8. Cost-benefit analysis to determine the costs associated with recovery site alternatives vis-à-vis their distance from the primary site.

Business continuity strategy summarizes the preventive and recovery strategies that must be carried out between disaster occurrence and business resumption after the incident.

The preparation of a *task list* will help in the strategy formulation process (Annexure A).

We define three phases of business continuity planning, implementing, and monitoring function. Basically an organizational BCMS includes all tasks and activities that are performed before, during, and after the crisis.

Preplanning Phase

In this stage, the practitioner should focus on freezing the BCM requirements and increasing organizational preparedness to face a crisis situation (Figure 5.4).

It includes spreading awareness for security, known vulnerabilities, and threats.

Initial activities

■ Setting the business continuity policy
■ Determining the business continuity program objectives
■ Determining the business continuity program scope
■ Defining governance
■ Accountability for the overall business continuity program
■ Delegated responsibility for implementation of the individual components of the business continuity program
■ Defined roles and responsibilities within the business continuity program

Figure 5.4 (i) Phases of business continuity strategy formulation.

The practitioner assigned the task of preparing the BCM strategy, has to first focus on BCM strategies for the business units within the organization, and then consolidate the plans into an organization-wide strategy. The following steps may be followed in this direction.

Mission Statement for Business Continuity

A short mission statement containing the purpose, roles and responsibilities, scope, goals, objectives, and methods of evaluation can be formulated. It gives the BCM project impetus and the necessary direction to initiate action.

BCM Objectives

The business continuity objectives are the real premise to begin with since they convey the management attitude and commitment toward the BCM program. BCM objectives may include the following:

1. Protection of assets.
2. Measures to limit loss during disruption.
3. Minimize business loss and loss of customer goodwill.
4. Improving prompt salvage of assets during disaster.
5. Ensuring orderly evacuation of personnel and moving them to safety. Providing resources for BCM and ensuring proper coordination between BCM teams by properly structuring them across locations and providing for their backups in case any of them is not available during crisis.
6. Reduction of response time through planning and exercising.

Ascertain the Budget

At the time of management presentation, the budget for BCM and ITDR is sanctioned by the management. It is best to bifurcate the budget into its various components and time when it has to be expended.

Refer to Annexure C at the end of the section for an illustrative budget breakdown structure.

Evaluate the Different Recovery Options

The following are the recovery options available (Figure 5.5):

1. *Prevention*: It is a good strategy that aims at reducing the chances of the disaster happening. It consists of deterrent controls that reduce the likelihood of the threats occurring. Preventive controls safeguard the vulnerable areas to ward off any threat that occurs and reduce its impact. Having these measures in place is always more cost-effective than attempting recovery after the interruption.

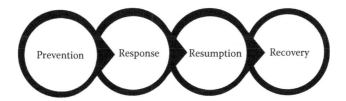

Figure 5.5 **Options for business continuity strategies.**

After the RA, when threats, risks, and vulnerabilities are identified, a strategy based on using deterrent and preventive controls to reduce the likelihood of risks materializing in the first place makes strategy makers to concentrate on BCM strategies that deal with residual risks only.

The following are few types of preventive controls that can be adopted by the enterprise:

a. *Ensure security of the facilities*: It is an example of a deterrent control that obstructs unauthorized entry to the installation/facilities by imposing physical access controls such as guards, biometric access control, and surveillance systems at the location.

b. *Personnel procedures*: Critical locations can be made restricted zones, entry to authorized personnel only, and a log of entry other than authorized personnel has to be maintained. Identification badge is a good way of identifying personnel and ensuring that they are confined to their authorized work spaces only.

c. *Infrastructure planning*: It includes capacity-planning measures like using an appropriate sized UPS, proper backup power, smoke detectors, fire extinguishers placed at strategic locations in the facility, waterproofing, fire-resistant containers, cabinets and walls, monitoring weather forecasts, and so on.

d. *Application controls*: They help run business processes. Hence proper access control, antivirus software, encryption algorithms, firewalls for peripheral security, intrusion detection systems to study anomalous behavior over the network, annual vulnerability assessments and penetration testing to overrule risk from open ports, and so on may be deployed as preventive controls.

e. *Data storage controls*: Off-site storage of backups and a proper predefined backup policy and procedures for backup, storage, testing, restoration, and purging after retention dates expire are controls connected to data storage.

f. *Security policy in place*: The confidentiality, integrity, and availability of organizational assets and information systems and its appropriate usage by the appropriate personnel is the backbone of the security policy of the enterprise, and this has to be developed, adopted by the board of directors, and reviewed on a periodic basis. Management oversight on compliance to security policy and periodic audit of security practices followed by the enterprise is a good preventive control.

Planning for prevention must be cautiously done, so as to ascertain that it is not too restrictive for smooth business nor it should obstruct venturing into new business opportunities that can be capitalized in future.

2. *Response*: In this stage, the first responses to an incident should be delisted. The first response to an incident is to notify the right people. A point to note is that major recipients of BCM communication are:

   - CIOs and CTOs
   - IT directors and data center managers
   - Security and risk management officers
   - BC/DR planners
   - Data center architects
   - Application owners

Notification of impending disaster can be given by issuing prior warning through the appointed communication channels to employees, visitors, and/or customers on the premises. This, however, involves deployment of diagnostic or detective controls. Such controls either continuously scan themselves for a symptom of interruption (network, servers) or collect such information from external sources (natural calamities).

Timely notification can ensure orderly shutdown of machines and systems and if necessary have an orderly evacuation of premises made in case of risk to premises. This is one of the first response steps to move to safety all personnel on the premises and to alert the police, fire service, and hospitals. This is required only if the interruption is of the nature of an accident, act of sabotage, or natural calamity.

Precise notification procedures must be documented, and call lists for persons to be contacted and informed should exist both at primary site and at the backup site to facilitate mobilization of notification procedures. Notification can be done using various tools: pager, short message service (SMS), phone, and e-mail.

The escalation procedure as per the severity of the incident as predetermined and the chain of command defined as per the severity criteria will enable the triggering of the appropriate business continuity plan (BCP) or invocation of DR plan as the case may be.

Call tree: It is set up as part of the BCP whereby an initial set of people to be notified is documented, and they in turn would notify the next set of people associated with them. The notification to be provided depends on the role of the personnel in the recovery procedures (See Chapter 9 for call-tree examples).

The following groups would be involved:

a. *Management* would need constant information on status of disruption. They need information on initial assessment so as to classify the incident under different levels of security and decide whether to invoke the DR plan or merely resort to fix the problem using troubleshooting methods. Management may also have to deal with public, press, and stakeholders.

b. *Technical team*: Soon after the damage assessment is done, the technical team will start its preparedness. They look at the BCM management to convey the severity of the disaster according to preset severity levels. These parameters should differentiate between an interruption and a disaster, and also rate the severity of the event. Time of repair, restoration, and resumption are heavily dependent on whether or not DR is invoked.

The type and extent of the disaster declared would indicate which portions of the BCP need to be implemented. Accordingly, the BCP team is notified, and resumption activities are started. While the damage assessment team and technical team are working, the rest of the BCP team is placed on alert for a possible activation of the BCP plan.

c. *Operations team* would execute the actual operations of the BCP. They would be responsible for business recovery of their most critical processes in the time limit that has been prescribed.

3. *Resumption*: It involves resuming only the time-sensitive business processes, either immediately after the interruption or after the declared mean time between failures (MTBF).

All operations are not fully recovered. The focus shifts to the command center once the BCM teams declare the severity of the disaster and invoke the appropriate plan of action. The resumption and subsequently the recovery activities are coordinated after this point.

Command center is a facility located near to the primary facility and has adequate communication facilities, PCs, printers, fax machines, and office equipment to support the activities of the team. The first decision to be taken is—whether the critical operations can be resumed at the normal business site or at an alternate site. In situations when access to the primary site is denied or the site is damaged beyond use, the operations could move to an alternate site.

The choice for alternate processing sites falls under the following categories:

a. *Hot site*: A hot site is a fully functional data center with hardware, software, personnel, and customer data. It is a 24/7 staffing; it is ready to be operational within a small span of time. In case of extremely small RTOs and RPOs, it would be good to have the systems up and running in a short time. Organization such as financial institutions where they hold a lot of customer data and have lot of customer-facing applications has to go for a hot site option.

b. *Warm site*: A warm site is an equipped data center with hardware, software, network services, and personnel. The element missing here is customer data. An organization can install additional equipment and introduces customer data when a disaster occurs.

c. *Cold site*: A cold site is a type of data center which has its own associated infrastructure that includes power, telecommunications, and environmental controls designed to support IT systems, applications, and data which are installed only when disaster strikes, and the DR plan is activated. Since the equipment has to be installed at the time of outage, this option can only be used when the business systems can be down for an extended period of time.

d. *Mobile site*: A mobile site is a portable van or trailer that can be used as an emergency-processing center at the time of disaster. It provides an excellent alternative to the above three options. After a disaster, the trailer can move to site, all essential equipment, and supplies can be loaded onto it, and then connection for power and communication are added to it before it can be made functional.

   The control point here is that it has to be ensured that the vendor who provides the trailer has enough number to provide to all clients in that location with whom he or she has contracted and also that training in these operations has been provided to the people who are going to work for and on these trailers.

e. *Mirrored site*: A mirror site is identical in all aspects to the primary site, right down to the information availability. It is equivalent to having a redundant site in normal times and is naturally the most expensive option. At the alternate site (or primary site, if still usable), the work environment is restored. Communication, networks, and workstations are set up and contact with the external world can be resumed.

f. *Manual mode*: It is possible that an organization might choose to function in the manual mode until the critical IT services can resume. If the recovery alternative (described in a later section) permits, the critical functions can also be resumed in the automated mode very quickly.

   Recovery: It addresses the start-up of less time-sensitive processes. The time duration of this naturally depends on the time taken for resumption of the time-sensitive functions. It could involve starting up these services at an alternate location. At the site of recovery (either primary or alternative), the operating system is restored on the standby system. Necessary applications are restored in the order of their criticality. When the applications to serve the critical functions are restored, data restoration from backup tapes or media obtained from the off-site storage can be initiated. Data must also be synchronized, that is, to rebuild data accurately to a predetermined point of time before the interruption. The point to which the restoration is done depends on the requirements of the critical services.

Validation of data: Business data come from different sources, each of which must be reconstructed to reach the desired state of data integrity. The synchronized data must be reviewed and validated. This is mandatory because under crisis situation, there will not be any test environment, and applications may be resumed in production environment directly. A strategy, checklist, or method for data validation must be defined so that once the reliability of data is ascertained, backlog of transactions can be processed.

4. *Restoration*: It is the process of repairing and restoring the primary site. At the end of this, the business operations are resumed in totality from the original site or a completely new site. While the recovery team is supporting operations from the alternate site, restoration of the primary site for full functionality is initiated. In case the original building/work area or primary facility is beyond repair, then a new site is restored. It is possible that the team members of the recovery and restoration team are common. It must be ensured that the site has the necessary infrastructure, equipment, hardware, software, and communication facilities.

It is necessary to test whether the site is capable of handling full operations. The operational data must then be uploaded at this site, and the emergency site must be gradually dismantled. Planning for all activities described above will include defining a time span within which they must be executed. This time duration is defined keeping in mind the recovery of the organization.

The BCP team must remember that if at any point of time, they exceed this planned time, then the contingency must be escalated to the command center at once, and immediate solutions must be worked out, or else they might miss their recovery targets.

Having discussed the recovery options, it will be necessary to note that organizations choose their recovery options based on predefined criteria in respect of

a. Advantages/disadvantages.
b. Cost.
c. Option of mitigation and control measures.

Consider requirements of off-site alternate facilities for operations during crisis and enlist the type of

a. Facilities required.
b. Utilities required.
c. Communication facilities required.
d. Time span for which such facilities need to be arranged.

Unit strategies have to be identified first that are suited to maintain the demand of RTOs and RPOs that have been approved by the management. Points under consideration in this context are

a. Timeframes.
b. Location.

    c. Number of people required with special mention of specialized skills required at units.

    d. Requirement of raw material/equipment/communication media/need for internet facilities, and so on.

A review of technology continuity issues for support services to ensure that BCM strategies are aligned to technology infrastructure and applications makes BCM planning more effective. A cost-benefit analysis must be made to ensure that strategies selected and their implementation costs fit into the BCM budget approved by the management.

Awareness and Training

Information dissemination before, during, and after a disaster is crucial. Continuously embedding BCM awareness in the form of intranet messages or one-liners under corporate e-mails gives out a healthy sign within and outside to those receiving the e-mails. Awareness is necessary to make BCM initiatives effective since response in emergencies can be enhanced by prior knowledge and training. This can be achieved through:

    a. Coordination with functional departments within the enterprise

    b. Designing awareness efforts with enterprise culture

    c. Uploading write ups, newsletters, briefings, and intranet pages for employees to view at leisure

    d. Having a slot on basic BCM awareness in induction programs for new entrants

    e. Conducting BCM workshops to discuss real-life incidents in and around the enterprise and to discuss the lessons learned from the recovery procedures at these incidents

    f. Involving staff to participate in the planning and execution of tests and exercises for business continuity

    g. Development of unambiguous and clear instructions and incident-handling procedures for major types of incidents that are most likely to occur or to which organization is vulnerable to

    h. Periodically hosting a business continuity week and spreading promotional material at entrances and canteens

Training to develop BCM capabilities:

    a. BCM training during induction

    b. Initiating program management

    c. Risk assessment workshops

    d. Training in crisis communication

    e. Developing training programs to be given on a periodic basis to refresh employee awareness and BCM skills

Other Factors

1. *All locations* should align with and coordinate all segments of the business continuity strategy. There is a need to develop uniform BCM policies and procedures across geographic locations and manage changes to these documents.
2. *Contracts and SLAs* should include specific clauses addressing continuity requirements.
3. *BCM consideration* should be included in system development life cycle (SDLC) and change management policies and procedures.
4. *Mobile devices* are now supporting critical functions/processes, and use of multiple types of communication (voice, text, video, social networks) during crisis may be considered. This will include contracts with mobile device vendors to have BCM requirements that specify the time limit within which the lost/stolen or damaged devices will be replaced.

Planning and Development

In the previous stage, prior planning and exploring of available options are made to facilitate the development of a BCM program (Figure 5.6). In this part, we shall see the planning for business continuity and development of the business continuity pan. Planning for continuity is planning for contingencies. Contingency planning is defined as the process of developing advance arrangements and procedures that enable an enterprise to respond to an event that could occur by chance or unforeseen circumstances. This exercise covers:

1. BCM team organization
2. Finalizing the BCM requirements
3. Evaluating recovery alternatives in the light of BCM objectives
4. Documenting the BCM strategy

Business Continuity Team Organization

A BCM strategy has to consider responsibility matrix for BCM within the organization. At the apex is the management representation (Figure 5.7).

Figure 5.6 (ii) Phases of business continuity strategy formulation.

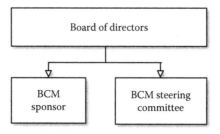

Figure 5.7 BCM management.

BCM sponsor can be the CEO or the chief operating officer (COO) of the organization; he or she is responsible for promoting business continuity expectations and culture throughout the enterprise.

BCM steering committee (BCMSC): A BCMSC will be formed to collectively take decisions on BCM-related issues. The BCMSC is the primary decision-making group for the BCM program, has an oversight for BCM at the corporate level, and reviews and approves the BCM program.

BCMSC comprises of senior management representing all primary functional and support areas, determines the scope, provides resources, develops timeframes, and defines responsibilities for the BCM program. It may consist of three to five members, represented by board members, BCM sponsor, generally the CEO/COO and BCM coordinator.

Business continuity management (BCM) coordinator is an individual who has overall responsibility for BCM at each specific location. The BCM coordinator helps the management to set recovery objectives, developing, and monitoring schedules and budgets. The BCM coordinator utilizes BCM personnel and implements the BCM strategies of the organization. He coordinates exercises and activities in crisis situations, and he is responsible for regular updates to BCM documentation.

Regional coordinators: In a large organization spread across many geographical or multinational locations, regional coordinators may be appointed who would be on site for disasters and communicate the status to other people in the organization. BCM coordinators monitor the planning, development, and implementation of the BCMS. They help the BCMSC to monitor project costs and timetables and take decisions on matters relating to BCM investment and administration. They in turn report to the management about the progress of the BCM.

When we talk about BCM management, it would be worthwhile to glance at the *BCM roles of the following executive management personnel*:

Role of CEO: The BCM program is controlled by the CEO who can optionally be the project sponsor. The Steering Committee has to report to him about the activities of BCM and at the time of disaster, it will be the CEO and in his absence an alternative executive such as COO who can declare a disaster.

Role of CIO: Role of CIO extends beyond safeguarding information systems assets and providing for continued availability of IT throughout the organization. As a part of the strategic planning for IT infrastructure, he or she has an important function toward planning for business continuity and disaster recovery. Availability requirements in crisis have to be mapped with critical processes, bearing in mind the risk appetite and resource constraints.

When developing and maturing a BCM strategy, CIOs work with COOs, chief risk officers (CROs), and BCM professionals and:

- Consider the legal and regulatory, political, cultural, environmental, and contractual factors applicable to the enterprise.
- Document the alignment of BCM to strategic business objectives, key performance indicators, key availability risk indicators, and the enterprise risk management program.
- Assess the adequacy of BCM program by benchmarking with best practices, prevalent standards, and sometimes even an existing BCM framework in the organization.
- Work toward closing the gaps that have been identified between capabilities that can be provided versus the recovery expectation from business. This precludes identification of single points of contact (SPOCs) in different departments that will get together for forming BCM teams and carry out the BCM activities (Figure 5.8).

Types of BCM Teams

1. *Emergency response team (ERT)*: It is the immediate reaction and response to an emergency situation commonly focusing on ensuring life safety and reducing the severity of the incident. The ERT should be drawn from a range of locations to reduce severity of impact to facilities, technology, and employees.

   An ERT is comprised of primary team members and alternate members at each major location responsible for emergency response. The alternate members perform the task when the primary member is not available for some reason. They need to:
   a. Take BCM training
   b. Participate in BCM exercises
   c. Capable of handling physical and emotional stressful situations and counsel employees during crisis

   The incident commander is in charge of the ERT. The incident commander is the individual responsible for the command and control of all aspects of a crisis. The incident commander must have the authority and ability to make quick decisions in critical situations. As the person who is in charge of the response efforts, the incident commander should be an officer of the organization.

   Chain of command is the order of authority within the organization. During a crisis, the chain of command is not necessarily the same organizational

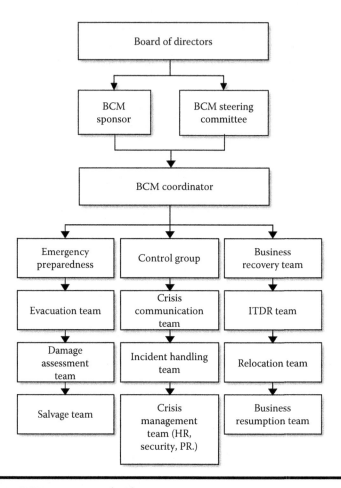

Figure 5.8 BCM team organization.

command order used during times of normal operations. The actual incident commander will be the available individual who is highest on the chain of command? Overall incident command is relinquished to responding civil authorities at their request.

2. *The damage assessment team* is among the earliest (along with the management) to be notified of the event. They would be required at the site at the earliest to evaluate the extent of the damage inflicted. In case the site itself has been subject to damage, then they should start their work as soon as an entry is allowed. The damage assessment should be as per the plan adopted by the management. This means that prior knowledge of strategic assets and processes that are crucial to business must prevail. Their assessment and report have to be closely aligned to the business continuity priorities.

The major areas to be examined by the damage assessment team are:

a. Cause of disruption
b. Whether there is scope to contain the disruption by segmenting/partitioning the premises
c. Examine the extent of infrastructure and equipment damage
d. Enlist all services that are affected by the disruption
e. Enlist all vital records that have been destroyed/damaged
f. Ascertain what can be salvaged from the damage site
g. Note down what needs immediate repair, restoration, or replacement
h. Requirement for insurance claims if applicable

The damage assessment team will assess the damage and convey the severity to the management and the extent to which the business is inoperable. They will provide for stabilization and resumption of operations caused by a crisis in the recovery phase.

3. *Evacuation team* is appointed at each location, and it consists of fire wardens on every floor. Their chief function is to cause an orderly evacuation of premises and take attendance at assembly point to ensure that employees have been evacuated from the facilities affected by crisis.

4. *Salvage team* is responsible for securing valuable property and equipment. They should commence salvage operations as soon as it is safe to do so.

5. *Control group*: Strategy must provide for a control group who will give direction and control during the emergency. This group will operate from an Emergency Operations Center also known as *command center*. Their functions include the following:

a. Direct operation of the ERTs
b. Coordinate rescue operations by orderly evacuation of personnel and on-site visitors
c. Communicating with employees
d. Assist in medical support and first aid
e. Gather and analyze information required for further emergency decisions to be taken by the management
f. Communicate essential information to local authorities
g. Involving in development and testing of emergency plans

BCM strategy has to be taken care to see that alternate locations for command centers have been identified and documented in the strategy document. Strategy has to document the circumstances when the primary facility has to shut its operations and revert to alternate facility. This will envisage procedures for orderly shutdown of equipment, utilities, and the facility as a whole. Emergency response procedures must be laid and damage control must be provided for.

6. *Crisis management team* (*CMT*) involves the following functions:

   – Identifying a crisis situation
   – Setting protocol for timing and manner for incident response

  – Communicating both internally and externally
  – Leading and directing the recovery process

The suitable structure and size of a CMT depend on culture, type, size, and configuration of an organization. Size of team is dependent on the hierarchical structure, the taller the organization chart, bigger the size of the CMT. Other factors that affect the CMT structure for a particular organization include the following:

a. Style of management; whether it is autocratic or democratic, whether it is centralized or decentralized
b. The available recovery options to choose from

In the event of a disaster, a CMT is highly important in maintaining clear lines of communication both internally and externally. This team greatly assists in the event of a disaster through understanding the crisis, making key decisions, and providing a stable framework for the other teams to communicate and work together.

Crisis team can be functionally bifurcated into:

a. *Crisis IT team*: If disaster strikes and the corporate website or internal lines of communication are broken, the crisis IT team will be crucial. A crisis IT team salvages data and routes around damaged servers quickly. Similarly, the crisis IT team should comprise of security experts. Increasingly, the disasters are man-made. A highly damaging piece of malware or any data leak will need to be contained and solved as soon as possible.

b. *Crisis security team*: It exists to secure tangible goods, sensitive files that may be exposed during a disaster, and employees themselves. This team physically safeguards a company's assets. They need to be on site to respond to major incident and provide relief to normal on-site security, which may suffer in case of a local disaster.

c. *Crisis HR*: The crisis HR team's role is to step in during an event that directly threatens the life of employees. Giving psychological support during crisis and post crisis and keeping their morale high can make recovery efforts come up faster.

d. *Crisis PR*: *This team concentrates on* keeping organizational image positive. Keeping a favorable image as a company that performs reliably and is able to humanely treat its employees during disasters is a key element in keeping business moving forward.

e. *Crisis communication team*: *Crisis communication* is a key factor between the command group and the ERT, and key personnel must have understanding of all available communication channels and procedures to be used in an emergency (Figure 5.9). Practitioner to consider creating more awareness among employees of threats, hazards, and impending disasters, the appropriate actions to be taken before, during or after an emergency. After an event, normal communication channels may not

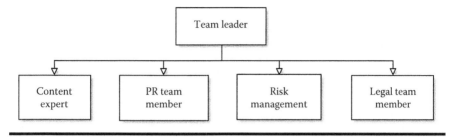

Figure 5.9 Crisis communication team.

exist. Effective communication is key to success of crisis response and to minimize confusion:

- Activation of BCM team and support teams
- Prioritization of activities and coordinating till plan invocation
- Call out recovery leaders and other personnel needed during crisis
- Help coordinate command center where applicable
- Public announcements and preparing press releases
- Coordinating preparation of detailed damage assessments:
    i. Business process
    ii. Facility
    iii. Systems
- Overseas damage assessment and control activities
- Coordinating news conferences and interviews
- Interfacing with media people
- Safeguarding organization's reputation and brand image during the crisis

Note: Also refer to crisis communication plan later in this section.

7. *Incident handling team* is responsible for central command and control of the incident and assists the critical processes in implementing their recovery plans. The team works to the procedures within the Incident Management Plan and liaises both with the business unit management team and the senior management team. They are responsible for handling security incidents from end to end. The process of detecting, analyzing, responding to, and improving from disruptive events is known as incident management. To accomplish this goal, an organization establishes processes that

    - Detect and identify events
    - Triage and analyze events to predict whether an incident is underway
    - Respond and recover from an incident
    - Improve the organization's capabilities for responding to a future incident

8. *Business recovery team* is a group of individuals responsible for maintaining the business recovery procedures and coordinating the recovery of business

functions and processes. There may be different recovery teams as designed by the recovery plans allocating recovery functions to the different people on the recovery teams.

9. *Disaster recovery team* (*ITDR*) deals with major catastrophic events that deny access to the normal facility for an extended period. Frequently, disaster recovery plans (DRPs) refers to an IT-focused plan designed to restore operability of the target system, application, or computer facility, and an alternate site after an emergency. IT is the backbone of business recovery. ITDR deals with data required to start business processing at alternate site and serves IT services at alternate site. It includes backup management and off-site storage of data. The DRP scope may overlap that of an IT contingency plan; however, the DRP is narrower in scope and does not address minor disruptions that do not require relocation. Dependent on the agency's needs, several DRPs may be appended to the BCP.

10. *Relocation team* is a bunch from generally the admin department who facilitate relocation of employees during an incident to off-site facilities temporarily. Some impacts may render a facility temporarily uninhabitable. For a day or two, work-from-home strategies may suffice—but they are not suitable if the outage lasts from three to five days onwards. Knowing where local, alternate space may be available (e.g., workspace sharing or hoteling vendors, neighboring buildings or other tenants with extra space) may provide better long-term temporary solutions. The relocation team must maintain a good working relationship with a landlord or building owner. It can give good dividends at the time of a disruption.

Having quick access to those contacts—within the business continuity plan—will ensure adequate time to make phone and network connections to make such spaces usable. In case of destruction of primary facility, it is this contact that enables the relocation team to start sourcing replacement facilities quickly.

11. *Business resumption team* comprises of BCM team members who are responsible for a documented set of actions to be performed during an incident ensuring that business processes can resume processing within the predefined timescales. Planning for business continuity is done with the objective of being able to perform the most critical functions within the RTOs accepted during BIA phase and to restore data and pick up on the backlog caused by disruption and enable the business recovery team to resume its critical operations within the timescale defined. Also the efforts to return to business as usual perpetually are always underlined.

Having discussed the various teams that can be formed by the organizations, a point to note is that a functional bifurcation of tasks to be performed during a crisis throws light on the type of expertise and capability to carry out certain typical functions (Figure 5.10).

Finance

- Representing on the BCM Steering Committee
- Ensuring compliances are done on time during crisis
- Provide petty cash to recovery team during crisis
- Coordinating payments to contract staff at recovery sites
- Identifying losses
- Processing insurance claims
- Tracking expenditure and providing funds for BCM activities
- Ensuring appropriate accounting controls are maintained

IT

Availability of information systems
Backups and restoration at alternate site
IT facilities at alternate site
Data center activities
Data cleansing and security

HR

- Administer smooth evacuation and ensure that all employees are accounted for
- Location-wise headcount
- Contact employees' families where needed
- Coordinating temporary relocation of staff (travel and accommodation)
- Hiring contract persons at alternate location
- Ensuring continuation of salaries and benefits to all employees at proper time
- Providing assistance to individual employees if requested
- Maintain call list of emergency personnel
- Contact lists for vendors and labor contractors
- Proforma drafts of crisis communication
- Salary processing in crisis

Admin.

- Liaison with civil authorities
- Damage assessment and salvage
- Provide BC coordinator with a report on:
  i. Missing staff injuries and/or loss of life
  ii. Extent of damage to facility
  iii. Damage to equipment (hardware, network components, etc.)
- Preparing the alternate location and contract facilities
- Arranging for physical security and initiating orderly evacuation in crisis
- Transportation of equipment and personnel to alternate site
- Redirecting mail and courier services to alternate location
- Arranging for interim telephone facility at alternate location

Operations

- Orderly evacuation
- Coordination with other departments to get critical processes up and about within appointed RTOs
- Providing for covering data needs and processing backlogs
- Communication with vendors and customers
- Coordinating resumption of operations

Figure 5.10   Functional allocation of BCM duties.

Review the BCM Strategy Requirements

Review the BCM strategy requirements on the backdrop of BIA/RA findings, it has to be ascertained what the BCM requirements include the following:

- Personnel
- Telephones/mobiles/pagers
- Internet/extranet
- E-mail/voicemail
- Videoconferencing
- PCs/desktops
- Dedicated printers
- FAX/telex
- Buffer for spools
- Copier
- Filing cabinets
- Dispatch room for post/couriers
- Special forms/stationery that includes letterheads, preprinted forms, and so on
- Software applications
- Logistics, which includes travel arrangements and packers and movers

Note: The above list is an inclusive list; requirements may vary from organization to organization. The choice of recovery objective guides the choice of strategy in various sections of the business at unit level. It is important to have a consistent method for evaluation. Hence a baseline should be established for guiding BCM strategy formulation, and it should be matched against requirements for business as defined by the BIA/RA.

Evaluating Recovery Alternatives in the Light of BCM Objectives

We need to first ascertain the type of outage that is likely to occur in the organization:

1. A technology failure that may cause a disruption to information systems processing but will not affect premises
2. Facilities disaster like fire and bomb blast, which makes primary site unavailable for business processes
3. A city outage that makes the entire city not reachable and unavailable due to curfew order, heavy rains, or any other crisis
4. A country outage where the country itself is not operational due to global disaster such as terrorism, war, and so on

Let us view some important functional departments as shown below:

Documenting the BCM Strategy

Choice of strategy depends to a large extent on which of the above situations we are preparing for. Generally, organizations do not prepare for a country outage simply because it is costly and probability of such outage is very less.

Organizations most commonly prepare for

1. Technology outage.
2. City outage.
3. Facilities outage.

Strategy options have been identified in preplanning stage. They range from alternate processing sites, work from home, and reciprocal agreements; every organization and the individual units within the organization may choose different alternatives for recovery for the time that full resumption of activities take place.

Consolidate unit and enterprise strategies: After selecting individual unit strategies, it is important to prioritize requirements considering availability of physical resources and personnel at required locations and to perform a cost-benefit analysis of strategies for arriving at enterprise strategy.

We shall consider a case study here to get the flavor of how organizations do their actual strategy planning.

Case Study—Sriman Health Insurance

BCM budget: Let us say we have a management budget of $200,000 each. Based on the facts of the case, we shall formulate BCM strategy for them.

Details of Company

Sriman is a relatively new player in the market. It has got operations PAN India with 36 offices distributed over different locations. They have an Asia Pacific office governed from Singapore and a head office situated in Canada.

Assuming that our practitioner's team has conducted a BIA and RA, only for their India offices and business, it would be good to look at the tabulated finding that was presented to the management:

Total Head Count: 700 employees in India.

Main locations in scope: 36 branches, 1 head office.

List of "in scope applications": health secure, receipting appl. Onix, Custocare, Investcare, Oracle, securepay, Froste, and Peoplesay. List of people and other resources have been tabulated below.

The following four functions have been identified as critical (Tables 5.1 through 5.5):

Table 5.1 Table of Critical Functions

Functions	Located at	RTO	RPO	MTD	IT Apps Used	Key People (No.)	Vital Records	Other Resources Needed
Operations	36 locations	24 hours	12 hours	32 hours	Health secure, receipting appl. Onix, Custocare	8	SLAs, policies, communication	Sensitive stationery; letterheads, logos, stamps
Finance	Mumbai	24 hours	14 hours	34 hours	Investcare, Oracle, securepay	3	Bills, bank statements	Cheque books, pass books
HR	Mumbai	28 hours	15 hours	32 hours	Froste	2	Employee records, salary records, leave records	Contact list
Admin	Mumbai	30 hours	24 hours	36 hours	Peoplesay	2	Contracts, facility agreements, and so on	Contact list, musters, attendance sheets

Table 5.2 **Operations**

Subprocesses	Location	Internal Interdependency	External Interdependency	Vital Records	IT Applications
Branch operations	36 locations	Finance, admin, underwriting, customer care	Vendor for printing, data entry, vendor for medical reports	Policy documents, SLAs	Receipting appl. Onix
Underwriting	Mumbai	Branch ops, finance	Vendor for medical reports		Health secure, Onix, e-mail, workflow
Customer service	Mumbai	Branch ops, claims, finance			Web, e-mails, Custocare
Claims	Mumbai	Underwriting, branch operations, customer service	Vendor	Claims documents	Vendor app

Table 5.3 Finance

Subprocesses	Location	Internal Interdependency	External Interdependency	Vital Records	IT Applications
Receipting	Mumbai	Operations	Communication from branches	Bank slips, communication	Receipting application
Investment	Mumbai	—	Brokers, fin. institutions	Broker slips, communication	Voice recording, invest care
Payments	Mumbai	Operations, HR, admin	Banks	—	Onix
Compliance	Mumbai	—	Regulatory bodies, tax authorities	Compliance doc. communication	Onix
Legal and regulatory	Mumbai	—	Regulatory bodies, tax authorities	Compliance doc. communication	Onix

Table 5.4   HR Operations

Subprocesses	Location	Internal Interdependency	External Interdependency	Vital Records	IT Applications
Appointment of people	Mumbai	Operations, admin, finance	Recruitment agents	Appointment letters	—
Organizing appraisals	Mumbai	Operations, admin, finance			
Training	All locations	Operations, admin, finance			

Table 5.5 Administration Department

Subprocesses	Location	Internal Interdependency	External Interdependency	Vital Records	IT Applications
Contract management for branches	All locations	Finance, HR	Facilities brokers	Contracts, communication	Oracle
Procurement of supplies	Mumbai	Finance	Vendors for supplies	Invoices, purchase order, challans	Oracle
Physical security	All locations	—	Security agency	Contracts, communication	Oracle

Table 5.6   Requirement Time for Recovery

Function/Department	RTO	RPO	MTD
Operations	24	12	32 hours
Finance	24	14	34 hours
Admin	28	24	36 hours
HR	30	15	32 hours

As we observe from the above charts, the MTDs on which we are going to base our BCM strategy is shown in Table 5.6.

IT has to prepare to build an infrastructure to support the MTDs approved by the management. At the same time, our budget for BCP/DRP is $20,000,000. We also need to assess the evaluation of existing capabilities and gaps identified during the BIA/RA exercise. This will help us to integrate mitigation controls into the BCMS. As a good measure, proper integration between the ITDR and BCM activities is necessary to build a comprehensive and fully supportive BCMS.

The risk analysis/gap report and recommendations in respect to Sriman Health Care (Table 5.7).

Solution

It will be beneficial if we make our assumptions list first:

1. The working of all branches is more or less similar.
2. Mumbai office is reporting to Singapore office on certain matters, and overall governance is from Canada.
3. The days of heavy load are from 26 to 30/31 of every month, and the busy months are December–March.
4. Our strategy will consider worst-case scenarios in order to cover heavy loads.
5. Management shall support awareness and training of employees to embed the BCM culture within the organization.

BCM Strategy of Sriman Health Insurance

There will be two business continuity strategies:

1. Branch units
2. HO

Type of disasters for which strategies to be formulated:

1. Facility outage
2. Systems going down
3. Earthquake, fire, and pandemic
4. Transport strike and people outage

Table 5.7 Risk Impact Table

Function	Observation	Asset	Risk	Prob.	ALE	Impact
Operations	IT systems downtime	Business processing	Operational disruption	0.66	$180,000	**$118,800**
Finance (investment)	Single point of failure	Invest care	Financial loss	0.4	$220,000	**$88,000**
Operations (underwriting)	10 underwriters in one location	Specialized skill	Single point of failure (location)	0.45	$210,000	**$94,500**
Operations (branch ops)	Single vendor across India	Printing of policies	Single point of failure	0.15	$120,000	**$18,000**
Operations (vendor document storage)	There is no documented recovery plan for fire hazard at the installation	Vital documents	Loss of vital documents	0.20	$358,000	**$71,600**
Operations (data center)	Located in proximity to the original facility	DC assets	Affected by the same disaster in that location	0.21	$41,000	**$8,610**
IT (applications managed from Singapore)	IT has no control over applications managed from Singapore e-mail, workflow systems, no BCP/DRP for these applications in Singapore	E-mail systems Workflow system	Reverse risk, if Singapore is down, India operations will be disrupted	0.15	$50,000	**$7,500**

(Continued)

Table 5.7 (*Continued*) Risk Impact Table

Function	Observation	Asset	Risk	Prob.	ALE	Impact
Admin. (SLAs)	SLAs are not kept in scanned form	Physical SLA copies	Destruction	0.01	$5,000	**$50**
HR (awareness)	Very low BCM awareness and security training	Key personnel	Operational loss	0.19	$12,000	**$2,280**
IT data center	Monitored guard station is not having guard	DC physical security	Security incident may be unnoticed	0.03	$22,100	**$663**
Admin. (facilities)	Fire exit doors are jammed and do not open easily	Facility	Evacuation will be disrupted	0.25	$32,550	**$8,138**
IT (backups)	Only data backups are taken, application backups are not kept offsite	Data	Wrong versions loaded in emergency	0.012	$18,900	**$227**

Branch recovery teams (two to three) will report to the branch operations controller and the overall BCM coordinator. The chief functions of these team members will be as follows:

1. Maintain call list of branch personnel
2. Maintain log of all persons in office on any working day
3. Well-documented procedures for orderly evacuation of people during disaster
4. Contact list of nearby branch offices and their contact persons
5. Spreading load of transaction processing on nearby branches designated in advance
6. Crisis communication and escalation of issues to HO during crisis

It has to be noted that branches methodology toward business continuity to focus around:

1. Security of people
2. Security of vital records
3. Processing of critical business processes

Critical department at branches is branch operations with RTO 24, RPO 12, and MTD of 32. An incident when discovered has to be escalated, and troubleshooting has to be done. If in spite of efforts, problem cannot be solved, then the appropriate authorities have to declare a disaster and invoke the relevant BCP.

Notification procedures to be formulated for crisis communication and escalation procedures.

Recommendations for Remediation Noted during BIA/RA (Preventive Measures)

1. Special attention to investment application, which must have availability during trading hours. A reciprocal agreement with vendor can be considered to allow some space for two members of the investment team to go to their office and work during period of disruption.
2. Alternate vendor for printing can be considered in order to mitigate single point of failure.
3. Specialized skill like underwriting that takes time to procure can be spread across 3–4 locations/branches so as to reduce single point of failure due to location.
4. System of application backups must be introduced.
5. Admin. to check all emergency exit doors periodically to prevent them from being jarred and rusted.
6. HR to incorporate BCM awareness training during induction and arrange for online awareness for all employees on a periodic basis.
7. IT infrastructure and facilities to be revisited so as to remove anomalies such as monitored workstation being left unguarded.

8. A system of keeping scanned copies of SLAs should be introduced so that a soft copy backup exists at off-site location.
9. Data center is in proximity to the primary site. The DR should mitigate proximity issues and provide for location convenience and ability to give recovery in case both primary site and DC are down.
10. In document storage vendor's installation if their BCP/DR does not provide for fire hazard, then our documents may be at a risk of being destroyed by fire. SLAs to include "right to audit" clause and special stipulation for inclusion of fire preventive measures in storage location.

It is important that if applications that are critical are being controlled by an overseas office, they must have a BCM plan in place in line with organization's policy since business continuity is an organization-wide exercise. If the failure at overseas end has a material impact on our operations, then preparing a BCM strategy and plan only for India will get diluted. The reverse risk can take the enterprise unawares. Hence uniform BCM strategies must be followed globally. If this is not done, the risk must be registered in the risk register.

Possible recovery options identified were:

1. Do nothing (take as acceptable risk).
2. Defer action (due to budgetary constraint).
3. Develop reciprocal agreements.
4. Develop alternate processing site (DR site).
5. Revert to alternate source of service (to prevent single point of failure).
6. Reduce impact through mitigation measures (prevention).

In the context of the above, either one of the following strategies has to be adopted after due deliberation with the departmental heads. Given the budget and the findings, practitioners will be faced with the objective of getting maximum value for the BCM investment.

The total strength of the enterprise is 700 spread across 36 branches and a head office in Mumbai. Budget to be bifurcated for BCM and ITFR purposes.

ITDR has proposed a budget of $1,000,000 for investing in technologies including the following:

1. Additional leased line for online backup.
2. Servers for replication from data center to ITDR site.
3. New systems for linking monitoring/alert systems to mobiles of the BCM-coordinating teams.
4. High-speed scanners to scan documents.
5. Software enabling online awareness training to employees.
6. Have a fall back for those applications controlled from overseas office, if they are not operational due to disruption.

BCM management is given the budget outer limit of $100,000 to coordinate its preventive and corrective measures:

1. Review the SLAs and have them include a right to audit clause where necessary. In case of vendors charging differentially for BCM to revise the agreement, go for a BCM capability contract with vendors.
2. Spreading the printing work between alternate vendors.
3. Appointing fall-back underwriters at alternate branch sites to avoid single point of failure if HO is down.
4. Spending on fire drills and testing of facilities to ensure that they will work during crisis.
5. Appointment of guards for monitored guard stations.

After documenting the strategy, plans of action have to be finalized. This will fall into:

- Emergency response plan (branch)
- Emergency response plan (HO)
- Evacuation plan (each branch)
- Evacuation plan (HO)
- Crisis management plan
- BCP
- Business recovery plan
- Business resumption plan
- Incident management plan

Sriman has plans for:

Facility outage: They have a network of branches and a work-from-home model by which they can spread the load of processing during the crisis period. In case of prolonged crisis, a leased site is there as Option B.

Contracted labor to cover unavailability of personnel in case of strikes, lockouts, or spread of pandemic diseases.

Alternate vendors to spread the procurement load to prevent single point of failure.

Alternate communication service providers to prevent single failure of communication line. Sriman's plans are coordinated with reporting to the BCMSC and regular reporting to management. They have change management for plans embedded within the BCMS and regular schedules for drills and exercises. Annual review of plans is provided, and awareness for BCM is a continuous process.

There is no prescribed format to document strategy. But every organization has some standard formats for general purpose like plans and policies, which can be adopted to document BCM strategy as well. Choice is up to the planning team.

Word format can be used for documentation. Any documentation for business continuity must provide review, update, and testing after changes occur to business, environment, or to the BCM personnel.

Note: The above is not an end-to-end solution but merely depicts how to analyze and what to document.

Implementation and Maintenance

The success of the BCMS implementation lies in the embedding of BCM principles into the culture or fabric of the organization (Figure 5.11). This can be achieved by increasing awareness through:

■ Consultation with key departments in the organization
■ Aligning awareness to the organization's culture
■ Articles on business continuity within the organization's newsletters, briefings, intranet pages, and through the organization's induction program
■ Business continuity management workshops, which examine lessons learned from real-life internal and external incidents
■ Inclusion in team meeting and project meeting agenda
■ Involvement of deputizing staff in tests and exercises
■ Establishing and maintaining an awareness campaign
■ Skills training

Review of plans: A periodic review of BCPs is necessary to ensure that they are working and are current. This review may include review of:

■ Mission-critical activities
■ Impact analyses
■ Vulnerabilities
■ Threats and hazards
■ The overall business continuity strategy
■ The organization's risk appetite
■ The organization's business continuity capability
■ The degree to which business continuity solutions remain appropriate
■ The progress of testing, exercising, and training
■ Independent audit of BCPs

Figure 5.11   (iii) Phases of business continuity strategy formulation.

Updating of plans: Change is a constant factor in a dynamic business environment where need to updates to plans arises on account of:

- Names of key individuals
- Contact details
- Photographs, maps, and charts
- Third-party response documentation
- Site access information
- Insurance claim procedures
- Communication procedures
- Links into the organization's change management process

Introduction of BCM Applications to Review and Update BCM Plans

It is possible to drive the business continuity program using a custom made or off-the-shelf application. This application can help to ensure the selection of cost-effective recovery options.

BCM applications can provide for the following features:

- Time-tested methodology based on prevalent standards that are used to develop meaningful and cost-effective BCM strategy.
- Deliverables defined to comply with BCM standards.
- Documenting project management including project timetables and dates of deliverables and a status map showing level of completion for project implementation.
- Helps map off-site capability with BCM requirements; this ensures optimum utilization of resources.
- Creates a BCM framework for BCM to standardize future initiatives to be undertaken in a cost-effective manner.
- Helps pick up the most appropriate option for off-site recovery of critical functions during crisis.

It is a more systematic way of managing the BCM program. An effective BCM program should equip an organization to ensure services that are critical to our objectives to continue despite the occurrence of a potentially disruptive event. Effective BCM programs require "before and after" comparisons at each phase.

Organization has to keep their business focus and implement the following steps:

- *Strategize and plan*: Draft a charter to gain agreement on the vision for the initiative, in alignment with business goals. Scope the initiative, and establish resources and budget. Integrate with strategic IT and business plans.

- *Drive change management*: Set up a system to communicate and socialize ideas via multiple channels. Get buy-in from stakeholders at all levels. Assess progress, and drive stakeholder commitment to the change.
- *Execute*: Optimally align BCM initiative with business goals. Regularly update and drive new initiatives to the program in response to changing business requirements.
- *Measure and improve*: Measure success of the program by studying impact on business outcomes. Seek feedback from stakeholders. Drive improvements through process changes and upgrades.

To supplement the BCM efforts, a practitioner can also suggest certain additional measures such as

1. Creating a BCM awareness week.
2. Launching a BCM suggestion box where there would be a small gift for the accepted suggestion.
3. Lunch time speakers to spread concept knowledge.
4. A wellness program.
5. Specific employee assistance program.
6. Creating an awareness among managers and supervisors to identify early signs of disorder related to employees such as
   - Illness/frequent pain.
   - Abnormal behavior.
   - Withdrawal symptoms.
   - Low morale.
7. As a preventive measure, the company HR policy should provide for
   - Compulsory annual leave.
   - Rotation of duties.
   - BCM compliance and participation to form part of the KRA to be considered during the periodic appraisals.

Business Continuity Follows the PDCA Cycle (Plan-Do-Check-Act)

Continuous changes occur in technology, business, legal environment, regulatory landscape, and business needs to cope with increased competition. Hence BCM program needs to be maintained. The following are ways to ensure proper updates and maintenance (Figure 5.12):

- Releasing a written mission statement.
- Communicating BCM plan to employees, visitors, contractors, and making the plan accessible to employees for their review.
- Training the team and employees on their roles and responsibilities in the event of an incident.
- Posting emergency contact numbers and your evacuation instructions.
- Conducting drills and establishing a periodic plan reassessment for improvement.

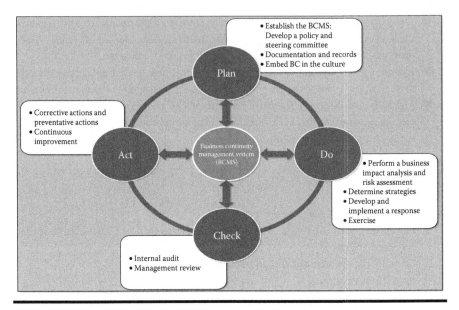

Figure 5.12 PDCA cycle.

Details of the review periods and frequency of testing and training may be included in a separate "Maintenance and Review document." This document specifies how and when the BCP will be reviewed and tested and the process for maintaining the plan. The intervals between tests and reviews will depend on the organization, its complexity, and rate of change. A training schedule may also be included.

The organization should provide for the independent audit of its BCM competence and capability to identify actual and potential shortcomings. Independent audits can be conducted by competent external or internal persons.

Once BCM has been embedded into the organization as an ongoing management process, it enters an iterative cycle being reviewed at regular intervals and updated when necessary.

Business Continuity Management Plans

Business continuity management—"Holistic management process that identifies potential impacts that threaten an organization and provides a framework for building resilience with the capability for an effective response that safeguards the interests of its key stakeholders, reputation, brand, and value-creating activities."

Business Imperatives

1. Growth/strategy
2. Efficiency
3. Compliance (Figure 5.13)

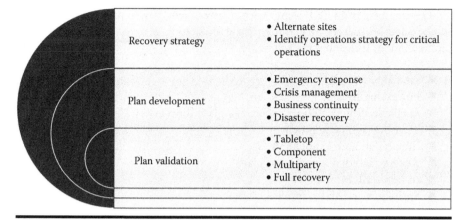

Figure 5.13   Stages in business continuity management.

We have discussed the recovery strategy formulation with choice of alternate sites, strategy for key BCM personnel, and the strategy for critical operations. The next step is plan development.

Plan Development

Emergency Response Plan (ERP)

An ERP is a detailed written document that lays down the nature and type of emergencies that are likely/probable and defines who will do what during a particular situation. Emergency incidents can create hazards for people in affected areas. Preparing before emergency is vital in order to ensure that employers and employees have the necessary equipment and resources, know what to do and where to go, and the ERTs know what tasks to execute during crisis (Figure 5.14).

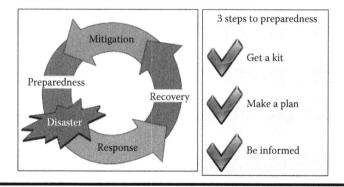

Figure 5.14   Plan development steps.

Development of an ERP begins with an assessment of what measures are already in place and procedures by making review of documents to see what has been put into operation. It includes the following:

- First aid kits
- Fire extinguishers
- Available shelters/ability to shelter in place if necessary
- Transportation equipment
- Evacuation routes if defined
- Review facility diagrams and plans
- In-house ERTs
- Sprinklers and alarm systems
- Security systems, surveillance systems, and security personnel

Note: It will be good to know the laws and compliance applicable to the facility just in case it has to be considered in our planning.

Coordination with external agencies:

- Fire department
- Police department
- Local authorities (civil)
- Hospitals

All activities that must be carried out during a crisis incident fall in the category of "emergency operations." It is important that these activities are properly designed and documented to ensure speedy and efficient execution during crisis. They can be grouped as per function and assigned to different response teams.

Objectives of the plan are

1. Reducing impact during emergency.
2. Meeting legal and social responsibilities.
3. Preventing fatalities and serious injury to workers.
4. Reducing damage to property and assets.
5. Accelerating resumption procedures.

A "management by committee" approach can be adopted. The BCMSC can also take over responsibility for planning and preparedness activities. They can form an ERT to work under their guidance and supervision. A chain of command should be set to make the authority responsibility clear and the path of communication and escalation simpler to understand and follow. There is no ambiguity in command, and this ensures that everyone knows the plan of action.

An ERT is an assembly of primary and alternate members at each major location responsible for the response to a crisis. All members are personnel who are familiar with their department's responsibilities. Alternate members execute their responsibilities in the absence or unavailability of the primary member. All primary and alternate members need to be knowledgeable of overall BCM operations. Members must also be available during a crisis. ERT members and/or ERT alternate members are required to attend plan exercises organized by the BCM coordinator.

First lines of defense in emergencies: ERT members are trained for potential crises and are physically capable of carrying out their duties. Team members need to know about vulnerabilities and toxic hazards in workplace, and should be able to identify when to evacuate personnel or when to rely on outside help.

Specialized training (one or more members of ERT) in the following capabilities:

1. The use of different types of fire extinguishers
2. First aid, including lifts and bandaging
3. Procedures for orderly shutdown and evacuation
4. If the organization has hazardous materials on site, to deal with them so that they do not accelerate the impact of the disaster (e.g., chemical spill control procedures)

The damage assessment team assesses and documents damages caused by a crisis. The recovery team is designated to provide for stabilization and resumption of operations caused by a crisis. Other teams to perform specific functions may be designated by individual departments as necessary.

Team members should be drawn from a range of geographical locations to reduce the probability of severe impact to multiple members from a community-wide crisis. Team members should be capable of handling physically and emotionally stressful situations. Renters and single employees will likely have fewer personal responsibilities after a community-wide crisis. Vacations should be coordinated so that a large number of ERT members are not out of the area at any given time.

Incident commander: Is the person in charge of the ERT. The incident commander is the individual responsible for the command and control of all aspects of a crisis. The incident commander must have the authority and ability to make quick decisions in critical situations. As the person who is in charge of the response efforts, the incident commander should be an officer of the organization. For a significant, organization-wide crisis event, it is not uncommon to find the COO, and not the CEO, at the top of the chain of command for emergency response purposes.

The chain of command is the order of authority within the organization. During a crisis, the chain of command is not necessarily the same organizational command order used during times of normal operations. The actual incident commander will be the available individual who is highest on the chain of command. The ERT is headed by the incident commander and comprised of management personnel representing areas of the organization that have critical plan execution responsibilities. Overall incident command is relinquished to responding civil authorities at their request. Other teams are involved in the BCM organization (Figure 5.15).

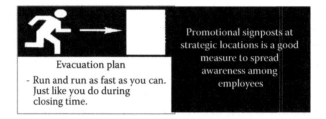

Evacuation plan
- Run and run as fast as you can. Just like you do during closing time.

Promotional signposts at strategic locations is a good measure to spread awareness among employees

Figure 5.15   Evacuation signposts.

It is necessary to determine the conditions under which an evacuation would be necessary. The primary and secondary evacuation routes have to be designated in advance. They have to be clearly marked and well lit. Post signs or arrows pointing to the emergency exit routes.

It is advisable to install emergency lighting in case a power outage occurs during an evacuation. Ensure that evacuation routes and emergency exits are: ~ Wide enough to accommodate the number of evacuating people ~ Clear and unobstructed at all times ~ Unlikely to expose evacuating people to additional hazards. Ideally an evacuation team per floor, which consists of fire wardens who will help others to evacuate during emergency and be accountable for the attendance taken at the assembly point, is an absolute necessity. Preset evacuation procedures well documented and distributed to employees and regular drills would facilitate evacuation without panic.

Note: A separate list of pregnant women and employees with physical handicapped must be prepared in advance and available with the evacuation team, so that their evacuation is escorted by the fire wardens till they reach the assembly point in safety.

Emergency drills to be undertaken at least once a year. Also documentation of the drill experience as to what went wrong should be done so that the evacuation plan can be improvised.

Accounting for evacuees: BCM teams to possess the call list of employees with contact numbers of home, next of kin so that they can be summoned immediately when needed. At designated assembly points, a head count of all employees present on site and all visitors as per visitor's log should be taken. In case of partial evacuation, procedures for further evacuation in case the disaster spreading to other areas has to be drafted and chain of command are defined.

First aid kit: After a disaster or emergency situation, emergency services (fire, police, and medical) may be disrupted or unavailable for some time. It may be necessary to provide immediate care for an injured person if medical professionals cannot be reached. It is important to have a complete first aid kit and first aid training. The plan must specify what steps will be taken to ensure that all injured staff receive immediate first aid and follow-up medical care including any physical rehabilitation that might be necessary as the result of injuries.

Note: A practical demonstration of different types of lifts of injured personnel and techniques of bandaging can be given after an evacuation drill. It has been observed that some employees turn out to be well trained in first aid and nursing and come ahead as volunteers. Evacuated employees should be sent home, and employees involved in the recovery procedures can be sent to off-site location. If there is need, a shelter place defined by the plan has to be used to house the evacuees. Develop a list of necessary emergency supplies such as water, food, and medical supplies at the shelter.

Plan needs to be circulated; employees must understand the components of ERP:

1. Who will be in charge during an emergency? Identification of personnel and defining their roles and responsibilities are important.
2. What should employee training include? Potential threats, hazards, and protective actions?
3. Search and rescue efforts should only be conducted by properly trained and equipped professionals. Death or serious injury can occur if untrained employees reenter a damaged or contaminated facility.

Sample Emergency Response Plan

Company name: **Location:**

Date completed: **Signed:**

Name of emergency operations coordinator (EOC)

Name of Person	Department	Contact (Office)	Contact (Home)	e-mail
Primary EOC				
Secondary EOC				

Note: The emergency operations coordinator (EOC) is the person who serves as the main contact person for the company in an emergency. The EOC is responsible for making decisions and following the steps described in this ERP. In the event of an emergency occurring within or affecting the worksite, the primary contact will serve as the EOC. If the primary contact is unable to fulfil the EOC duties, the secondary contact will take on this role. Primary contact.

Emergency Contact Numbers

- Fire station
- Ambulance
- Police
- Hospital
- Others

Potential Emergencies

1.
2.
3.
4.
5.

Location of Emergency Equipment

Fire alarm
Fire extinguisher
Fire hose
Panic alarm button
Personal protective equipment (PPE)
Emergency communication equipment
Others

Employees Trained in the Use of Emergency Equipment

Provide a list of employees trained in emergency equipment use along with their location.

Early Warning Signals

- Devices such as smoke detectors and heat detectors
- Clinical thermometers inside data centers to monitor temperature
- Warning messages from weather service or local authorities
- Switchboard operators or word of mouth reports

This will help in timely evacuation and notification of authorities such as fire/police department.

Training Requirements for Emergency Response

Type of Training	Frequency
Induction awareness training	When new employee joins
General BCM training	Annual
Train the trainer training to BCM teams	Quarterly
Training before BCM testing	Six monthly

Notification Lists

■ Call list for customers
■ Call list for vendors

First Aid

Type of first aid kit:	**Location of first aid kit:**
Other supplies:	**Transportation for ill or injured employees:**
Name of first aid attendant:	**Location:**

(First aid attendant is the employee trained in first aid. If the work is in shifts, then the shift of work to be mentioned and for each shift, the first aid attendant must be identified.)

Emergency Communication

Communication will be in accordance to the crisis management plan. Chain of command has to be strictly adhered to.

Evacuation Plans

Refer to evacuation plans for your location.
Please find building and site maps posted in the procedures.
Please observe all emergency exits have been specifically marked.
Evacuation drills shall be conducted two times a year at all locations.

Shelters in Place

In case employees have to move to shelter for some time, the essential supplies that will be provided will be

1. Tea/coffee.
2. Drinking water.
3. Food.
4. Other items that will be given in a personalized kit form.

Note: Such provision needs to be made at all locations.

Employees' Emergency Contact List

Role	Name	Current Position/Function	E-mail	Phone	Emergency
Business continuity plan coordinator			Bus: Home:	Bus: Home: Cell:	
Backup coordinator			Bus: Home:	Bus: Home: Cell:	
Planning team members			Bus: Home:	Bus: Home: Cell:	
Backup team members			Bus: Home:	Bus: Home: Cell:	
Local site managers			Bus: Home:	Bus: Home: Cell:	
			Bus: Home:	Bus: Home: Cell:	

Plan Review

The plan will be reviewed by the BCMSC every 12 months.

Date last reviewed: Sign:

Next review date: Sign:

Crisis Management Plan

Crisis may be defined as an emergency or out-of-ordinary situation caused due to human error or inappropriate employee behavior, which may last for a brief period, or can be extended over a long period, or can apply to a single entity, or can spread over many entities (Figure 5.16).

1. Emergency/out-of-the-ordinary situation
2. Human error/inappropriate behavior
3. Brief or extended
4. Can involve other organizations
5. Good thing (award/achievement)

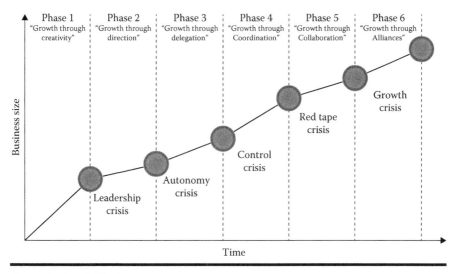

Figure 5.16   Crisis type.

Crisis management has usually been defined as the role that senior management has during a business continuity incident. It includes the following:

■ Identifying a crisis situation
■ Deciding how and when to respond
■ Communicating both internally and externally
■ Leading and directing the recovery process

An effective crisis management plan should

1. Identify members of the CMT.
2. Document what criteria will be used to determine a crisis.
3. Establish monitoring systems and practices to detect early warning signals of any potential crisis.
4. Specify who will be the spokesperson in the event of a crisis.
5. Provide a list of key emergency contacts.
6. Document who will need to be notified in the event of a crisis.
7. Identify a process for assessing the incident and its potential severity, and assessing the impact on the building and employees.
8. Identify procedures for responding to the crisis and emergency assembly points where employees can go.
9. Provide a process for testing the effectiveness of the crisis management plan and updating it on a regular basis (Figure 5.17).

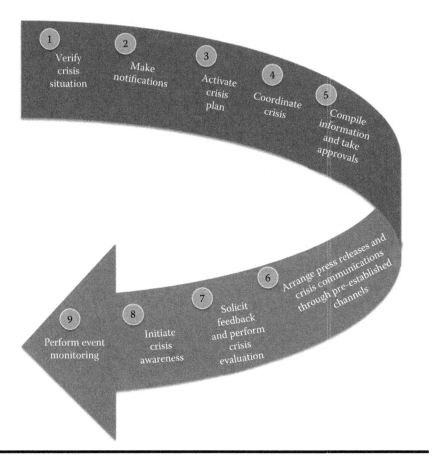

Figure 5.17   Crisis plan.

Developing Crisis Plan

- Start with a needs assessment
- Human resources
- Technological support
- Training
- Space
- Supplies
- Travel
- Funding mechanisms
- Planning needs

Signed Endorsement from Director

- Is a must—signed and dated
- Provides accountability
- Integrates plan into overall EOC plans

Command and Control

- Directs release of public information
- Coordinates with partners
- Advises the director
- Knows incident-specific policy, science, and situation
- Works with experts to create situation-specific materials
- Tests messages and materials for cultural appropriateness

Prevention of Crisis

- Ensure policies and plans in respect of communication during crisis are written, publicized, and practiced
- Ensure that the policies are consistent across all locations
- Consider the interest of all stakeholders while formulating crisis-related policies and procedures

Big crises are those that lead to big effects, and they may be expected or unexpected. The cause can be of natural origin (e.g., weather, earthquake) or man-made, resulting from a political occurrence, judgmental error, fraud, and intentional or accidental malfeasance. Whatever the root causes, the effects of the crisis must be managed. The primary focus of crisis management planning should be preparedness of a methodology to respond to events. Once a crisis has occurred, the enterprise is in reactive mode, and a poor response can have devastating effects on the organization.

Crisis management is usually carried out by a CMT. The BCM standard BS25999 has redefined these terms somewhat introducing an "Incident Management Plan" (IMP), which covers the acute stage of an "incident." In theory, an incident could potentially be contained and thus never become a crisis so that an IMP has a slightly wider scope than traditional CMT plans.

The size of the organization and the location of its functional/operational offices determine the role and composition of the CMT. For smaller organizations, a business continuity event is a business survival issue, and the recovery is managed directly from the top, everyone is involved in response and recovery activities, and the chain of command is held at the top.

Factors that Affect the CMT Structure

- Management styles, whether it is autocratic, democratic, or proactive.
- The range of strategies open to the organization during a recovery. i.e., how much decision-making needs to be made.

Very hierarchical organizations are usually used to all key decisions being made by those at the top and then cascaded down. Flatter management style organizations are used to more participation in key decisions and more localized decision-making.

Some organizations document detailed steps for their CMT's to follow through a crisis, others only draw up vague guidelines to go with the overall policy and strategy and rely on the experience of their senior people to do the right thing at the right time. BS25999 standard suggests the following should be included in crisis management plans at least at some level of detail:

- Roles and responsibilities
- Plan invocation
- Task and action lists
- Emergency contacts
- People activities (site evacuation and muster site mobilization, accounting for staff, safety issues, and staff communications)
- Media response
- Stakeholder management
- Incident management location
- Any other useful information

The crisis will be something pertinent to the organization and be the type of crisis that can be escalated gradually, giving the CMT members time to think through the timing of invoking plans and the risk/cost calculations they would face in a real crisis. The interactions between the members are critical to its success; if the team splits into two or more factions that are working against each other, then the team composition needs to be changed. For this reason, facilitation of crisis plan exercises preferably coordinated or witnessed by external third-party specialists is advisable.

BCM Program Execution During a Crisis

- Crisis/IMPs
- Crisis communications plans
- A damage assessment
- Life and safety checks
- Business response, resumption, recovery, and restoration plan execution
- Technical response, resumption, recovery, and restoration plan execution

The same wide variety applies to the CMT plan. Some organizations document detailed steps for their CMTs to follow through a crisis, others only draw up vague guidelines to go with the overall policy and strategy and rely on the experience of their senior people to do the right thing at the right time. BS25999 standard suggests the following should be included in all plans at least at some level of detail:

- Roles and responsibilities
- Plan invocation
- Task and action lists
- Emergency contacts
- People activities (site evacuation and muster site mobilization, accounting for staff, safety issues, and staff communications)
- Media response
- Stakeholder management

Information systems audit and control association (ISACA) in its audit assurance program for crisis management prescribes that, "The crisis management program should utilize a risk-based approach to establish scenarios that require a crisis management plan, and the program is linked to enterprise risk and continuity plans." It further prescribes creation of crisis scenarios to establish crisis response and management. It recommends preparation of a list of probable scenarios based on a risk-based approach and recommends the inclusion of high-impact crisis scenarios even though their probability may be low (Figure 5.18).

Develop and document the action plans to facilitate communication of critical continuity information. Coordinate and exercise with stakeholders and the media

Figure 5.18   Crisis communication plan.

to ensure clarity during crisis communications. In order to formalize the crisis communication plan, the following activities need to be performed:

1. Establish a crisis communications program.
2. Develop processes and procedures to establish crisis communication channels.
3. Establish proactive crisis communication plan that can be adaptable to changes.
4. Exercise crisis communications for the program.
5. Implement crisis communication plan at time of disaster event.
6. Define crisis communications method and schedule—Identify notification process and or tools.
7. Identify groups to receive communications and develop communication processes and procedures for each identified group:
    a. Internal groups (examples include corporate, lines of business, and stakeholders)
    b. External groups (examples include media, customers, vendors, suppliers, public, local, state, and government agencies)
    c. Media (examples include print, radio, television, and internet)
    d. Stakeholders
8. Ensure communications align with organizational requirement.
9. Agree upon frequency of communications (pre, post, and interim).
10. Media—Identify designated communications spokesperson (corporate communications, public relations, etc.). Generally, the CEO is assigned the task of addressing the media and stakeholders.
11. Identify most effective methods for communications (press release, press conference, notification via radio, TV and other, etc). Care should be taken to ensure consistency in messaging throughout the organization. This can only be prescribed since at the time of crisis, one has to make do with limited channels which may be available and hence the plan has to be flexible.
12. *Assist* in the development of the external agencies exercise requirements as appropriate. It would be promotional to invite external agencies to participate in BCM drills and exercises as appropriate.
13. Maintain knowledge of current laws and regulations to support emergency management.

Designate spokesperson: The following points need to be considered in respect of designated spokesperson during crisis:

1. Their name should be there in the plan annexure.
2. Ensure their back up is also defined.
3. Educate spokesperson in emergency risk principles.
4. Mock exercise in media and public address.
5. Include secure procedures for emergency response.

Notification procedures: Call lists and call trees have been used for notifying personnel/management during crisis. But modern notification is replacing manual call-tree processes. These automated systems can be linked to human resource (HR) databases to update employee information efficiently and in a timely manner, thus reducing the risk of using outdated contact information during a critical time. Messages can be distributed using voice, SMS, or e-mail and received using mobile devices.

Storing BCPs and DRPs off site has been part of best practices for a long time, but now with the proliferation of mobile devices making plans accessible via these devices is also becoming an area of focus for parties involved in the different areas of BCM.

Efficiency can be improved if employees can begin recovery tasks soon after the disaster is declared instead of having to wait until the plans can be retrieved from the off-site location. Proper communication with employees and suppliers also can improve efficiency. Mobile devices allow continuity coordinators to contact key personnel and direct them where to go, what to do, or simply provide status updates to keep uncertainty and panic to a minimum.

Social networks are also increasingly used for fast and effective communication during crisis. Social media can be used to promptly provide customers and employees with crisis-related information. But security considerations must be considered while using social media. Sensitive information should not be notified over social media, and there should be trained people who are qualified to make effective use of many communication channels to get the message through during crisis.

Considerations in developing the crisis message are as follows:

- Develop message.
- Identify audiences.
- What do media want to know?
- Show empathy.

Matters to be documented in advance include the following:

- 24/7 contact information for everyone
- Instructions for posting to your web site
- Instructions for changing voicemail messages
- Prewritten templates for "likely" emergencies

Media Communication

In order to prepare messages, it must be deliberated upon as to what media is going to look for.

- What happened?
- Who is in charge?
- Has the crisis been contained?

- Are victims being helped?
- What can we expect?
- Why did this happen?
- Did you have forewarning?

Media Contact List

It is advisable to have a media list prepared in advance. It is also beneficial to maintain relationship with media since they can be helpful during crisis.

- Critically important contact list.
- Nonduty contacts too.
- It should not be on scraps of paper but in diaries and also on laptops in electronic form.
- E-mails, fax numbers, and backdoor entries must be established.
- Currency of contacts to be tested as any failure in contact list can be costly (Figure 5.19).

Response to Inquiries (you are authorized to give out the following information)

Date: _____ Time: _____ Approved by:

_____

This is an evolving emergency and I know that, just like we do, you want as much information as possible right now. While we work to get your questions answered as quickly as possible, I want to tell you what we can confirm right now:

At approximately, _____ (time), a (brief description of what happened)

_____

_____

_____ _____.

At this point, we do not know the number of (persons ill, persons exposed, injuries, deaths, etc.).

We have a system (plan, procedure, operation) in place for just such an emergency and we are being assisted by (police, FBI, EOC) as part of that plan.

The situation is (under)(not yet under) control, and we are working with (Local, State, Federal) authorities to (e.g., contain this situation, determine how this happened, determine what actions may be needed by individuals and the community to prevent this from happening again).

We will continue to gather information and release it to you as soon as possible. I will be back to you within (amount of time, 2 hours or less) to give you an update. As soon as we have more confirmed information, it will be provided. We ask for your patience as we respond to this emergency.

Figure 5.19 Proforma of initial press statement.

Next media step

- When interviewing, be prepared to make one or two points specific and stick to them.
- Establish relationships BEFORE a crisis.
- Deal with truth, get the true status out.
- Include a statement of empathy and commit to "seeing it through."

Public expectations and concerns—It will be interesting to note what public is interested to know:

- Are my family and I safe?
- What have you found that may affect me?
- What can I do to protect myself and my family?
- Who caused this?
- Can you fix it?

Since the public image is very important for your organization, it needs tact to tackle public queries. In case the going is bad and you do not want to comment at that moment, you can try some alternatives that may sound better than no comment, then you may try one of the following:

- "We have just learned about this and are trying to get more information."
- I am sorry, I am not the authority on this, let me have Mr. X call you right back.
- "We are preparing a statement on that now. Can I fax it to you in about two hours?"

To maintain credibility, it will be a good idea to

- Summarize your points.
- Provide supporting documents in simple form.
- Offer to answer questions during writing process.
- Be available!!
- Read/watch/listen to the story.

Crisis Communication Plan (Suggestive)

1. Name of location
2. Person in charge
3. Purpose of plan
4. Objectives of crisis communication
5. Scope and exclusions
6. Crisis communication policy statement

7. Develop guidelines:
   a. Communication with ERTs
   b. Escalation procedures
   c. Communication standards and protocols
8. Document existing processes in place:
   a. Crisis communication team
   b. Crisis communication methods and schedules including schedule for crisis plan exercise
   c. Location of the designated meeting place
   d. Name of person who will gather and compile information for communication
   e. The communication that needs to be in writing
   f. The information flow for communicating
   g. Team who will declare a disaster
   h. Persons who will handle incoming calls, e-mails, and so on
   i. Finance person to meet crisis expenses
   j. Customers/external agencies to be notified during crisis
   k. Notification procedures
9. Establish triggering procedure for activating crisis communication plan:
   - Assess the impact on communication operations and staffing.
   - Determine the role of organizational departments in the crisis communication process.
   - Activate media and internet monitoring as soon as plan is activated.
   - Quickly identify the affected people and their initial communication requirements.
10. Activities to support the first 48 hours:
    - Name of person who shall make the first assessment
    - Format for documenting facts
    - Person who will arrange the requisite resources
    - Media team to handle media and public response
    - Exercising initial activities to ensure they go smoothly
    - System by which key partners will be alerted of the crisis
11. Documenting crisis communication plan exercise results:
    Crisis communication plan to be tested as per policy (ideally once in six months) (Figure 5.20)
    Open issues
    Lessons learned
    Updates recommended based on findings
    Proposed date of completion
    Plan last reviewed
    Plan last updated
    Date of next review

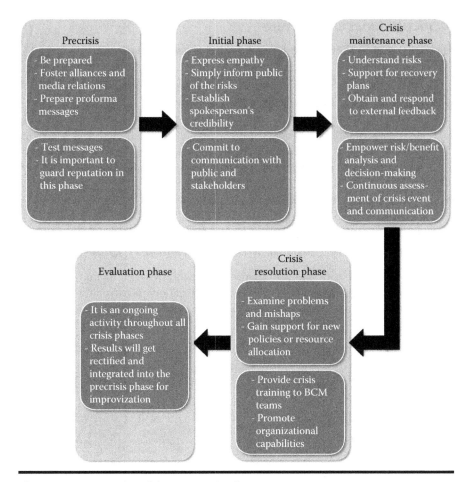

Figure 5.20   Steps in crisis communication.

Failure to implement a crisis management plan may result in:

Financial loss	Inability to repair or resolve a crisis
Loss of life	Inefficient use of resources
Loss of property	Bankruptcy
Loss of critical information	Loss of reputation/customer confidence
Unreasonable response teams	Legal/regulatory noncompliance and liability

Incident Management Plans

The contents of an IMP include the following:

- Emergency contact details, details of the incident management location.
- Activities, including people, process, and technology.
- Communications, including internal, media, emergency responders, voluntary services, and stakeholders.
- Annexes, including photographs, maps, and charts; third-party response documentation; site access information; and insurance claim procedures.

Note: Please refer to Annexure Section for some specific IMPs.

Business Recovery Plans or Business Continuity Plans

A recovery plan for business is associated on its capability to conduct uninterrupted business processes even during a disaster. Organizations plan for their business continuity and make strategic and tactical plans to survive during a crisis or disaster (Figure 5.21).

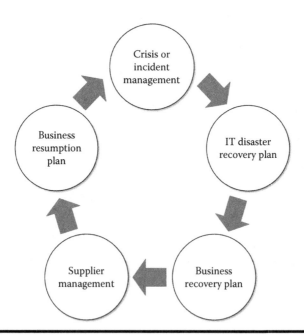

Figure 5.21   Components of a business recovery plan.

Components of a business recovery plan are

- Recovery strategies.
- Team organizational structure and responsibilities.
- Preparedness measures.
- Notification procedures and checklists for internal and external parties.
- Incident response steps and how team members are mobilized to respond.
- Key systems and tools.
- Vital records recovery.
- Recovery steps of each specific business function.
- Interdependence with other systems.
- Plan resource guides (crash books) that contain
  - Recovery task checklists.
  - Phone contact lists for employees.
  - Contractors and vendors.
  - Reporting forms.
  - Location emergency procedures.
- Emergency procedures describe the actions to be taken following an incident that jeopardizes.
- *Business operations and/or human life*: This should include procedures for handling public relations and liaison with appropriate public authorities, for example, police, fire, and local government.
- Emergency procedures include the step-by-step instructions on how to react when a specific emergency occurs. The types of emergencies can depend on the organization's geographical location and business model. The emergencies identified in the business impact analysis as the most likely to occur should have procedures developed and documented. Examples of emergency procedures include how to respond to a bomb threat or fire and an institution's response to a pandemic outbreak. An incident response plan per identified incident can be prepared along with incident response procedures.
- A business recovery strategy to include records retention dates and supply chain recovery strategy.
- Business operations risk mitigation controls.
- Work area recovery arrangements for business personnel.

Business Resumption Plans

The business resumption plan deals with how, where, when, and who will be responsible, and what they will do when a significant event occurs. This event can range from any type of incident from technology failure, natural disaster,

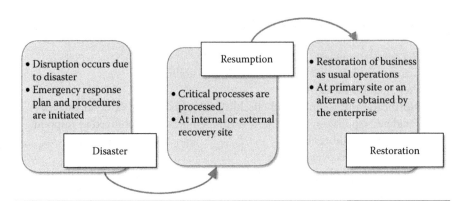

Figure 5.22   Different parts of disaster recovery.

human errors, malicious code, fraudulent activity, or any other event that disrupts business.

If such disruption occurs, there will be a need to reconstruct critical infrastructure to facilitate business to resume their critical operations from the primary site or if primary site is unavailable, from alternate site in the time scale defined by its RTOs.

This point is the intersection of the BCP with the disaster recovery plan. A well-planned implemented and tested plan is effective in getting the business resumption process within defined timelines possible (Figure 5.22).

Components of BRP

- Task and action lists
- Ownership and management of the business resumption process
- High-level options for longer term replacement of key staff, premises, systems, services, equipment, and machinery
- Salvage and recovery of assets from premises affected by an incident
- Insurance claims for assets lost or destroyed by an incident
- Communications, including internal and stakeholders
- The subsequent impact of an incident on cash flow, staff, customers, and insurance premium

Business resumption plans identify preset arrangements that serve as a standby for getting vital functions operating again with minimum delay. The BRP provides for the provision of necessary resources including people, information equipment finance, services, and accommodations. It helps organizations to survive an unplanned interruption by ensuring speedy resumption.

Example Business Resumption Plan

Plan prepared by:

Location:
Reviewed by:
Date of next review:

1. *Composition of the business resumption planning committee*:
   Project leader:
   Committee selection:
   Authority-responsibility chart:
   Roles and responsibilities matrix:
   Periodicity of committee meetings (as per policy):
   Periodic management overview of project:
2. *Perform a business resumption capability assessment*:
   a. Mapping of business divisions with their RTOs and RPOs
   b. Fill up the security checklist
   c. Document the resource requirement analysis per division
   d. Refer to risk analysis and BIA reports
   e. Establish mitigation controls
3. *Make a list of essential components for recovery*:
   a. Hardware
   b. Software system and application software
   c. Communications
   d. Physical facilities available for recovery
   e. People
   f. Data backups
   g. Vendor support during crisis
   h. Essential forms, supplies, and vital records
   i. Office equipment necessary at resumption site
   j. Funding during crisis
   k. Arrangement for logistics to reach the resumption site
   l. Security for information systems
4. *Design the business resumption plan for recovery operations*:
   a. Team organization and call list
   b. Damage assessment team and roles
   c. User liaison team
   d. Crisis communication team
   e. Operations team
   f. Security backup team
   g. Procurement responsibilities and facilities support for administrative matters

    h. IT team

    i. Risk manager for risk assessment and approval

5. *Conduct BRP implementation training*:

    Arrange a team-training session for the team members in emergency procedures, use of emergency equipment such as fire extinguishers and the method of data retrieval.

6. *Test the BRP*: The BRP must be tested at least annually. The test script or scenario needs to be developed, and responsibility for the same needs to be affixed. Results must be evaluated, and a report must be submitted to the BCM management.

7. *Follow-up* on the lessons learned and remediation measures decided upon by the management has to be done so that timescales are religiously adhered to. After making changes to plan where necessary, the plan must show updated version with date, sanctioning authority, and new version number for the plan.

As is evident, the nomenclature of the BCM plans may vary, but the process to be enacted commences from declaration of disaster or even before. As soon as an incident occurs, notification of BCM management, initial assessment of situation, firefighting for containing disaster and ultimately declaring a disaster. The DR plan gets activated, and critical functions have to be commenced from alternate site. As we read on the plans, we may notice some overlaps which may be possible because the same task may have to be performed in the next phase/s but with a different purpose. An effective integration of ITDR and BCM plans for achieving the business continuity objectives and resuming operations within the timescales that have been defined is crucial for the success of the BCMS.

Postincident review: A postincident review is necessary to understand how the recovery process had been handled. It is an opportunity to look into the incident handling successes and delineate areas of improvement. The review should take place within a reasonable period of time (to be stipulated) after the event. As soon as incident is resolved, feedback from participants have to be sought, and notes have to be integrated to bring out the issues emerging from the incident, the mistakes or lessons learned, and the part of the response that could be carried out flawlessly as per plan.

Information to arrive at results can be sought from the command center's operation log and initial recovery-tracking log. Review results must be circulated to all participants requesting them to check their area and put in some additional point that may have been missed out. Finally consolidation of findings to be done and depending on the time slots agreed upon, a tracker log can be prepared jotting down the designated time and person responsible for resolving the identified issue. An owner and analysis of issues and a tracking log as to the time of resolution of issue and assigning responsibilities to dissolve the log should be assigned.

(Please note this is not an exhaustive plan.)

Annexures

Annexure A: BCM Task List

1. *Threat avoidance*: This can be achieved by any of the following ways:
   a. Removal of source from where threat originates
   b. Remediating the situations that may lead to materialization of threat
2. *Preventive controls*: This can check the potential threat before it materializes. Preventive controls can be enforced through the establishment of proper infrastructure to protect data and systems and also arranging to set up a robust and flexible response organization for BCM workers. It includes the following:
   a. Setting up of stable communication infrastructure and communication arrangements and processes between personnel.
   b. Providing fall-back scenarios.
   c. Building redundancy for critical components.
3. *Identify threats/risk-inventory*: This needs to be done during planning process by:
   a. Preparing scenarios to get an insight into threats and vulnerabilities.
   b. Identification of vital services and key resources required.
   c. Consider interdependencies in determination of resources.
   Lower the impact from threats: This can be achieved by drawing up, implementing, exercising, and overseeing response plan and communication plan to list down all activities to be carried out before, during, and after the threat event.
   The following factors will be included in this initiative:
   a. Training of BCM personnel
   b. Regularly exercising plans
   c. Testing facilities, systems, and available organizational capabilities
   d. Maintaining stocks of vital goods and emergency supplies
   e. Optimizing distribution of scarce organizational resources, which are required for recovery of business operations
   f. Setting up channels for effective risk communication
4. *Incident-handling procedures*: This can be ensured by

    a. Logistics support for emergencies.

    b. Incident response procedures that include the following:

        i. Existence of BCM policies and detailed procedures.

        ii. Medical assistance, mental health care, preventive health measures, and so on.

        iii. Firefighting devices, measuring decontamination, handling of hazardous substances, and so on.

        iv. BCM personnel's coordination among themselves.

        v. Rapport with local authorities.

5. *Early warning systems*: Gather information and forecasts of water levels, disruptions to IT, spread of viruses, and set the procedure on the following:

    a. Person responsible for giving warning/information.

    b. Person who will evaluate the information and take decisions.

    c. Benchmark on how other organizations plan to combat the threat.

    d. *Set proper escalation levels*: Escalate to the level of control appropriate for the crisis.

    e. List down consequences of incidents, decisions to be taken, and constraints justifying the decisions.

    f. Note down postcrisis actions to be taken.

6. *Establishing the desired security level*:

    a. Secure the procurement of essential supplies

    b. Security against some specific risks

7. *Incident-handling procedures*:

    a. Ensure safety of crisis team

    b. Logistics for incident handling

    c. Containment procedures to limit disaster

    d. Ensure supply of essential supplies

    e. Optimum allocation of scarce resources

8. *Activate employees' understanding of roles in crisis handling and control*:

    a. Defining BCM teams and documenting roles and responsibilities.

    b. Testing plans and monitoring whether BCM personnel are effectively carrying out responsibilities as per assigned roles.

    c. Ensuring continuous improvisation, knowledge sharing, and effective communication in order to support BCM initiatives.

9. *Crisis communication* to inform employees and direct them during the crisis:

    a. Coordination of crisis messages through predefined channels of communication.

    b. Use of predefined escalation procedures prior to declaration of disaster.

    c. Use of unambiguous and clear messages for crisis communication.

    d. Ensuring that possible actions to be taken are communicated to the team along with proformas for crisis communication.

10. *Planning for resumption/restoration*: It involves returning to "business as usual." This can be done once

    a. Facilities are restored and employees return to primary facility.

    b. Insurance claims are redeemed.

    c. Salvage has been disposed and repairs completed where required.

11. *Evaluation*: A postmortem analysis of actions taken, lessons learned, mitigation recommended, and monitoring of implementation of mitigation measures, which can include

    a. Preventive measures.

    b. Preparation and exercises.

    c. Response after an event.

    d. Postincident measures taken.

Annexure B: Emergency Preparedness Plan and Team

Step 1: Establish an emergency preparedness team: Clear and specific assignment of responsibilities to the emergency preparedness team members is necessary for ensuring a good understanding of business objectives and recovery objectives. The team will work and research on the risks applicable to the enterprise and search for cost-effective means for mitigating these risks. The team leader for this team should be capable of evaluating the situation and taking proper decisions.

Key roles and responsibilities for the team: (planning and implementation)

1. Develop the BCP.
2. Establish emergency alerts and monitor the same.
3. Develop cross-training plan and prepare training schedules.
4. Identify key vendors/suppliers/trading partners and determine that they have BCM arrangements in place.
5. Assess potential financial impact on business of any potential emergency that may strike on the organization.
6. Ensure that essential supplies (emergency safety equipment, such as personal protective equipment, or in the event of a pandemic, hygiene supplies like hand sanitizers, cleaning products, masks, protective barriers, etc.) are adequately stocked.
7. Make trial run of the business continuity plan and ensure that local site manager(s) will be able to implement the BCP.
8. **Call List for BCM Team Members**

Role	Name	Current Position/ Function	E-mail	Phone	Emergency
Business continuity plan coordinator			Bus: Home:	Bus: Home: Cell:	
Backup coordinator			Bus: Home:	Bus: Home: Cell:	
Planning team members			Bus: Home:	Bus: Home: Cell:	
Backup team members			Bus: Home:	Bus: Home: Cell:	
Local site managers			Bus: Home:	Bus: Home: Cell:	
			Bus: Home:	Bus: Home: Cell:	

Policies, procedures, and organization
1. Establish policies such as compensation and absences, return to work procedures, telecommuting, flexible work hours, and travel restrictions.
2. Define chain of command and levels of escalation for business continuity implementation. Establish authorities' who will trigger the BCP and invoke the plan.
3. Establish safety procedures for workplace. For instance, in case of spread of Swine Flu, preventive medical measures and personnel policies during the continuation of the outflow of the disease and fall backs on account of excessive absenteeism.

Communications
1. Maintain good communications and manage relations with all staff levels.
2. Advise senior management.
3. Instill importance of the BCP throughout the organization.
4. Liaison with local government agencies.

5. Prepare and disseminate timely and accurate information to all employees.
6. Educate staff about possible emergencies. For example, in the advent of a pandemic, give information on signs and symptoms of influenza, modes of transmission, personal and family protection, and response strategies.
7. Evaluate using various forms of technology to maintain communications.
8. Help prepare training on the subject.
9. Local site managers should implement the plan.
10. Set up systems to monitor employees for an emergency.

Step 2: Identify essential services/functions:

During an emergency, business may experience a disruption in operations due to:

– High staff absenteeism
– Unavailability of supplies and materials
– Interruptions to services like power, transportation, and communications

Consequences of unavailability of essential services

– A service when not delivered creates an impact on the health and safety of individuals.
– A service that may lead to the failure of a business unit if activities are not performed in a specified time period. (Prepare call list of vendors and contractors.)

Call List for Vendors and Contractors

S. No.	Company	Contact Name	Emergency Telephone	Business Telephone
1				
2				
3				
4				
5				

– In some organizations, services that must be performed to satisfy regulatory requirements.
– A service where if not performed, the impact may be immediate or may occur over a certain time period.

The business may have to modify, reduce, or remove specific services to cope with the impacts arising from an emergency either affecting some units or affecting the enterprise as a whole.

Prioritize essential services:

1. Prepare a ranking template listing unit-wise requirements for essential services and make a prioritized list depending on criticality of the service.
2. Ranking can be based on the following criteria:

   Priority I: Most essential services/functions

   Priority II: Services that can be suspended for a short period of time (say one month)

   Priority III: Services that can be suspended for an extended period of time (more than one month)

Step 3: Identify required skill sets and requirement for staff reallocation: Prepare a ranking template listing unit-wise requirements for essential services and make a prioritized list depending on criticality of the service. BIA will give a unit-wise requirement for staff and skills to perform and maintain essential services/functions. The planning team can use this skill set mapping to develop the continuity plan. A list of tasks or a task list as described earlier in Annexure A can be used to assign specific tasks to individuals such as IT support, back up team, and CMT.

Step 4: Identify potential issues: Prepare a ranking template listing unit-wise requirements for essential services and make a prioritized list depending on criticality of the service. Discuss what will happen if you have to reduce, modify, or eliminate essential services or functions. A potential threat list can be prepared, and scenario analysis can be made.

A separate incident-handling procedure can be documented for major types of incidents. Care to be taken to include precise roles and responsibilities of designated personnel for each essential service/function.

Step 5: Prepare a plan for each essential service/function: Incident-handling plans may be prepared for each incident that has been identified in the BIA/RA exercise.

This can cover the units or area that can be hit by the incident and should include the following:

1. Description of the incident.
2. BCM team members who will deal with the incident.
3. Backup individuals in case the designated personnel are unavailable due to some reason.
4. Likely impact from the incident and procedures to reduce impact and contain the incident at the earliest.
5. Procedures for notification of BCM management, for arranging staff relocation, and procurement of alternate resources, and suppliers must be laid down.

6. The need for personnel to resume operations and their key contacts must be readily available and form part of the incident-handling plan.

7. Contact list of important customers to whom communication will have to be made in case of incident occurrence must be prepared. Also include the purpose for communication during crisis situation to such customers.

8. Other business partners that include internal business units who rely on organization's communication during crisis such as corporate insurance, internal security, facilities, public relations, and legal entities.

9. Emergency response agencies such as the local police, ambulance services, fire stations, utility companies, and their contact numbers must be kept handy.

Step 6: Compare with "preparedness checklist": Review the plan and ascertain whether any element has been missed out or needs additional documentation. Availability of a preparedness checklist would assist in comparing and serving as a tick list to check all procedures have been covered completely and effectively. Check whether a trained and tested workforce is present, and whether they are able to display their abilities in dealing with the list of incidents mentioned.

Check to see that appropriate communication means are provided for employees' communication, and awareness training is provided by dissemination of brochures and newsletters through which the emergency procedures and security messages are reached to employees. Ensure that there exists a platform for communicating emergency status and actions to employees, vendors, suppliers, and customers inside and outside the worksite in a consistent and timely way.

Coordinating with external organizations like insurance companies, health insurance companies, and health care facilities to understand their capabilities to respond in times of disaster. It is advisable to have PR relationship managers in the team in order to maintain good relationship with trade associations, chambers of commerce, and to enhance emergency response efforts.

Step 7: Review with the emergency preparedness team: The emergency preparedness team must possess a copy of the BCP of the enterprise and review the same to ensure that:

BCP is consistent for all business units and departments.

BCP addresses all critical elements for recovery.

BCMSC to monitor the progress of emergency preparedness procedures.

Step 8: Revise, test, and update the plan. It is essential to perform trial runs, test the plan, and identify any gaps or weaknesses that need to be rectified.

Annexure C

Component Breakdown Structure for BCM Budget

S. No.	Particulars	January–March	April–June	July–September	October–December	Total $
1	**Staffing**					
	BCM consultant					
	Senior analyst					
	Administrator					
	Contractors					
2	**Emergency Operation Center**					
	Office space					
	Furniture					
	Telecom					
	Electricity					
	Internet					
	Supplies					
	Postage					

(Continued)

S. No.	Particulars	January–March	April–June	July–September	October–December	Total $
	Emergency funds					
	Mobile emergency processing van					
	Others					
3	**BCM Operations**					
	Risk analysts					
	BIA consultants					
	Policies and procedures doc.					
	Plan development					
	BCM documentation					
	Plan exercising					
	Maintenance					
	Training					
	Awareness campaign					
	Incident handling					
	Records management					
	Auditing BCM arrangements					

(Continued)

S. No.	Particulars	January–March	April–June	July–September	October–December	Total $
4	**ITDR Management**					
	DR technology					
	DR software					
	System software					
	Hot site					
	Cold site					
	Data backup/restoration					
	Alternate office space					
	Notification systems					
	Emergency command center					
	Others					

(Continued)

S. No.	Particulars	January–March	April–June	July–September	October–December	Total $
5	**Employee Education**					
	Webinars/Podcasts					
	Conferences					
	Subscriptions					
	Professional accreditation					
6	**Miscellaneous Expenses**					
	Travel					
	Other expenses					

Annexure D: Crisis Communication Form—Incident Media Call Sheet

Date: ....   Time: ....
Deadline:...........hrs........today..........a.m.....today...........p.m......ASAP.........
Others..........
Media Outlet--

- ▪ National   TV...... Radio...... Livewire....... Magazine......... Other..........
- ▪ Local
- ▪ International

Caller's Name.......................
Caller's Contact Information:
Phone.......
FAX...........
E-mail.............
Request

- ▪ SME questions
- ▪ Fact check
- ▪ Update
- ▪ Return call to press officer

Action Needed: ....
Return call expected from press officer
Return call expected from SME
Press Assistant suggested priority:

- ▪ Level A
- ▪ Level B
- ▪ Level C

No action needed:

    i. PA answered query
    ii. PA referred to Internet
    iii. PA referred to CIO
    iv. Other

    Taken by-..........   Designation: ....

Annexure E: Incident Declaration Criteria

Crisis incidents vary in intensity and location. All incidents are to be declared and qualified as high, medium, or low when they meet the following criteria. Incidents are to be declared based on an assessment of the gravity of the situation, criticality of the service impacted, sensitivity of information threatened or compromised, and potential for harm to this organization.

A list of potential specific criteria for each class and severity of incident is given below. This is only a suggestive list and should be tailored/customized as per the organization's operating environment.

Level One incidents: These refer to serious and significant incidents; they have a high potential for damage and need immediate handling. High-severity incidents like earthquake, building collapse, terrorist attacks, hacking attack, DOS attacks, unauthorized copying of copyrighted material, and so on fall under the category of Level One.

Level Two incidents are potentially serious and should be handled the same day that the incident occurs or that notification of the incident is given. Incidents that fall under this category include the following:

- Fraudulent action resulting in employee termination
- Intrusion detection system (IDS) reports unauthorized use of a system that is processing or storing organizational data
- Property destruction/theft in relation to a cyber security incident
- Any misuse of organizational property, facilities, and services
- Impact to business caused by virus/worms if the infection is the result of security policy violations on the part of employees
- Undocumented or unapproved vulnerability scans

Level Three incidents: These incidents are of low on severity; they must be investigated no more than three working days after the incident occurs. They include the following:

- Loss or compromise of a personal password
- Suspected sharing of individually assigned accounts
- Minor misuse of organizational property, facilities, and services
- Unsuccessful scans/probes (internal and external)
- Detected computer virus/worms (depending on impact to business unit)

Annexure F: Incident Management Plan Template

Definition: An incident response plan (IRP) is a set of written instructions for detecting, responding to, and limiting the effects of an information. Given below is a sample IMP:

Name of author of plan: **Date:**

Authorization by members of executive management

Name of Executive Manager	Date	Sign

Brief Description of Incident Handling Procedures

Critical Services

S. No.	Name of Process	Time Criticality (RTO)	Process Time Objective (RPO)

Plan Triggering Procedures

Responsibility Authority Matrix for Incident

S. No.	Name of BCM Team Member	Sign	Contact Number	Responsibility

Communication Channels for Communicating During Crisis

Situation	Mode of Communication

Key Contacts

List the key contact information essential to the service and this plan. Include the process owners, stakeholders, internal, and external support.

Name	Role	Company Name	Mobile	Fall-Back Phone

Incident Response Team

Identify roles essential for incident management, as well as primary and backup/alternate personnel to perform those roles.

Incident Response Role	Primary Team Member	Alternate Team Member	Contact Primary Member	Contact Alternate Member

IT Assets Required for incident handling

List all information and technology assets, its location, and its role during crisis.

Asset Name	Description	Physical Location	Logical Location	Backup Strategy and Schedule

Details of Processing Sites

Site Type	Location	Work to be Performed During Crisis
Primary site		
Alternate site		
Branch site		

Incident Management Checklist

S. No.	Activity to be Performed	Y	N	In Progress

Testing Schedule

Plan to be tested every quarter; participants will be BCM coordinator, incident commander, and other BCM members to be specified.

Name of Tester	Details	Lessons Learned	Report Signed By	Comments

Annexure G: Incident-Handling Log

S. No.	Actions Taken	Comments
1	Action taken to identify and salvage affected resources	
2	Actions taken to put preventive controls to contain/ prevent similar incidents	
3	Actions taken to remediate the incident	
4	Actions taken for orderly evacuation of facility where necessary	

Annexure H

Disaster declaration procedures include the chain of command to be followed in case of:

Type of Incident	Escalation Procedure	Authority to Invoke BCP Plan
Level One disaster		
Level Two disaster		
Level Three disaster		

Annexure I

Damage Assessment Form

S. No.	Equipment	Condition	Salvage	Comments
		OK (undamaged)	Y	
		DBU (damaged but usable)	N	
		DS (damaged, requires salvage before use)		
		D (destroyed, requires reconstruction)		

Date prepared:
Date reviewed:
Signature of reviewer:

Annexure J: Incident-Handling Procedures

Incident-Handling Procedures—Earthquake

Introduction: The objectives of earthquake planning are

1. To minimize potential for injury/death of employees and customers.
2. To evaluate and reduce hazards.
3. To reduce expenses caused by loss and liability.
4. To put tested procedures and equipment in place.
5. To plan for business resumption following an earthquake.

Earthquake Emergency Response Procedures

During a major earthquake, you may hear a roaring or rumbling sound that gradually grows louder. You may feel a rolling sensation that starts out gently and, within a second or two, grows violent. Alternatively, you may experience a violent jolt. A moment or two later, you may feel the shaking, and it is difficult to move or stand.

If your office is in a vulnerable seismic zone, you need to prepare for the earthquake disaster. The best way to deal with the disaster is to plan, prepare, and practice the procedures you need to adopt in case of it happening.

Practice Drills

By planning and practicing what to do if an earthquake strikes, you can learn to react correctly and automatically when the shaking begins. During an earthquake, most deaths and injuries are caused by collapsing building materials and heavy falling objects, such as bookcases, cabinets, and heating units. Participating in an earthquake drill will help understand what to do during an earthquake.

Major Considerations during an Earthquake Drill

- *DROP down onto your hands and knees;* this position protects you from falling but still allows you to move if necessary.
- *COVER* your head and neck (and your entire body if possible) under the shelter of a sturdy table or desk. If there is no shelter nearby, get down near an interior wall or next to low-lying furniture that will not fall on you, and cover your head and neck with your arms and hands. Try to stay clear of windows or glass that could shatter or objects that could fall on you.
- *HOLD ON to your shelter* (or to your head and neck) until the shaking stops. Be prepared to move with your shelter if the shaking shifts it around.

Before

■ Maintain current call list for employees and vendors housed in the branch. Keep them in a safe, easily accessible place.
■ Keep the BCM emergency kit in a safe, easily accessible place.
■ Participate fully in drills and exercises for enhancing response readiness.
■ Train staff to have a working knowledge of response protocols and how to use them. Plan safe areas for staff members who may not fit under their work table to use during an earthquake.
■ Secure all cabinets, doors, and supplies so they are less likely to fall.
■ Know your office floor plan, emergency escape staircase, surrounding area, know the work area in case you have to move in darkness if light goes out during the emergency.
■ Before an earthquake, quickly secure items that could fall and cause injuries.
■ Store critical supplies including basic food items, medicines, and water.
■ Plan proper communication methods for dealing with many people. (Refer crisis communication plan).

During an Earthquake

When disaster strikes, people may be inside the office or on field outside. Hence it is advisable to educate them as to what they must do in either cases:

1. *During: Inside*:
   a. Duck, cover, and hold at first sign of an earthquake. Hold on to furniture legs if the furniture moves. If there is not a table or desk near you, cover your face and head with your arms and couch in an inside corner of the building.
   b. Keep calm.
   c. Stay away from glass, windows, outside doors, and walls.
   d. Use stairs, not lifts.
   e. Walk never run.
   f. Use a doorway for shelter only if it is in close proximity to you and if you know it is an older building and the doorway is a strongly supported, load-bearing doorway.
   g. Stay inside until shaking stops, and it is safe to go outside. Be aware that the electricity may go out or the sprinkler systems and/or fire alarms may turn on.
   h. Stay indoors unless otherwise directed by BCM team members.
   i. Take cover under solid furniture or doorways.
   j. Move away from anything that could fall on someone.
   k. Curl into "turtle position" and protect the head. If outdoors:
   l. Stay clear of buildings and tall structures, trees, high walls, electricity lines—anything that could fall on someone.
   m. If evacuated, remain at assembly point or as directed by warden/person in charge until all clear is given.

2. *During: Outside*:
   - Stay outside.
   - Move away from buildings, street lights, and utility wires.
   - Once out in the open, stay there until the shaking stops. Most earthquake-related casualties result from collapsing walls, flying glass, and falling objects.

After an Earthquake

1. Take account of all staff and outsiders reported to be onsite at the time of disaster.
2. Make note of all missing people and injured students or staff.
3. Implement and coordinate emergency search operations.
4. Decide on the need for evacuation and other critical issues.
5. Keep a record of events, decisions, and actions.
6. Keep everyone together.
7. Do not let staff leave your site unless the proper authorities have told you it is all right to leave.
8. DO NOT TALK WITH THE MEDIA. Let only communication officer who will be in charge of this event do this task. Be very careful about information shared with outsiders.
9. When the event is completed, fill out required paperwork and debrief with the proper authorities and/or BCM personnel.
10. Look out for live electric wires and any other hazards.
11. Prepare for aftershocks; more things could fall.
12. Turn off electricity, gas, and water at mains.
13. Treat any injuries.
14. If there is a gas smell, evacuate building as for gas leak.
15. Conserve water and try to stop any leaks.
16. If power is cut, keep refrigerator and freezer doors closed as much as possible.
17. Ensure utilities are in working order before reoccupying buildings (contact utility company, if required).

Evacuation Instructions and Plans

- Follow instructions of evacuation team leader.
- Conduct earthquake emergency drills once in every six months.
- Assess site buildings for structural adequacy (get professional advice).
- Include potential earthquake hazards on inspection checklists (e.g., wall and ceiling fittings appropriately secured).
- Secure all heavy equipment.
- Store heaviest objects in lower shelves of cupboards.
- Store breakable items (e.g., glass, crockery) in cupboards that will not spring open.

- Be prepared to roll out the branch evacuation plan. The emergency evacuation team will guide personnel safely through the procedures.
- Mark where your emergency food, water, first aid kits, and fire extinguishers are located.
- Mark where the utility switches or valves are located so that they can be turned off, if possible.
- Indicate the location of the assembly area for meeting after evacuation.

Insurance Checklist

- If earthquake is a potential threat, earthquake insurance must be included in your insurance policy.
- Insurance must match the value of property, and regular valuation of property needs to be performed.
- Ensure that business interruption is included in the organization's insurance policy.
- Determine whether insurance taken provides for funding of an off-site location and whether the temporary substitute location be covered under the policy.
- Ascertain whether the insurance coverage limit in the general liability section is adequate for the organization.

Earthquake safety kit: It is good to have an *earthquake safety* kit ready for emergencies. This should include the following:

1. A first aid kit
2. Flashlights
3. Batteries
4. A portable radio
5. Water

Establish Priorities

Take time before an earthquake strikes to write an emergency priority list, including the following:

- Important items to be hand carried by you (BCM Kit).
- Items to be removed by car or truck if one is available.
- Things to do if time permits, such as locking doors and windows and turning off the utilities.

Gather and Store Important Documents in a Fire-Proof Safe

- Contracts
- Cheques

■ Unentered forms
■ Shop and establishment license

Note: Preparedness and preventive measures and proper education of employees serve to minimize the impact from disaster and facilitate the recovery process.

Incident Response Procedures for Floods Hazard

Definition: A flood emergency exists if floodwater is uncontrolled and flowing beyond the area where the source of water is normally contained or controlled.

Policy

The IRP for flooding has been developed to establish appropriate procedures for responding to a flood emergency that affects the organization and its branch offices.

Notification Procedures

Branches shall notify local authorities upon discovery of flood possibility. Alternatively, they can receive flood alerts from local public announcement systems or local media. The "on-call" safety officer will immediately be summoned who in turn shall notify the BCM management, and BCM coordinator should exercise his authority of initiating the emergency response procedures.

Incident Response in Case of Building Floods

1. The facilities administration shall determine the cause of the floods.
2. If water clogging is happening within the building, the health and safety officer shall conduct a hazard assessment of flooded areas prior to entry by responsible personnel.
3. All electrical equipment shall be de-energized for safety purposes.
4. Facilities operations shall take measures to stop the flow of water by shutting off valves controlling the flow of water.
5. Building personnel to move equipment/supplies to unaffected areas if possible.
6. All personnel not involved in recovery procedures shall be safely moved to safe area.
7. Building facilities management shall restrict access to affected areas by appropriate means.

A separate team can be assigned to deal with water-related incidents. It can comprise of

1. Health and safety officer.
2. Facilities manager.
3. Risk manager.

The health and safety officer in the branch shall act as on-scene incident commander of the team. The local police authorities get included in the team at the time of incident. The roles and responsibilities of each team player are as follows:

a. *The police department shall be responsible for*
   – Notifying the "On-Call" safety officer in the event of a flood and providing him contact list for facilities personnel on site.
   – Notifying the "on-Call" safety officer in case of a severe weather alert.
   – Initiating preventive evacuation of building by orders of ERT and securing area to prevent unauthorized intrusions.

b. *Facilities operations (Admin) will be responsible for*
   i. Calling the local authorities when a flood occurs and providing them with contact list to call appropriate personnel.
   ii. Flood prevention measures such as placing sandbags, setting up of generators, or submersible pumps.
   iii. De-energizing and locking out equipment/assets in the affected area if it can be done safely.
   iv. Checking outside drainage systems for "at-risk" buildings.
   v. Access to mechanical rooms for remediation and installation by contractors.
   vi. Securing access to branch facility.
   vii. Containing flood and initiating minor clean-up by appropriate contractors or initiating remedial repairs in case of major damage.

c. *Facilities admin will be responsible for*:
   1. Notifying Central Branch Operations and BCM coordinator in case of rising water levels
   2. Attempting to contain the flood and initial clean-up measures
   3. Working along with building facilities to constantly check outside drainage
   4. Managing outside contractors for remediation
   5. Coordinating work schedules for contractors with building manager risk department and health and safety officer
   6. Coordinating with risk management and health and safety officer for declaration of area to be safe for reoccupancy

d. *Facilities to treat the remediation measures as a project and appoint a responsible project manager immediately*: The PM to coordinate with risk and environmental safety to appoint a remediation contractor to carry out the remediation procedures. The following activities need to be carried out:
   i. Managing and supervising remediation contractors
   ii. Coordination for replacement of building parts
   iii. Communicate the building costs with risk department
   iv. Coordinating with building facilities management to gain access to office area
   v. Declare office ready for reoccupancy

e. *Health and safety officer aboard the branch shall ensure that*:
  i. Response to floods is met in a timely manner with appropriate measures to control and ensure safety of respondents and recover from the flood.
  ii. Acting as an incident commander (assigning BCM personnel key roles and responsibilities).
  iii. Contacting contractors to obtain supplies. (sand bags, submersible pumps, generators, etc.).
  iv. Acting as a liaison with authorities (police, BMC, fire department).
  v. Notifying BCM management of the incident and providing regular status reports.
  vi. Reviewing and amending IRP according to actual circumstances.
  vii. Contacting remediation contractors if damaged building materials are to be removed or dried, and disinfected water has to be obtained.
  viii. Declaring affected area safe for reoccupancy.
  ix. Reviewing IRP and amending it on the basis of "lessons learned."
f. *Logistics shall be taken care by admin. operations*:
  – Restock supplies, equipment, medications, food, and water
  – Ensure communication and IT/IS operations return to normal
  – Provide stress management and mental health support to staff
g. *Risk management shall be responsible for*
  i. Responding with appropriate action and instructions to recover from the flood.
  ii. Coordinating with contractors for clean-up or removal of debris or damaged assets after the flood.
  iii. Contacting and coordinating with insurance company for claims.
  iv. Coordinating with health and safety officer to declare affected area ready and safe for reoccupancy.

Reoccupancy: The above team shall assess areas affected by a flood for reoccupancy. Affected areas shall be declared ready for reoccupancy when the construction work is complete and safe for occupants. They shall ensure all wall and floor openings are closed up; tools and equipment have been removed from the area and ventilation; and fire alarm and fire suppression systems have been reinstated and in working condition.

Infection control: The above team shall, where there is possibility that water from flooding can pose additional hazards, appoint a remediation contractor to completely clean up the area to mitigate the additional risks/hazards. These measures may include infection control by use of disinfecting agents to clean affected areas when drying of or removal of building material is complete. The remediation contractor should decontaminate any equipment that is in the affected area during flooding from hazardous water.

Incident follow-up: A follow-up meeting to be held after the flood. The meeting shall include all departments that responded to the flood and is intended to obtain the "lessons learned" by probing into what went wrong during the incident response process.

Note: Each incident is typical and have unique method of dealing with them. Hence the incident commander for different incidents can be different depending on the skill sets required to deal with the disaster.

Incident Response Procedures for Terrorist Attacks

Definition: The FBI defines "*Terrorism* as the unlawful use of force and violence against persons or property to intimidate or coerce a government, the civilian population, or any segment thereof, in furtherance of political or social objectives." A terrorist attack affects a wider spectrum of people and organizations; it is advisable to follow what authorities instruct and be in close touch with social news media such as radio and television.

1. *Bomb threat—first possibility is that of bomb threat*: In this case, it will be beneficial to follow the following checklist:
   Threatening caller/bomb checklist
   a. Check caller ID for return phone number—record number immediately.
   b. Take call as serious threat but stay calm.
   c. Immediately start bomb threat checklist—record comments verbatim if possible.
   d. Keep caller talking and on line.
   e. Listen closely to the voice of the caller—note sex, age, accent, speech impediments, and voice.
   f. Note the characteristics (drunk, monotone, high pitched) and attitude (angry, calm, excited, etc.).
   g. Pay attention to background noises that may assist the authorities (street noise, bar noise, home noise).
   h. Ask caller when the bomb is set to go off and where it is located.
   i. Advise caller that building is occupied, and death and injury to innocent people could occur.
   j. Notify supervisor immediately—DO NOT notify others unless instructed to do so.

Voice Characteristics _____
Background noises _____
Ask: Where is bomb? _____

Advise caller: People could be hurt.

Write down exactly what caller says.

All this first information can be on the basis of subjective intelligence and first-hand approximation of person who has talked over phone. But in no circumstances, it should go unreported even if the receiver is of the opinion that it is just a prank played by somebody. Writing down what caller says will help give an idea of the probable intent of the caller.

2. *Bomb blast*: The second possibility is a bomb blast inside the building of the relevant branch. It will lead to a lot of commotion. Procedure to be followed will be:

   - All employees will be escorted to an area of safety, or there will be an orderly evacuation of premises.
   - Employees will be urged by BCM team to remain calm and be patient.
   - Since this is a local emergency, officials from fire brigade, police, and so on will also be involved, BCM team will follow the advice of local emergency officials.
   - For updated information on surrounding area, it will be advisable to resort to radio/television for news and instructions.
   - If the event occurs near you, check for injuries. Arrange to provide first aid and get help for seriously injured people.
   - If the event occurs near your office, while you are there, check for damage using a flashlight. Do not light matches or candles or turn on electrical switches. Check for fires, fire hazards, and other hazards. Sniff for gas leaks, starting at the water heater. If you smell gas or suspect a leak, turn off the main gas valve, open windows, and get everyone outside quickly.
   - In such disasters, the authorities assume the role of incident commander.

Consequences of a Terrorist Attack

- There can be significant numbers of casualties and/or damage to buildings and the infrastructure. So employers need up-to-date information about any medical needs you may have and on how to contact your designated beneficiaries. Call list for essential services should be part of the BCM kit, and help has to be summoned immediately.
- Heavy law enforcement involvement at local, state, and national levels follows a terrorist attack due to the event's criminal nature.
- Health and mental health resources in the affected communities can be strained to their limits, maybe even overwhelmed.

- Extensive media coverage, strong public fear, and international implications, and consequences can continue for a prolonged period.
- Workplaces and schools may be closed, and there may be restrictions on domestic and international travel.
- You may have to evacuate your building area for your safety. A roll call has to be taken, and communication procedures with those not in office or the relatives of injured employees should be initiated.
- Shut off any other damaged utilities.
- Call your family contact—do not use the telephone again unless it is a life-threatening emergency.
- Check on employees who are disabled or pregnant, and see that they are comfortable or comfortably evacuated from the building.
- If no multiple blast is reported in surrounding area or city, then employees can be permitted to go home.
- Clean-up may take many months and so the business recovery team to set relocation plan into action and get the resumption process going.
- If the situation is chaotic, then BCM team has to accommodate employees in office or other safe area and provide basic amenities such as food and water.
- BCM recovery personnel will coordinate with vendors, alternate site officials, and data center to set up the recovery process.

After the Incident Procedures

Reporting: An account of exact nature of blast, areas affected, equipment affected by blast, number of injured personnel during the incident, and whether the IRP was properly activated and executed. Lessons learned should be documented, and remedial measures have to be executed.

Psychological trauma: Such incidents are not forgettable easily and the shock trauma lingers for some time. To deal with this, organizations should conduct special counseling sessions and organize some destress activities to motivate employees and bring them back to original form.

Note: Terrorism is becoming more and more prevalent, and hence organizations can volunteer in spreading social awareness to bomb threats. Employees have to be trained to be alert and report suspicious things lying around or strange parcels lying inside or outside the organization building.

Appendix

BCM Audit/Assurance Program (Illustrative)

S. No.	Heading	Person to be Contacted in Relevant Area of Audit	Document Reviewed	Pending Points
I	**Pre-audit Plan**			
1	Review of audit charter to define audit objectives.		Audit Charter; RFP; BCM policy	
2	Discuss the audit objectives with auditee management.			
3	Familiarize with the standards, regulations, and best practices that apply to the industry and BCM program.		ISO 22301 COBIT 5	
4	Map the boundaries of audit review and document exclusions if any.			
5	Understand the compliance status and attempt to identify where deficiencies exist prior to the audit			
6	Physical locations under audit purview.		RFP; Charter	
7	Arrange a kick-off meeting.			
8	Take stock of all single points of contact/BCM team.		BCM team structure	

(Continued)

S. No.	Heading	Person to be Contacted in Relevant Area of Audit	Document Reviewed	Pending Points
9	Plan the audit strategy and calendar and communicate to auditee.			
10	Agree upon milestones and adopt a project management approach.			
II	**Planning the Audit Proceedings**			
1	Finalize audit team and allocate the areas of audit. Make the audit program and take sign-off from team.		Audit program	
2	Enlist the crisis situations covered by the BCM plan.		Scenario analysis	
3	Match the crisis situations with a list of threats both internal and external that can lead to the crisis situation.		Threat lists	
4	Arrange for an awareness session on BCM/risk.		Risk register	
5	Assess business processes under scope and list down strategic assets in the running of these processes.		Asset register	
6	Identify and document risks Adopt a risk-based approach to audit to utilize audit resources optimally.			
7	Identify the business risk associated to the crisis situations selected for BCM program.	Business managers		

(Continued)

S. No.	Heading	Person to be Contacted in Relevant Area of Audit	Document Reviewed	Pending Points
8	Align identified business risks to crisis situations.	Business managers		
9	Evaluate the overall audit risk for performing the BCM review.			
10	Adjust the scope of audit based on the results of the risk assessment.			
11	Tabulate the risks, check they are entered in risk register and discuss management intent of treating risk and document results.			
12	Identify the drivers including policies, procedures, standards adopted by the enterprise that can be instrumental to achieving the assurance objectives.			
13	Communicate the success drivers with process owners and stakeholders and obtain agreement for audit procedures.			
III	**Define Audit Resources required for audit**	BCM team members		
1	A list of audit resources/team is prepared.			
2	Time schedule is submitted for audit along with team.			

(Continued)

S. No.	Heading	Person to be Contacted in Relevant Area of Audit	Document Reviewed	Pending Points
IV	**Define Milestones and Deliverables at the End of Each Phase of Audit**			
1	Document flow of deliverables; status reports, initial findings, gap report, minutes of update meetings, etc.			
2	Pre-fix dates for management reports as specified by RFP.			
V	**Assessing Crisis Preparedness**			
1	Determine that a crisis governance committee has been established with executive sponsorship from top management.			
2	Obtain the crisis management objectives.			
3	Establish that key business managers are represented on the crisis committee and a C-level executive is a sponsor.			
4	Ascertain that crisis team has set levels of crisis and escalation procedures.			
5	Determine whether the program and associated plans focus on the organization's mission-critical activities?			
6	Ascertain that the Crisis Committee has formulated a crisis communication plan and approved it.			

(Continued)

S. No.	Heading	Person to be Contacted in Relevant Area of Audit	Document Reviewed	Pending Points
7	Auditor should review the minutes of the crisis management committee to check the level of management monitoring.			
8	Crisis management plans are made ready to be rolled at the time of crisis.			
VI	**Conduct a BIA and Adopt a Risk-based Crisis Management Program**			
1	Determine whether organization has a clearly defined and documented business impact analysis (BIA) process in place.		BIA	
2	Find out whether BIA was carried out in the past 12 months, if yes, obtain and review the BIA report.			
3	Ascertain that the Recovery Time Objectives (RTOs) and the Recovery Point Objectives (RPOs) for mission critical systems are identified.			
4	Determine whether the risks and vulnerabilities for mission critical systems have been identified.		Risk register Risk map	

(Continued)

S. No.	Heading	Person to be Contacted in Relevant Area of Audit	Document Reviewed	Pending Points
5	Determine a risk-based approach to assess enterprise risk and develop scenarios for the crisis management plan has been adopted.			
6	Examine risk assessments carried out are aligned to business continuity objectives for crisis preparedness.			
7	Verify all identifiable risks; financial, operational, strategic, IT, legal, security, compliance, are evaluated.		Threat list	
8	Determine that all identified risks are communicated to management/process owners.			
9	Determine that ITDR processes are aligned to crisis management processes.	IT team		
10	Determine that a process, procedure or methodology based on management decision or some standard is adopted and executed. Criteria for risk mitigation and prioritization must be checked.			
11	Determine that there is management oversight on compliance to these standards/methodologies adopted.		BCM management	
12	Determine there is designated budget.		BCM sponsor	

(Continued)

S. No.	Heading	Person to be Contacted in Relevant Area of Audit	Document Reviewed	Pending Points
VII	**Examining Crisis Strategy**			
1	Find out whether organization has a clearly defined, documented and approved overall Crisis Management strategy.			
2	Determine that there is a clearly defined, documented and approved resource recovery strategy.			
3	Ascertain that BCM strategies are properly aligned with business strategies.			
4	Determine whether there is an approved framework for recovering from crisis.			
5	Ascertain whether strategy consists of both technical (e.g., IT, telecoms) and non-technical (e.g., people) issues involved with crisis.			
6	Ensure that strategy is including other parts of the organization (e.g., office locations, production sites).			
7	Make sure that internal and external sourcing of products and services is considered as a part of the strategy for crisis response.			

(Continued)

S. No.	Heading	Person to be Contacted in Relevant Area of Audit	Document Reviewed	Pending Points
8	Examine plan templates and sample plans available to support the planning process.			
VIII	**Identify Crisis Scenarios**			
1	Obtain list of crisis scenarios.			
2	Assess whether risk scenarios are based on risk management, prioritization, and mitigation.			
3	Examine all high impact high probability scenarios as well as low probability but high impact scenarios are considered.			
IX	**Legal and Regulatory Compliance**	Compliance officer	Contracts, books	
1	Assess contact list of regulators and legal entities.			
2	Awareness of regulatory requirements to be followed must be assessed.			
3	Identification of regulatory/legal issues are considered in the crisis scenarios.			
4	Communication with regulators during crisis is configured in crisis plan.			

(Continued)

S. No.	Heading	Person to be Contacted in Relevant Area of Audit	Document Reviewed	Pending Points
X	**Crisis Management Plan Components**			
1	Commitment from senior management in the crisis management team/committee.			
2	A crisis team leader is assigned to the task of handling crisis scenarios.			
3	Proper communication channel is established between crisis coordinator, project sponsor, and the business process owners.	Crisis coordinator		
4	Determine whether the levels of severity have been assigned to crisis and proper escalation procedures and procedures for crisis declaration have been laid.			
5	Ascertain that a subject matter expert has been assigned to assess crisis and report or escalate for triggering crisis response plan.			
6	Ensure that risk assessment covers all outcomes and risks associated with scenarios that aids further in defining severity levels which helps in formulating crisis response procedures.			

(Continued)

S. No.	Heading	Person to be Contacted in Relevant Area of Audit	Document Reviewed	Pending Points
7	Crisis committee to approve of all crisis related procedures including crisis declaration.			
XI	**BCM Personnel**			
1	Auditor to ensure that proper representation of SME from all divisions within the organization exists.			
2	Ascertain that BCM roles and responsibilities have been clearly defined, documented, and approved key performance indicators (KPIs) have been set.			
3	Check whether the program is monitored, reviewed, and evaluated in terms of KPIs.			
4	Check whether "train the trainer" training is given to all BCM personnel.			
5	Ensure that each BCM role been assigned to a primary and alternate individual, both undergo same training.			
XII	**Crisis Communication**			
1	Determine who will be the spokesperson to address the media and stakeholders during the continuation of the crisis.			

(Continued)

S. No.	Heading	Person to be Contacted in Relevant Area of Audit	Document Reviewed	Pending Points
2	Determine that competent personnel are assigned the task of writing the crisis communication to be addressed at the time of each type of crisis scenario that is identified.			
3	Ascertain the communication infrastructure is adequate and redundancy exists.			
4	Determine that the intranet is properly configured to disseminate information to employees.			
5	Determine who will be the spokesperson to address the media and stakeholders during the continuation of the crisis.			
6	Ensure that the plan has current (internal and external) contact lists.			
7	Determine whether the plan include a list of key service providers and suppliers.			
8	Ensure that the plan include a list of emergencies first responders, e.g., police, fire.			
9	Ensure crisis communication plan and call lists are tested.			

(Continued)

S. No.	Heading	Person to be Contacted in Relevant Area of Audit	Document Reviewed	Pending Points
10	Ascertain and examine the central announcement systems to be used to alert employees in different sections during a crisis.			
11	Ascertain that central announcement systems are maintained and tested on a regular basis.			
12	Ascertain that communication channels with external stakeholders and authorities is established and maintained. Contact lists are kept updated.			
13	Establish whether the stakeholders are aware of the crisis communication plan.			
14	Determine whether there are standby contacts with media and other public-facing organizations have been established.			
15	Determine that the web site use to communicate to public during crisis is determined, configured, and ready to use during crisis.			
16	Toll free number to accept/answer stakeholder calls is arranged to be used in crisis.			

(Continued)

S. No.	Heading	Person to be Contacted in Relevant Area of Audit	Document Reviewed	Pending Points
XIII	**Consider Third Party Vendors**			
1	Obtain information on vendor contracts and examine the SLAs for strategic contracts.		SLAs NDAs	
2	Ascertain whether the program suppliers (internal and/or outsourced providers) have up-to-date and tested plans?			
3	Determine whether an external vendor requirement is identified for vital services such as legal, equipment, public relations, or some essential services.			
4	Determine contracts are valid, active, and monitored.			
5	Determine that a Nondisclosure agreement is signed with each vendor.			
6	A "right to audit" clause or receipt of third party audit report is provided in the contract.			

(Continued)

S. No.	Heading	Person to be Contacted in Relevant Area of Audit	Document Reviewed	Pending Points
XIV	**Assess Emergency Operations Center Assets/Processes**			
1	Assess whether there exists an Emergency Operations Centre as per the BCM Plan.			
2	Does the site exist in crowded locality or in outskirts of the city?			
3	Determine whether the EOC contains a processing facility and infrastructure for information processing is maintained.			
4	Ascertain whether an alternate EOC is identified in case primary EOC is not available during crisis.			
5	Are physical security controls such as swipe card, CC TV cameras, fire extinguishers, temperature controllers are in place at the EOC/alternate EOC.			
6	Determine whether EOC possesses copy of BCM plans.			
7	Check that crisis plan provides for logistics for personnel being sent to EOC for carrying out critical operations as per plan.			

(Continued)

S. No.	Heading	Person to be Contacted in Relevant Area of Audit	Document Reviewed	Pending Points
XV	**Testing of Crisis Plan**			
1	Has competence (and crisis management) been demonstrated through exercises, tests, or plan activations?			
2	Observe that plans get updated based on exercise results.			
3	Determine that the exercise schedule support different types of exercise techniques.			
4	Ascertain whether desktop walkthrough exercises are conducted, at least annually.			
5	Find out whether other live exercises, involving the shutdown of systems, are conducted at least once a year.			
6	Determine whether exercises are conducted by qualified personnel or under the supervision of a subject matter expert.			
7	Ascertain whether the organization has clearly defined, documented, and approved exercise guidelines.			
8	Evaluate post-exercise evaluation and reporting processes if any defined, approved, and documented.			

(Continued)

S. No.	Heading	Person to be Contacted in Relevant Area of Audit	Document Reviewed	Pending Points
XVI	**Maintenance of Crisis Program**			
1	Look for a clearly defined, documented, and approved maintenance program.			
2	Determine whether the maintenance program addresses all IT disaster recovery activities.			
3	Determine whether the maintenance program addresses all IT suppliers, their Service Level Agreements.			
4	Identify whether noncompliant maintenance issues are escalated to ensure they are made compliant.			
5	Examine the maintenance process and ascertain that it has a clearly defined, documented, and approved process for incorporating all changes to strategy and/or plans into exercising, training, and awareness programs.			
6	Check whether plans are audited annually.			
7	Find out whether there exists a clearly defined, documented, and approved audit cycle and program.			
8	Find out if there is a process for continuous improvement of the overall crisis management program.			

(Continued)

S. No.	Heading	Person to be Contacted in Relevant Area of Audit	Document Reviewed	Pending Points
XVII	**Audit Conclusion and Reporting**			
1	Conducting interviews with management and other company stakeholders to determine their involvement in business continuity planning efforts.		Audit report (prior)	
2	Reviewing the BCM document to determine its completeness, accuracy, and timeliness.			
3	Reviewing supporting BCM documents, such as procedural manuals, guidelines, and training materials.			
4	Evaluating the effectiveness of BCP and DRC plans by reviewing plan testing results or the results of actual disasters where the BCP or DRP was used. This can be accomplished by asking questions such as: Did it work? What did not work and why? Was the process improved?			
5	Analysing the audit report's conclusion and recommendations.			
6	Audit report should certify that plans are up-to-date.			
7	Auditor must mention all critical systems and business functions included in the plan.			

(Continued)

S. No.	Heading	Person to be Contacted in Relevant Area of Audit	Document Reviewed	Pending Points
8	Auditor must mention on the assessment of roles and responsibilities to the BCM personnel.			
9	Auditor must mention risk methodology, risk assessment, and risk treatment strategies adopted by the organization.			
10	Location of data backups and plans for exercise and testing of backups and storage media must be assessed and note.			
11	Auditors to comment on plan testing, results, and documentation of "lessons learnt."			
12	Auditors must note where plans are stored and whether offsite storage is done.			
13	Auditors to set priority areas, identify continuous monitoring rules.			
14	Auditors should define audit frequency/extent, configure continuous audit parameters.			
15	Auditors should collate audit findings and report to the right levels of management and obtain response and conduct follow-up on observations and remediation measures.			

Chapter 6

Information Technology Is All Pervasive in an Organization

Introduction

Information technology (IT) is all pervasive. What used to be a support department that ran the basic infrastructure, IT 333 has evolved into a business enabler; the role of IT has turned from tactical to strategic. IT now finds a place in business committees, planning forums, and BCM teams, and it drives and supports business initiatives by enabling process improvement and helping in resource optimization.

IT has multiple roles: as a functional department and as a DR enabler (ITDR), participating in the response, recovery, and resumption processes immediately after a disaster. The rapid pace of business and technology changes coupled with increasing performance expectations from customers, employees, and management applies a constant pressure on IT infrastructures and supporting teams to provide around-the-clock availability and to minimize planned and unplanned disruptions.

To adapt and respond to such demands under both normal and adverse conditions, the enterprise should incorporate robust technology adoption policies and procedures and recovery solutions that are tested periodically as part of the BCM program. IT has a defined budget as a function and a budget for the DR function, and it has to plot the ROI for each function.

Organizations are constantly reengineering business processes and optimizing resources making technology an engine to gear speed in computation and creating a baseline for optimizing the cost of running the business. It would be worth mentioning the role of some technologies that have turned IT into such a great enabler.

Emerging Technologies in Business

Internet technologies and web applications are playing a major role in defining business and have enabled the extension of IT services over large distributed networks. Let us have a brief look at some of the enabling technologies that impact business:

1. *Data warehousing*: It is a virtual concept whereby a central repository of data/information created from different disparate sources or legacy systems is used to give users instant access and usability of the data/information. This helps improve and speed up transactional processes and business decision-making (Figure 6.1).

   This is immensely useful when the same data are used by different functions for different reasons, and they need to represent them in different formats for end use. It gives views against writes, and it maintains the integrity of the database. Data warehousing has an enabling impact on business decision-making.

2. *Business analytics*: This has been defined as a practice of iterative, methodical exploration of an organization's data with emphasis on statistical analysis. Business analytics is used by companies committed to data-driven decision-making. It consists of solutions to build analysis models and simulations to create scenarios, to understand realities, and to predict future states. Business

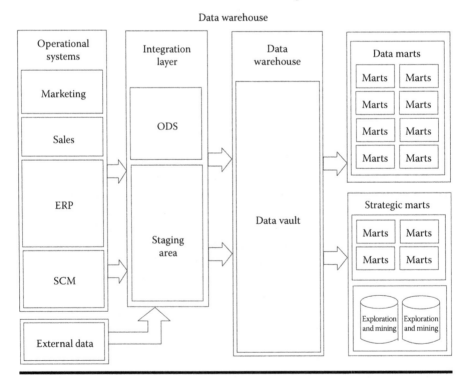

Figure 6.1 Data warehouse.

analytics includes data mining, predictive analytics, applied analytics, and statistics and is delivered as an application suitable for a business user.

3. *Digital performance dashboards*: This provides the capability to measure performance as it is occurring in stock market (Figure 6.2).

   A well-designed digital performance dashboard encourages real-time engagement, empowerment, and self-management and a monitoring of risk levels. Digitizing the process has brought in accuracy and standardization in monitoring processes.

4. *Data visualization*: This technology deals with the emerging science of displaying data and information to convey ideas and conclusions effectively, both in terms of aesthetic form and functionality. Data visualization attempts to achieve a balance between form and function, thereby reducing perceptions and opinions about different individual's interpretations about the end result. This is an emerging science as practitioners use data visualization technique to better convey their ideas and explain concepts. It enables error reduction and correct interpretation of the results, and the corrective actions are based on evidence and not just opinions.

5. *Mobile technology*: The mobile devices such as laptops, notebooks, tablets, and phones brought in a new culture. Organizational activities were now scheduled through schedulers, conference calls, and e-mails that could be accessed with mobile devices. But this brought in a risk of protecting data on these devices. Proliferation of enterprise data on employee's personal device(s) has given rise to risk to the very existence of enterprises. But many enterprises have addressed these risks and decided to integrate personal devices with corporate and business applications giving rise to BYOD (bring your own devices) concept. The level of workforce mobilization created with this IT shift (mindset) soon became an integral part of business strategy and advantageous to enterprises.

6. *Development of business tools on mobiles*: Availability of e-mails on personal handheld devices was the biggest positive impact as it enhanced employee productivity and collaboration. But it opened up corporate tools such as CRM, ERP, and so on that were sitting behind the firewall. It had a positive impact on customer servicing as well, since now it is possible to give the apps to the customers and customers. The next wave of technology is moving toward mobile apps of core applications to steer the business processes and communications to give customers and employees connectivity on a 24/7 basis, to enable customers to bank around the clock, and to establish a lot of customer satisfaction and goodwill.

Note: The technology mentioned above is just illustrative. Technology evolves by the second; new innovations, newer methods of developing technology such as agile computing, and new ways of doing business through e-commerce are making a lot of headway into the business enabler.

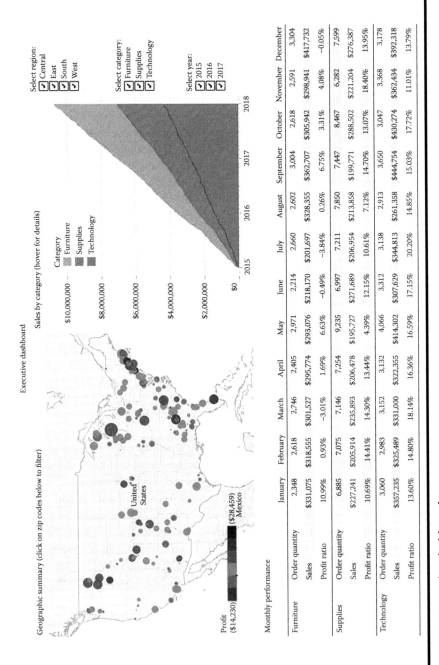

Figure 6.2 Executive dashboard.

Features of IT in an Enabling Capacity

Computer-aided business design and computer-generated applications have reduced the constraints of IT resources to IT's support of the business. This is helping business leaders to:

1. *Align with business goals and objectives*: This involves analyzing and improving business processes and improvising processes for attainment of enterprise goals and objectives. The key is to align business requirements with technology and design business processes around the technology adopted.
2. *Set strategies*: Business strategies have to be techno-savvy to make them more benefit oriented by saving on costs and time of execution. It is recommended to view end-to-end processes in order to frame strategies.
3. *Use technology to computer-generated applications*: This capability is essential for IT to owe from focusing on applications to business operations. This will help customize applications keeping in mind business requirements.
4. *Monitor the performance of aligned operations*: Use KPI and metric results to monitor progress toward achieving the desired business goals. IT must help analyze results and determine additional process adjustments that may be necessary to achieve the business goal. The manner in which IT should be channelized to achieve this objective of being a business enabler is to ensure that:
   - *Business process performance enhancement*: IT must take the initiative in analyzing business processes, adapting to change in business' strategy conditions and regulatory requirements supporting innovation, and adapting to changes in the business's strategy.
   - *Providing business design standards, controls, and compliance*: Standards and controls for defining business operations provide the basis for ensuring compliance with regulations and corporate direction.
   - *Reducing the resources required for IT infrastructure*: Committing IT to developing business designs and computer-generating complete applications will help IT reduce costs. Eliminating the cost of programming is the obvious cost reduction. Managing the costs of the data center is another.

Businesses today are under more pressure than ever to deliver value to stakeholders, particularly when undertaking mergers, acquisitions, or asset disposals. Under the current economic conditions, management teams will require additional effort in streamlining operations of acquired businesses to deliver success in the absence of financial engineering. IT is fastly becoming a key lever, which management can use to deliver operational benefits and to drive deal value. The strategic initiatives behind a transaction rely on IT, and businesses can no longer ignore IT or view it as a back-office function if they want to achieve maximum deal value.

Today "IT" mainly addresses the following:

1. *IT infrastructure needs*: hardware, software, utilities, network resources, and IT services to other departments bound by timescales (TATs) entered or fixed in advance for which IT is accountable.
2. *IT systems architecture*: selecting various IT components for connecting networks and offices all over the organization.
3. *IT system development* of new systems or customizing off-the-shelf systems to meet user requirements and to maintain segregated environments in respect of test and production environments.
4. *Role in DR operations*: Besides the above roles, IT has an active role in planning the DR function based on approved RTOs and RPOs, in organizing the backups and preventive controls in respect of information systems, and in enabling the business functions to resume operations from alternate site or any other within the Recovery Time Objective during a disaster.

In this section, we shall delve into these diverse roles of IT and see how they impact business decisions and recovery during crisis situations.

Information Technology Infrastructure

IT infrastructure refers to the composite hardware, software, network resources, and services required for the existence, operation, and management of an enterprise IT environment (Figure 6.3).

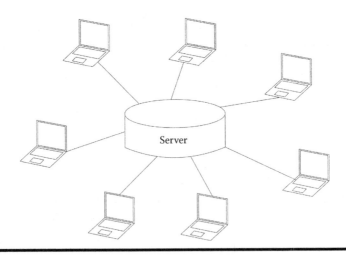

Figure 6.3   IT infrastructure.

Every organization needs a strong infrastructure that facilitates interconnectivity with all other basic facilities and services in order to carry out its activities. Different organizations need varied infrastructures in terms of hardware, software, facilities, services, and so on. In some cases, specific infrastructure is required to fulfill the business/operational or compliance requirements.

Advances in telecommunications, more user-friendly technology, improved data storage solutions, cost-effective virtualized environments, and cloud computing are enabling enterprises to increase data storage capabilities, to become agile, and to improve business resilience.

The Need for an Information Systems Infrastructure

The information systems infrastructure consists of hardware, software, networks, data facilities, human resources, and services to support decision-making process. The business processes consist of activities performed to achieve the goals and objectives.

Large global organizations are slowly developing their IT infrastructure in line with globally accepted practices, standards, and guidelines in order to design a fault-tolerant enterprise where fall back redundancy exists, and the distributed structures enables the removal of single dependencies that may result in "single points of failure."

Some of these activities are primary, and some are support activities. Primary activities are related to the core processes in the value chain, and supporting processes are processes that are required to perform supporting activities in the value chain such as accounting, human resources, and so on.

The success of business depends on the authenticity of its underlying information systems infrastructure, though degree of dependence on it may differ. Today we live in an extended organization concept, while it is necessary to keep constant interaction between customers as well as suppliers. Intelligence/market reports to be obtained since accurate and timely information is necessary to support business processes and to make business decisions (Figure 6.4).

Thus we find that organizations rely on a complex, interrelated information systems infrastructure to exist and survive in a competitive digital world. The process/function of information gathering and evaluating information for decision support for business is known as "business intelligence." So today organizations depend upon the following components:

■ Hardware
■ Software
■ Communications and collaboration
■ Data and knowledge
■ Facilities

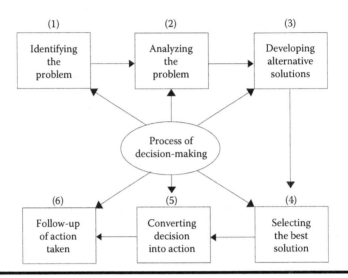

Figure 6.4   Decision-making process.

- Human resources
- Technology development
- Support activities

We shall now move to see how the above-mentioned components and different infrastructure solutions help to support an organization's competitive strategy, decision-making, and business processes.

Managing the Hardware Infrastructure

Planning the hardware infrastructure also has undergone a paradigm change. Companies often face difficult decisions regarding their hardware. Information systems executives therefore face countless complex questions, such as the following:

- Which hardware technologies should be chosen?
- What time interval should the equipment be replaced?
- How can the information systems be secured best?
- What performance and storage are needed today? Next year?
- How can reliability be assured?

Many organizations now turn to on-demand computing for fluctuating computation needs, grid computing for solving large-scale problems, and autonomic computing for increasing reliability.

On-demand computing: In this concept, the allotment of scarce resources that are not used at all times of day can be distributed to users on a pay per use basis. Some high-bandwidth applications such as videoconferencing may be needed only on certain days of the week. For instance, user department running a complex data mining algorithm would receive more processing power than a user merely doing some word processing. In this way, optimum use of resources can be done thus reducing overall cost of using costly services.

Utility computing: Sometimes, it is more convenient for organizations to "rent" resources from an external provider. This form of on-demand computing is referred to as utility computing, where the resources in terms of processing, data storage, or networking are rented on an as-needed basis, and the organization receives a bill for the services used from the provider at the end of each month. Availability is the major constraint and that can be resolved by proper contractual agreements with the vendor.

Grid computing refers to combining the computing power of a large number of smaller, independent, and networked computers (often regular desktop PCs) into a cohesive system in order to solve problems that can only be solved using super computers. In order to use the grid-computing method, large computing tasks are broken into small chunks, each of which can then be completed by the individual computers. However, as the individual computers are also in regular use, the individual calculations are performed during the computers' idle time so as to maximize the use of existing resources (Figure 6.5).

Grid computing is particularly useful for global companies. Some resources are always lying idle for some time throughout the network and

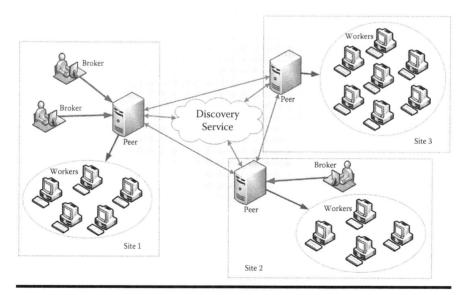

Figure 6.5 Grid computing.

grid leverages that make grid computing feasible and advantageous. Globally, there is a leverage in differences in night and day. But a limiting factor here is the demand on network infrastructure or the software managing the distribution of the tasks.

A point to note is that many of the grids work on the speed of the slowest machine on the network, thus slowing down the grid. The only solution is to have dedicated grids that perform tasks only for the grid. It is composed of a number of homogeneous computers not merely unutilized resources. In dedicated grids, there is a saving in cost of software and an ease of management.

Edge computing: Another recent trend in IS hardware infrastructure management is edge computing. With the decrease in the cost for processing and data storage, computing tasks are now often solved at the edge of a company's network. In other words, rather than having massive, centralized computers and databases, multiple smaller servers are located closer to the individual users.

This way, resources in terms of network bandwidth and access time are saved. If a computer needs several hours to compute a certain problem, it might be a good choice to send the task over a network to a more powerful computer that might be able to solve that problem faster. However, as the costs for computing power have decreased tremendously over the past years, many problems can now be computed locally.

To save resources, many businesses use edge computing for their online commerce sites. In such cases, customers interact with the servers of an edge-computing service provider (such as Akamai). These servers, in turn, communicate with the business computers.

This form of edge computing helps to reduce wait times for the consumers, as the e-commerce sites are replicated on Akamai's servers, while at the same time reducing the number of requests to the company's own infrastructure. This process not only saves valuable resources such as bandwidth but also offers superior performance that would otherwise be too expensive for organizations to offer.

Managing the Software Infrastructure

Operating systems and application software and utilities are dominating the information systems environment, and businesses are increasing their dependence on these systems including the business intelligence applications.

However, continuously upgrading operating systems and applications software can be costly, hence organizations are turning to open source software, to integrate different software tools, or to using application service providers (ASPs) for their software needs. A large number of web sites are powered by the Linux operating system. Apache web server and Firefox web browser are other instances of open source. As organizations manage their software infrastructure, there are several issues that must be carefully managed, such as software bugs and licensing.

Managing software licensing: Software licensing has been a major issue for software companies as they lose in piracy and unlicensed users. Software licensing is defined as the permission and rights that are imposed on applications and the use of software. Although freeware or shareware is freely available, the copyright owners often retain their rights and do not provide access to the program's source code. The second type of licensing is enterprise licensing. Enterprise licensing contains limitations of liability and warranty disclaimers that protect the software vendor from being sued if their software does not operate as expected.

Managing bugs: With the increased complexity of software, it is imperative that errors or bugs will be present or will develop no matter whether such applications are operating systems, web sites, or enterprise-wide software. Normally, software developers account for these unforeseen problems by incorporating a patch management system into the application. Patch management is typically based on an online system that checks a web service for available patches. If the software vendor offers a new patch, the application will download and install the patch in order to fix the software bug. We will recall Microsoft has given a lot of patches to their operating systems software, and it is easily downloadable. Some patches are used to fix security holes that could be exploited by intruders.

Communications and collaboration: Networking and communication software and other components that facilitate the interconnection of different computers, enabling collaboration literally around the world is a critical subsystem in most organizations. E-mail servers and communication software are also required for internal or external communication (Figure 6.6).

Organizations also need to decide whether to utilize tools such as instant messaging and which applications to use for such services. Videoconferencing is one such collaboration tool that gives cost saving and place utility at the same time providing connectivity across the globe.

Note: Organizations set the communication infrastructure for communicating with internal and external parties, vendors, stakeholders, employees, and so on, and this infrastructure and these channels are used for crisis communication during crisis.

Data and Knowledge

Data and knowledge are the most critical assets of an organization. Managing data and information is not just a business need but a legal and regulatory requirement.

Figure 6.6   Videoconferencing facilities.

Capacity, reliability, and performance of these assets must be organized. Online retail companies such as Flipcart, Amazon, and others need databases to store customer information, product information, inventory, transactions, and so on. Insurance companies have a large amount of data including legacy data that they are required to maintain and keep the integrity, authenticity, and confidentiality of this database, which is the chief concern for their security department.

Note: Data storage, security, retention, access, and data movement over networks are IT service areas by itself. We shall delve in detail when we touch upon ITDR later on in this section.

Facilities

An organization's information systems infrastructure always needs to be secured to prevent it from outside intruders, given various threats to IS infrastructure components (such as storm, power outages, earthquakes, etc.); organizations have to take great care on where and how to house the infrastructure.

As the sophistication of computing devices, servers, and routers goes on increasing, there are special environmental considerations that govern the area where they are located. Since these devices generate a lot of heat, it is necessary that the cooling and temperature of the facility should be monitored and should meet stipulations given by the vendors.

Physical security of data center is of paramount importance, and the facilities must be safeguarded and tested periodically. Controls such as access control, CCTV cameras, biometric entry points, and deadman doors are recommended (Figure 6.7).

Figure 6.7   Deadman doors.

Deadman doors work on the principle that at one time, only one person can gain access to a facility. It is guarded by two doors; when the access is demanded, person steps in through the first door; the first door closes before second door opens thus granting access to the visitor. This prevents an unauthorized person to get access along with an authorized person (piggybacking). It is used in sensitive installations with high-security stipulations.

Web Services

Organizations make use of web services to integrate information from different applications, running on different platforms and increasing interoperability. It enables a service-oriented architecture (SOA), and it chiefly leads to integration of different vendor independent services and can be used to integrate data and capabilities of different systems running on different platforms. This capability—and the reusability of different services—allows businesses to quickly react to changes in the business environment.

Managing the Human Resource Infrastructure

Adopting the latest technology and infrastructure entails deployment of a highly trained workforce. Availability of necessary human resource infrastructure is not there in many rural areas. Gradually, certain skills are known to abound in certain locations. For instance, some cities, such as Bangalore and Pune in India, have emerged as IT hubs, and human resources are concentrated in these areas. Likewise, IT companies get headquartered in Silicon Valley California or Seattle, Washington.

Organizations have to devise ways to attract people and formulate policies to procure an adequate supply of trained professionals to run the complex and hi-end technology. Many organizations give retention bonus at the end of the year; others plan career progression, sponsor training, and education.

Typically, after receiving continuing education benefits, employees may be made to sign a bond assuring minimum number of years they will stay with the organization and bound by a sum to be paid if they break the bond.

Other human resource policies, such as work from home, flexitime, and competitive packages, also help in attracting and retaining talent along with development of human infrastructure in selected areas; other infrastructural facilities such as roads, power outages, traffic, and climatic conditions affect the life in these areas, and there is a need to improve the infrastructure in all ways to make it congenial for the workforce to work. Every organization is unique in terms of IT infrastructure, the business applications that run business processes, and the support services infrastructure.

The main considerations that governs IT are:

1. Availability
2. Confidentiality
3. Integrity

Technology supports business by providing support functions. These include the following:

■ Providing a secure IT infrastructure to carry out the business processes
■ Maintaining a complete inventory of all IT assets
■ Providing for backups for data and applications and maintaining off-site copies for business continuity
■ Providing security for business processes
■ Maintaining data center to provide data continuity for the organization

Building an IT infrastructure, maintaining it, and enhancing it are important, but protecting the infrastructure is equally important.

Confidentiality: Organizations hold public information on their servers. Such information is bound by privacy laws and other standards like PCI DSS where applicable. The impact from noncompliance is financial penalties and confiscation of business license in some places. Hence, it is obligatory for organizations to plan for safeguarding the data.

Maintaining integrity of data is protecting it from being changed in an unauthorized manner. The integrity of data stored in databases versus integrity of data/information passing through telecommunication channels outside the organization, all, comes under the purview of data security. Use of checksums, integrity checkers, and CRC checks help compute whether integrity of data is preserved. Maintaining proper version control over data distributed at different locations also contributes toward maintenance of data integrity.

Availability of data: In our entire experience in the BCM sector, we have noticed that users are very sceptical over nonavailability of information systems or technically speaking "downtime." Organizations plan their infrastructure and data centres in particular to provide high availability. They provide self-generating power to survive for two or three days; they have fire resistant walls; and they hold superior quality fire-suppressant equipment, air-conditioning systems, and so on to give reliability an assurance of high availability of systems.

Consider that data owners may belong to the functional departments but the custodians of data belong to the IT department, and they are responsible for the security of the data. Having said that it emerges out that IT has a big role to play in the DR strategy and implementation.

IT Disaster Recovery Plan

Disaster recovery of information technology (IT) components support restoring operations critical to the resumption of business, including regaining access to data (records, hardware, software, etc.), communications (e-mail, phone, etc.), workspace, and other business processes after a disaster. A well-established and thoroughly tested disaster recovery plan must be developed in harmony with the BCM plan to increase the probability of successfully recovering vital organization records.

Business environment is changing; enterprises are moving toward real-time environments that operate on 24/7. In a client-centric market, expectations from clients can be demanding, and there is a need for faster connectivity and a 24/7 availability of critical infrastructure for continuity of service (Figure 6.8).

Operations always look for business recovery. Business recovery strategy provides protection of vital records, data backups storage preservation of data, and a means to meet the agreed RTOs and RPOs. This will include the following:

1. Review of vendors
2. Priority clause in outsourcing agreements
3. Choice of hot, cold, warm, mobile, or other option for recovering processing

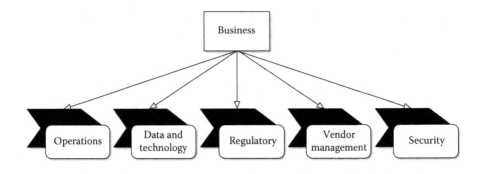

Figure 6.8   Business components of ITDR.

4. Guarantee of delivery clause in vendor agreements
5. Arrangement of alternate staff
6. Providing for redundancies in components to be used in recovery
7. Cross training of staff
8. Workarounds
9. Stock piling of critical supplies for shelters
10. Minimum IT requirements including hardware requirements, software applications to be loaded, and networking requirements
11. Cost-benefit analysis and timeline for implementation

Data disaster has been defined as "any event that can cause a significant disruption in operational and/or computer processing capabilities for a period of time, which affects the operations of the business." The causes of disaster may range from the following:

1. Failure of a support function to a critical business function.
2. The service cannot be restored within the RTO fixed for the business function.

Storage and Server Options

1. *Conventional backup*: This involves backing up the various servers and storing them at off-site location.
2. *Redundant array of inexpensive disks (RAID) servers*: This is advantageous as it introduces redundancy within the server that renders security from data loss. It is an array of redundant disks used to store data.

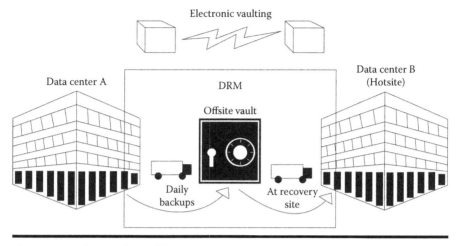

Figure 6.9   Electronic vaulting.

3. *Remote journaling*: It is the process of collecting the writes to the logs and journals and transmitting them to a remote site. It can be done in real time, that is, by simultaneously transmitting the writes or can be achieved by extracting the writes and periodically transmitting them. It does not update the database but only sends the logs, so that recovery can be achieved to the point of last transmission. This can mean nearly no loss of data. Remote journaling is not a stand-alone method and needs a starting point on which the logs are applied.

4. *Electronic vaulting*: This transmits data electronically and automatically creates the backup offsite (Figure 6.9).

No physical transport of data is necessary. It enables fast transfer of data to an offsite location, and the frequency of backup can be increased without the need for manual supervision. Vaulting at the hot site gives a very good RPO. When used with remote journaling—also sent to the hot site—it drastically reduces the outage time, thus achieving good RTO too. The only limiting factor in this method is the cost of the bandwidth that has to be available for transfer of data.

Data Backup

An integral function of IT support is to take daily backups. The objective of taking backups is to save data without corruption in a manner that reduces storage space and the impact on bandwidth usage and computing resources. There are six main methods for taking backups:

1. *Full backup*: It is a full copy of the entire data taken on a preset schedule (daily, weekly, monthly) and stored on removable storage media. It is mostly an automatic function, and backup files are compressed although this methodology requires a lot of storage space.

Advantage of this method is that restoration becomes easy. Restoration needs file name, location, and date from which to restore the data. Restoration becomes simple once backup files from the stipulated date and time are made available. But taking full backup creates multiple copies of data that may not have changed, and it takes a lot of storage space as well. Hence it would be good to explore other methodologies as per requirement.

2. *Incremental backups*: It consists of backing up only those files that have been created or changed since the last backup. The benefit being that the volume of data backups is reduced substantially, which saves storage space on backup media and utilizes lesser network bandwidth. However, such backups increase the computing overhead because each source file has to be compared with the last full backup and the incremental iterations to ascertain whether data are new or changed.

   Likewise locating a file to restore may involve going through several iterations and taking care to see that only the most recent version of each file is used. Many organizations' backup strategies include a combination of full and incremental backups at different periodicities. For instance, they may choose incremental backups to be taken daily and a full backup to be taken weekly, when the network usage is not heavy. (nonpeak time).

3. *Differential backup*: In this method, each backup stores the new and updated files since the last full backup. For instance, if the full backup was taken on the last day of the last week, then if the file was changed on Tuesday, that file will be a part of every backup till that week ends until at the end of the week, a full backup is taken. The last full backup and the last differential backup are needed to initiate recovery. Differential backups need more space and network bandwidth compared to incremental backups.

4. *Virtual full backups*: Full virtual backups use a database to track and manage backed-up data that helps avoid some of the pitfalls of other backup methods. A full copy or replica is taken once and does not need to be taken again so long as the storage medium typically a network-attached storage location remains unchanged. The virtual full backup periodically synchronizes backup data to the database. Virtual full backups are usually performed automatically by backup software. Restoration of one file or an entire disk is a matter of choosing a preferred recovery point and the file or files that are to be recovered.

5. *Synthetic full backup*: This method combines the existing full backup that is indistinguishable from a full backup. Advantage of this method is the reduced restore times. Restoring a synthetic full backup does not require the backup operator to restore multiple tape sets as an incremental backup does. Synthetic full backups provide all of the advantages of a true full backup but offer the decreased backup times and decrease bandwidth usage of an incremental backup.

6. *Incremental forever backups*: This method is used by disk-to-disk tape backup systems. An incremental forever backup begins by taking a full backup of the

data set. After that point, only incremental backups are taken. A differentiating feature of this method is the availability of data. Restoring an incremental backup requires the tape containing the full backup and every subsequent backup up to the backup that you want to restore.

The backup server typically stores all of the backup sets on either a large disk array or in a tape library. It automates the process of restoration, so that users do not have to ascertain which tapes need to be restored. The process of restoration of the incremental data becomes completely transparent and is akin to the restoration of a full backup.

Data Marts

Rather than storing all enterprise data in one data warehouse, many organizations have created multiple data marts, each containing a subset of the data for a single aspect of a company's business—for example, finance, inventory, or personnel. Data mart is a limited scope data warehouse. It contains selected information from the data warehouse such that each separate data mart is customized for the decision support applications of a particular end-user group.

For example, an organization may have several data marts, such as a marketing data mart or a finance data mart, that are customized for a particular type of user. Data marts are generally featured by small and medium-sized businesses who cannot afford to have data warehouse due to the huge outlay involved.

Choosing the Right Backup Strategy

Organizations choose their backup strategy as per their requirement to be up and about after a crisis. Backup methodology is based on the following:

1. What is the service level agreement (SLA) in regard to the RTO and RPO signed in the business impact analysis (BIA) and RA stage?
2. Hat is the organizational policy regarding storing backup tapes at off-site location.
3. What types of backups do the application support and whether backups are made using a software?

While new emerging methods of backups such as synthetic full backups and incremental forever backups modernize the backup process, the method selected must align well with the type of business requirement, and efforts should be directed toward optimization of cost keeping in mind maximization of benefits.

The most recommended strategy for backups is 3-2-1, which includes three copies of backups, one copy onsite, two media for storage of data, and one copy of backups on an off-site location.

Disk Replication (Mirroring, Shadowing)

Mirroring is a good option where the requirement is zero data loss. It is a synchronous process of writing the data to the replicated server in the same way as writing the data to the primary server. It protects from disk failures and provides an up-to-date copy of the data, thus providing an excellent RPO. In this method, a point of control is the adequacy of the bandwidth which may sometimes cause performance degradation. Hence mirror sites are not kept at long distances. If the replicated server is placed at the hot site, only logs of uncommitted work have to be run for complete recovery thus reducing the RTO to a small lapse.

The question is how does it work? There is a signal exchanged between the servers at preset intervals. When there is failure in communication, the replicated server informs the primary server of possible problems in primary server. This can cause a manually planned switch to the replicated server or can be set up for an autoswitch. It gives two options here: mirroring and shadowing.

To face the challenges posed by new business and regulatory trends, enterprises need to adopt technologies that enable high-availability systems, real-time communications, and faster recovery times while minimizing IT cost. Advances in telecommunications, more user-friendly technology, improved data storage solutions, cost-effective virtualized environments, and cloud computing are enabling enterprises to increase data storage capabilities, to become agile, and to improve business resilience. There is a significant trend to achieve organizational resilience through server virtualization and cloud-computing technology.

Server virtualization and cloud computing assist in reducing planned outages by equipping the business to move applications to temporary during system maintenance, firmware upgrades, critical patching, and DR testing. Unplanned outages can also be minimized due to the ability to take configuration snapshots of mission-critical virtual machines and to restore them using similar hardware devices in shorter periods of time within the same data center or across geographic areas.

Server Virtualization

Virtual desktop infrastructure (VDI) has a positive impact on BCM by enabling distributed work forces and access to critical applications during a disaster. Employees will be able to access the applications via Internet configured using virtual desktops. This can protect reputation loss resulting from a break in customer support during an outage. Leveraging VDI as part of the BCM strategy can help reduce the cost associated with work area recovery because the efforts to recover physical facilities may be spread over longer periods of time without sacrificing productivity or efficiency.

Business Recovery in a Cloud

Organization's decision to adopt cloud computing has a big impact on IT since critical business operations get affected. Organizations need an enterprise-wide approach that takes in the cross-functional effects of cloud computing. The approach may vary depending on the chosen cloud service model, deployment model, and the maturity of existing business and IT processes. The lessons learned from outsourcing apply in the cloud as cloud service providers (CSPs) practices become popular.

Cloud Services: Computing

Cloud backups help to keep organizational backups; it is more advisable for data for which the security aspect is not significant since cloud storage always comes with security concerns. Ensuring continuity for cloud services is the responsibility of the cloud service provider; however, the enterprise must be diligent during contract negotiations and establish SLAs that clearly define continuity expectations for critical applications and, if necessary, must maintain internal contingency plans to alleviate vendor failure to meet SLAs (Figure 6.10).

Choice of cloud services can range from a private cloud dedicated for the enterprise to a public cloud that hosts more than one enterprise data. A private cloud takes all of the infrastructure technology that runs a public cloud and stores it on premise. Users achieve the same functionality and ability to access their data through a web browser. However, instead of sharing the computing power with the general public, the computing power is shared among users at one company.

Contrary to the public cloud model, a private cloud requires an IT department to perform maintenance and upkeep. But it is an expensive option, and only large enterprises hosting large amount of data can justify use of private cloud.

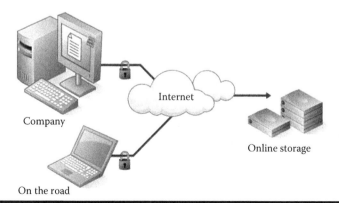

Figure 6.10 DR services in cloud.

Backup to the Public Cloud

Use of Infrastructure as a Service (IaaS) to reduce running costs is increasing among many organizations as part of their public cloud adoption. Public cloud vendors leverage public cloud storage by facilitating the backup of the virtual data centre to more than one storage provider including Amazon, Azure, and Google cloud storage platforms.

The backup and replication cloud enables organizations to consider cloud as an off-site DR target to store their backups using built-in encryption to comply with any security requirements. Such facility provides the ultimate solution for IT operation continuity from the DR site. Replication technology used by some cloud providers helps achieve best RTOs and RPOs through deployment of near continuous data protection (near CDP) approach.

Other trends, such as mobile devices and social networks, are improving the way enterprises communicate, interact, and collaborate with customers, suppliers, employees, government agencies, and peers during a business disruption. While virtualization and cloud are transforming IT service delivery, the rate of change to infrastructure is accelerating, sometimes out of control.

Hardware upgrades, software updates, middleware patches, security, and DR assurance in response to the need to continuously verify and ensure that protection processes remain current and capable of delivering SLAs contracted with the line of business and application owners.

Whatever the cause of outages, assuring recovery and continuity can only be done through a much higher level of automation and orchestration across the different layers of the service delivery stack from the network to the application.

Legacy mechanisms for DR testing are mostly manual, expensive, disruptive, and infrequent—yearly, for most organizations. There are products available that automate DR testing and make it more iterative. Such automated systems do not cause interference in production, and the backups are taken at preset regularity (hourly, daily, or some other iterative cycle).

Use of IT Services to Improve Resiliency

IT services that help in the betterment of resilience within the organization are "Backup as a Service (BaaS)," "Storage as a Service (STaaS)," "DR as a service (DRaaS)," and "Software as a Service (SaaS)." The main advantage of these services is that they can help enterprises improve resiliency while maintaining the initial investment cost and keeping down the operating cost. Let us view these services in brief.

Backup as a Service (BaaS)

Backup as a service provides a set of capabilities that pure "SaaS" or public cloud-based online backup services do not. It is a consultative approach to determine customer needs and an ideal solution. It results in the provision of customized service contracts and products based on requirements and SLAs (Figure 6.11).

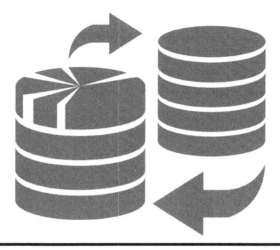

Figure 6.11 BaaS.

Such managed services' capabilities include configuration and implementation, monitoring, reporting, assistance with first backup and/or full recovery, and initiation of restores. Products are available to be used by service providers that can enhance the service offerings for backups to their customer base.

Storage as a Service (STaaS)

A lot of service providers provide storage as a service; they help organizations to build and deploy performance-optimized storage and data protection services with low cost and predictable service levels. They provide on premise public cloud and hybrid users, they help IT administrators and IT teams to maintain the service by delivering 24/7 proactive support and seamless upgrades coupled with a suitably drafted SLA that provides a 24/7 uptime.

DR as a Service

DRaaS is targeted at enterprises deploying DR on physical, private cloud, or public cloud. The solution's multitenancy capabilities and comprehensive coverage of the DR life cycle make it the leading management solution to enable hybrid DR deployments. It enables features such as multitenancy, prepackaged best practice workflows, and automation of the DR process that makes it possible for the service organizations to offer scalable, secure, and automated DR services.

To be able to deploy and manage DR solutions, service providers must use tools to monitor and automate their DR process. Without using tools, service providers cannot scale their services and cannot assure customer that they are able to meet SLAs. DRaaS enables enterprise IT teams to offer robust DR services with stringent SLAs to their business teams. This solution offers a "pay per use" option, which is a very cost-effective alternative to maintaining a second location for DR purposes.

Software as a Service

Gartner defines *SaaS* as software that is owned, delivered, and managed remotely by one or more providers. The provider delivers software based on one set of common code and data definitions that are consumed in a one-to-many model by all contracted customers at any time on a pay-for-use basis or as a subscription based on use metrics. SaaS is a method of software delivery that allows data to be accessed from any device with an Internet connection and web browser.

In this web-based model, software vendors host and maintain the servers, databases, and code that constitute an application. This is a significant departure from the on-premise software delivery model. First, companies do not have to invest in extensive hardware to host the software, and this in turn allows buyers to outsource most of the IT responsibilities typically required to troubleshoot and maintain the software. The SaaS vendor takes care of it all (Figure 6.12).

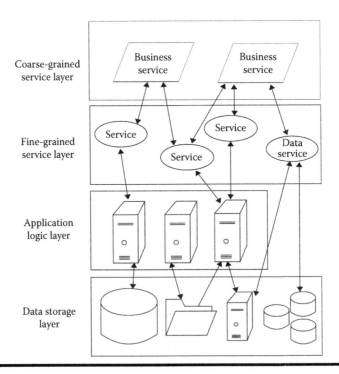

Figure 6.12   Software as service (SaaS).

In addition to allowing remote access via the web to the software applications and data, SaaS also differs from on-premise software in its pricing model. Enterprises have to purchase license for on-premise software; in addition, they have to pay for its maintenance and sometimes for the latest upgrades. In contrast, SaaS allows buyers to pay an annual or monthly subscription fee, which typically includes the software license, support, and most other fees. A major benefit of SaaS is being able to spread out costs over time.

In terms of data ownership, buyers should ensure there is a clause in their SLA that clearly states that they own the data. Most SaaS contracts have built-in and prepaid contingencies that will provide access to your data if the vendors go out of business. Most of the SaaS vendors will allow their clients to export their data and back it up locally any time they want.

Security of organizational data is of prime consideration when allowing third-party service providers to maintain business critical data. However, with online banking and online payroll systems becoming the norm today, the security issue seems to be a bit of a red herring. Few things are more important than our bank accounts, yet most of us are comfortable with putting this information in the cloud. SaaS vendors have to undergo stringent security procedures such as SSAE16 Type I and Type II audits that test the data centre's level of security.

Evaluation of Business Continuity Strategy of Critical Vendors

The shift of IT services to specialized third-party service providers is driving higher expectations of greater utilization and efficiency. While there are both financial and performance improvements associated with a greater resource and infrastructure mix (internal IT, outsourcing, and offshoring), there are also new threats and vulnerabilities to business performance, security, and continuity arising from growing interdependencies with third-party service providers.

These interdependencies make it all the more critical to anticipate and plan how to respond in the event of a disruption or natural disaster affecting a third-party service provider.

Performing an evaluation of vendors for assessing the business continuity capabilities is now being exercised by organizations mainly because the standards for BCM are recommending that it should be done. A "right to audit clause" is preferred in the contract, and it is possible to visit the vendors' installation for a survey or audit.

There are time and resource constraints to carry out such evaluation. Alternatively, a questionnaire mapping the chief information that the organization wishes to obtain from vendors must be drafted and communicated to vendors (Table 6.1).

The following table summarizes these five questions that you should ask your suppliers, as well as high-quality answers you should expect, and possible follow-up questions for each topic.

Table 6.1 Tier II Metrics for BCM

Your Question	The Answer You Should Expect	Possible Follow-Up Question(s)
1. How have you handled the scoping of your BCM program, and how does it impact the recoverability of products/services offered to our organization?	We performed a business impact analysis (BIA) that aligns our internal business operations to each of our customers' products and services. For the products/services we deliver to your organization, we are performing risk mitigation and recovery planning.	Specific to the scope of your preparedness efforts, are you addressing all aspects of recoverability, meaning your facilities, people, technology, suppliers, and equipment/ resources?
2. Please describe your strategy to recover aspects of your business that deliver our products/services.	The answer to this will be situation specific, although the reply should describe how and where key business and technology processes are recovered, as well as supply chain risk management activities.	When will these capabilities be available following a disruptive event and at what level of performance?
3. How have you validated that your business continuity strategies work as designed?	We perform annual exercises (tests) of our business continuity strategies and involve those that will be leading the response and recovery efforts. We set exercise objectives, success criteria, and compare results to predetermined objectives.	What is the scope of your exercises—a loss of primary work locations, a loss of technology, other?
4. Is the management proactively involved in reviewing and improving the BCM program?	We have a steering committee that meets on a quarterly basis to offer input on scoping and objectives, as well as feedback on our BCM program.	

(Continued)

Table 6.1 (*Continued*) Tier II Metrics for BCM

Your Question	The Answer You Should Expect	Possible Follow-Up Question(s)
5. How do you tackle improvement opportunities in order to ensure your organization is best prepared to address our organization's needs?	We track corrective and preventive actions in a list that is reviewed and reprioritized monthly by our business continuity team and quarterly by our steering committee.	Which of these are the sources of the corrective and preventive actions (exercises, audits, business impact analyses, risk assessments, management reviews)?

But simply administering a questionnaire is not enough. There is a need for a two-way dialog to share preparedness techniques and expectations. To ensure readiness, organizations can work with the vendor's supply chain management team to draft an enforceable SLA, which includes their preparedness efforts over a long term (maybe two or three years).

Besides, standards have been developed such as SSAE 16 and ISAE 3402 that prescribe Type I and Type II audits of vendors to ascertain the design efficiency and effectiveness of controls implemented at vendor's installation. Underlying principles in these standards are to ensure security (confidentiality, integrity, and availability of data and systems) governed by principles of trust. Vendor evaluation has grown in significance due to an increase in the outsourced services. Refer to the COBIT framework given below.

COBIT 5 defines the roles and responsibilities of the different stakeholders in the contractual agreements. The RACI (responsible, accountable, consulted, and informed) chart is as shown in Table 6.2. Let us consider the role of each of the following personnel:

1. *C-level executives*: They are accountable for the vendor management process; the extent of accountability depends on the scale of outsourcing.
2. *Business process officers*: Business process officers should be actively involved in the vendor management life cycle.
3. *Procurement*: Many responsibilities within the vendor management life cycle belong to the procurement function.
4. *Legal*: To effectively mitigate vendor-related risk, the legal function should be involved throughout the entire vendor management life cycle.

Table 6.2   COBIT 5 Framework for Vendor Management

Vendor Management RACI Chart				
Contractual Relationship Life Cycle				
Stakeholders	*Setup*	*Contract*	*Operations*	*Transition Out*
C-level executives	A	A	A	A
Business process owners	R	R	I	R
Procurement	R	R	I	R
Legal	R	R	C	C
Risk function	C	C	R	R
Compliance and audit	C	C	C	C
IT	R	R	R	R
Security	R	C	R	C
Human resources (HR)	C	C	C	C

5. *Risk function*: The risk function should be consulted throughout the vendor management life cycle to obtain a complete view on risk that is related to the relationship, services, or products.
6. *Compliance and audit*: The compliance and audit functions should be consulted throughout the vendor management life cycle to ensure compliance with internal and external laws, regulations, and policies.
7. *IT*: The IT role is significant because its members may be more familiar with the products and services and their market availability.
8. *Human resources (HR)*: The HR has to ensure compliance with the enterprise's worker statutes, local regulations, and code of conduct and labor law.

Legal and Regulatory Considerations in a Business Recovery

The disperse storage or processing of data exposes enterprises to potential legal and regulatory risk. In some cases, there may be no legal precedent to define roles, responsibilities, and liabilities of data owners and service providers across jurisdictions. Therefore, it is vital that enterprises secure, under contract, the right to know the ultimate location of its BCM strategies.

Failure to implement the necessary processes to address disruptive events can result in penalties, even if the enterprise is not obligated to meet a particular regulatory requirement for BCM. Internal or external SLAs or contractual obligations may include clauses related to availability service levels or production commitments that should be maintained.

Security of Operations, a Key Consideration in Recovery Planning

Security is an important component of the ITDR. In the backdrop of global operations, it has become imperative that the security of operations should be preserved.

Separation of duties: This procedural control is intended to meet certain regulatory and audit system requirements by helping ensure that one single individual does not have total control over a programming process without appropriate review points or requiring other individuals to perform certain tasks within the process prior to final user acceptance. For example, someone other than the original developer would be responsible for loading the program to the production environment from a staging library.

Version and configuration control: Refers to maintaining control over the versions of software checked out for update being loaded to staging or production libraries, and so on. This would include the monitoring of error reports associated with this activity and taking appropriate corrective action.

Periodic testing: Involves taking a test case and periodically running the system with known data, which have predictable results. The intent is to ensure the system still performs as expected and does not produce inconsistent results.

Random checking: Production checking of defined data and results.

Access control of software: In some applications, the coding techniques and other information contained within the program are sensitive to disclosure, or unauthorized access could have an economic impact. Therefore, the source code must be protected from unauthorized access.

Virus checking: All software destined for a PC platform, regardless of source, should be scanned by an authorized virus-scanning program for computer viruses before it is loaded into production on the PC or placed on a file server for distribution. Some applications would have periodic testing as part of a software quality assurance plan.

A phased approach in enforcing security controls will most likely produce better results. The allocation of roles and responsibilities should develop the initial implementation plan. This plan should consider using a phased approach—first to identify from the risk assessment data those applications that are critical by order of magnitude to the organization (such as time-critical business functions first, etc.) and then defining security parameters.

Security training programs must be developed and must be ready to implement at regular intervals to make team members aware of the policy, procedures, and preventive controls to be exercised in carrying out business operations.

Another important aspect faced by security professionals in the conduct of their duties is to tackle cultural aspects arising from cross-country business operations. If the organization is geographically limited to one continent and one nation, then the challenges to information security are a little less severe. However, in an era of globalization, as business expands to other nations and continents, the information security challenges and threats increase tremendously.

Some major challenges to be dealt with includes the following:

1. Factors that negatively motivate people to indulge in unauthorized, illegal activities and to understand how they can be diverted toward complying with organizational policies and security procedures.
2. Misunderstandings may be caused due to disparity in culture and language barriers caused by interaction of people who work on global operations.

Managing risk effectively enables senior management to make better decisions for aligning BCM with business and IT strategies to eliminate redundancies; to manage resources efficiently; and to still meet shareholder, customer, and regulatory expectations and requirements for resilience and recovery capabilities.

IT Disaster Recovery Management Program Office

The IT disaster recovery management (IT DRM) program office is responsible for planning, building, running, and governing the implementation of the IT disaster recovery program. The office is responsible for ensuring that appropriate preparedness, response and recovery policies, standards, risk mitigation controls, procedures, plans, and solutions exist and are applied for all IT services throughout the enterprise (Figure 6.13).

This office is responsible for determining the methods used to implement and enforce IT DRM policies; for measuring and reporting on the level of compliance to such policies; and for advising the enterprise on IT DRM preparedness, response, and recovery-related issues on a day-to-day basis. The IT DRM office ensures, in particular, that IT DRM awareness is increased, and that all risk mitigation controls, plans, and solutions are exercised on a regular basis.

The office is responsible for reporting the status and effectiveness of the IT DRM program to the BCM program office leader and executive management team. The IT DRM leader is typically a member of the BCM steering committee as well as the crisis/incident management team.

For organizations that have a multiple data center footprint, local, and regional IT DRM program offices may be set up to manage the IT DRM program initiative for those locations. Each of these local/region program offices would then report directly into the enterprise IT.

DRM program office and, in some cases—for example, country and major geographic region—also report into local/regional management.

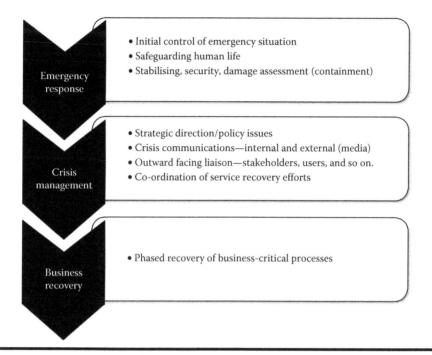

Figure 6.13   IT DRM program.

IT DRM Team Organization

The BCM leader, in collaboration with executive management and the BCM steering committee, determines the formation and reporting relationships of the BCM organization.

Refer below for ITDR Program Office Sample:

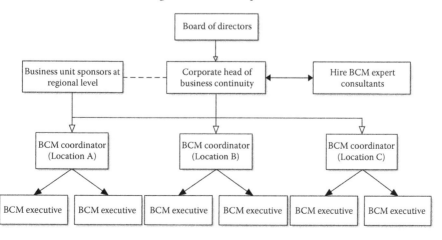

This includes appointing and managing individuals with appropriate skill sets to the BCM team, as well as requesting the appointment of BCM coordinators in all business units to be part of the enterprise-wide BCM implementation team.

All business-unit BCM coordinators will be empowered by their respective management teams to fully represent them in the development and exercising of all components of the organization's BCM program. Typically, the BCM coordinator reports to the business unit for which it has BCM responsibility and would have a dotted-line reporting relationship into the local/regional/enterprise BCM program office.

In addition, there may be a BCM program site coordinator for each location. The site coordinator would be in charge at the time of a crisis and coordinate all response, recovery, and restoration activities. There are a number of business units that have responsibilities over and above ensuring that their department/business unit is recovered when a crisis strikes.

These business units, along with their crisis-specific responsibilities, follow:

- *Public/investor relations and corporate communications*: Coordinating internal and external crisis communications and messaging throughout the life cycle of the crisis.
- *Human resources*: Coordinating communications regarding the impact of the crisis to employees and their families.
- *Travel*: Coordinating travel-related activities for recovery staff, stranded employees, and those injured.
- *Financial services*: Managing crisis-related expenditures over and above day-to-day operations levels.
- *Insurance*: Managing all insurance claims to the organization's property and casualty policy insurance providers.

BCM Governance Decisions

BCM governance is the program governance, which is initiated by the top management to establish a business continuity management system commensurate with the scale and size of the business and organization.

BCM governance has eight domains:

- *Vision, mission, principles, and policies*: High-level statements about how BCM is valuable to the business and the rules to govern the execution and management of the BCM program
- *Program management*: Decisions about how the BCM program will be implemented, measured, and improved upon over time
- *Budgets and investments*: Decisions about how much and where to invest in BCM, including project approvals and justification techniques (via demand governance processes)

- *Architecture*: A set of policies, processes, standards, and rules that govern the preparedness and activation of BCM (includes data, technology, processes, applications, and facilities)
- *Risk assessment and BIA*: The foundation for the BCM program and subsequent mitigation strategies and tactics
- *Recovery strategies and solutions (business and IT)*: An integrated set of strategy and solution choices to guide the organization in satisfying BCM needs
- *Supply chain risk management*: Decisions about all vendor relationships, including due diligence to ensure vendors meet availability requirements or, if not, to decide on alternate sources
- *Activation and execution*: Decisions about how and by whom BCM will be activated and executed, as well as when a disaster will be declared

BCM Program Implementation and Management Processes and Mechanisms

Once the BCM program sponsorship and governance are established, the next step is to develop a set of BCM program implementation and management processes and mechanisms.

Preliminary Steps

Before commencing on this task, it would pay to perform a need analysis.

1. *Needs assessment*: This can involve talking with stakeholders, analyzing existing data, doing surveys to identify need, and looking what other programs and activities are already occurring. The purpose is to define if there is a need and to detail as much as possible what that need is, so that the program can be designed to meet the need. The following factors need consideration as follows:
   - Identify applicable BCM standards, regulations, and contractual obligations for recovery.
   - Inventory organizational resources/assets: workforce, facilities, suppliers, IT, vital records, special equipment, and forms.
2. *Review of literature, previous experience*: A review of the literature is a summary of the research findings from the past, which relate to the program. It ranges from an informal look at publications in relevant area to highly structured systematic reviews. Such reviews are performed by evaluators who have been there around and who possess information about past precedents and incidents and can add value to the BCM program.
3. *Document analysis*: Analysis of documents such as formal reports, minutes of meetings, memos, and print media reports or electronic media transcripts to make an analysis either quantitative and/or qualitative that can give input for the BCM program development.

Developing the BCM Program

BCM program must be commensurated to the size and spread of the organization's business processes. As seen in the diagram below, business sites are on one side and ITDR components of platform, telephony, networks, data, applications, and information security are on the other side. The BCM program management coordinates between the BCM coordinators and the ITDR management to fulfill their BCM requirements (Figure 6.14).

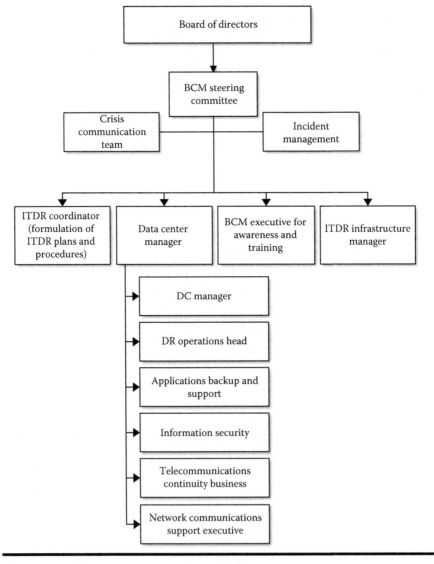

Figure 6.14   BCM program operating model.

The BCM program is based on requirements and key program development components (business recovery, IT service continuity management, crisis/incident management, supplier contingency) that address the key organizational resources/ assets: workforce, facilities, suppliers, IT, vital records, special equipment, and forms. Linkage between assets and BCM components has to be performed, and the same has to be further linked to recovery strategies. BCM program team will customize the BCM program as per the need for recovery of critical business operations and considering the time and cost constraints.

Disaster Recovery Scenario

It is always advantageous to build scenarios and base plans around the findings from such scenarios. Let us say we want to address a scenario where there is a loss of access to the data center and the data-processing capabilities of those systems and the network connectivity. Although loss of access to the facility may be more probable, this disaster recovery plan will only address recovery of the critical systems and essential communications. This scenario also assumes that all equipment in the computer room is not salvageable and that all critical telecommunications capability has been lost.

Emergency response plan assuming that a disaster is declared, key personnel will take immediate action to alert the disaster recovery site and the backup site for immediate action. Activities will include, without limitation, the following:

1. Delivery of the authorized user data and software archived in off-site storage to the disaster recovery center
2. Connecting network lines to the disaster recovery center
3. Operating the critical applications on the configuration at the disaster recovery center
4. Provide critical coverage at the disaster recovery center
5. Provide workspace and required equipment

In this scenario, different alternatives may be considered. Let us say Unit A does not wish to relocate to DR site. Their requirements are fulfilled by a fully configured Laptop and a VPN connection linking them to DR site. They are the work from anywhere team and the business-unit managers undertake to coordinate with the IT team for the resumption of their operations from these laptops.

Another alternative that can be envisaged is that there is a DR hot or warm site that will be made ready for operations, and IT teams will help the business team to start working from the DR site. Admin team members will arrange for their logistics (travel arrangements).

There will be one more possibility that the existing team cannot travel or relocate. In this case, HR will have to have readiness of contacting their agencies for the procurement of personnel with the desired skill sets, which will have been predefined during BIA stage. These contracted personnel will carry on the critical processing work till the restoration of primary data center is done.

As we see, disaster scenario development makes us walk through the situation, and all points related to the incident come to the forefront and help the BCM program personnel do a more realistic planning. Disaster scenarios can be used to test BCM programs as well as to inspire participation in risk workshops held with the purpose of mapping threats and vulnerabilities.

Implement and Validate

Once plan is prepared, it is necessary to implement it and have it validated. Also certain gaps may have been observed during the first step that needs to be addressed. The following activities need to be carried out:

- Implement risk mitigation measures
- Implement recovery strategy solutions
- Implement BCM program management tools
- Exercise recovery plans leveraging a variety of test methods (walkthrough, tabletop, unit, full, simulation)
- Incorporate feedback from exercise results into BCM processes and recovery plans as needed
- Based on exercise results, modify or update RTO/RPOs, recovery strategies, solutions, and plans, as required
- Facilitate plan invocation and debrief for business disruptions

Monitor and Manage

- Define the ongoing business case for BCM.
- Implement BCM metrics and scorecards—refer to the Establish a BCM Program Management and Status Measurement Process section in this research.
- Update KPIs and KRIs as appropriate for changes in the business.
- Ensure recovery plans are reviewed and updated on a regular basis.
- Conduct internal training and awareness.
- Review and report gap analyses and program metrics for program maturity.
- Facilitate and manage requests for BCM program audits.
- Facilitate business interruption insurance coverage (if applicable).
- Facilitate BCM program certification (if applicable).
- Integrate BCM practices with the business and IT project life cycles.
- Review and update the BCM program management practices.

BCM Program Metrics

BCM program managers are reporting to management, stakeholders, staff, HR, external auditors, customers, regulators, insurance companies, and the work force on the efficacy of the BCM program. BCM program metrics are used for such reporting as well as day-to-day management of the BCM program. Metrics should be reported at the enterprise, division, legal entity, business process/function, and location levels; different organizations have different levels to add.

The most common form of metrics is pure counts: how many recovery sites, how many employees have key skills, and so on. Other metric form is much more scientific as it is based on analytics and can be used to manage and improve the maturity of the BCM program. Defining and capturing the data for BCM program metrics are the responsibility of the BCM program office as well as the BCM program implementation organization. Monthly reporting to business units and quarterly or biannual reporting to executive management is normally followed.

Tier One Metrics in Business Continuity Programs

Within business continuity, we can identify various high-level metrics, which we can call "tier one." The best method is to set up a gap analysis excel sheet in the following form (Table 6.3).

By the below table, it is simple to compare the metric to what is currently being used. Remediation actions can then be identified and applied.

Tier Two Metrics in Business Continuity Programs

Tier two metrics are more granular and are more imminent in technology-based DR plans that deal with protection and recovery of data, prevention of cyber threats from compromising critical systems and data, recovery and restarting of critical servers, recovery of critical network infrastructure services, and relocation of staff to alternate work locations. Let us examine some Tier two metrics in Table 6.4.

Cost effectiveness is by far the best metric for evaluating recovery strategies. All types of impacts and the mitigating strategies to be quantified in terms of loss and cost of remediation in order to enable management to do a cost-benefit analysis to arrive at whether to live with or to accept the risk of no control or to build a remediating measure for the gaps are identified.

Table 6.3   BCM Metrics Table

Action Area	Metric	Current Position	Desired Situation	Recommended Status

Table 6.4 Area wise Metrics Table

Tier Two Action Areas	Examples of Metrics
Data recovery	1. Backup files to be picked for storage by time specified 2. Time to recover critical files within one hour 3. Backlog data to be entered within 24 hours of resumption
Server recovery	1. Time to restart and reboot file servers within agreed timeframe after a disaster 2. Time to physically replace servers in designated racks within 30 minutes 3. Number of errors during reboot is less than two
Data network recovery	1. Time to recover, restart, and reconfigure network routers within one hour of outage 2. Time needed to test and validate network performance before transmitting live data within one hour of outage 3. Maximum time needed to physically replace damaged network devices within four hours
Voice equipment recovery	1. Time needed to restart voice system following outage within one hour of outage 2. Maximum time for service company to arrive on site following service call within four hours 3. Time needed to resynchronize DS-1/PRI circuits with switch within four hours
Activation of hot site	1. Time needed to confirm approval from the hot site firm for recovery space within one hour of contact 2. Time needed to restart critical systems at hot site within four hours of outage 3. Time needed to relocate staff to hot site within four hours of reporting outage

Although this factor is rational, there are some nonrevenue impacts that are not measurable but hold potential to do substantial damage to the business. These include the following:

■ Loss of credibility and customer goodwill
■ Leading to noncompliance with certain regulatory requirement
■ Environmental damage

Reputation and goodwill are at stake, and management should consider customer/public facing applications, activities, and crisis communication to be of prime importance. There is also a need to link critical roles to critical resources and to a more critical resource, that is, a monetary resource to provide for continuity and the trade-off among the need to recover, the cost of failure, and the cost to recover.

Trade-off is a difficult task, and it is the responsibility of top management to provide and commit resources. Thus it can be observed from the above discussion that all metrics are generally built around the yardsticks of time and costs.

Considerations for DR Siting

A disaster recovery (DR) site is the facility that an organization uses to recover and restore its technology infrastructure and operations when its primary data center becomes unavailable. The choice of the kind of DR site suitable for the organization and its location requires careful evaluation based on cost and benefits analysis.

There are two types of DR options available to organizations: internal dedicated site and external site. Internal DR site is owned, maintained, and operated by the organization, whereas the external site is owned and operated by an outsider. Organizations which are large scale and have aggressive RTOs most likely prefer a dedicated internal DR site earmarked for the purpose. The internal site is typically a second data center and allows a company to recover and resume operations after a disaster at the primary center.

IT may not always be economical to hold a second data center establishment. Hence, more and more organizations are opting for the second option. Distance is a major consideration in the choice of recovery site. While proximity to primary processing site renders tighter synchronization and easier staff management, it is important that it should be on a different power grid than the primary site so that they are not both impacted by the same disaster. On the other hand, if the two sites are too far away, then it can be costly and replication can become difficult.

It is precisely due to these considerations and depending on the exigencies imposed by the business continuity needs, organizations may choose to plan for a second DR site. Again the DR budget will govern whether the remote DR site should be a self-owned site or a contracted site.

Considerations in Designing the DR Plant

A careful examination of surrounding region, a study of available public utility services, transportation, environment, weather, and even the crime statistics needs to be undertaken. Another factor is that members of the emergency recovery team may be reluctant to travel and go to work at a significant distance for possibly an extended period of time. There may be personal or family issues (Figure 6.15).

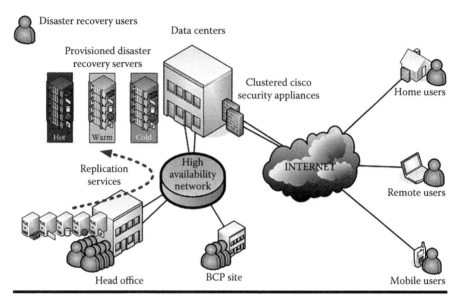

Figure 6.15   Designing DR plant.

Review the risk assessment findings to identify the areas of least chances of occurrence for disruptive events/incidents. At the same time it is to be borne in mind that one has to gauge consequences if at all such events occur. Any facility selected should be reasonably secure and should have good physical and information security provisions to prevent unauthorized access. Use an experienced architect to design the data centers and similar facilities.

A distance of 10 to 50 miles from the primary data center should be kept as a minimum benchmark for locating the DR site. Always consider the impact of a remotely located data center on your staff, especially if it may be necessary for staff to relocate their place of work to a remote location for an extended period of time.

The most important challenge that organizations face today is the recovery of processes as near to normal as possible. The most prevalent method is to go for a contracted site with necessary infrastructure and telecommunication facilities, and at the time of disaster, the backups and data will be loaded on from backup site, and till the disruption lasts, processing will take place from the contracted DR site.

Considerations in Building Own DR Site

1. Management can control the availability of key resources on site at the time of disaster and can plan with vendors close to the DR site to supply essential supplies, equipment, and communication equipment at the DR center at the time of crisis.
2. It can give more security to confidential data processed at the DR site.

3. It gives more security as there is no need to intermingle data with other organizations and no compromise of confidentiality of data.
4. Spare bandwidth can be used for processing in peak periods, and this will take off the load and result in speedy processing.

Most third-party recovery site vendors encourage regular testing of the facility in accordance with a scheduled DR plan test. Most of the times, DR testing or "right to audit" clause is a part of the SLA entered into with the DR vendor. An annual test of facility is highly advisable as a minimum, although a biyearly testing would increase the DR budget.

Disadvantages of dedicated own site:

1. Increased start up investment
2. Costs for staffing and maintenance of backup site

Advantages of an outsourced disaster recovery site include the following:

1. Minimum or no costs of setting up.
2. Staffing costs are shared, and technology infrastructure is available at DR location.
3. Physical security is the responsibility of the outsourced parties.
4. Since the vendor is in the business of providing DR, the on-site subject matter expertise exists on a 24/7 basis.

Disadvantages of outsourced DR site vendor:

1. Confidentiality and integrity of data can be at stake.
2. Facilities may be contracted to many clients and if there is an outage in a particular area, it is possible that every client will want to have priority on the availability of DR site resulting in confusion.
3. The SLA may not provide for order of preference in case of global disaster. It may not include testing provisions.

The processes will be recovered at the Disaster Recovery Services provider name and location of the Hot Site. The Disaster Recovery Services provider name is responsible for ensuring that the system configurations and the associated network requirements are accurate and technically feasible at all times. Therefore, yearly testing will be a part of the alternate processing strategy.

Also, the associated network connectivity will be recovered, within the disaster recovery scenario, using the alternate processing strategy. Recovery phases' recovery activities will be conducted in a phased approach. The emphasis will be to recover the critical applications effectively and efficiently. Critical applications will be recovered over a period of time after data center activation.

Updates to the DR Plan

A formal review of a disaster recovery plan should be conducted yearly, and a quarterly Disaster Recovery Readiness Assessment Audit should be conducted as well. The purpose of the reviews and the audits is to identify any changes to ensure that these and any other updates identified since the previous review has been captured.

Audit/History

Information documenting the software change such as the work request detailing the work to be performed, test plans, test results, corrective actions, approvals, who performed the work, and other pertinent documentation required by the business.

These reviews will require the time and attention of all plan holders and participants, especially those that have hardware and network responsibilities. The proper maintenance of the plan will be the responsibility of ALL holders of the plan. They will be responsible for incorporating approved changes/revisions to the plan, and keeping it current and ready.

The DR plan may require updates if problems or changes include some or any of the following:

1. New critical applications are introduced, or critical customers are added.
2. Increased application complexity.
3. Personnel changes.
4. Mission changes.
5. Priority changes.
6. New equipment acquisitions.
7. Changes in backup procedures.
8. Changes to hardware, software, network, and applications.
9. DR test procedures and results.

Disaster Recovery Testing

The purpose of DR plan testing is to specifically identify and document the task plan and procedures to be implemented in a testing environment. This test plan includes test parameters, objectives, measurement criteria, test methodology, task plan charts, and time lines to validate the effectiveness of the current disaster recovery plan.

The disaster recovery plan will be tested to ensure that the business has the ability to continue the critical business processes in the event of a disaster. Testing can be accomplished by executing the disaster implementation plan, or it may be desirable to execute a subset of the plan. It is extremely necessary to validate that recovery procedures outlined in the plan are executable and accurate.

Another factor is to train personnel who will take responsibility for executing the DR plan. Test results and problems encountered must be documented, and plan should be improvised based on "lessons learned" from the test. When performing a Disaster Recovery Test, it is very important to use only that information, which is recalled from the off-site storage facility. This will contribute toward simulating the conditions of an actual disaster.

Administration/Maintenance of the Plan

DR plan maintenance is important to ensure currency of what is to be recovered and procedures governing the recovery. This means keeping the test plan and implementation plan current and in sync with business changes has to be emphasized. All changes to be documented in the form of updates to the plan.

Emerging Technology Benefits for BCM

1. *Financial and strategic objectives* can be achieved through effective utilization of emerging technologies within a BCM program. However to realize these objectives, the enterprise needs to first address new risk introduced through the adoption of new technologies to minimize negative impacts and maximize benefits. Managing risk effectively enables senior management to make better decisions for aligning BCM with business and IT strategies to eliminate redundancies, to manage resources efficiently, and still to meet shareholder, customer and regulatory expectations, and requirements for resilience and recovery capabilities.

2. *Improved resilience*: Server virtualization and cloud computing help reduce planned outages by providing the ability to move applications to temporary environments during system maintenance, firmware upgrades, critical patching, and DR testing.

3. *Unplanned outages* can also be minimized due to the ability to take configuration snapshots of mission-critical virtual machines and to restore them using similar hardware devices in shorter periods of time within the same data center or across geographic areas.

4. *Managing risk effectively* enables senior management to make better decisions for aligning BCM with business and IT strategies to eliminate redundancies, to manage resources efficiently, and still to meet shareholder, customer and regulatory expectations, and requirements for resilience and recovery capabilities.

5. *VDI* has a positive impact on BCM because it enables more distributed work forces and access to critical applications during a disaster. As long as employees can access the Internet, they will have access to applications configured to be delivered using virtual desktops; this can minimize productivity loss and reputational damage resulting from poor customer support during an outage.

Leveraging VDI as part of the BCM strategy can help reduce the cost associated with work area recovery because the efforts to recover physical facilities may be spread over longer periods of time without sacrificing productivity or efficiency.

Conclusion

BCM has evolved tremendously in the last ten years, new standards have evolved and are still evolving to keep pace with new technology and innovations and the new way of doing business.

Today's age is the age of e-Commerce, m-Commerce, and online businesses. All these developments are fueled by the information technology backbone, which has emerged not only as a functional department among other departments but which acts as a support function to keep information systems up and running, and as a champion in the IT DR activity to enable business to recover from disaster situations.

The introduction of the new standard BS25999 is the latest step to raise the standard bar. Its evolution into the ISO 22301 standard has given business continuity a global standard based on Societal Security. The need for BCM in the organizations is now being dictated by regulatory norms and owners of business, auditors, other stakeholders, all are working toward different standards to build organizational resilience.

Chapter 7

Business Continuity Tests and Exercises

Introduction

Business continuity plans do not hold just cosmetic value. They are the key to organizational resilience. Their success lies in how best they are executed in crisis and how team members exhibit a thorough understanding of the steps to be followed after a crisis. Training and drills are instrumental in instilling in team players a natural responsiveness based on business continuity management (BCM) plans.

Although it is true that every incident is unique, the plan execution cannot go on in its entirety. But tests and exercises create the platform for the BCM teams to show readiness to follow the plan and to adapt it to suit the need of the hour. BCM personnel understand their roles including sending notifications and participating in an orderly shutdown of facility.

In Figure 7.1, it is observed that a fully tested plan has the minimum risk, whereas if you do not have a tested plan, you may escape if you are lucky or you may face a huge impact and you may be exposed to the maximum risk, which is shown as the third point. People are most important and BCM teams must work toward protection of people first. Also, people have to be made aware of hazards, threats, and how to react during a disaster. Business continuity planning/disaster recovery (BCP/DR) drills and exercises assist in making people responsive and in

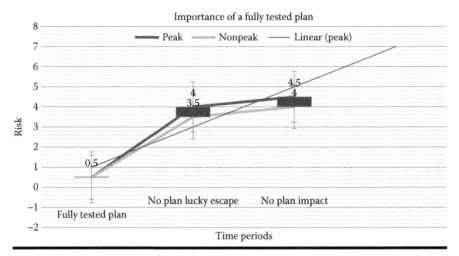

Figure 7.1   Plan testing.

training the BCM teams to cope with different sorts of disasters. Performing tests and exercises and making postexercise evaluations lead to continuous improvement and fine tuning of plans.

Nature of Tests and Exercises

An exercise is defined as a planned rehearsal of a possible incident designed to evaluate an organization's capability to manage that incident, to provide an opportunity to improve the organization's future responses, and to enhance the relevant competences of those involved (Figure 7.2).

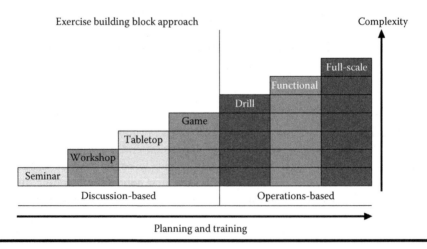

Figure 7.2   Nature of tests and exercises.

Some organizations differentiate the terms exercise and test, but there is no requirement to use these terms in specific circumstances. The focus of plan testing should be to improve the organization's performance in an actual event. It is important to note that there are many types of exercises; all of these have to be appropriately timed and conducted at different periodicity to provide assurance and value to the BCM management.

Key players in the tests and exercises: Before we commence our test planning, it is important to understand the role of people involved in the tests and exercises. The following people play a vital role:

1. *Facilitator* is a person who leads the exercise; he or she performs the following:
   a. Facilitates the exercise
   b. Regulates participants
   c. Serves as a link between key staff and decision makers
   d. Consists of elected/appointed officials

   The use of senior level facilitators, who have a detailed understanding of the BCM plan, is a key to the success of any exercise, but especially a Tabletop exercise (TTX). The facilitator can be from external agencies: he or she guides and maintains the focus and pace of the exercise. Facilitators enable the plan leaders to concentrate on their role in the exercise and not grope to get everybody focused on the topic of discussion. The qualities of a good facilitator include the following:
   i. Excellent presentation skills
   ii. Proven leadership abilities and comfort with exercise format
   iii. Knowledge of the business and/or industry
   iv. Understanding of business and location-specific risks
   v. Sufficient experience with the organization's business continuity program, especially those elements being exercised

   Before the exercise, the planner(s) and facilitator(s) should contact the respective leaders whom they will assist during the exercise, in order to coordinate the exercise plan and to gain an understanding of the organization and its members. In addition to good facilitation skills, the facilitator must also have a complete understanding of the missions, organization, BCM plan, and other relevant information.

   Following the exercise, the facilitator leads the analysis of exercise data and assists in the preparation of the after-action report (AAR) to capture key lessons learned. Key facilitator actions include setting the stage for the exercise, coordinate and control exercise execution, and manage the postexercise activities. Simple, high-level one-pagers that introduce the process is a great way to help exercise participants feel comfortable.

2. *Observers/reporters* witness the exercise merely as onlookers and give their comments on the way they saw the exercise enacted. They observe player actions and later act as evaluators and report what went well and what went wrong

so that the plan can be improvised. The number of observers needed would depend upon the size and scope of the exercise. Observer responsibilities include the following:

a. Participate in critiques and development of the after-action report
b. Brief the controller during the exercise when problems arise
c. Keep a log of all observations and events

3. *Recovery team(s) members* who need to know the plan and procedures and their role at the time of crisis.
4. *Time keepers* who keep a track of time taken for response and execution of exercise to compare whether it meets preset timelines.
5. *Auditor/reviewers* in some cases auditors express their intent to witness the exercise to check the currency and performance of the test. Their status is the same as that of the observers.
6. *Suppliers* in case suppliers need to supply some equipment, material or services during disruption, they must be a part of the exercise.
7. *Out-sourced services providers* connected to the business recovery plan need to be a part of the exercise team.

Before we plan tests and exercises, it will be good to understand what is it that we want to test? While building the business continuity plans, we would like to test the components that make the plans. So, we go for component testing.

Component test: A component test is a test that focuses on the miscellaneous components of a business continuity plan. Some examples of components to be tested include the following:

■ Test staff members' knowledge of their business unit plan
■ Confirm availability of correct version at all locations
■ Confirm hard copy records from off-site location are retrievable
■ Contact staff, suppliers and other vendors and service providers
■ Check lead time for supply of critical equipment
■ Check important lists are still current
■ Confirm readiness at alternate site
■ Recall documents from off-site storage and check the lead time

It is the small things or components which when they fail during the crisis can cause big damage to the recovery exercise and fail the plan. Besides testing of components is less expensive and less cumbersome than running the entire plan.

Let us illustrate using notification test. People are mobile and the attrition rate is hitting enterprises and people get transferred. In this condition, the call lists have to be constantly updated to change names and add new members. Hence notification test is useful to ascertain that the people to be notified would indeed be there on the crisis day to receive the notifications.

Notification Test: It is a type of component test whereby the call list of persons, roles, and/or organizations to be contacted as a part of an information, or plan

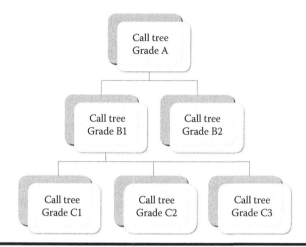

Figure 7.3 Notification lists testing.

invocation procedure is tested to do an existence check. Notification test is a test for the recovery team members to notify designated staff members via a contact list as documented in the BCM plan (Figure 7.3).

Note: Crisis communication network is one of the most efficient and effective means of communicating news/notifications to all relevant staff, during the actual crisis.

As against component testing that endeavors to test one part of the plan, an integrated test of all components tests the plan in entirety right from its people to resources to external relationships and tests the impact on stakeholders and customers.

Organizations differ in their size, nature of business, and geographical spread. Organizational culture varies across different locations. Organizations may choose to test their plans at varied frequency and in parts. Testing should be scheduled and conducted in a way that does not put essential business functions of the organization at risk.

The testing methods should be practical, cost-effective and appropriate, and designed to promote confidence. The test schedule for a contingency plan should indicate how and when each element of the plan should be tested. It is recommended that specific components of the plan should be tested separately.

Sometimes components of a plan fail, due to incorrect assumptions having been made, oversights, changes in services, systems, equipment, processes or personnel. The rate of organizational and technical change increases the vulnerability of such plans and leads to obsolescence. But if failure of component is discovered in time, the plan can still be kept operational.

One of the key building blocks of an exercise is the determination of the type of exercise that will be used. Commonly, this depends on the familiarity of the organization and exercise participants with business continuity and their previous exercise experience. "A business continuity management (BCM) capability cannot be considered reliable until it has been exercised" (BS 25999-1)

Tests and exercises are of different types and can be categorized on two broad criteria

1. Discussion-based
2. Operations-based

Discussion-Based Exercises

Commonly used are walkthroughs, workshops, and orientation seminars that are used to give basic training to team members to familiarize them with emergency response, business continuity and crisis communications plans, and their roles and responsibilities as defined in the plans.

Plan Orientation or Plan Walkthrough

When a business continuity or a crisis management plan has been formulated, it is beneficial to walkthrough the document informally with those expected to implement it. The facilitator performs the task of giving orientation to the BCM team about plans and procedures. This includes the following:

1. Introducing participants to the plans and procedures
2. Introducing new plans or revise old plans
3. Helping orient new staff or leadership

Purpose

1. Familiarize staff to organization's emergency response plan
2. Ensure team members understand their BCM roles
3. Familiarize current staff to changing information or procedures
4. Bring together various departments for better understanding and coordination
5. Identify planning and response priorities prior to plan development

Methods

1. Talk through
2. Brain storming
3. Case study
4. Training workshop

Use

1. Review identified issues
2. Prioritize issues
3. Brainstorm realistic action steps

Good For

1. Educating, building awareness
2. Gathering new ideas or feedback
3. Exercising before a plan is started
4. Exercising before a plan is finalized

The effort would include a team meeting facilitated by a designated team leader. It is just a paper walkthrough to ensure that team members understand their roles and responsibilities. A seminar exercise is also a kind of plan walkthrough test.

Game

A game is a simulation of operations that often involves two or more teams, usually in a competitive environment, using rules, data, and procedure designed to depict an actual or assumed real-life situation. This can be configured to create awareness activities (for new employees) during induction to get basic concepts tested in the form of quiz game or group exercise during induction.

Live Play

Exercise activity that is as close as safely practicable to the expected response to a real incident.

Workshop (Scenario-Based)

To establish which scenarios are to be covered by our continuity plan, a workshop can be held involving selected employees from the organization. An illustrative scenario can be "Data center out of service." Other examples of scenarios may include:

1. Critical systems out of service
2. Critical virtual server out of service
3. SQL server out of service
4. Extensive virus outbreak
5. Hacker attack
6. Key supplier goes out of business
7. Leak of information

Desk Check Exercise

A desk check normally involves only the plan owner and perhaps a disinterested third-party. The goal of this type of effort is simply to ensure that content inside the plan is not outdated (e.g., contact information) and that the plan is still current. It normally includes a simple page-by-page reading and updating of the plan itself.

Objectives

1. Ensure that team members are accurate.
2. Ensure that internal and external contact numbers are current.

Checklist Exercise

Involves a structured walkthrough of BCP plan. The team comes together with a prior knowledge of the test scenario. Each member plays a designated role and walks through the activities assigned to him/her in the continuity plan. Tactical exercise involves an actual simulation. There will be a coordinator for each test, who will announce the intermediate events for the scenario—as if they were happening.

Desktop Exercises or Tabletop Exercises (TTXs)

This exercise is a discussion-based exercise where team members meet in an informal, classroom setting to discuss their roles during an emergency and their responses to a particular emergency situation. A facilitator guides participants through a discussion of one or more scenarios. The duration of a Tabletop exercise depends on the audience, the topic being exercised and the exercise objectives. Many Tabletop exercises can be conducted in a few hours, so they are cost-effective tools to validate plans and capabilities (Figure 7.4).

TTX is held in an informal setting intended to generate discussion of various issues regarding a hypothetical, simulated emergency incident; It brings the BCM team members together for a session to work collaboratively through a realistic scenario to identify challenges and build rapport in solving them together.

Figure 7.4 Tabletop exercise or TTX.

The main features of a TTX are as follows:

■ Gaps in business continuity plans get identified.
■ It specifically directs the discussion of the BCM operations to focus on response to an emergency event.
■ The spotlight is always on processes, discussions and decision-making process, and not minute details.

Objectives of a tabletop exercise include the following:

1. Understanding concepts and identifying plan strengths and weaknesses.
2. Triggering awareness and acceptance of BCM plans.
3. Highlighting areas for improvement within current plans, policies and procedures.
4. Problem-solving and discussions based on scenarios and decisions based on these to be implemented. All responses on discussions to be recorded.

Preparing a scenario for a tabletop exercise:

As a part of preliminary preparations, it would be good to know that the team composition of who are going to participate in the exercise, the plan to be tested, and the objectives of the test. Points to be taken into consideration include the following:

1. The scenario should be comprehensible and acceptable to the team.
2. Avoid complicated scenarios as it is not necessary to have complex scenarios to spot the weak points in plans and their performance. Incident triggers; raising the incident management team; communicating with all employees; coordinating with third parties; media and social media; business continuity plans being out of date, incomplete or unrealistic.
3. Keep abreast of latest news and major incidents/events that have occurred; it will help in scenario building.
4. After selecting a scenario, it is essential to make it live by a series of injects. The injects supply the team with more information, problems, and even questions as the exercise unfolds. Depending on the type of exercise you might only need three major injects to keep a team busy for a couple of hours: or you may want to simulate a more realistic steady stream of live feeds.
5. The principals are the same regardless of the exercise type. Work out the story, break it into chapters or events (the injects) and then decide the best way to feed these into the exercise.
6. Injects can be supplied in many ways, so be creative. Even using some PowerPoint, screenshots and some cutting and pasting you can feed information through from a mocked up CNN News page or a mocked up Twitter account. On a more elaborate exercise, you could prerecord interviews with executives and neighbors. You might also use reporters live on the scene, or organize live phone calls to provide more information or ask the team for help. An occasional (mock) press person phoning into the room and asking for a comment on the situation can also add some color (Figure 7.5).

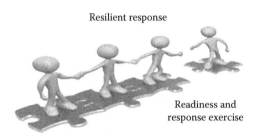

Resilient response

Readiness and
response exercise

Figure 7.5 Readiness and response planning for TTX.

Let us observe how injects work:

1. *Day one.* Local weather forecasters are predicting more heavy rain for the week ahead and potential city center flooding if this continues.

   Facilitator may prompt: Is this an incident?/who decides?/what, if any, action will you take?

2. *Day two.* Television News forecast; rivers in the city center are expected to flood sometime tomorrow night. The local council advises that tonight they will close several roads around the city (including organization's site) due to rivers bursting. They recommend that the public avoid all nonessential travel into the city.

   Facilitator may prompt: What are your priorities? What is the message to staff and customers, how will you get it out? What about parents with children in schools that are closed? Is it safe to keep operating?

3. *Day three.* Last night roads were closed and your site isolated, a local electricity substation also flooded and you are running on emergency power; that is just lights for security. A contract cleaner at the site is off work and has been tweeting your site is down.

   Facilitator may prompt: Where is your team now working from?/What are the priorities?/Media Message/Twitter response?/Recovery plans/what about that customer who is due to visit?

4. *Day four.* It is stopped raining. Water is going down and the power has been restored on site, and roads are likely to open today.

   Facilitator may prompt: The priorities?/Can you get staff back to work today?/What if it rains some more?

Some control points to be considered:

1. Plan well ahead to fix a date.
2. Have the exercise sponsor send out the invitation and have the right people attend.
3. Keep the scenario and injects secret from anyone involved in the exercise.
4. Set the expectation for participants (e.g., In advance of this exercise you should be familiar with the business continuity plans for your area and be prepared to play your role in the incident management team…).

5. Set the expectations of people outside the exercise. (i.e., Will you need people outside of the incident management team to contribute?).
6. Coach any new players in an otherwise experienced team ahead of the exercise so they know what to expect and how to engage.
7. Housekeeping to help arrange for the food and drinks and facilitate communication throughout the exercise.
8. It is advisable to have business continuity plan copies in the room during the exercise.

Hotwash: A debrief with the exercise planning team; controllers and evaluators is held immediately after the exercise. It enables the observers/evaluators to collect observations and thoughts about the way the exercise was conducted and make a preliminary analysis of the same. This wash up exercise in respect of the scenario above is simple as it merely refers to a short-term loss of access to the facility. In a hotwash, team members discuss what went well? What should we do more of? What should we do differently? In large, more complex exercises the full review could take several days and require follow-up interviews/investigations.

Documenting results: All the teams participating should give a formal feedback about the outcome of the test, and their feedbacks should be documented for improving your overall continuity plan.

An *after-action report* (*AAR*) is prepared to document the exercise. It helps to highlight strengths and areas for improvement. It demonstrates the capabilities being exercised AAR should address strengths and weaknesses of the planning process as they affect the ability to develop and eventually conduct an effective exercise. Normally, the AAR does not focus on such things as the scenario used in the exercise. Rather, the AAR intent is to capture shortfalls in existing policies, procedures, capabilities or resources that affect the successful execution of the BCM plan. Other suggested topics for inclusion in the AAR include:

1. Design of the exercise: Any problems noted and recommendations for future exercises.
2. Exercise site(s): Adequacy of the site and support for the exercise.
3. Adequacy of communications and information systems.
4. Access to required vital records and databases.
5. The relocation process and recovery process and problems noted.
6. Adequacy of the administrative support for the exercise.
7. Adequacy of the timeline available for the exercise development process, and where more time may be needed in the future.

Corrective Action Plan (*CAP*): Corrective actions are the mandated, actionable steps outlined in improvement plans that are intended to resolve preparedness gaps and shortcomings experienced in exercises or postevent evaluations.

BCM Plan Revision with the completion of the exercise, the leadership team now has a basis for developing a more effective plan. The recommendations from the exercise, contained in the AAR, should be coordinated with executives and incorporated into the appropriate sections and annexures within the plan during the annual review and update of the plan.

Note: A Tabletop exercise is a testing of the plan and *not* the people. It is a platform where key organizational personnel discuss simulated scenarios in an informal setting to validate the BCM plan. The effort ends with an evaluation of gaps observed, the fulfillment of test objectives and a remediation mandate accompanied with a time deadline to complete it.

The team goes through the entire plan, performing all the activities, from notification to restoration. If this exercise is a planned or notified exercise, then it will be generally designed in such a way that the activities of the entire team are covered.

Operations-Based Exercises

The following exercises fall in the category of operations-based exercises:

Drill

A drill is a practical exercise in managing operations which simulates damage and injuries in a hypothetical emergency. Such exercises are also referred to as procedure verification exercise or validation exercise. In a drill, participants face mock situations using the skills and techniques that would have applied in real situations (Figure 7.6).

Drills allow for the evaluation of procedures, tools, skills, and individual and institutional capacity in relation to disaster preparedness and response. Drills are carried

Figure 7.6 Operations-based exercises.

out in "real" time and each of the participants assumes the role that he or she customarily performs in his/her regular work. Others will perform as victims or other roles.

Objectives of Drills

1. Test the relevance and effectiveness of plans, protocols, procedures, guidelines, and other operational mechanisms for emergency response.
2. Evaluate abilities and the use of techniques, tools, resources, and actions related to the organization of emergency response operations.
3. Improve coordination and application of specific techniques for risk reduction and control of consequences on the part of multiple actors and organizations.

The drill takes place in real time. The exercise primarily consists of practical actions, performed by participants who have experience in emergency management, including persons who can play specific roles. The time for the drill are measured beginning with the activation of alarms or an order given to begin operations.

Drills are effective methods for training and for evaluating or validating preparedness and response efforts in a variety of areas, including: Identification of responsibilities, confirmation of established roles, use of techniques, evaluation of performance and skills, and use of resources. Drills presupposes an established, organizational structure for emergency management which has an action plan; Clear identification of the elements to be evaluated during the drill; A risk scenario that considers hazards, vulnerabilities, and capacities; A location with suitable physical and environmental conditions for recreating the emergency situations with minimal risk to participants; Institutional backing, financial resources, and adequate logistical support.

Types of Drills

Drills have different characteristics depending on the number of persons who will be involved, whether those involved have prior knowledge that it will take place, and the degree of complexity. They can be classified as: Partial or full-scale drills: A partial drill would be a simulation of the arrival of injured at the emergency department of a hospital; the complete evacuation of a workplace would be a full-scale drill.

Preannounced or surprise drills: This depends on whether the participants and the public are informed prior to the exercise, or whether only the coordinating committees know of it. Unannounced or surprise drills must be part of a process that includes earlier exercises that were announced, and should be used only when there are established response plans

Organizational structure for drills: A team should be formed to undertake the tasks of organizing and executing the drill, under the supervision of a coordinator. Preparing for and executing drills. Throughout the preparatory process, it is necessary to maintain close contact with the different working groups to approve content, validate the tools, establish guidelines, monitor compliance with the activity schedule, correct deviations, and for other aspects of coordination to ensure proper development of the exercise.

Coordinated, supervised activities usually employed to exercise a single specific operation, procedure or function in a single agency

1. Test of individual emergency response functions involves actual field response
2. Practice or test under realistic conditions
3. Involve all levels of responders
4. Planning cycle: One month
5. Test time: 10 to 60 minutes

A drill focuses on a small part of the plan to practice it and perfect it. The following are a few examples of drills

1. A fire drill
2. Drill for practicing the Emergency Operations Centre (EOC) operations
3. IT systems recovery drill
4. Radio test

A drill instructs through repetition and practice. Focus is on one part of the emergency response plan. It is best used to test effectiveness of staff training response time, interdepartmental coordination and capabilities of resources and equipment. It would pay to orient the BCM staff clearly before the drill.

Functional Exercise

A fully simulated interactive exercise that tests the capability of an organization to respond to an event.

- Tests multiple functions of the organization's operational plan.
- A coordinated response to a situation in a time-pressured realistic simulation.

Focuses on the coordination, integration, and interaction of an organization's policies, procedures, roles, and responsibilities before, during, or after the simulated event. Functional exercises allow personnel to validate plans and readiness by performing their duties in a simulated operational environment.

Activities for a functional exercise are scenario-driven, such as the failure of a critical business function or a specific hazard scenario. Functional exercises are designed to exercise specific team members, procedures and resources (e.g., communications, warning, notifications and equipment setup).

Illustration-Crisis Communication Plan Exercise

Communication is the key to the success of the business continuity management system (BCMS). Hence it would be a good strategy to test the crisis communication plan regularly. It is generally observed that lack of prompt communication cause crisis response to fail in situations of crisis. Crisis communication testing becomes important and these are designed keeping in mind scope of planning and the level of automation in the crisis communication process.

For instance, some organizations have installed mass notification tools. Testing would help evaluate the tool's performance as well as expose the recipients to the way such notifications will be received by them. Normally, this type of event involves actually contacting business partners and employees, not simply reviewing contact the contact lists.

Objectives

1. Validate the contact information of key stakeholders.
2. Train participants in the use of mass notification and specify their role in the communication/response.
3. Properly configure/customize mass notification tools.
4. Identify communication gaps/bottlenecks where timely communication could falter in an event.

Exercise Communications Plans for the Program

The crisis communication plan must be documented and exercise standards and guidelines have to be communicated to employees. The scope and objectives of the plan should be clearly set and exercise schedules must be determined including call-out procedures for key personnel.

Testing recovery at an alternative site, running services, systems or business processes in parallel with recovery operations away from the main site:

1. Complete rehearsals announced and unannounced testing that the organization, personnel, equipment, facilities, and business processes can cope with incidents.
2. Document crisis communications exercise results (1) open issues, (2) lessons learned, and (3) update communications plans based on findings.
3. Implement crisis communication plan; crisis management declaration team authorizes implementation.
4. Tests of supplier facilities and services, ensuring externally provided services and products will meet the contracted commitment.
5. Awareness, training and exercising workforce BCM awareness training programs business response, resumption recovery, and restoration plan exercises technical response, resumption recovery, and restoration plan exercises.

Communication to BCM and escalating the incident till it is declared as a disaster and DR plan is invoked and communication with internal and external parties during the disaster is important and should be regulated. Hence testing the correct manner and timing of crisis communication is significant in salvaging reputation and public image.

It is a test of multiple functions and the test of the coordinated response in a time-pressured realistic simulation without deploying resources. It is a test of whether the organization can respond to a simulated event. These tests have following purpose-it tests the comprehensive response capacity of multiple organizations by simulating a real event as closely as possible

Full-Scale Exercise

This test evaluates the operational capability of in an interactive manner over a substantial period. It presents complex and detailed events in real time, mobilizes personnel, resources, emergency response teams and equipment. The disadvantage is that it can be expensive; and cause disruption to normal business operations. These tests are conducted in a stressful environment that simulates actual response conditions. It requires the mobilization and actual movement of emergency personnel, equipment, and resources. It checks most of the functions of the emergency plans.

Test time: Two to eight hours.

Planning cycle: Four months' minimum (These exercises require conscious and deliberate planning and the organizer must assume end-to-end control).

Simulation Exercise

Exercise in which a group of players, usually representing a control center or management team, reacts to a simulated incident notionally happening elsewhere. Sometimes known as a functional exercise, are focused on management control. These test an organization's responses to a scenario-driven event. Exercise controllers inject preprogrammed challenges throughout the exercise (Figure 7.7).

Figure 7.7 Simulation exercise.

Depending on the organization's level of readiness, the stress level and intensity can be increased by positioning participants in different areas, and using phone and radios to make it realistic. This exercise uses established business continuity resources, such as the recovery site, backup equipment, services from recovery vendors and transportation. It can require sending teams to alternate sites to restart technology as well as business functions.

It uses established business continuity resources, such as recovery sites, backup systems, and other specialized services. Teams may be sent to alternate sites to restart technology as well as business functions. Simulations may also uncover staff issues regarding the nature of their tasks. In effect, a simulation is a full-scale test without failing over or commencing processing at alternate site.

Incident Simulation: The best way to prepare for a crisis is to practice, usually through a simulation exercise of a scenario. In these types of exercise, a mock crisis is outlined to the team and they should work through the steps and face the consequences of their decisions. Typically, the crisis will be something pertinent to the organization and be the type of crisis that can be escalated gradually, giving the crisis management team (CMT) members time to think through the timing of invoking plans and the risk/cost calculations they would face in a real crisis. These exercises test performance of the entire team.

Partial Simulation: Selected business units are chosen to run the full simulation tests. They have a detailed scope and full testing within their units.

Surprise simulations can also be performed. It is usually the last type of exercise in the testing of the continuity plan and gives a picture of the actual preparedness of the team. When simulations are planned, the knowledge is there that the simulation is an exercise. But surprise simulations though they are painstaking, give a more realistic report on the performance of the team. In fact, surprise simulations test preparedness and the reflexive reactions of the BCM team in responding to a disaster.

Full Simulation Tests: Is also known as "mock disaster test" or "full interruption test" and it aims at testing many components in the business recovery plans. Testing is expensive and causes normal operations to be interrupted and must be conducted carefully. Adequate time should be allotted for the testing. A well-designed full-scale exercise is a good test of an organization's ability to successfully respond to an emergency.

Other exercises that may be designed or configured can depend on type of business and complexity of plan. Let us see some such tests.

Technical Recovery Testing

Both modular and full, ensuring equipment or systems (e.g., medical devices, information systems) can be restored effectively; this can be categorized as component testing also.

IT Environment (Systems and Application) Walkthrough

This test involves conducting an announced or unannounced disaster simulation and executing documented system recovery procedures. Many IT environments are extremely complicated, and plans may be built around recovering specific applications or systems rather than the entire data center loss. In these circumstances, testing the loss of a data center could be highly disruptive and expensive. A well-designed walkthrough can be an effective exercise to bring disparate parties together in the only way that can be accomplished practically.

Objectives

- Verify that critical systems and data can be recovered in a large-scale event.
- Determine whether internal resources in individual system or application plans can fulfill their responsibilities, given the loss of multiple systems/applications.
- Coordinate the use of response/recovery resources across multiple locations/lines of business.
- Ensure the adequacy of supporting resources (e.g., human resources [HR], procurement) to the IT response.

Alternate Site Testing

This test of all restoration/recovery components at an alternate site should include a test of the organization's ability to relocate staff to the alternate site, as well as a validation that recovery processes and IT assets operate at the alternate site, as designed.

Objectives

- Demonstrate the actual capability to continue key processes at the alternate site.
- Identify whether privacy, security, and financial controls can be maintained in the alternate operating environment.
- Train participants on any revised procedures to complete key processes at the alternate site.
- Evaluate the sufficiency and effectiveness of IT assets at the alternate site.
- Ensure the plan to transport employees is reasonable based on the likely disaster scenarios identified in the BCM risk assessment.

End-to-End Testing

This test of alternate site facilities should include both business and IT. An end-to-end test differs from an alternate site in that critical suppliers/business partners and customers—internal or external—are included within the scope. This test typically validates connectivity to the organization's production site.

Objectives

1. To check the ability to perform key processes at a predetermined level without significant issues.
2. To reconcile the effective capacity of the continuity strategy with the performance expectations assumed or documented in the continuity plan.

Alternatively testing of alternate site can be done by testing its processing capability without disrupting normal operations at the primary site.

Tests and exercises are to be planned keeping in mind the readiness and the objectives which govern the testing. Level of participants is also important. Focus should be on what is to be tested, this will determine what tests should be selected. We have desk checks, walkthroughs, drills, workshops, and so on. The main takeaway from all these exercises are level of confidence and assurance on the effectiveness of their BCM plans (Figure 7.8).

Intermittently if there is an incident in between, it trickles the testing of the plans and one must focus on what went wrong. The next point of contention is how often should you exercise your plans? A cost element is involved in testing as well.

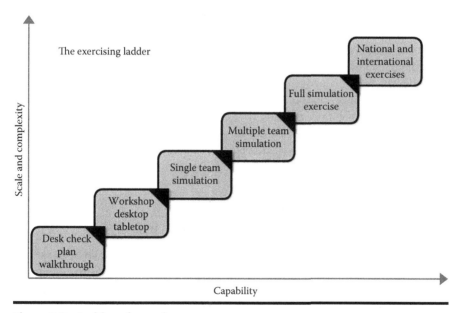

Figure 7.8   Ladder of exercises.

Frequency of Tests and Exercises

As a student, if I must appear for a paper on Mathematics, I have to sit down prior to the exam and solve as many sums as I can. Practice makes us perfect and it is this principle that applies to tests and exercises too. No matter circumstances may be different, but the regularity of exercises builds in a sort of resilience, brings agility to the mind and develops certain reflexes that help initiate the recovery process.

All major BC standards require some sort of test and exercise regime to be an integral part of the BCM program. Generally, a large-scale exercise of the BCM programs and BC plans should be conducted at least annually. More frequent testing may be required for complicated environments and those with a great impact (e.g., loss) to the organization. Several component tests should also be scheduled at regular intervals throughout the year. Requirements for exercises can be documented either inside the plan itself or in the entity-level BCM policy.

Several component tests should also be scheduled at regular intervals throughout the year. It is important to assess the health of the BCM program of an organization by determining what type of testing they have done at least once in the past year. What elements of your BCM program have you exercised at least once in the past year?

- Departmental business recovery exercise
- Site-specific business recovery exercise
- Alternate site (work area recover) exercise
- Mock crisis/emergency management exercise
- None

However, merely fixing frequency of exercises is not always an effective way since repeating same tests can cause stagnant outcomes and bored team members participating in the test. Frequency to be sufficient to ensure that the program is becoming progressively more mature. Besides the facilitators must introduce some novelty to the test and make it exciting and lively.

Many mature organizations test business continuity processes one or two times a year; however, this can be increased by such factors as:

1. Changes in business processes.
2. Changes in technology.
3. A change in BCP team membership.
4. Anticipated events that may result in a potential business.

Regardless of the actual frequency the focus of tests and exercises should be to aim at a continuous improvement of the BCM program. It is necessary to understand the business and the nature of the BCM plans in place. It would be good to obtain the following:

1. Site plans/layouts/process flows.
2. BCPs/incident management plans.
3. What they do/how it works/what goes wrong/what they worry might go wrong.

4. Any special customers/suppliers/third parties of concern?

5. Any useful information in the risk register?

Prior knowledge of business and business continuity plans gives insight into the type of scenarios that can be built to test the plans.

Debrief Teams of Testing Methodologies

It would be good to educate and gear up the team into readiness to conduct drills and exercises planned for testing. The facilitator needs to assess the capabilities of the team members and accordingly assign tasks. Executive team members are busy; hence they may not have time for training sessions. A short process updates or briefing, will add value, especially if they have not had chance to read the plans fully.

Parts of BCM Testing

Tests and exercises are training ground for the BCM teams. It may be possible that at the time of disaster, the team may not have immediate access to the plans, there would be panic and chaos around, at such times, the earlier "drills" would serve to remind them of their activities and provide some level of confidence (Figure 7.9).

Test Scenarios: The best way for a CMT to prepare itself for a crisis is to practice, usually through a simulation exercise of a specific scenario. In these types of exercises, a mock crisis is outlined to the CMT who then must work through the steps and face the consequences of their decisions.

A scenario is a description of:

■ The incident, that is, (the nature and scale of)
■ The lead-up to the incident, consisting of the (underlying) cause
■ The trigger which creates the incident
■ The context of the events, indicating general circumstances and the degree of vulnerability and resistance of people, object and society, to the extent relevant to the incident described
■ The consequences of the incident, indicating nature and scale with an overall description of the response and the control measures
■ The effects of the incident on the continuity of vital infrastructure

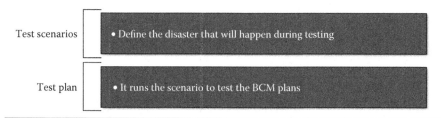

Figure 7.9 Two parts of BCM testing.

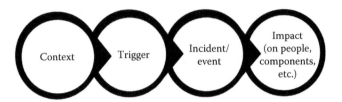

Figure 7.10 Components of scenarios.

Scenario Planning

Scenario planning has been defined as a strategic planning method, expressly developed to test the viability of alternative strategies. According to Global Business Network, which provides scenario-based consulting, scenarios are not predictions. Rather, they are plausible accounts of how relevant external forces—such as the future political environment, scientific and technological developments, social dynamics, and economic conditions—might interact and evolve in the future (Figure 7.10).

In scenario planning, an organization typically creates three or four scenarios that capture a range of possibilities; examines the opportunities and threats that each may bring; and makes short- and long-term strategic decisions based on these analyses.

Each scenario is divided into three stages to help you consider the immediate impact, the short-term and the longer-term implications and to think about the actions you could take.

Development of Scenarios

Scenarios are tools for understanding possible future events and preparing organizations to respond to worst-case situations by fine tuning their plans to meet eventualities. The base premise is that there are certain events that have happened in the last two to three years and many events that are anticipated to happen, and based on these past and anticipated events, BCM plans are formulated.

A scenario is developed after obtaining input from all specialist fields within the organization. The nature of scenario, the cause and environment in which it is to be run are important factors. A multidisciplinary working group can be performed for developing scenarios.

Key Points in Scenarios

1. The task of who performs the scenario writing, who prepares the probability and impact scores and who makes the capability analysis. The membership of the group that scores the likelihood and the impact can be totally different from the group that writes the scenario or the group that performs the capability analysis.

2. In respect of the confidentiality of the available information, it is conceivable that for the threat scenarios, a select group of experts can be appointed (staff of the intelligence or national police services, etc.). When composing the working groups, care must be taken to ensure that all specialist fields that are relevant to the scenario are represented.
3. If the work of an expert is to be used, it has to be determined how experts' work can be organized. Think about efficiency, use of their time and discussion between experts. Determine whether experts can provide continuous input into the process, or whether it will suffice to have a one-off contribution from an expert. (Refer Annexure A for considerations for use of experts)

Requirements of a Scenario

1. It must be realistic; it should depict events that can occur in future.
2. It must be structured consistently and logically.
3. It must be doable, and acceptable by the team.
4. It must specify the time horizon that it will take to roll out.
5. It must be unique and meet the security objectives of testing.

Developing Test Scenarios: Organizations need to create realistic scenario, which approximate to the types of incidents they may experience and the types of problems that are likely to be associated with those incidents.

No Blame Scenario

Another factor to consider is the culture of the organization involved in the plan test. Some prefer a "no blame" scenario such as severe weather or terrorism—where the company is an innocent victim. But naturally, as good scenario writers we will throw in injects that attempt to hinder the company's response. This should drive the simulation because although the initial incident was not the company's fault, if their reaction is seen as tardy or in some way lacking then staff, clients and the media will soon start to complain.

Alternatively, some organizations are forward looking and choose scenarios in which they bear some of the blame. This might involve data loss, product recall or perhaps the crisis scenario of the present moment—cybercrime.

Scenarios Rehearsing Lack of People

This scenario may comprise of a shortage of personnel due to

- Contagious illness
- Strike
- Transport outage
- Building closure (see "lack of access" column)
- Using recovery location

Ex. Pandemic Flu

A typical scenario in this category is "Pandemic flu" since it is potentially catastrophic. It is a human/people outage and has nothing to do with technology. It is a condition of dealing with mass absenteeism and how the organization plans to meet such contingencies and still manage to run its critical operations within the agreed recovery time objectives (RTOs). A point to note here is that the scenario is not so significant as the resultant impacts and how the players react as the scenario unfolds.

Scenarios to Rehearse "Lack of Access"

The players of this scenario cover the following:

1. Loss, damage or denial of access to key infrastructure
2. Application failures
3. Nonperformance of providers, distributors or third parties
4. Corruption of key information
5. Sabotage, extortion, commercial espionage or other such event
6. Deliberate infiltration into systems
7. Attacks on critical information system applications
8. Facility evacuation

IT is an important component of most business processes. Availability of IT systems and its support is most important for organizations. Gartner survey has revealed that 30% of businesses fail within four months of an IT disaster striking them.

Scenarios to Rehearse Lack of Rehearsing "Lack of Infrastructure"

Scenarios can be built around any of the following conditions and results noted

1. Power outage
2. Gas outage
3. Water outage
4. IT network outage
5. Loss of IT files
6. Technology connection outage
7. Loss of data
8. System application outage
9. Telecoms outage
10. Flood

Scenarios that are hazard specific: These are constructed to test crisis management response to specific hazards. Threats include data theft, bomb blast, power failure, downtime, and so on. If any such hazard is made live discussion points triggered give valuable inputs in improvising existing arrangements.

A multidisciplinary group may consist of representatives of the various (specialist) departments and be chaired by the person of the specialist group most affected. The working group may decide to develop the scenario itself, or an external consultant may be asked to develop the scenario. In that case, it is advisable for the working group to set the terms of reference within which the scenario is to be developed. In both cases, it must be ensured that the scenario devised offers sufficient leads to be able to carry out the risk assessment in the next stage.

The scenario must be concrete enough so as to be able to assess which capabilities are necessary, which are already available and whether there are capabilities that need to be reinforced. The input of experts can be guaranteed by including these experts in the working group.

Hazard specific exercise scenarios may be developed based on the operating environment; including data breach, hostile takeover, unauthorized communication (i.e., social media), terrorist event, or regulatory activity. The overall facilitation time of the exercise will vary depending on the type of exercise selected (and in many cases, the time management commits to the exercise). In general, exercises range in length from two to four hours.

Illustrative Examples

Blackout

Initial Information

You arrive at your office on Thursday morning to find out that the storm force winds overnight appear to have caused a tree to fall across power lines, cutting off the electricity. Your office/building has no power. Points for discussion:

- What, if any, is the immediate impact on your business?
- What are your initial priorities?
- Are there any Health and Safety issues?

Update It is Now 11.00: Power has not been restored. You have been told that although work is underway to fix the problem as soon as possible, power is unlikely to be available today. Points for discussion:

1. What, if any, is the short-term impact on your business?
2. What are your short-term priorities?
3. What information would you now give to members of your team, where would you get this from and are all, including out of hour, contact details up-to-date?
4. What response and/or recovery plans are you going to initiate?

Longer-Term Implications

Thankfully, power was restored overnight and by midday on Friday, you are able to resume near normal activities, but you are left with a backlog of information to record electronically and several outstanding queries from customers. A couple of members of staff are burdened with most of these but others have offered to help.

Points for discussion:

1. What, if any, is the long-term impact on your business?
2. What are your long-term priorities?
3. Are there any actions that you could take now to reduce the likelihood or impact of this happening in the future?
4. Do your BC and recovery plans have all the information you required to manage this scenario? Blackout! In relation to this scenario.
5. Many premises do not have a backup generator so alternative working arrangements may need to be made in order to keep critical functions active.
6. Digital phones are reliant on electricity so would not work in the event of a power cut (once any battery power had run out).
7. UPS systems are not designed to work for a long time.
8. Home working may be possible but the Information & Communication Technology (ICT) connections may not be operational. With so many areas affected (fire alarms, heating, technologies), the impact of a power cut would be like loss of a building.
9. As a power failure, would undoubtedly affect your current work place, you need to consider where you could work from as an alternative, that is, Work Area Recovery site.
10. The following technologies could be unavailable through a power cut. For example, phone, ICT, radio base station, CCTV, and security swipe cards.
11. There may be Health and Safety issues arising from a power cut, for example, emergency lighting in stairwells is not designed to work for a long time.
12. There may be access issues as elevators may not work.

Note: The above hazard makes a good scenario. The main limitation being the backlog of processing that should be entered after the outage.

Downtime

Initial Information

A leaking water pipe was discovered in the early hours of this morning by security guards patrolling the office building. Unfortunately, the leak could not be stopped before water got into several PCs. At 6 a.m. this morning, the IT was shut down until damage could be assessed and alternative arrangements or repairs made. It is now 9 a.m. and, although the building has only suffered minimal isolated damage, no e-mail or internet access is available at your place of work. There are no data communications possible.

Points for discussion:

1. What, if any, is the immediate impact on your business?
2. What are your initial priorities?
3. Are there any Health and Safety issues?

Update It is 3 *p.m.*: And no systems are available as the machines damaged were those concerned with logging into various applications. Other machines have had to be moved to allow repairs to take place. The data blackout is complete (i.e., no internet, e-mail or software systems which rely on logging in over the internet). It is likely that there will be no systems for at least a week, while repairs take place and systems are restarted. The phone system is connected to the ICT and that is down as well.

Points for discussion:

1. What, if any, is the short-term impact on your business?
2. What are your short-term priorities?
3. What information would you now give to members of your team, where would you get this from and are all, including out of hour, contact details up-to-date?
4. What response and/or recovery plans are you going to initiate?

Longer-Term Implications

With nowhere for ICT to be relocated and no backup system capable of taking over all activities, it took two weeks for the resumption of access to applications, e-mail and the Internet. Despite best efforts the impact was widely felt across your organization and it will be a long time before the media stories about the effects dissipate.

Points for discussion:

1. What, if any, is the long-term impact on your business?
2. What are your long-term priorities?
3. Are there any actions that you could take now to reduce the likelihood or impact of this happening in the future?
4. Do your BC and recovery plans have all the information you required to manage this scenario? Downtime! In relation to this scenario
5. In the event of such an incident, which applications and users will be prioritized for recovery?
6. It is possible that in the event of problems accessing electronic data some critical activities may need support to cope with a more manual style of working.
7. The website and IP phone system would also be down and it is possible that staff would be deployed elsewhere.

Note: The purpose here is to emphasize on the need for communication and Internet facilities to give service to customers and resolve complaints/queries. Systems down for more than a week can cause damage to goodwill and customer confidence. Hence redundancies are desired and telecom continuity is asked for.

Terrorism

Initial Information: At first it sounded as if a tire had burst on the street but as you rush outside to see what had happened, you can hear people screaming, car alarms and smell something burning. The scene outside is like a horror film, most of the windows in the area have been shattered, there are people walking around in a daze and some are obviously bleeding, there seems to be a body lying on the ground across the street. A bomb attack in here?

Points for discussion:

- What, if any, is the immediate impact on your business? Maybe your office is not a target, but people accounting is essential.
- What are your initial priorities? Whether to stop the large delivery due in two hours?
- Are there any Health and Safety issues? Update it seems as if there was a large explosion in the street close to your office. Your local radio station has stopped their normal scheduled programs and is broadcasting eye witness accounts from the scene. People are in a state of shock and trauma; most of them want to go home. Need to communicate and counsel employees.

Police have cordoned off the area which includes the car park where most of your staff cars are parked. Your staff are nervous and want to go home. You have a large delivery scheduled to arrive in two hours.

Points for discussion:

1. What, if any, is the short-term impact on your business?
2. What are your short-term priorities?
3. What information would you now give to members of your team, where would you get this from and are all, including out of hour, contact details up-to-date?
4. What response and/or recovery plans are you going to initiate?

Longer-term implications: You have still not been able to get back into your original premise and have been working from temporary facilities since. Staff are not happy with this and your customers find the arrangements inconvenient as the car park is not as close as it was. Deliveries are being taken in a warehouse some distance away.

Points for discussion:

1. What, if any, is the long-term impact on your business?
2. What are your long-term priorities? Are there any actions that you could take now to reduce the likelihood or impact of this happening in the future?

3. Do your BC and recovery plans have all the information you required to manage this scenario? Expect the unexpected—terrorism in relation to this scenario.
4. Consider having a Grab Bag available so that in the event of a sudden departure from your normal place of work all necessary vital information is to hand.
5. Staff may need counseling after such an event. You could consider having contact details for a suitable organization available.
6. Staff travel arrangements may be severely disrupted; you may want to support them in making alternative arrangements. The Business Lincolnshire website has more info.

Note: With the right wording of the scenario, a near to real situation can be created and all relevant points in connection to that disaster discussed and issues can be resolved.

Debrief

Immediately following an exercise, it is crucial (and necessary) to have a verbal debrief, "hotwash" and lessons learned discussion with participants to answer any questions, solicit feedback and outline how the exercise outcomes will impact future planning activities. Although numerous means of soliciting feedback from participants exist, including paper-based or internet surveys and interviews, it is best to ask for written and on-the-spot feedback using easy-to-answer questions with a ratings scale:

1. To what degree did the exercise meet your expectations?
2. Please rate your satisfaction with the overall time/duration of the exercise session.
3. Please rate the overall style and quality of presentation materials.
4. How effectively did the facilitator present information?
5. Other: (recommendations for improvement, additional training needs, new topics, etc.).

Although feedback is important for continuous improvement, it is also a means of accounting for participants for training and audit purposes. Similarly, a summary document that captures key exercise details is perfect for historical records, audit documentation and review by senior leaders (i.e., Business Continuity Steering Committee) and may include:

1. Exercise results
2. Strengths
3. Opportunities for improvement
4. Lessons learned
5. Actions items/corrective actions

Just like a plan that sits unexercised on a shelf, exercise results that are documented and left unattended to do little to improve organizational resiliency. As such, action items and opportunities for improvement captured during the exercise should be entered into an issue log or corrective actions database so that they may be recorded, delegated and tracked to completion. While testing, frequency varies based on operating industry and standards; it is best to exercise business continuity plans and capabilities at least annually or following significant organizational changes.

Assumptions in Building Scenarios

1. All scenarios are possible although the likelihood for different scenarios may vary.
2. The scenario has an impact on, facility, assets, security, safety, and so on.

Hazard list for incident scenarios: A consensus on the inventory of incidents, the joint inventory of empirical data on the incidents and the cause and effect is important.

Make a joint inventory of available empirical data concerning the current context and the effect of risk management measures. Document available empirical data and/or include references in the scenario. Empirical data refers to design or model calculations, case histories, research results, trend analyses, amended legislation and demands, oversight of enforcement and so on.

The incident scenarios identified (both hazards and threats) can be split into two groups:

1. *Incidents that are already realistic* right now with a certain likelihood; examples of this are major floods or a pandemic.
2. *Incidents which are subject to developments,* and where the described impact will only become realistic in the longer-term; examples of this are scenarios based on the impact of the ageing population or climate change.

The conditions that the selection of incident scenarios needs to meet are the same for both types of scenario: the likelihood of occurrence becomes different and hence the prioritization of long-term incidents may be postponed. The scenario development for the period in the long-term should be based on the currently available knowledge and predictable trends.

Example Scenarios

1. Catastrophe industrial incident
2. Economic crisis
3. Enterprise function failure
4. WEATHER related incident
5. Terrorist attack
6. Pandemic outbreak

Aftermath of Disaster

Disasters are a testing time for everyone. The aftermath of a disaster can be felt on the employee morale and health. So, while we prepare to test the plans and build scenarios, we must factor the human element as well.

Reason Why Organizations Must Plan for People Reactions?

Employees are the organization's most valuable asset. To survive a disaster, organizations need to give support to its employees to deal with shock and stress. Tests of plans should combine building of mental preparedness and agility to deal with disaster. Many organizations have an outside specialist to talk to employees and advise them on stress management especially during crisis situations.

After-effects of disaster: When disaster strikes suddenly and there is loss of property and human life, it leads to trauma and stress among the people. People undergo psychological after-effects; they are generally spread over three distinct stages.

The first 24 hours: Employees may show symptoms of numbness or denial, be physically sick or anxious, or may withdraw from contact with others. In a city outage, the employee has to worry about the safety of his family as well as fulfill his organizational tasks. Some cases employees themselves take lead and suppress their anxiety to meet the crisis.

The first week: After the first phase, employees may feel isolated, anxious about the future, or angry/irritated at the situation. They may also withdraw from contact with each other or may exhibit demanding behavior.

Long-term effects: These effects depend on how well employees have come to terms with the situation. Employees having sense of ownership toward the organization and who believe organization has taken adequate measures to salvage the situation will show commitment to the organization. Employees who are still under stress or trauma will work with lower levels of commitment or to leave the company. These symptoms are common after any crisis; hence, scenario planning should introduce preparedness for stress as well.

Cycle testing consists of a series of exercises utilizing multiple methodologies that often increase in complexity and length from one phase to the next. The results of each test are assessed individually; improvements and error corrections are applied to the plan prior to beginning the next phase. At the end of the cycle the entire plan has been completely evaluated, in fact the plan goes through perfecting through iterations. Small logistical errors that could prove to be major obstacles in full-scale testing are isolated and removed from the plan. Testing in cycles has a cumulative impact on the organization, infusing disaster recovery preparedness at all levels.

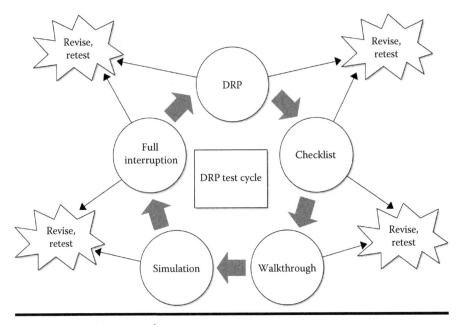

Figure 7.11 DRP test cycle.

Cyclical Testing of the Disaster Recovery Plan

Cyclic recovery tests provide an efficient pathway to *disaster recovery plan* (DRP) maintenance by early recognition and correction of such problems. At the end of each exercise and prior to the next, comprehensive debriefing, audit and analysis are required to update the current test plan as well as each of the following phases of the cycle (Figure 7.11).

Preparing a Test Plan

A test and exercise plan must meet the organization's business continuity objectives. It should be adequate to get assurance on the business recovery and response to crisis incidents. The following points to be adhered:

1. Obtaining executive sponsorship for testing and exercise program development.
2. Developing a realistic, progressive and cost-effective program.
3. Document the testing and exercise standards and guidelines to be used.
4. Defined testing and exercise program assumptions and limitations.
5. Identify exercise types to be included that will create a comprehensive exercise program based on the recovery strategies implemented and the RTO and recovery point objective (RPO) defined by the entity for its operations. These may include operational, facility and technical exercises and testing such as:
   a. Life safety exercises
   b. Plan walk–through/Tabletop review

    c. Scenario-based Tabletop exercise
    d. Call notification exercise
    e. Alternate site exercise
    f. Standalone platform, infrastructure or application recovery test
    g. Full end-to-end functional exercise of an operation or technology
    h. Comprehensive exercise of all recovery strategies required to recover the time sensitive operations and technology from a single site
    i. Integrated technology exercise with internal and external interdependencies

The success of a testing exercise depends upon the efficacy of the test plan. The following steps must be followed:

Step 1: Determine exercise requirements for each exercise to be conducted.
    a. *Set the exercise objectives*: The facilitator needs to set the exercise objectives. The following are some guidelines:
        i. Visualize the change you desire to see because of the exercise.
        ii. Initiate validation of team's capability associated with emergency response arrangements; communication systems; evacuation routines; incident control rooms; coordination with emergency services; media response; social media response; incident management; business continuity plans; crisis management plans; off-site recovery plans; IT disaster recovery; IT system penetration; supplier incident management; employee communications; incident management tools, and so on.
        iii. If outcomes are measurable, then objective setting is simple. For example, meeting preset RTOs.
        iv. Determine whether the team deputies are participating in the exercise or not. They could exercise separately or serve as observers/note takers/advisors during the main team exercise.
        v. After finalizing the test objectives, they must be approved by the BCM sponsor. Their support will give credibility to the testing and ensure that team members take the tests seriously. Also the lessons learned will be reviewed and corrective action taken where necessary.
    b. Define and document in-scope/out-of-scope requirements.
    c. Define exercise notification process.
        i. Announced/planned
        ii. Unannounced/surprised
Step 2: Schedule tests and exercises to be conducted.
Develop a multiyear progressive schedule building on lessons learned and mastery of recovery processes (Table 7.1).
Develop specific schedule for tests and exercises to be conducted on an annual basis or as frequently as necessary to ensure competency and to meet regulatory requirements.

Table 7.1   Test Schedule

Name of Test	Frequency/Year	Year 1	Year 2	Year 3
Evacuation drill	2	1/7, 2/12		
Checklist exercise	4	1/3, 1/6, 1/9, 1/12		
Tabletop exercise	3	1/2, 3/4, 5/9		
Notification test	4	1/3, 1/6, 1/9, 1/12		
Simulation test	1	8/10		
Functional test	2	1/3, 2/9		

Define and document evaluation criteria aligned with exercise objectives and scope:
   a. Quantitative
   b. Qualitative

Step 3: Identify pre-exercise activities.
   a. Identify resources required to conduct the exercise.
   b. Identify participants team members, IT representatives, vendors, and so on.
   c. Ensure all understand the objectives of the exercise and their roles.
   d. Provide an inventory of hardware, software and physical assets required for the exercise (e.g., PC/laptop, security access, telephone, applications, and printers).
   e. Document and communicate specifications for the exercise environment.
   f. Specify production versus test environments.
   g. Time for test—business day versus weekend.
   h. Provide a timetable of events and circulate to all participants, facilitators and adjudicators.
   i. Establish the conditions for "back-out" or test and exercise cancellation plan.

Step 4: Conduct exercise.
   a. Should an incident occur during an exercise you should have a predetermined mechanism for cancelling the exercise and invoking the actual continuity process.
   b. Record exercise process.
   c. Document exercise results via the activation and maintenance of the issues log.
   d. Declare end of exercise.
   e. Shut down procedures.
   f. Perform clean-up activities.

Step 5: Identify postexercise activities.
   a. Conduct debriefing sessions to review exercise results and identify actions for improvements.

    b. Postexercise reporting.

    c. Provide a comprehensive summary with recommendations.

    d. Document action plan report.

    e. Identify open issues.

    f. Identify actionable items with responsibilities and timeframes for resolution.

Step 6: Monitor (and escalate where necessary) progress to completion of agreed actions.

    a. Communicate exercise results.

    b. Document lessons learned.

    c. Document expected versus actual results.

    d. Document unexpected results.

Step 7: Establish plan maintenance program.

    a. Define plan maintenance method and schedule.

    b. Define ownership of plan data.

    c. Prepare maintenance schedules and review procedures.

    d. Select maintenance tools.

    e. Monitor maintenance activities.

    f. Establish plan update process.

    g. Ensure that scheduled plan maintenance addresses all documented recommendations.

Step 8: Define change control process.

    a. Analyze business changes with planning implications.

    b. Develop change control procedures to monitor changes.

    c. Create proper version control; develop plan re-issue, distribution, and circulation procedures.

    d. Identify plan distribution lists for circulation.

    e. Develop a process to update plans based on response to audit findings.

    f. Set guidelines for feedback of changes to planning function.

    g. Implement change control process.

Step 9: Identify or establish appropriate standards.

    a. Review process owner expectations based on industry standards and organizational as well as "client" service expectations.

    b. Develop an organizational standard with a recurring review and enhancement/continuous improvement process.

    c. Based on industry and/or national/international standards as well as organizational and/or client expectations.

    d. Frequency and scope appropriate for the organization.

    e. Approved by leadership.

Step 10: Establish a business continuity program audit process.

    a. Define schedule for self-assessment audit.

    b. Prepare to support other audits which may occur.

    c. Document audit standards and guidelines.

    d. Select/develop any needed audit tools.

    e. Establish audit schedule.

    f. Conduct/monitor audit activities.

The areas to be covered by audit include

    a. Audit the plan documentation control procedures.

    b. Audit version control process and documentation.

    c. Audit distribution lists and associated processes.

    d. Audit change control process.

Review management response to audit findings.

    a. Confirm responses have been submitted and action plans documented.

    b. Verify completed actions have been captured in the plan and supporting documentation.

Communicate test and exercise/audit results and recommendations.

    a. Identify appropriate stakeholders

    b. Process owners

    c. Governance coordinators

    d. Senior leadership/operations oversight

Select appropriate communication methods and communicate in a timely manner.

    a. Reporting level of detail

    b. Where appropriate, consider graphic representations or comparison reports targeted by audience

Step 11: Establish a feedback/validation loop to confirm appropriate actions have been taken as a result of reported findings.

    a. Issues tracking

    b. Date item opened

    c. Owner of issue

    d. Date item closed

The design team develops the test from start to finish. Members should have strong knowledge of the overall business. They should also have detailed knowledge in their area or department. The team usually has three to seven members, more if needed.

The desired features in the design team include

- Creative
- Functional under pressure
- Able to stay on schedule
- Detail-oriented
- Willing to challenge
- Good at keeping secrets
- Not participating in the test

Choose test scenarios: And state the expected results. Prepare test design description and list test case description and test procedures. Plan the test execution and write test incident report and test log to summarize points in the test summary report.

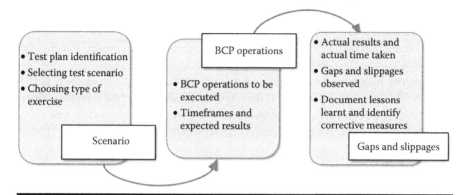

Figure 7.12 Components of a test plan.

A bit of creativity and imagination goes in writing an interesting test plan. The occasional injects into scenario builds the resilience and responsiveness and true performance of players can be observed. Players exercise the plan with a good humored setting and a bit of refreshments arranged by the organizer, puts a lot of motivation to the test room (Figure 7.12).

As seen from the above diagram, the test plans should be carefully designed to suit the organization's requirements. Tests and exercises should be scheduled so that the efficacy of plans can be tested. In a constantly changing business environment plans need to have change management procedures in place and plans are updated and kept current and executable after changes are effected.

Considerations Governing Design of Exercises

1. Determine exercise criteria and program frequency
2. Develop test scenarios, teams and evaluation criteria
3. Provision for documenting "Lessons Learned"

Understanding the role of BCM personnel and facilitators: Actual exercise facilitation and delivery can take several shapes based on the type of the exercise, complexity of the scenario, participant familiarity with business continuity, and access to technology. To increase the realism of the scenario and garner engagement from participants, the following approaches may be considered:

1. Exercise activation utilizing (and testing) an automated emergency notification system
2. PowerPoint slides that illustrates the scenario and provides situational updates by time period
3. Paper-based, verbal or digital injects that provide additional details on the scenario
4. "Breaking news" videos that illustrate the scenario or changing conditions

5. Remote or work-from-home testing via virtual private network and/or teleconference
6. Interaction with key suppliers, first responders or other interested stakeholders

Perhaps the biggest recommendation for business continuity practitioners is that they should thoroughly understand their audience, especially if the exercise includes senior management. Participant profiles and their expected participation and direction should be studied to get maximum effectiveness from the exercise.

Formal Change Control Process

This formal change control process should then ensure that the updated plans are distributed and reinforced by regular reviews of the complete plan. Examples of situations that might necessitate updating plans include:

1. Changes in business objectives or strategy
2. Service changes
3. Acquisition of new systems or replacement or upgrading of operational systems
4. Acquisition of new hardware
5. Relocation of facilities and resources
6. Changes in key personnel or their roles
7. Response to changes in legislation or national guidance
8. Changes in contractors, suppliers or services
9. Changes in processes
10. Changes in risk
11. Changes in backup and standby arrangements
12. Deficiencies found during testing

Change Control: Any changes to the scope or detailed content of business continuity plans can, unless they are carefully controlled, impact on the total effectiveness of those plans. Procedures should be included within the organization's change management program to ensure that business continuity matters are appropriately addressed.

Define Change Control Process

1. Analyze business changes with planning implications
2. Develop change control procedures to monitor changes—create proper version control; develop plan re-issue, distribution, and circulation procedures— identify plan distribution lists for circulation—process to update plans based on response to Audit findings
3. Set guidelines for feedback of changes to planning function
4. Implement change control process

Responsibility should be assigned for the identification of changes in business arrangements not yet reflected in each plan and the assessment of how the plan should be amended to accommodate them.

A formal change control process therefore, needs to be in place to assess the likely effect of any such changes, their significance for all plans, with time schedules and their likely impact on resource requirements. There should be multiple, controlled copies of the business continuity plans, held in widely separate locations. At least one should be kept at the remote backup and standby locations.

This will ensure that, in the event of a widespread disaster, at least some copies can be found. All updates should be logged in a central register. It is important to keep all copies updated to the same level. This will be the responsibility of the holders of individual copies, who will be advised by the coordinator of the changes to be entered. All changes should be recorded and the version number of the plan logged on each copy.

Business Continuity Plan Exercise, Audit, and Maintenance

1. Establish an testing and exercise program which documents plan exercise requirements including the planning, scheduling, facilitation, communications, auditing, and postreview documentation.
2. Establish maintenance program to keep plans current and relevant.
3. Establish an audit process which will validate compliance with standards, review solutions, verify appropriate levels of maintenance and exercise activities and validate the plans are current, accurate and complete.
4. Communicate test and exercise results and recommendations.
5. A documentation of testing and exercise standards and guideline must be made.
6. An identification of type of tests and exercises to be made that should include business, facility and technical testing.

Identify Postexercise Activities

1. Conduct debriefing sessions to review exercise results and identify actions for improvements.
2. Postexercise Reporting
   a. Provide a comprehensive summary with recommendations
   b. Document action plan report—identify open issues—identify actionable items with responsibilities and timeframes for resolution
   c. Monitor (and escalate where necessary) progress to completion of agreed actions
   d. Communicate exercise Results—Document Lessons Learned—Document expected versus actual results—Document unexpected results

Establish Plan Maintenance Program

1. Define Plan Maintenance Method and Schedule
2. Define ownership of plan data
3. Prepare maintenance schedules and review procedures
4. Select maintenance tools
5. Monitor maintenance activities
6. Establish plan update process
7. Ensure that scheduled plan maintenance addresses all documented recommendations

Evaluating BCM Plans

The primary objective of any disaster recovery plan is to enable organizations to maintain its business continuity, minimize damage, and prevent loss. The critical part of any BCM plan would be its workability. The common anxiety of BCM plan managers is; "will my plan work?" The best assurance to that question is to practice the plan regularly. Along with practicing plans, a proper change management system to be installed to update plans regularly according to changes.

Once an exercise type is agreed upon, it will be necessary to determine the scenario(s) that will guide exercise participants and encourage the usage of, review and feedback on their business continuity plans. The following list provides general examples of scenarios, organized by resource type, which may be considered and customized based on an organization's unique resources, needs, dependencies, or operating environment.

- *Loss of facility*: Continuing the delivery of critical products and services following the loss of a key facility (i.e., fire)
  - *Loss of people*: Continuing the delivery of critical products and services with a reduced workforce (i.e., pandemic)
  - *Loss of technology*: Continuing the delivery of critical products and services without access to technology or systems (i.e., data center failure)
  - *Loss of equipment*: Continuing the delivery of critical products and services following the loss of key equipment (i.e., metal press)
  - *Loss of suppliers*: Continuing the delivery of critical products and services (i.e., payroll processing)

Maintaining and reviewing business continuity plans: Business continuity plans should be maintained by being subject to regular review and update, to ensure their continuing effectiveness. Responsibility should be assigned for regular reviews of each business continuity plan to an individual acting under the control of business continuity planning team and the coordinator. The identification of changes in business arrangements not yet reflected in the business continuity plans should be followed by an appropriate update of the plan.

Set Up the Next Exercise

Toward the end of the exercise, I like to ask for the teams for their ideas for the next exercise. What do they think needs to be covered next time, who should attend and when should it be scheduled? With a captive audience, its great timing and you will often get some good ideas for future objectives or scenarios.

The takeaway from an exercise is what the participants learned and what was documented and a feedback on how the participants feel and whether they are confident that their plan will be enacted as desired?

"Plans are useless, but planning is everything." Business continuity plans attempt to provide for and address the unpredictable. The actual scenario of a disaster as it unfolds may not be what the planners anticipated, but the business continuity planning process should provide the flexibility to respond to changing circumstances. Planning and exercises brings in discipline and responsiveness which will create preparedness to disaster.

Annexures

Annexure A: Considerations in Taking Help of Experts

1. The source of know-how of expert to be ascertained. (empirical data, model calculations); assumptions used should be subject to checks.
2. Empirical data must be checked against the latest circumstances that may influence (the likelihood of) or the occurrence of future circumstances. While determining correction factors, experts should adhere to formal calculation rules of probability.
3. Record as many references, sources, assumptions, and uncertainties. Make a distinction between uncertainties (due to lack of knowledge) and differences of views between experts.
4. Determine how to achieve the greatest possible convergence between the various expert opinions, while maintaining individual views and to a "best" outcome, and how the best can be reported, including the uncertainties and differences of views.
5. Experts have to adhere to formal calculation rules of probability.
6. Determine how the expert can best be helped in coming to an independent determination of his/her own interpretation and estimates.
7. The more explicit the knowledge sources, assumptions and uncertainties are, the easier it will be to manage discussions between experts and substantiate and follow-up choices made. It is good to record as many references, sources, assumptions and uncertainties.
8. Make a distinction between uncertainties (due to lack of knowledge) and differences of views between experts.

Annexure B: Scenario Task List

1. Proactively avoiding potential threats to organizational safety and security:
   a. Removing the source
   b. Minimizing threat occurrence by reducing the circumstances that may lead to materialization of threat (avoidance measures)
2. Mitigation measures to limit (source) a potential threat before it occurs (prevention):
   a. Limiting the threat by spatial layout
   b. Limiting the threat by setting up an appropriate infrastructure by building of road network, protecting data and information through proper nondisclosure agreements (NDAs) with local and international clients
   c. Timely decisions in response to market forces and economic downturn within the industry
   d. Increasing the awareness to risk and risk mitigation measures among the employees, vendors, and other stakeholders
3. Create preparedness to limit impact of threats if and when they occur (preparation):
   a. Developing, implementing, testing, and monitoring emergency response plan, crisis communication plan to increase timely response and minimization of impact during an incident. This can be enhanced by
      i. Conducting training and exercises regularly for employees.
      ii. Involving multidisciplinary organizations including media, local authorities, regional administration and people as a whole. This will enable
         A. Training of personnel through exercising.
         B. Exercise to test arrangements, systems, and available capabilities.
      iii. Create a buffer of food supplies, emergency supplies, and vital goods.
      iv. Optimum allocation of BCM resources for maximizing success of BCM(prioritization).
   b. Drawing up, implementing, exercising, and overseeing continuity plans.
   c. Setting up a clear information structure for communication during crisis.
   d. Setting up channels for risk monitoring and reporting.
   e. Setting up emergency response/incident-handling procedures.
      i. Ensure logistics support for emergency services
      ii. Preparation of emergency response plans that include
         A. Crisis management and coordination.
         B. Fire service processes.
         C. Medical facilities for medical assistance and mental health care for postincident stress.
         D. Communication and assistance from police authorities for maintaining law and order, controlling traffic, cordoning off facilities after a structural disaster, identification of victims of the disaster at hand.

      E. Multidisciplinary processes (information, warning, clearance, evacuation), relief operations, basic necessities, environment, making roads passable, collection of contaminated goods).

  f. Setting up and maintaining a flexible, proactive response mechanism by

     i. Setting up a consistent communication infrastructure and crisis communication arrangements and procedures for the business continuity teams to follow in case of a crisis/disaster.

     ii. Providing fall-back mechanisms and scenarios.

     iii. Configuring sufficient redundancies where there is a possibility of failure due to single dependencies.

4. Attempt to limit the impact of an imminent incident

  a. Continuously monitor for imminent events and early warning indicators (examples: forecasts of rising water levels, detection of virus, etc.) and set a procedure as to who shall set alert and the action plan (e.g., evacuation and shutting down of systems).

  b. Evaluate information and take decisions on how to contain the impact.

  c. In the case of a global disaster, it will be beneficial to exchange and disseminate information between organizations to check what measures they are taking to avert disaster and if possible doing a combined effort to contain the impact.

  d. Increasing awareness to enhance inbuilt resilience among employees and increase their ability to cope and participate during crisis.

  e. Set escalation levels in advance and escalate to the level of control appropriate for the crisis.

  f. Crisis alert systems and emergency alarms to alert employees.

  g. Decision-making and crisis coordination

     i. Involve all relevant personnel in the decision-making process for crisis

     ii. Take stock of the situation based on available information

     iii. Evaluate potential scenarios for the crisis (generally assuming worst case)

     iv. Take decisions in respect of operational and administrative matters at the preset levels

     v. Coordinate/manage execution of decisions by BCM management

     vi. Note the consequences of the decisions taken (e.g., time required, road and transport capacity, social and political/administrative disruption)

     vii. Prepare postcrisis situation and lessons learned

  h. Incident fighting

     i. Implement incident-handling procedures:

       A. Oversee the safety of people

       B. Ensure logistical support for incident fighting

     ii. Attempt to reduce or restrict the source of the threat

     iii. Take measures to reduce the spread of the threat (example in case of fire, in one part, preventive measures can be taken to ensure that it does not spread to other parts of the facility.)

      iv. Ensure that the impact of threat on personnel is minimized by
  - A. Ensuring provision of basic/vital supplies.
  - B. Optimal allocation of scarce resources during crisis.
  - C. Demonstrating the use of organizational emergency facilities (e.g., emergency exits) and emergency resources (hand-held fire extinguishers).

   i. Crisis communication to public:
  - i. Draw up environment analysis with external players involved including media.
  - ii. Clear and unambiguous crisis communication prewritten where necessary to be delivered by authorized individual especially to media and stakeholders. Means can vary from a broadcast channel to website communication or merely addressing a crowd.
  - iii. Ensure that progress and possible alternatives for action are contained in any communications with the public.

5. Repair the impairment and consequences (aftercare):
  - a. Resume normal operations after repairing affected site and making it accessible again:
    - i. Return of relocated employees to primary facility
    - ii. Recovery of business and cash flow
  - b. Take measures to reduce the aftermath from the crisis by stress-reducing activities, office picnics, and psychological aftercare.
  - c. Compensate the loss sustained by monetary compensation for the dead and injured.

6. Consider and implement support measures for A, B, C, D, and E.
  - a. These do not by themselves make any direct contribution to security: set up the policy process:
    - i. Maintain network of contacts with relevant services, organizations, firms, and authorities (nationally and internationally).
    - ii. Introduce the importance of safety and security measures in the policy processes.
  - b. Maintain risk inventory and identify threats
    - i. Carry out forecasts and forward studies and produce scenarios
      - A. Gain an insight into (the source of) threats
      - B. Gain an insight into the vulnerabilities
        1. Identification of vital sectors
        2. Identifications of vital services, processes, and objects within the vital sectors
      - C. Gain an insight into the vulnerabilities of vital sectors, including intersector dependencies

    c. Creating the desired security level:
        i. Requirements of certainty of supply
        ii. Security requirements for specific risks
        iii. Tests against best practices (enforcement and oversight)
7. Consider and implement measures intended to support A, B, C, D, and E.
    a. Decide what procedures need to be undertaken to achieve a desired level of security and tasks per incident undertaken for interoperability of process, equipment, and training.
    b. Prioritize tasks per the criticality ranking given based on quantitative evaluation of risk.
    c. General constraints for a safety and security system.
        i. Task allocation, responsibilities, and powers between actors and players
            A. There is a need to explain employees what type of ability is required, whether to participate or to actively cope with disaster incident.
            B. Informs the stakeholders about the BCM plans.
        ii. Encourage citizens to be active (coping and citizen participation)
            A. Inform citizens about their role.
            B. Create preconditions so that people understand their role.
        iii. Activate vital BCM infrastructure that includes BCM teams, IT, and logistics, facilities, and so on and monitor them so that they play their role effectively and on time.
    d. Evaluate actions taken and lessons learned, and implement mitigation measures for inadequacies identified during the incident and monitor remediation process.
        i. Evaluate preventive measures
        ii. Evaluate preparation and exercises
        iii. Evaluate response after an event
        iv. Evaluates the aftercare measures

Annexure C: Tabletop Exercise Walkthrough Scenario

A desktop walkthrough exercise is useful for testing the business continuity plan without disrupting normal business.

    Suggested format:

Attendance: Key staff

Team Lead: Manager

Structure: Injects to be distributed or displayed in sequence giving sufficient time to review the plan and discussing issues posed by the injects.

Inject One

Time: Monday 6:30 p.m.

The fire alarm has buzzed, and there is news of fire on the 17th floor of the building. The admin staff has confirmed the fire, but evacuation of premises was not yet ordered. Employees were getting jumpy and tensed up.

Questions discussed were as follows:

1. Are the incident response plan and procedures for fire hazard existing?
2. Who will receive the fire call and respond with building authorities?
3. In case of partial fire, how soon should the evacuation of employees be effected?
4. Who will trigger evacuation?
5. Are HR procedures on to talk to employees and assure them of their safety?

Inject Two

At 7:50 p.m., the fire authorities have tried to contain the fire. But it has spread to the next floor. It has become necessary to evacuate the building, and all offices have been intimated to prepare for an orderly evacuation.

Questions discussed were as follows:

- Is the crisis communication team corresponding and taking constant status of the incident?
- Does the spread of fire to the next floor trigger the security considerations and the evacuation procedures are initiated?
- Are fire wardens carrying the contact lists and instructing the employees to assemble at assembly point? What business continuity arrangements would be considered at this stage?
- What instructions would be given to staff and how?

Inject Three

At 10 p.m., building is vacated, but the fire has spread to five or six floors including the floor of our office. Authorities have cordoned the facility, and it is not going to be available for the next few days.

Questions discussed were as follows:

- Who would trigger the DR?
- What instructions would be given to staff, customers, and suppliers and how?
- How would operational backlogs be managed?
- What might the longer-term issues be and how would they be addressed?

Check whether plan is designed to cope with the incident

- Check that initial response procedures cover the requirement of the scenario.
- Is there any scope for improvement of the existing plan in light of the discussions?
- Are roles and responsibilities for evacuation properly understood by the team members?
- Is plan validated in terms of declaration procedures, evacuation and adhering to prewritten plan?

Chapter 8

Aligning IT with Business Requirement

Introduction

The term disaster recovery (DR) is slowly becoming old fashioned. ITDR is being replaced by IT resilience, representing an organization's capability to prevent, respond to, and recover from disaster. There is now a need for organizations to move beyond disaster recovery and include resiliency that is more focused on continuous availability and continuous improvement. A stable infrastructure and good support from applications running the organization's business give sustainability and resilience, and result in a fair ROI on BCM investments (Figure 8.1).

When we say IT is all pervasive, it has the tenacity to cause a great impact on business if something goes wrong. Hence alignment of IT with business requirements is very important. Gartner and Forrester research now support IT resiliency as it has a focus on the need to serve customers and help business to stay competitive; it concentrates on the more likely disruptions rather than catastrophic disasters.

Business resiliency leverages the technologies such as replication, continuous data protection, and snapshots to enhance resiliency, and in the process reduce recovery time objectives. While RTOs used to be in the range of 6 to 18 hours, it has now been possible to reduce it to four hours. IT resiliency measures downtime in minutes or hours.

The following factors contribute to IT resiliency:

1. *Availability of systems*: As organizations are working in an integrated environment, the availability of all systems in unison is significant to continuity of operations.

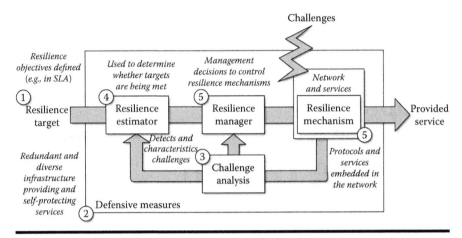

Figure 8.1   IT Infrastructure for a small enterprise.

2. *Ascertain the cost of downtime*: Impact of downtime can be grave: loss of employee productivity, lost business opportunities, and loss of customer confidence apart from revenue losses. Yet, empirical research has shown that more than 50% of the organizations do not calculate the cost of downtime. In fact, it is difficult to find a log of the dates and duration when they suffered downtime.

3. *Alignment of technology with business objectives*: Investment in resiliency should be carefully made so as to get maximum ROI and achieve the objective of resiliency. Businesses can consider failover and replication options in their planning. Technology is not one size that fits all, and so it has to be customized as per business requirements.

Considerations in Requirement Analysis and Specifications

Organizations have witnessed system failure and costly application software being abandoned only because they were not effective. It has been determined that one of the primary reasons why software projects fail is because requirements of the project were not captured properly. Current software applications often operate over multiple platforms and across many locations around the globe. Often during the project lifecycle, the demands keep varying and this can also have an impact in eliciting proper requirements.

Those systems are effective that are "fit for purpose." Hence requirements definition and analysis is an integral part of development of IT systems, failing which the impact can be substantial on finance and business. Requirement analysis covers those tasks to determine the needs of a proposed software solution or product, often involving requirements of various stakeholders associated with the solution.

Requirement analysis is a key component in the software development lifecycle and is usually the initial step before the project commences. Requirements gathering can be a difficult and exhaustive process. Some of the most prevalent methods are given below:

1. *Prototyping*: This involves interviews/interaction with users representing all departments or aspects of the existing system. A preliminary system is created for the new system and the first prototype is created from this initial design. This is usually a scaled-down system and represents an approximation of the features of the final product (screens, interactive formats).

   Constant interaction with users is made and they add further value/features to the prototype and an iterative process commences where users and developers show prototypes and go on perfecting it. This step continues till an acceptable prototype is made. The final system is made from the final prototype. This system is evaluated and tested.

2. *Storyboards*: Storyboards help developers visualize the sequence and interconnectedness of their work. They allow for a "big picture" approach that may be very useful in requirements gathering.

3. *Modeling*: A requirements modeling can be done on a simple whiteboard or any other method. User requirements are parsed around the different kinds of feasibilities to arrive at a workable solution. This method focuses around system's external behavior from its internal design.
   - Describe the users' and stakeholders' needs with clarity in natural language.
   - Define a consistent glossary of terms that can be used by users, developers, and testers.
   - Reduce gaps and inconsistencies in the requirements.
   - Plan the order in which features will be developed.
   - Use the models as a basis for system tests, making a clear relationship between the tests and the requirements. When the requirements change, this relationship enables the updating of tests.

   A partially working application, even if very much simplified, generally forms the most stimulating basis for discussion of the requirements with users. The model is an effective way to summarize the results of those discussions. It is specifically used in agile computing.

4. *State transition diagrams*: Allow developers and users to see how a program might behave. This anticipation of events is useful when discussing requirements (Figure 8.2).

   Objects have both behavior and state or, in other words, they do things and they know things. Some objects do and know more things, or at least

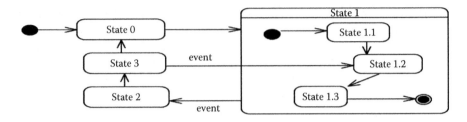

Figure 8.2   State-transition diagram.

more complicated things, than other objects. Some objects are incredibly complicated, so complex that developers can have difficulty understanding them. To understand complex classes better, particularly those that act in different manners depending on their state, state machine diagrams are used to describe requirements in its different transition states.

A state represents a stage in the behavior pattern of an object, and it is possible to have initial states and final states. An initial state, also called a creation state, is the one that an object is in when it is first created, whereas a final state is one in which no transitions lead out of. A transition is a progression from one state to another and will be triggered by an event that is either internal or external to the object.

5. *Use cases*: Use cases are created to capture functional requirements in the software development lifecycle. Use cases can be utilized through the following:
   a. Scenarios describe how the product will be used in specific situations.
   b. Written narratives describe the role of an actor (user or device) as it interacts with the system.
   c. Use cases designed from the actor or user's point of view.
   d. Not all actors can be identified during the first iteration of requirements elicitation, but it is important to identify the primary actors before developing the use cases.

Functional specifications help build a system that corresponds with user requirements. A use-case diagram is a helpful visual resource and a well-written use case is an excellent tool in the requirements gathering process (Figures 8.3 and 8.4).

Facilitated application specification technique (FAST) consists of two types:

1. It involves arranging a meeting between customers and developers at a neutral site and then helping customers to identify the problem, propose elements of solution, and negotiate different approaches. This helps get the first set of requirements.
2. Alternatively, the rules for participation can be set in advance and agenda fixed. A brainstorming session is encouraged and the appointed facilitator

Use case template

Use case ID (UC-1)		Use case name	**Name**
Created by		Last updated by	
Date created		Date last updated	
Actor			
Description			
Preconditions			
Post conditions			
Priority: (low/medium/high)			
Frequency of use			
Normal course		**UC-1: Case**	
		Actor actions	**System responses**
		1.	2.
		3.	4.
		5.	6.
Alternative course			
		Actor actions	**System responses**
Exceptions			
		Actor actions	**System responses**
Includes (another use case id)			
Special requirements			
Assumptions			
Notes and issues			

Figure 8.3 Use case template.

	GuardingEarth	MagicMaps	MagicMaps DB	Community	Location	MapService	Routing	Security	TrafficInfo
Issues	2								
Preview Issue	✓								
Report An Issue	✓								
Locations				1	4				
Add To Favourites					✓				
Find nearest points of inter...					✓				
Find Place					✓				
Share Map				✓	✓				
Map Navigation						6			
Routing				1			7		2
Add To Route							✓		
Change Drive Mode							✓		
Find Route							✓		
Reroute due to traffic							✓		✓
Share Route				✓			✓		
Show Route							✓		
Update Traffic Info							✓		✓
System Access								2	

Figure 8.4 Spreadsheet based used case example.

leads the discussion with use of sheets, flipcharts, whiteboards, and so on and the objective is to arrive at a consensus on the preliminary requirements for the proposed solution.

Based on the scope and nature of a specific software project, requirement analysis is carried out by an independent business analyst or a team of analysts to capture requirements. A requirements analysis involves capturing both functional and non-functional requirements and requires both technical and business expertise. To ensure effective capturing of requirement organizations follow a holistic process involving these broad steps:

1. *Requirements scope*: The scope and boundary of the proposed software solution is drawn based on business requirements and goals.
2. *Stakeholder identification*: Identifying stakeholders such as customers, end-users, system administrators, and so on is the next step in requirements analysis. This is one of the most important steps in the whole process, as proper identification of stakeholders enables the business analyst to draw a road map for gathering requirements.
3. *Requirements elicitation/requirements gathering*: Postidentification of stakeholders, requirements soliciting task commences. This is done by using personal interviews, focus groups, market study, surveys, and research.
4. *Requirement analysis*: Once user data is gathered, structured analysis is carried out on this data to determine models. Usually use cases are developed to analyze the data on various parameters depending on the larger goals of the software solution.
5. *Software requirement specification and signoff*: Once the captured data is analyzed, these are put together in the form of a software requirement specification (SRS) document. This document serves as a blueprint for the design or development teams to start building the solution on and is signed by user management to concur the accuracy of requirements defined for new system. The objectives of a requirement analysis can be listed as follows:
   a. Identify customer's needs
   b. Examine feasibility of proposed solution
   c. Perform economic and technical analysis
   d. Establish schedule and constraints
   e. Create system definitions
   f. Problem recognition and a focus on how to address problems
   g. Modeling
   h. Specification
   Analysis consists of review of both functional and nonfunctional requirements:
   - Functional requirements
     • Input/output

- Processing
- Error handling
- Nonfunctional requirements
  - Physical environment (equipment locations, multiple sites, etc.)
  - Interfaces (for example data medium)
  - User and human factors (for example who are the users, their skill level)
  - Performance (how well is the system functioning)
  - Documentation
  - Data (qualitative stuff)
  - Resources (finding, physical space)
  - Security (backup, firewall)
  - Quality assurance (maximum down time, MTBF, etc.)

As seen from the above, the objective of continuity is right from requirement analysis stage, and when BCM has to be embedded into the culture, it means inculcating it not only in people and process, but to align its technology to meet business requirements as well as business continuity requirements.

Application Impact Analysis

The application impact analysis (AIA) is a risk-based approach to determine application restoration priorities based on the needs of the business. It studies the impact on operations, business processes, and application dependencies (upstream/downstream) and, in turn, be in a better position to determine an application's recovery time objective (RTO). It takes the following into consideration:

1. Inventory of all desktop applications and local databases used within the enterprise.
2. Include standalone critical systems.
3. Determine the legal and regulatory implications as also impact to the goodwill of the business if customer-specific applications suffer a downtime.

The most effective way to check impact of applications is through testing and performance monitoring. In a distributed complex network and multiple applications running on the infrastructure it is imperative to check, test, and adapt the applications to best align with business requirements.

Application testing has to be performed to ensure software application reliability and project success software testing to assure on the following:

- Test if all defined requirements are met
- Test the performance of the application

■ Test each component
■ Test the components integrated with each other
■ Test the application end-to-end
■ Test the application in various environments
■ Test all the application paths
■ Test all the scenarios and then test some more

An application can be effective in standalone mode but in an integrated environment, it adversely impacts other applications' performance by degrading it or causing a system crash. Technology is all pervasive and it also acts as an enabler in planning for business continuity and plays vital part in business operations today.

The effectiveness of testing can be measured if the goal and purpose of the testing effort is clearly defined. Some of the testing goals are the following:

■ Testing in each phase of the development cycle to ensure that the "bugs" (defects) are eliminated at the earliest.
■ Testing to ensure no "bugs" creep through in the final product.
■ Testing to ensure the reliability of the software.
■ Above-all testing to ensure that the user expectations are met.

Unreliable software can severely hurt businesses and endanger lives depending on the criticality of the application. The simplest application poorly written can deteriorate the performance of your environment such as the servers, the network, and thereby causing an unwanted mess.

Coverage

The testing process and the test cases should cover

■ All the scenarios that can occur when using the software application.
■ Each business requirement that was defined for the project.
■ Specific levels of testing that should cover every line of code written for the application.

There are various levels of testing that focus on different aspects of the software application. The often-quoted V model best explains this (Figure 8.5).

The various levels of testing illustrated above are the following:

■ *Unit testing* should ensure that each and every line of code is tested.
■ *Integration testing* should ensure that the components can be integrated, and all the interfaces of each component are working correctly.

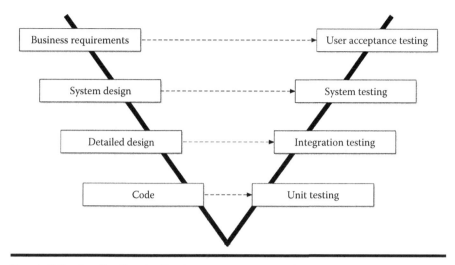

Figure 8.5   Application testing types.

- *System testing* should cover all the "paths"/scenarios possible when using the system. The system testing is done in an environment that is like the production environment, that is, the environment where the product will be finally deployed.
- *User acceptance testing* is done to check the application functions as desired.

An effective testing process will comprise the following steps:

1. Test strategy and planning
2. Review test strategy to ensure that it is aligned with the project goals
3. Design/write test cases
4. Review test cases to ensure proper test coverage
5. Execute test cases
6. Capture test results
7. Track defects
8. Capture relevant metrics
9. Analyze

An effective-testing strategy and process helps to minimize or eliminate bugs/defects. The extent to which it eliminates these postproduction defects is a good measure of the effectiveness of the testing strategy and process. Also in application-impact analysis, the interdependencies between applications are analyzed to check how much impact the nonavailability of one would have on other functions or businesses.

Impact of Security Concerns Caused by IT

Complexity of IT is increasing and maintenance of an adequate security architecture that aligns with business processes results in substantial impact on business. As Ron Weber, an information systems audit specialist notes security is but like onion-skin layers around the application. Chief applications are at the core of information systems processing, and business transactions are processed and stored with these applications and/or databases. Misalignment of IT with security of these applications leads to severe impacts on processes that can disrupt business for short or sometimes elongated periods.

In addition, the people and processes and policies supporting the technology becomes less effective due to misalignment. IT security is very critical for maintaining the confidentiality, integrity, and availability of information systems. Impact of nonavailability or disruption has been discussed in earlier sections. Let us briefly glance at some impacts resulting from misalignment:

1. Business loss due to loss of reputation caused by publicized data breaches in the organization.
2. Legal and financial impact caused by noncompliance to laws and regulations.
3. Rework of data due to loss of data due to interruptions in information systems or corruption of disks and drives due to virus, worms, or malware.
4. Loss of productivity due to security incident at the organization.

Telecommunication Continuity Needs and Implementation of the Same

Last Mile Circuit Protection

Telecom continuity has become crucial to the operation of complex corporate networks. So much we depend on our wired worlds, that we cannot imagine what might happen if primary telecommunications facilities were disrupted or become generally unreliable. Those who have faced problems have introduced redundancies in bits and pieces, but have not considered addressing the problem of telecom continuity as a whole for the entire organization (Figure 8.6).

Core networks generally offer a high level of resilience; however, the "last mile" connection to the customer is invariably the weakest connectivity link. Strategies to enhance the resilience of the "last mile" connection include gaining assurance from your provider that the geographic cable routes and points of presence are physically separate and that arrangements provide diversity of connection in the event of service degradation or failure.

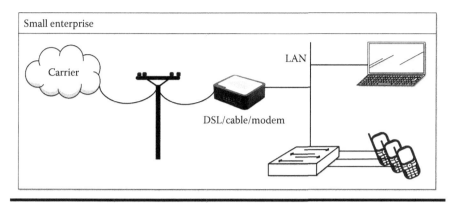

Figure 8.6   Last mile protection.

Last mile circuit protection is a redundant combination of local carrier T-1s, microwave and/or coaxial cable access to the local communications loop. This enables the facility to have access during a local carrier communication disaster. Alternate local carrier routing is also utilized in many networks.

Some organizations have initiated running separate feeds from different suppliers into different parts of a building. This affords greater protection, but it has also happened that some distance off, the separate feeds had the same route to the client—and this produced disastrous results.

Another area that impacts telecom performance is supplier bankruptcy. Some telecommunications agreements require clients to remain with their supplier regardless of quality of service during such a period because bankruptcy is specifically defined as a condition that preempts or supersedes any contractual escape provisions in case of vendor nonperformance. SLAs with vendors need to be reassessed to cover such situations.

Telecommunications continuity planning deals with contingency planning for interruptions in telecommunications services. Diverse routing routes traffic through split cable facilities or duplicate cable facilities. If different cable sheaths are used, the cable may be in the same conduit and therefore subject to the same interruptions as the cable it is backing up. With diverse routing, you can protect not only against cable failure but also against local exchange failure as there are two separate routes from two exchanges to your site.

The communication service subscriber can duplicate the facilities by having alternate routes, although the entrance to and from the customer premises may be in the same conduit. Alternative routing provides two different cables from the local exchange to your site, so you can protect against cable failure as your service will be maintained on the alternative route.

Five Guiding Principles for Enhancing the Resilience of Communications

1. *Look beyond technology at processes and the organizations*: When considering resilient telecommunications, considerable emphasis tends to be placed on the technical solutions (such as mobile phones). However, the processes used in communicating (such as agreed protocols that make conference calls work smoothly) and the way in which responders organize themselves to respond to emergencies should command equal attention and recognition, so all components should be considered together and not in isolation.

2. *Identify/review critical communication activities that underpin response arrangements*: To focus the selection of technical solutions on the need to communicate, it can be helpful to identify the critical communication activities. Critical activities are those that are essential to the effectiveness of response arrangements. For these activities, the focus can be maintained on the need to communicate by assessing the basic "technology free" communication requirements (such as sending or receiving specific crisis information rather than just phoning someone.

3. *Ensure diversity of your technical solutions*: For critical activities, the technological means to carry out the communication can then be considered with the objective of increasing overall telecommunications diversity. However, it can be difficult to assess how truly diverse technical solutions are because of the inherent dependency of one technical solution on another. For example, public mobile (cellular) networks are dependent to varying degrees on core communications networks (that deliver land-line telephone services)—failure or degradation of core networks can affect mobile services. Hence fall-back options must be explored and deployed.

4. *Adopt layered fall-back arrangements*: It is not feasible to have a technical solution available all the time. Availability is a consequence of the reliability of the system (associated with faults, and their repair) and the ability to cope with congestion (resulting from excessive demand). Adopting a layered fall-back approach to selecting technical solutions helps mitigate unavailability.

Impact from Data Unavailability/Corruption

Over years of experience, it has been observed that in 80% of the cases, organizations host their data centre within proximity of the primary site many times in the same city. Thus, when we consider the probability of crisis we plan for

1. Localized failure.
2. Facility failure.

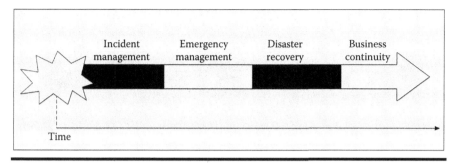

Figure 8.7   Incident response and recovery process.

3. City outage.
4. Technology failure.
5. People failure.
6. Failure of infrastructure.
7. Failure of machinery.

Data centre operations involve the following:

1. Distributed operations
2. Personnel, networks, power
3. All elements within IT environment

Recovery strategies are based on business requirements and after a cost-benefit analysis. All recovery strategies are based on MTPD.

As seen from Figure 8.7, when incident strikes, there is an initial assessment and damage assessment done. The escalations to appropriate authorities are made in the chain of command. Depending on severity level of the event, a DR plan will be invoked. There is a data loss in the period before the incident when last backup was taken, to the point of resumption of operations.

Work backlog: The backlog created by disaster from the time of last backup to the point of resumption, has to be cleared before the resumption processes commence.

Workaround procedures: These have to be developed for those IT services and business operations that may fail during a disruption and some manual or other workaround has to be determined for such processes (Figure 8.8).

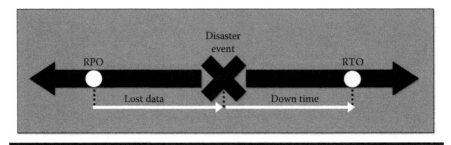

Figure 8.8 Workaround procedures for lost data.

Optimize Your Data Centre Environment

The data centre is the hub of your business operations—and you clearly recognize its critical importance. Even so, it is tough to accurately forecast growth and budgets due to rapidly increasing data and compute requirements—and the accompanying demand for additional power and cooling. High levels of physical and logical access controls must prevail at the data centre for maintaining the confidentiality of the data. But planning data centre within proximity of primary site makes it vulnerable to city outage.

Hence a DR site away from the prime site is important. Data can flow electronically to offsite DR site and be available at the time of DR recovery procedures. A resilient disaster recovery suite, developed in conjunction with the essential stakeholders, will ensure that data is available at the time of disaster.

By choosing the right partner/vendor for data centre colocation, organizations can reduce risk and impact from downtime, and can much more closely align their disaster recovery requirements with their business objectives. Failure on part of IT to align with the continuity requirements would pose a large business impact and may lead to financial loss as well as reputation loss.

Impact from Failure of Supply Chain

Supply chains today are complex and global, and for many are regularly disrupted, often opaque, and increasingly regulated. Coupled with the megatrends of accelerating urbanization, resource scarcity and the breath-taking pace of technology proliferation, supply chains continue to rapidly evolve and transform. Yet, most companies do not regularly assess the resilience of their supply chain:

- 90%[*] do not know if key suppliers have business continuity plans
- 75%[*] experience at least one major supply chain disruption a year

BCM Supply Chain Vendor Checklist

- Obtain list of suppliers and choose some critical suppliers on whom dependency is high. It is essential to vet these suppliers and it must be ensured that a "right to audit clause" exists in the contract/SLA with the vendor.
- Look for single dependencies and hence single point of failure. In case of dependence on single vendor, it is preferred to keep fall-back suppliers.
- Working with existing contracts: There is a cost involved in developing and maintaining a BCM programme. However, the underlying BCM questions can be put to suppliers through performance reviews to build a picture of capability in preparation for the time when a BCM capability can be required contractually.
- Vendor analysis should be under the oversight of the BCM manager. The BCM manager is there to provide expert advice and ask the procurement team a simple question: what do we do if a critical supplier fails? However good the risk mitigation measures undertaken, supply chain failure still needs to be considered, as you cannot outsource responsibility of your own BCP.
- Consider carefully those suppliers that want to sell you a BCP as an additional product, when you ask for their BCP. BCM is not a project-add-on, it is integral to the supplying organization's operational capability and a reasonable expectation to have them.
- Does the supplier have a business continuity management programme? Check that plans assume working differently or at a reduced level and that there is a need to prioritize resources and activities.
- Is their plan relevant to the product or service you are buying?

Your organization may be buying a product that is not of highest priority when disruption hits: other clients or product lines may take priority. Know where you stand.

- Is the scope of vendor's BCP appropriate? If the plan's scope is restricted to IT or telecoms, then you need to ask why other areas are not covered: sites and facilities, their supply chain, nonavailability of people, dependencies on credit lines or trade insurance, or overdependency on a single customer.
- Can they prove they can do what is in the plan? Is there evidence of an exercise and testing regime and embedding learnings? Is there evidence that the BCM people are working with the organization and not around it?
- Are there independent indicators of competency in BCM?

Increasing resilience and preventing the cost and revenue impacts of these disruptions affects the entire spectrum of supply chain risks—product, supplier, network, and environmental—as well as demand chain and back office technology. It requires a new approach—adopting a scenario focus to identify and manage the challenges and opportunities that encompass external events and internal lapses.

A supply chain resilience strategy focused on sustained performance that remains agile and fundamentally operations-focused. Companies that focus on supply chain resilience cohesively react to adverse events faster than the competition to take market share and outperform, in business performance. A resilient supply chain is a competitive advantage, reduces customer perception of assumed risks, and moves organization from simple risk management to risk resilient growth.

Practitioners can assist with supply chain resilience services, including:

■ Supply chain resilience strategy, organization, and management
■ Multitier supplier risk and resilience
■ Source to finished product integrity
■ Supply chain finance
■ Supply chain disruption/continuity analytics

Key Principles

1. Getting BCM in the supply chain is a risk mitigation measure. It is still necessary to factor supply chain failure in organization's BCP and how they would like to recover from such failure. Somewhere there will be a SLA slippage or a supply delay due to which business will suffer loss.
2. BCM needs to be part of the procurement strategy. The engagement with the supply chain requires a positive relationship and the usual issues of purchasing power and negotiating leverage apply with BCM. Procurement needs to make sure that the appropriate business continuity conversations have happened, if not carried out directly.
3. A focus on key suppliers first. Key suppliers are typically defined by how difficult they would be to replace should their product or service not be available to you over a time period that would cause significant operational performance problems. These key suppliers may well be those with the largest spend, but smaller niche suppliers may emerge from considering your business continuity requirements.
4. Work with suppliers to develop their business continuity capability. This is particularly important when dealing with off-shore service providers and for improving communication between parties should an incident occur.

Best Results Come from Alignment and Optimization

Alignment enables organizations to perform organizational processes and technological readiness while limiting overall business impact to its information technology, business processes, the supply chain, and its client base. Integration of processes and alignment with technology are key enablers for business. They limit the impact due to disruption (Figure 8.9).

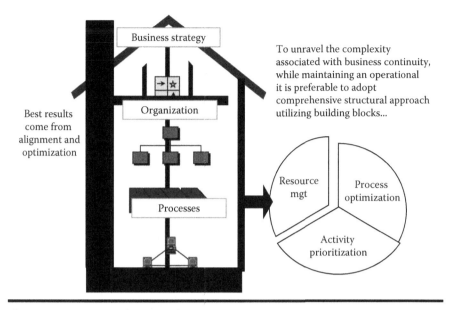

Figure 8.9 Integrated approach to BCM.

Information Technology Service Continuity Management

This is a process that deals with disasters impacting IT services. It maintains services to allow a business to continue to operate in the event of a disaster. IT service continuity management (ITSCM) is one of the methods used to achieve organizational resilience through integration of different components (Figure 8.10).

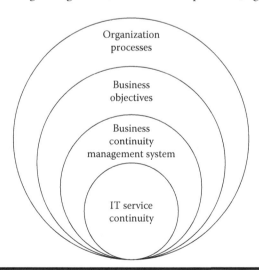

Figure 8.10 ITSCM environment within organizational context.

Why ITSCM?

- ITSCM covers IT services and its components
- Key to the survival of the business as a whole
- Risk reduction measures
- Recovery options
- Maintain the necessary ongoing recovery capability

ITSCM Processes

1. *Initiation* defines policy, scope, allocate resources, and set up project organization.
2. *Requirements and strategy* will need to be defined.
   a. A business impact analysis (BIA) has to be done.
   b. Service analysis will also have to be done. This will analyze essential IT services based on the SLA. Dependencies must also be assessed.
   c. Risks affecting the business will then have to be analyzed. The ITSC manager also has to identify the threats and vulnerabilities.
   d. ITSCM strategy must then be defined. The strategy can be risk reduction or recovery planning.
3. *Implement the plan*: This includes setting up the organization, developing the plan, and testing it.
4. *Operation management* requires training non-IT staff on the DRP. It requires regular review and testing. Any improvements or changes have to go through the change management process.

ITSCM Objectives

- Maintain service continuity plans (including IT) that support the organization's overall BCP plans.
- Complete regular BIA exercises.
- Ensure plans are maintained in line with changing business impacts and requirements.
- Conduct regular risk analysis and management exercises.
- Business participates in BCM activities.
- Provide guidance to other areas of the business and IT on continuity and recovery-related issues.

Risks Addressed by ITSCM

ITSCM addresses risks that cause sudden impact and endanger the business continuity of the organization. These include the following:

- Loss, damage, or denial of access to key infrastructure services
- Failure or nonperformance of critical providers, distributors, or other third parties
- Loss or corruption of key information
- Sabotage, extortion, or commercial espionage
- Deliberate infiltration or attack on critical information systems

ITSCM Must Be Aligned to the Business Continuity Lifecycle

- Business continuity management (BCM)
- BCM process involves reducing risk to an acceptable level
- Planning for the recovery of business processes should a risk materialize and a disruption to the business occur
- ITSCM must be a part of the overall business continuity plan and not dealt with in isolation
- ITSCM is the "technical component" of BCM, ITSCM, and ITIL

Service Level Management

- ITSCM is IT service-oriented.
- SLM provides a key interface as it defines what are the IT services within a service catalog and at what service levels they must be maintained.
- During a continuity "event," the service level manager is the interface to the business customers, not the service desk. As such, the service level manager should be baked into the ITSCM-invocation processes and brought in early during recovery activities.

The Business Value of ITSCM

- Potential lower insurance premiums.
- The IT organization can help the organization demonstrate to underwriters or insurers that they are proactively managing down their business risks.
- Regulatory requirement in some industries, a recovery capability is becoming a mandatory requirement such as health, defense, and financial industries.
- Business relationship—the requirement to work closely with the business to develop and maintain a continuity capability fosters a much closer working relationship between IT and the business areas.
- Positive marketing of contingency capabilities.
- Being able to demonstrate effective ITSCM capabilities enables an organization to provide high service levels to clients and customers and thus win business.

- Organizational credibility is increased.
- There is a responsibility on the directors of organizations to protect the shareholders' interest and those of their clients.

Service organizations are increasingly being asked by business partners, customers, and stakeholders to demonstrate their contingency facilities and may not be invited to tender for business unless they can demonstrate appropriate recovery capabilities.

Conclusion

Thus, we note that IT service continuity is closely associated with the overall business continuity plan and the disaster recovery plan. Business objectives should be met and alignment and integration are keywords to remember while planning service continuity with information technology. Our tasks include the following:

- Aligning business continuity policy with IT disaster recovery.
- Deploying nondisruptive and continuous DR testing.
- Guarantee that all components of an IT service are always fully recoverable.
- Report compliance deviations via dashboard, e-mail, or problem management systems.
- Measure and enforce RPO and RTO automatically.
- Failover individual applications at the push of a button.
- Scale recovery from individual applications to large data centers.

Business is most important for the organization; many components make the business and each component is a part of the BCM system. There is technology, there is a man running the technology, there are processes to run business systems, and there are a handful of stakeholders who are constantly querying information systems to ensure value creation for their business.

Going concern is more of an assumption for business and to fulfill this assumption, the whole lot of continuity activities must be planned, implemented, tested, and run in the background. So long as time stipulations are met and cost is kept under budgeted outlay, the success or otherwise of the BCM program is determined. We are just not wanting safety for our technology, we are aspiring for resilience in business and from unforeseen eventualities. The best metric is impact and in its qualitative or quantitative form the impact from events should be measured and risks related to the probability of occurrence from these events need to be addressed or mitigated.

Hence, we observe that risk assessment, business impact analysis, constant monitoring, external and internal audits, recommendations, mitigation, and testing are now regular processes carried out by enterprises to keep their business running without interruption as far as possible and in spite of controls if any incident occurs they are building the response and recovery mechanisms to bring business to normal within the time that they have predecided for recovery (RTOs, RPOs, MTPOD).

Even these efforts are incomplete, without mention of people, because "people first" is a universally accepted motto when it comes to disaster, people are the first asset that have to be directed to safety, people are the first asset that must be counseled when stressed after a major incident. Hence the domain of continuity is spread out among people, process, and technology, the three tenets of business and alignment is the key driver for success in achieving our business continuity objectives.

Chapter 9

Comparative Analysis of Requirements for Common Standards/ Compliances

Need for Standards for BCM

For the past several decades, business continuity has been working on guidelines provided by various bodies of knowledge and, following these guidelines, has assisted the formulation of good business continuity programs for enterprises. The Standards Development Organizations have made these guidelines a base to develop BCM standards to make it more auditable and sustainable.

To illustrate this point, a list of international business continuity standards is given as follows:

1. ISACA was established in 1969.
2. ITIL was formed in 1980.
3. DRI International was started in 1988.
4. BCI-GPG UK was started in 1994.
5. BS 25999 BSi was started in 2006.
6. ANAO Australian National Audit Office was started in 2009.
7. ISO 22301 was started in 2012.
8. COBIT % was started in in 2012.
9. BCMI BCM Guidelines 2013.

10. Guidance on Organizational Resilience BS 65000.
11. PAS 56 was started in 2003.

The economic, social, and global dimensions of business have made it imperative for business organizations to adopt global standards for ease of implementation and audit. They may deploy internal experts or external experts to assist them to choose a standard and align it with the provisions of the standard with or without obtaining certification of that standard. Customization is usually a necessary process in standards adoption and application.

Organizations follow many standards for information security and quality, and in the bargain, they are subjected to multiple audits in respect of certifications adopted, and for them compliance becomes an important function on its own. It will be beneficial if the organization does a comparative analysis of the requirements for each of the standard to identify the overlapping provisions so that mapping of compliances can be easy. BCM standards are closely linked to standards for information security, risk, and quality. In this section, we shall visit different standards and try to make a comparative analysis of the requirements for better maintenance of the standards.

BCM Standards

Organizations always prefer to adopt BCM standards appropriate for them. Why is it necessary to follow a standard?

- To observe acknowledged and recognized best practices.
- Standards have been developed by a consensus process involving industry professionals.
- To provide a common platform for program components.
- To establish measurable and auditable criteria.
- To outline a comprehensive program management view.
- To assist with risk management.
- Are an important element in supply chain risk mitigation.

A point to note is that standards may be place or country specific, or they may be function/process specific, that is, governance, risk, business continuity, third-party evaluation, and so on.

NFPA 1600 Standard on Disaster/Emergency Management and Business Continuity

The National Commission on Terrorist Attacks upon the United States (the 9/11 Commission) recognized NFPA 1600 as a National Preparedness Standard. Widely used by public, not-for-profit, nongovernmental, and private entities on a local,

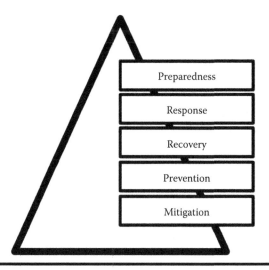

Figure 9.1   Total program approach.

regional, national, international, and global basis, NFPA 1600 has been adopted by the U.S. Department of Homeland Security as a voluntary consensus standard for emergency preparedness (Figure 9.1).

The standard follows a total program approach revolving around the business continuity phases of preparedness, response, recovery, prevention, and mitigation. It provides common elements techniques and processes. It aims at augmenting the disaster/emergency management programs to reduce and contain impacts from disasters.

The NFPA standard emphasizes program policies and management components, providing guidelines that address the analysis, planning, and implementation of the core elements of crisis management, business resumption planning, and information technology-based (IT) disaster recovery.

The essential elements for certification for this standard consists of development of a fully documented program to be run by a program coordinator as well as an advisory committee whose primary function is to administer, maintain, and review the organization's program. These aspects are in line with the analysis, planning, and implementation of the core elements of risk assessments, impact analyses, incident prevention strategies, mitigation strategies, resource management and logistics, incident management systems, and operational procedures in order to prevent, prepare for, and respond to a disaster or emergency situation.

The NFPA 1600 standard emphasizes a regular planning process in order to improve current strategies and confront newly identified problems.

ASIS SPC.1 ASIS International SPC.1-2009 Organizational Resilience: Security, Preparedness, and Continuity Management Systems

ASIS SPC.1

This standard provides guidance for management system audits for risk-based disciplines of risk, resilience, security, crisis, continuity, and recovery management. The standard uses an approach for auditing and conformity assessment consistent with the current versions of ISO 19011.

The competence of auditors is the foundation for conducting effective and credible audits; therefore, this standard provides competence criteria for auditors conducting conformity assessment of a management system to a risk and resilience-based management systems standard. Auditors understand much of their activities involving interactions between people; therefore, there is a need to build rapport, trust, and confidence while avoiding the creation of an adversarial atmosphere. An audit is a positive experience if the people being audited feel the audit adds value and may lead to opportunities for improvement.

This standard represents a management framework for BCM planning and decision-making to anticipate, prevent, prepare for, and respond to a disruption (Figure 9.2). The ASIS SPC.1 standard seeks to increase organizational and customer confidence by creating a safe and secure environment for both the organization and its stakeholders. It emphasizes the planning and implementation of the core elements, as well as the maintenance, review, and improvement element. The ASIS standard

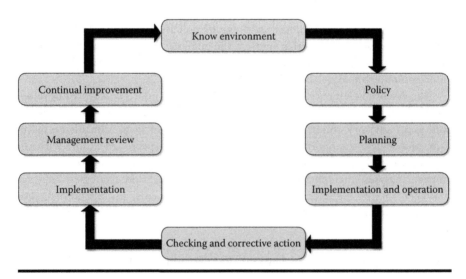

Figure 9.2   BCM management framework.

plans and implements its organizational resilience (OR) management policy by requiring management to provide evidence of its commitment to implement.

ASIS focuses on the maintenance, review, and improvement requirements that treat BCM as a continuous cycle rather than a onetime process. It provides auditable criteria for regular audits to establish, check, maintain, and improve its business continuity management system (BCMS). Like any other BCM guidelines, the standard requires internal audits, exercise and testing, management reviews, input and output reviews, program maintenance, and policies aimed at continuously improving the standard.

BS 25999 The British Standard 25999-2:2007

BS 25999 was designed to be an "auditable" standard, in that its structure is designed so that each step can be audited. Individual BC plans and associated program activities can be audited against the standard. The British Standards Institution (BSI) even has its own audit process in which organizations can submit their programs (for a fee) to be audited and certified for compliance with BS 25999.

BS 25999 speaks of building a BCMS and implementing BCM policy, management reviews, checking, evaluating, remediating gaps, exercising, and documenting lessons learned. It came with the sentiment of an organization-wide approach to business continuity and embedding it within the organizational culture so that impacts can be reduced, preventive controls would replace or at most would supplement the corrective plans, and losses can be contained.

British Standard describes detail-oriented continuity and recovery plans that organizations must enact for accreditation. The following is a list of mandatory documentation for certification under BS 25999:

1. BCM policy
2. Business impact analysis report
3. Incident-handling plan
4. Emergency response plan
5. Management oversight
6. Exercises

It requires specifics on how your organization will reestablish operations, communications, and policies during disasters and specifics on how to implement a media response strategy.

The British Standard specifies action and task details that need to be performed once the response plan is initiated, as well as the resources required for business continuity and business recovery efforts at different points in time.

The British Standard also emphasizes the maintenance, review, and improvement of the core elements. It requires your organization to develop and conduct exercises that are consistent within the scope of the BCM system, to hold postexercise reviews of each exercise, and to review its BCM arrangements to ensure continuing suitability, adequacy, and effectiveness.

This standard establishes an internal auditing system, management review of the BCM system, and review of inputs and outputs to ensure effectiveness and efficiency.

Special note: With the release of ISO 22301, BS 25999 has retired, and BSI has set an upgrade path for organizations with certifications under BS 25999.

Adopting a best practices standard and being certified in that involves a lot of planning and customization. Some standards allow scoping to be done; some exclusions are accepted while some have to be organization wide. The main determinant is commitment to preparedness for your organization, aligned to defined industry best practices for business continuity—demonstrated to your stakeholders, board of directors, executives, employees, customers, clients, external regulators, and supply chain.

Regulatory environments—Many businesses are required to operate within regulatory environments and must implement specific components in their business continuity program. Compliance and certification to a standard will complement the requirements for the regulations.

Sometimes certification gives value addition to business, customers feel secure and assured that dealing with certified organizations will assure quality processes within the organization and in case of resilience and continued availability of goods and services.

NFPA 1600 versus BS 25999

NFPA 1600 and its roots in emergency management would appear to be a more realistic standard, in that it addresses more of the above disaster continuity than BS 25999. However, neither standard explains when various activities should be activated, or what should be done, that is up to individual organizations.

BS 25999 is the British National Standard for business continuity. The first part of the standard, Part 1, the Code of Practice, and the second part, Part 2, Specification, comprise a document that focuses largely on business continuity. The document has been positioned for audit purposes, and organizations can submit their plans to a formal audit and certification process by the BSI, the author of BS 25999.

Currently, the American National Standard for business continuity is NFPA 1600: 2007, which addresses emergency management, incident response, and business continuity. The standard has been in place for several years and was initially launched as an emergency management standard. The NFPA has no audit process in place, but the structure of the document makes it easy to transform NFPA 1600 into an audit document.

In comparing the two documents, we see that both support the business continuity competencies as advocated by the Business Continuity Institute (BCI) and

DRI International (DRII). The level of detail exhibited by both standards is sufficient for launching a business continuity program.

NFPA 1600 is considered an American standard; therefore, it would not be used outside this country. By contrast, while BS 25999 is the designated British standard, it has gained recognition on the world scene, largely through the efforts of the BSI.

DRII/DRJ GAP versus BCMI GPG 2013

Identify and define all potential risks to the process/functions to include regulatory, legal, operational, technological, financial, informational, and physical securities. Geographic characteristics may also need to be factored in.

- Define applicable threats to the enterprise, such as hurricanes, tornadoes, floods, wildfires, civil unrest, acts of terrorism, mass transportation breakdowns, utility failures, and so on.
- Assess the probability of the threat.
- Assess the impact from the threat.
- Quantify/qualify the threat into a risk matrix.
- Identify potential mitigations to reduce, eliminate, or transfer the risk.

Professional Practice Subject Area Overview

1. *Program initiation and management*: Establish the need for a business continuity management program within the entity and identify the program components from understanding the entity's risks and vulnerabilities through development of resilience strategies and response, restoration and recovery plans. The objectives of this professional practice are to obtain the entity's support and funding and to build the organizational framework to develop the BCM program.

2. *Risk evaluation and control*: The objective is to identify the risks/threats and vulnerabilities that are both inherent and acquired, which can adversely affect the entity and its resources or can impact the entity's image. Once identified, threats and vulnerabilities will be assessed as to the likelihood that they would occur and the potential level of impact that would result. The entity can then focus on high probability and high impact events to identify where controls, mitigations, or management processes are nonexistent, weak, or ineffective.

3. *Business impact analysis*: Enterprises identify the likely and potential impacts from events on the entity or its processes and the criteria that will be used to quantify and qualify such impacts. The criteria to measure and assess the financial, customer, regulatory, and/or reputational impacts must be defined and accepted and then used consistently throughout the entity to define the

recovery time objective (RTO) and recovery point objective (RPO) for each of the entity's processes. The result of this analysis is to identify time-sensitive processes and the requirements to recover them in the timeframe that is acceptable to the entity.

4. *Business continuity strategies*: The data that were collected during the business impact analysis (BIA) and risk evaluation are used to identify available continuity and recovery strategies for the entity's operations and technology. Recommended strategies must be approved and funded and must meet both the recovery time and RPOs identified in the BIA. A cost-benefit analysis has to be performed on the recommended strategies to align the cost of implementing the strategy against the assets at risk.

5. *Emergency response and operations*: Defines the requirements to develop and implement the entity's plan for response to emergency situations that may impact safety of the entity's employees, visitors, or other assets. The emergency response plan documents how the entity will respond to emergencies in a coordinated, timely, and effective manner to address life safety and stabilization of emergency situations until the arrival of trained or external first responders.

6. *Plan implementation and documentation*: Business continuity plan is a set of documented processes and procedures, which will enable the entity to continue or recover time-sensitive processes to the minimum acceptable level within the timeframe acceptable to the entity. In this phase of the business continuity management program, the relevant teams design, develop, and implement the continuity strategies approved by the entity and document the recovery plans to be used in response to an incident or event.

7. *Awareness and training programs*: A program is developed and implemented to establish and maintain corporate awareness about BCM and to train the entity's staff so that they are prepared to respond during an event.

8. *Business continuity plan exercise, audit, and maintenance*: To establish an exercise, testing, maintenance, and audit program. To continue to be effective, a BCM program must implement a regular exercise schedule to establish confidence in a predictable and repeatable performance of recovery activities throughout the organization. As part of the change management program, the tracking and documentation of these activities provide an evaluation of the on-going state of readiness and allows for continuous improvement of recovery capabilities and ensures that plans remain current and relevant.

   Establishing an audit process will validate the plans are complete, accurate, and in compliance with organizational goals and industry standards as appropriate.

9. *Crisis communications*: Provides the framework to identify, develop, communicate, and exercise a crisis communications plan. A crisis communications plan addresses the need for effective and timely communication between the entity and all the stakeholders impacted or involved during the response and recovery efforts.

10. *Coordination with external agencies*: Defines the need to establish policies and procedures to coordinate response, continuity, and recovery activities with external agencies at the local, regional, and national levels while ensuring compliance with applicable statutes and regulations.

Hence we see DRII is a comprehensive standard that considers BCM as a project and goes by steps to identify, implement, exercise, and test and maintain a business continuity management program for the enterprise.

BCI GPG: The BCI Guidelines had been developed in the year 1994 and served many organizations as a useful practical guideline for BCM implementation. It was formulated as a standard guideline in 2013.

- Form a BCM strategy team.
- Identify the organization's business strategy, objectives, and legal and regulatory requirements, and understand how a continuity strategy will support these objectives.
- Tabulate a scoring system for impacts and probabilities and agree with the project sponsor.
- List threats to the urgent business processes determined in a BIA.
- Estimate the impact of the threat on the organization using a numerical scoring system.
- Determine the likelihood (probability or frequency) of each threat occurring and weight according to a numerical scoring system.
- Calculate a risk by combining the scores for impact and probability of each threat according to an agreed formula.
- Optionally prioritize the risks according to a formula that includes a measure of the ability to control that threat.
- Obtain the organization sponsor's approval and sign-off of these risk priorities.
- Review existing risk management control strategies, noting where the assessed risk level is out of step with the current risk management strategies for that threat.
- Consider appropriate measures to:

    1. Transfer the risk, for example, through insurance.
    2. Accept the risk, for example, where impact/probability is low.
    3. Reduce the risk, for example, through the introduction of further controls.
    4. Avoid the risk, for example, by removing the cause or source of the threat.

- Ensure that planned risk measures do not increase other risks. For example, outsourcing an activity may decrease some types of risk by increasing others.
- Obtain the organization sponsor's approval, a budget and sign-off for the proposed risk management controls.

ISO 22301 Was Published by the International Standardization Organization

ISO 22301 was published by the International Standardization Organization (ISO) in May 2012. ISO 22301 blends the requirements from several standards from the United States, Japan, Singapore, Canada, and Australia. ISO 22301—is the first comprehensive BCMSs standard developed by a true international body.

ISO 22301 Standard for Societal Security

ISO 22301 is a standard for Societal Security, and it has brought the BCM on a common language platform and put it on a pedestal of respect. Because of the respect afforded to ISO standards, it is also natural that entities—regardless of geography—will contribute toward standardization of BCM activities and initiatives worldwide (Figure 9.3).

Main features of ISO 22301 include the following:

1. A greater focus on improving and demonstrating evidence through documentation and defined control processes.
2. More emphasis on the wider context of BCMSs.
3. Definition of scope and justification of exclusions of particular areas of the overall program must be documented and approved for exclusion.

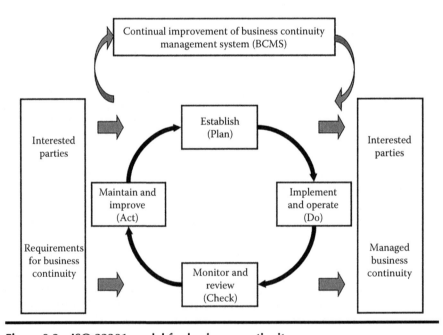

Figure 9.3 ISO 22301 model for business continuity.

4. Increased emphasis on the demonstration of executive management commitment.
5. More clearly defined parameters for executive management commitment.
6. More defined content for the required policy for business continuity.

It included the following distinctive definitions:

1. *Disruptive incident*: An event that stops business operations.
2. *Documented information*: Information required to be controlled and maintained by an organization and the medium on which it is contained.
3. *Maximum acceptable outage* (*MAO*): The time it would take for adverse impacts, which may arise as the result of not providing a product/service or performing an activity, to become unacceptable.
4. *Minimum business continuity objective* (*MBCO*): Minimum level of services and/or products that is acceptable to the organization to achieve its business objectives during a disruption.
5. *Maximum data loss*: The point to which information used by an activity must be restored to enable the activity to operate upon resumption, also referred to as RPO.
6. *Correction*: An action to eliminate a detected nonconformity.

The standard shows increased emphasis and details around the establishment of a communications process to ensure availability of the means of communications during a disruptive incident maintain and improve (Act), implement and operate (Do), monitor and review (Check), establish (Plan) interested parties requirements for business continuity interested parties managed business continuity continual improvement of BCMS. ISO 22301 is concise and includes many "shall" statements. ISO 22313 is a guidance and provides explanations and examples in relation to ISO 22301.

COBIT 5, Risk IT, and Val IT

COBIT 5 can be used jointly to provide decision-makers with a set of criteria for assessing the value created through the delivery of a high-quality BCM program. These frameworks can help answer strategic questions including the following:

- *Are we doing the right things?* What is our industry doing with respect to continuity management over emerging business trends and technologies, and how is our enterprise placed in relation to our peers?
- *Are we getting the benefits?* Based upon these comparisons is our BCM providing competitive advantage?
- *Are we doing them the right way?* How do we identify what is required to reach additional levels of cost-effective availability and business resiliency through future-state BCM strategies?

■ *Are we getting them done well?* How do we assess the level of maturity of our BCM program and supporting processes?

Enabling processes and the IT continuity planning audit/assurance program from ISACA provides a comprehensive guide to the assurance professional to plan and execute a business continuity assessment. Specific guidance on BCM is provided in the following COBIT 5 enabling processes:

1. *EDM03 ensure risk optimization*: Determine whether IT risk appetite is commensurate with business objectives and enterprise risk tolerance.
2. *APO02 manage strategy*: Determine whether the IT strategy is aligned with business objectives.
3. *APO09 manage service agreements*: Determine whether IT services and service levels meet current and future enterprise needs.
4. *APO10 manage suppliers*: Determine whether IT has processes to minimize risk associated with nonperforming suppliers.
5. *APO12 manage risk*: Determine whether the IT strategy supports business requirements to comply with external laws and regulations.
6. *BAI04 manage availability and capacity*: Determine whether IT has the necessary processes to predict performance and capacity requirements to maintain availability.
7. *BAI06 manage changes*: Determine whether risk associated with IT changes is properly assessed and reflected in the continuity strategy.
8. *DSS04 manage continuity*: Determine whether appropriate plans exist to enable the business and IT to respond to incident and disruptions in order to continue operations of critical business functions.

A *point to note* is that publications on crisis management, human aspects of continuity, exercising and testing, supply chain continuity and recovery management expand on areas in BS 25999-1. A standard BS 25777-ICT continuity management has come and gone as it was used in the development of ISO 27031 on ICT continuity management, and now it is withdrawn.

ISO 31000 (Risk)

ISO 31000:2009 gives a set of general options to be considered when risk is treated. The order of the list reflects preference. Importantly, the options deal with both risks that have downside and/or upside consequences. The options are:

1. Avoiding the risk by deciding not to start or continue with the activity that gives rise to the risk
2. Taking or increasing the risk in order to pursue an opportunity
3. Removing the risk source
4. Changing the likelihood

5. Changing the consequences
6. Sharing the risk with another party or parties (including contracts and risk financing)
7. Retaining the risk by informed decision

Clause 4 of the ISO 31000 standard concerns implementation of the risk management process through integration by using a management framework, which consists of the policies, arrangements, and organizational structures to implement, sustain, and improve the process. The standard not only describes the important elements that are required in such a framework but also describes how an organization should go about creating, implementing, and keeping these elements up to date and relevant.

Each organization needs to design or revise the risk management components of its management system to suit its business processes, structure, risk profile, and policies, and this is the purpose of a risk management plan. This implementation plan may extend over a considerable time as introducing soundly based risk management usually requires alignment with and even changes to the organization's culture and processes. Large or complex organizations may require a hierarchy of risk management plans but there should always be an overall plan for the organization that describes the broad strategies to be pursued.

There are some clear performance requirements that, if followed, ensure that risks are managed both effectively and efficiently. The principles of effective risk management in ISO 31000 are that it should

1. Create and protect value.
2. Be an integral part of all organizational processes.
3. Be part of decision-making.
4. Explicitly address uncertainty.
5. Be systematic, structured, and timely.
6. Be based on the best available information.
7. Be tailored.
8. Take into account human and cultural factors.
9. Be transparent and inclusive.
10. Be dynamic, iterative, and responsive to change.
11. Facilitate continual improvement of the organization (Figures 9.4 and 9.5).

ISO 31000 does not express a preference for either a quantitative or qualitative approach to risk analysis, as both have a role. Rather, it advises that:

■ The way in which consequences and likelihood are expressed and the way in which they are combined to determine a level of risk should reflect the type of risk, the information available, and the purpose for which the risk assessment output is to be used. These should all be consistent with the risk criteria.

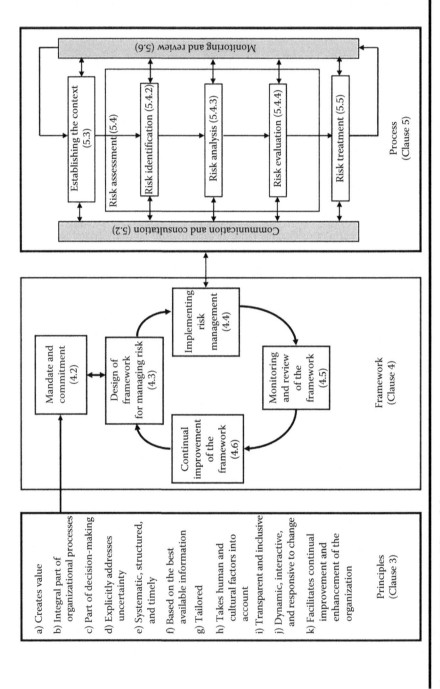

Figure 9.4   ISO 31000 risk model.

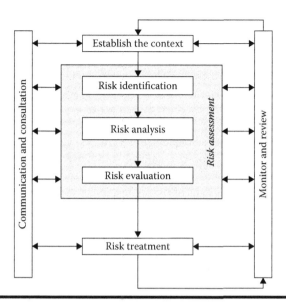

Figure 9.5 The risk management process from ISO 31000:2009.

■ The confidence in determination of the level of risk and its sensitivity to pre-conditions and assumptions should be considered in the analysis and communicated effectively to decision-makers and, as appropriate, other stakeholders.

■ Risk analysis can be undertaken with varying degrees of detail, depending on the risk, the purpose of the analysis, and the information, data, and resources available. Analysis can be qualitative, semi-quantitative, quantitative, or a combination of these, depending on the circumstances.

Risk evaluation then involves making a decision about the level of risk and the priority for attention through the application of the criteria developed when the context was established.

Business managers determine what IT needs to do to support their business; they set the targets for IT and are accountable for managing the associated risks. The risk IT framework explains IT risk, allows the enterprise to make appropriate risk-aware decisions and will enable users to integrate the management of IT risk into the overall enterprise risk management (ERM) of the organization.

1. Make well-informed decisions about the extent of the risk, the risk appetite, and the risk tolerance of the enterprise.
2. Understand how to respond to the risk.

Like COBIT and Val IT, risk IT is not a standard but a flexible framework. This means that enterprises can and should customize the components provided in the framework to suit their particular organization.

Risk IT consists of two publications: the Risk IT Framework and the Risk IT Practitioner Guide.

The Risk IT framework complements ISACA's COBIT, which provides a comprehensive framework for the control and governance of business-driven IT-based solutions and services. COBIT sets good practices for the means of risk management by providing a set of controls to mitigate IT risk (Figure 9.6).

The risk IT framework complements ISACA's COBIT, which provides a comprehensive framework for the control and governance of business-driven information-technology-based (IT-based) solutions and services. While COBIT sets good practices for the means of risk management by providing a set of controls to mitigate IT risk, Risk IT sets good practices for the ends by providing a framework for enterprises to identify, govern, and manage IT risk.

The risk IT framework is to be used to help implement IT governance and enterprises that have adopted (or are planning to adopt) COBIT as their IT governance framework can use risk IT to enhance risk management.

Risk IT is a framework to help organizations establish effective governance and management of IT risk. It is a part of ISACA's product portfolio on IT governance.

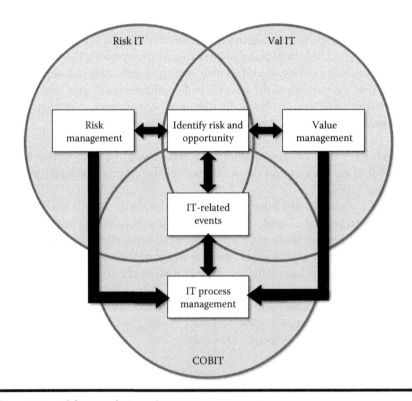

Figure 9.6   Risk IT, Val IT, and COBIT components.

The objective of risk IT is to

1. Allow enterprises to customize the components provided in the framework to suit their particular needs.
2. Provide end-to-end comprehensive view of all risks related to the use of IT and an appropriate treatment of risk related to operational issues.
3. Provide tangible business benefits and enable enterprises to make risk-aware decisions.
4. Enable integration with overall risk and compliance structures within the enterprise when assessing and managing IT risk and obtaining ROI out of risk investments.

The risk IT framework provides a set of governance practices for risk management and a generic list of common, potentially adverse, IT-related risk scenarios that could impact the realization of business objectives. Tools and techniques to understand concrete risks to business operations as opposed to generic checklists of controls or compliance requirements have been developed to achieve risk objectives.

Benefits of risk IT include the following:

1. A common language to help communication among business, IT, risk, and audit management.
2. End-to-end guidance on how to manage IT-related risks.
3. A complete risk profile to better understand risk, so as to better utilize enterprise resources.
4. A better understanding of the roles and responsibilities with regard to IT risk management (Figure 9.7).

The Risk IT Practitioner Guide is a support document for the risk IT framework that provides examples of possible techniques to address IT-related risk issues' more detailed guidance on how to approach the concepts covered in the process model. Concepts and techniques explored in more detail include the following:

1. Building scenarios, based on a set of generic IT risk scenarios
2. Building a risk map, using techniques to describe the impact and frequency of scenarios
3. Building impact criteria with business relevance
4. Defining KRIs

Alignment with ERM

1. Develop better understanding of IT-related risk and its financial implications
2. Fewer operational surprises and failures
3. Increased information quality

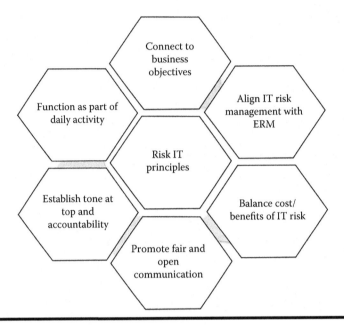

Figure 9.7   Risk IT principles.

4. Greater stakeholder confidence and reduced regulatory concerns
5. Innovative applications supporting new business initiatives

(Source: The risk IT framework ©2009 ISACA. All rights reserved. Used by permission.)

New standards, by their nature, reset goals and ways of thinking, and undoubtedly the publication of ISO 31000 now requires all risk management practitioners to examine their current ways of working and the language they use so that their customers, those who are faced with making decisions, obtain simple, consistent, useful, and unambiguous information.

Common Points between ISO 27001, PCI DSS, and ISO 22301

ISO 27001 is a standard for information security. It permits organizations to scope their critical systems and form a information systems management system that covers security of these systems. ISO 27001's requirements involve determining the scope of an information security management system (ISMS), which maps to PCI DSS requirements, to develop and maintain secure systems and applications, and to maintain a policy that addresses information security.

There are a few crossover and common ground between the Payment Card Industry Data Security Standard (PCI DSS) and ISO 27001. High-level areas where there are similarities between the two standards include organization and leadership.

Planning and operation actions to address risks and opportunities under ISO 27001 have crossover with many of the requirements of PCI DSS. These include the protection of stored cardholder data, restriction of physical access to cardholder data, and regular testing of security systems and processes. To address improvement, ISO 27001's focus on corrective action and continual improvement has crossover with PCI DSS, including tracking and monitoring all access to network resources and regularly testing systems and security.

ISO 27001's asset management and access control requirements map to those under PCI DSS around firewall configuration, system passwords, and protection of stored cardholder data. The supplier relationships focus within ISO 27001 has key crossover with PCI DSS in requirements such as restricting physical access to cardholder data, tracking, and monitoring supplier compliance and the need to conduct supplier risk analysis. Legal and contractual requirements and information security reviews as part of compliance issues under ISO 27001 map to all of the requirements of PCI DSS. ISO 22301 have the same key elements as ISO 27001 including internal audits, corrective actions, training and awareness, management reviews, and so on. ISO 27001 also includes business continuity controls; (Annexure A of the standard) such as addressing information security continuity and redundancies, which in turn map to requirements under PCI DSS including protection of stored cardholder data and the development and maintenance of secure systems and applications.

Areas such as risk management have particular crossover between the two standards and meeting the requirements under ISO 27001 will also mean compliance with ISO 22301.

Greater Focus across Standards for Third-Party Supplier Management

The rapid growth seen in outsourcing of business processes means third-party suppliers and partners are increasingly trusted with access to systems and sensitive information. Ever increasing amounts of data are being processed and stored within third parties which is why information security and business continuity standards are increasingly looking to address the issue of third-party supplier management.

There is now significant emphasis in ISO standards relating to information security and in PCI DSS on making sure suppliers, external parties and hosting providers are meeting their obligations in protecting cardholder data. Even where suppliers are simply providing storage services, such as data centers, they cannot turn a blind eye to the activities of their customers. For example, there is a risk that customers with access to server racks could access the data of others being held on the same rack. As well as hosting their own data, many organizations also host for third parties, introducing new risks which need to be considered.

Suppliers who do not hold data can be affected as many of the requirements under the standard cover the processing of data. While compliance with third-party supplier requirements under various standards may seem onerous, it can also be used as a competitive advantage and an opportunity to secure new business by demonstrating a robust approach to information security.

PCI DSS Standard: The latest version of PCI DSS highlights the responsibility of businesses to address potential weaknesses from third parties and makes clear that businesses are responsible for the PCI compliance of their vendors and suppliers with access to cardholder data. Third parties may be involved in storing, processing, or transmitting cardholder data on their behalf, or managing infrastructure such as routers, firewalls, databases, physical security, and servers.

Under the PCI DSS requirements, parties "should clearly identify the services and system components which are included in the scope of the service provider's PCI DSS assessment, the specific PCI DSS requirements covered by the service provider, and any requirements which are the responsibility of the service provider's customers to include in their own PCI DSS reviews." The 2013 version of ISO 27001 also dedicates an entire sector of Annex A to maintaining the "security of the organization's information and information-processing facilities that are accessed, processed, communicated to, or managed by external parties".

Compliance requires a process of risk assessment, background checks on potential suppliers or partners, and compliance monitoring. Access control is also a key issue both for ISO 27001 and PCI DSS. Third parties should have access only on a need-to-know basis rather than having wider access to data within a company. Businesses also need to address exactly what happens in terms of data and access when a relationship with a third-party comes to an end for whatever reason.

How PCI DSS Can Support Third-Party Aspects of ISO 27001 Audits

As part of ISO 27001 audits, organizations are required to provide evidence of conformity, something which they often have difficulty with in particular areas including supplier relationships. Extracting information from policies, procedures, records, and logs to provide evidence that changes to the provision of services by suppliers are managed can be time consuming and reduces opportunities for the audit to provide valuable opportunities for improvement. Referring to the organization's implementation of PCI DSS can provide evidence to meet a number of ISO 27001 requirements, such as the development of procedures to easily distinguish between onsite personnel and visitors. RED ISLAND: Through our role as a leading PCI DSS QSA company, we make it easier to take a combined approach to PCI DSS with ISO 27001 and/or ISO 22301 with integrated solutions, which can reduce the time and costs involved with compliance and maintenance.

ISO/PAS 2239:2007—Guideline for Incident Preparedness and Operational Continuity Management

The National Institute of Standards and Technology (NIST) SP800-30 Rev 1—Guide for Conducting Risk Assessments has a commercially developed business continuity maturity model (BCMM) for assessing state of preparedness. ITIL IT infrastructure library gives guidelines for business continuity planning process and documentation.

Overview of Information Security Standards and IT's Role

There are several standards that IT groups typically adhere to when developing response strategies. Some of the most common security best practices include NIST, ISO 27001, ISO 15408, and RFC 2196. Each of these standards outline best practices and specific procedures that IT should consider (and align to as necessary) when working to prevent or respond to cyber security threats. Specifically, when

- Developing a security program and defining access controls.
- Identifying and tracking breaches.
- Logging and backing up data to avoid destruction of evidence.
- Shutting down unauthorized access.
- Recovering and restoring system operations.

These standards typically include guidance for how IT should respond to assess the breadth and severity of information accessed, control the situation, and communicate cyber-attack incident impacts, strategies, and outcomes to leadership.

However, these standards may have a too narrow scope in helping an organization determine impacts and make appropriate decisions. More importantly, IT often applies the concepts in these standards to just IT groups.

Organizations have to align IT cybersecurity response fully to IT best practices, and if a corporate crisis management structure exists, it is useful to integrate IT's response into the existing business continuity structure, rather than having two separate response models. The following sections highlight some of the ways organizations can better align the two response structures to increase the effectiveness of response and strengthen organization recovery.

Enhance Leadership Teams and Align Response Strategies

One opportunity to align business continuity and IT cybersecurity response involves providing the appropriate organizational leadership the information necessary to enable effective response and decision-making. The leadership roles typically highlighted to receive periodic status reporting in IT-focused standards tend to be IT or security focused but may not include all areas of business operations that may ultimately be affected by an IT incident.

This takes advantage of the existing crisis management process, ensures leadership receives timely information, gives an insight and ownership of impact assessment and stakeholder communications response efforts to the leadership already responsible for these activities in response to all other events, and ensures adequate executive leadership and participation.

ASIS SPC.1 ASIS International SPC.1–2009 Organizational Resilience: Security, preparedness, and continuity management systems * is a management framework for action planning and decision-making to anticipate, prevent, and prepare for, and respond to a disruptive incident. The standard seeks to increase organizational and customer confidence by creating a safe and secure environment for both.

Management to Take a Call on Certification

If an organization desires to certify to a standard, it must conduct a third-party review by an authorized certification body to validate the company's preparedness to a standard. However, in some cases, an internal assessment followed by a self-declaration of conformity to the standard can meet its corporate goals. The following are the steps for certification:

Step 1: Management commitment: BCM is a top—down process, and commitment of top management is necessary to secure the requisite resources to implement the BCMS. An initial BIA and risk assessment would enable the executive management to get a fuller understanding of process dependencies and risks faced by the organization. On the basis of a cost-benefit analysis, the management will then commit definite budget and resources needed for the BCM initiatives to be conducted.

Step 2: Choice of standard: Selecting an appropriate standard for business continuity should be enabled by subject matter expert either in the organization or an external consultant, who shall suggest a standard based on the overall business environment and the culture of the organization.

Step 3: Delineate the scope: BCM initiatives have to be organization wide. Yet after the BIA/RA stage, prioritization of recovery can be made possible. Those processes that can wait for some time before they are to be performed and who do not have interdependencies with critical processes can then be excluded from scope. In scope assets, processes, applications can be considered, and focus of BCM procedures can be directed toward these assets. At the time of certification, this scope needs to be agreed with the certifying body.

Step 4: Align with legal and regulatory requirements: Many organizations initiate the BCM implementation only because it is mandatory as per industry regulators or legal requirements. Some processes may be undertaken to meet these requirements, and they may be included among the list of critical processes simply because of fines and penalties for noncompliance that has a direct impact on the finances of the company.

Alignment of organizational processes to legal and regulatory provisions will help in identifying gaps that must be addressed for complying with the standard (Figure 9.8).

Step 5: Implement the components within the selected scope: Making a detailed study of the standard under consideration, evaluating the various components, and designing the BCM program to steer the processes in scope to meet the stipulations laid by each component of the standard are necessary for fulfilling the standard adopted. Certification will be obtained only if there is full compliance to each component of the standard.

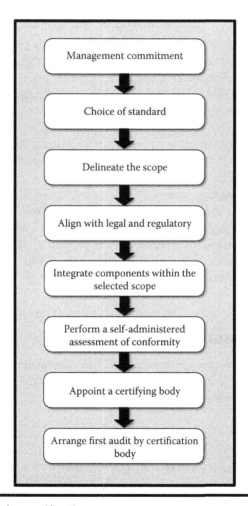

Figure 9.8 Steps for certification.

Step 6: Self-administer an assessment of conformity: Once all the components of the standard have been implemented, it enables the organization to perform the assessment of conformity or otherwise to all components of the standard. This self-assessment is an alternative to get an independent audit since such an assessment can be costly.

The readiness for certification can be determined, and the progress of the project can be measured, and this will keep the management commitment intact.

Step 7: Appoint a certifying body: Once the BCM program of the organization is in place, self-assessment has brought out the readiness of the enterprise to comply with selected standards, a certifying body has to be appointed to examine the program and certify the organization with the standard. Selecting a third-party certifying body must be on the basis of the experience on the part of the certifying body in the industry to which the organization belongs.

Once the selection of firm is made, there is need for a responsible member of the BCM team to proactively manage the audit process and channelize resources needed access to documentation that are requisitioned by the auditors. A good communication and interchange of queries and their satisfactory resolutions can make the process smoother and effective.

Step 8: Complete an audit by the certifying body: The certifying body conducts a preliminary audit to examine the BCM program as existing in the organization to check conformity with the selected standard. Near the completion of the BCM program, all mandatory documentation according to specifications of the standard has to be completed.

Some organization undertake a preparedness audit to be undertaken by an independent consultant, generally a SME who will be able to assess processes, identify gaps, and enable the organization to remediate them so that conformity to standard is enabled. Such preaudit gives a desired confidence to the management that the certification process will be smooth going and successful without much delay.

BCM Audit Assurance Program

The audit and assurance program for BCM covers comprehensively each aspect of BCM beginning with planning, BIA, RA, and ends with risk mitigation and certification. Refer to Annexure A.

Annexure A

Assessment Maturity versus Target Maturity

The spider graph is an example of the assessment results and maturity target for a specific enterprise (Figure 9.9).

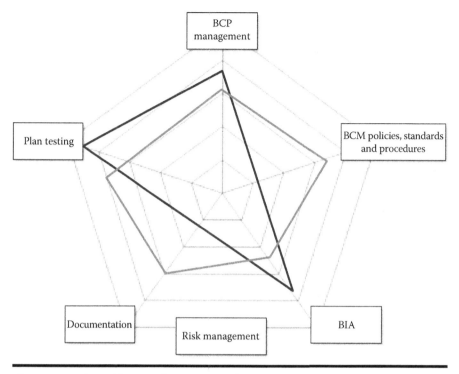

Figure 9.9   The spider graph-BCM maturity.

The assessment maturity of BCM processes and the target maturity will have a gap as seen between red line that is what is assessed, and the blue line shows what is target maturity for the certification. Point to be noted here is that it begins defini-tion from documentation, which is mandatory and has to be present for prelimi-nary assessment to take place. It may be updated after assessment to eliminate gaps.

Conclusion

As we have seen above, the different standards and frameworks on risk, security, and business continuity remain the same more or less. It is a variation of perception sometimes. In the U.S. DRI standard, a RA is prescribed to be preceded by an BIA, whereas UK standard BS 25999 and later on ISO 22301 recommend a BIA to be performed first and the RA to be performed just before the conclusion of the BIA.

Which standard to follow, which framework to adopt, and which guidelines to adopt are sometimes confusing prepositions. Basic awareness of BCM is necessary to plan the organizational BCMS. Likewise, for security, the planning team must be aware of the basic tenets of security. Geographical location of business, type of business, and commonly followed practices govern choice of these standards and guidelines.

For instance, SOX provisions apply to the United States, J-SOX applies to Japan, and Europe follows a different version. In such situations, it would be prudent to take stock of the mandatory standards and regulations to be followed by business. Whether a SSAE 16 or vendor audit is mandated by customers or is it giving value add to business if you have certification for third-party audit? If security-related issues are most important, then one must consider ISO 27001 implementation or resilience as the need of the hour? ISO 22301 is a comprehensive standard that is globally accepted at the moment for business continuity.

There is commonality between standards. By following basic documentation requirements, an intelligent compliance manager can make the enterprise ready for more than one certification. But is that our end objective? Cost of certification and cost of maintaining the certification are equally important considerations for the management. This is the reason why even after readiness, organizations sometimes delay the certification process.

So many different standards are available; it is difficult to select the best fit. At the same time, organizations have to be in business and prepare for the worst-case scenarios. Information is the most valuable asset, and security is at premium. Governance has been mandated, and assurance has become regular. In all these requirements and considering the financial availability for certification, organizations have to optimize on such decisions and derive value optimization for the business. Benchmarking with similar businesses will help take decisions and get value add for business.

Appendix:
Annexures, Templates, Questionnaires, BIA and RA Forms, Graphs, and Illustrations

1. BIA Questionnaire "What" Questions...

Date: *Department: IT*

S. No.	Question			
1	What areas of growth and the presence of technology are outpacing the process of monitoring and management of IT-related risks within your enterprise?			
2	Are IT risks being defined and documented in risk register?			
3	Is there a regular risk assessment system in the enterprise and are risks updated in the risk register if maintained?			
4	Does the enterprise possess the right of IT skills and capabilities to assess IT risks adequately?			

(Continued)

Date: Department: IT

S. No.	Question			
5	What are the chief business objectives and does IT portfolio align with these objectives?			
6	Is there a procurement policy for IT in place? Are there long-term and short-term plans for IT?			
7	Is user requirement analysis a part of IT procedure?			

   2. Critical systems/application survey for business impact analysis.
      1. *Name of Department:*   *Function/Division:*
      2. *Location of Department:*   *Date of completion of survey:*
      3. *Name of person completing survey:*   *Contact Number:*
      4. *Name of Business Head:*   *Contact number:*
      5. *Brief description of business process:*

      6. *Please inventory all application systems used by your department and fill the following table*

Operational Impact	Severity	Day 1	Day 2	Day 3	Day 4	Day 5	Wk. 1	Wk. 2	Wk. 3	Wk. 4
Application 1										
Cash flow										
Compliance gap										
Customer service										
Employee resignations										
Financial reporting										

(Continued)

Operational Impact	Severity	Day 1	Day 2	Day 3	Day 4	Day 5	Wk. 1	Wk. 2	Wk. 3	Wk. 4
Regulatory reporting										
Goodwill										
Legal obligations										
Reputation										
Others (specify)										
Application 2										
Cash flow										
Compliance gap										
Customer service										
Employee resignations										
Financial reporting										
Regulatory reporting										
Goodwill										
Legal obligations										
Reputation										
Others (specify)										

Please note the severity levels to be set on a scale of 0–4, where 4 denotes highest severity. Impacts are only illustrative, and every department can include all critical applications in this format.

7. *Recovery time objective (RTO)/recovery point objective (RPO)*: Please summarize your criticality for different applications into a table depicting RTO/RPOs

Application Name	Prioritize with Top Severity First	RTO (hours)	RPO How Frequently Do You Backup?	How Many Customers Are Impacted by Outage?	Is There Any Workaround for the Application?	Which Are Peak Periods for the Application?	How Much Revenue Is Lost per Day of Outage? ($)
App. 1	4			More than 100	Y		
App. 2	3			More than 50	N		
App. 3	2						

8. *Chart for critical processing periods for applications*

Application Name	Jan.	Feb.	Mar.	Apr.	May	Jun.	Jul.	Aug.	Sept.	Oct.	Nov.	Dec.
App. 1												
App. 2												
App. 3												
App. 4												

9. *Chart for tabulating operational loss over a period of time*

Application	Nature of Loss	Loss in Hours	Loss on Day 1	Loss in Week 1	Loss in Month 1
App. 1	Penalties				
App. 2	Interest				

10. *Upstream/downstream dependencies*

Applications on Which Other Systems Depend	What Data Are Passed?	What Is the Loss If Data Cannot Pass due to Outage? ($)	Does This Dependency Make the Supporting Process Critical?	
App. 2			Y/N	

11. *Name of Primary Contact*:   *Contact Number*:

Note: All data provided in this survey will be treated as confidential and shall be utilized only for conducting the BIA by our personnel.

3. Business dependencies.

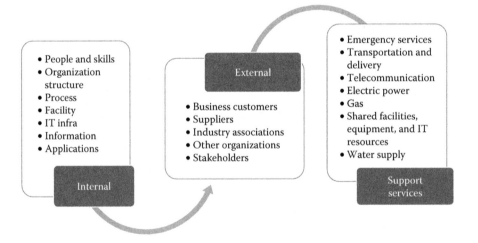

4. Data points for business impact analysis (BIA).

Data Point	Description	IT Dependencies
Business function or process	Short description of the business function or process (we will use "function" from here on).	Describe primary IT systems used for this business function.
Dependencies	Description of the dependencies to this function. What are the input and output points to this function? What has to happen or be available in order for this function to occur? What input is received either from internal or external sources, that is, required to perform this business function? How would the disruption of this business function impact other parts of the business? How and when would this disruption to other functions occur?	Describe IT systems that impact or are impacted by this business function. Are there any internal or external IT dependencies?
Resource dependencies	Is this business function dependent upon any key job functions? If so, which and to what extent? Is this business function dependent upon any unique resources? If so, what and to what extent (contractors, special equipment, etc.)?	Describe secondary/support computer/IT systems required for this business function to occur.
Personnel dependencies	Is this function dependent on specialized skill, knowledge, or expertise? What are the key positions or roles associated with this function? What would happen if people in these roles were unavailable?	Describe key roles, positions, knowledge, expertise, experience, and certification needed to work with this particular IT system or IT/business function.
Impact profile	When does this function occur? Is it hourly, daily, quarterly, or seasonally? Is there a specific time of day/week/year that this function is more at risk? Is there a specific time at which the business is more at risk if this function does not occur (tax time, payroll periods, year-end inventory, etc.)?	Describe the critical timeline related to this function/process and related IT systems, if any.

(*Continued*)

Data Point	Description	IT Dependencies
Operational	If this function did not occur, when and how would it impact the business? Would the impact be on time or recurring? Describe the operational impact of this function not occurring.	Describe the impact on IT if this business function does not occur. Describe the impact on IT if this business function does not occur.
Financial	If this function did not occur, what would be the financial impact to the business? When would the financial impact be felt or noticed? Would it be one time or recurring? Describe the financial impact of this function not occurring. Backlog. Describe the financial impact of this function not occurring.	
Backlog	At what point would work become backlogged?	Describe how a backlog would impact IT systems and other related or support systems work.
Recovery	What types of resources would be needed to support the function? How many resources would be needed and in what timeframe (phones, desks, computers, printers, etc.)?	What resources, skills, and knowledge would be required to recover IT systems related to this business function?
Time to recover	What is the minimum time needed to recover this business function if disrupted? What is the maximum time this business function could be unavailable?	How long would it take to recover, restore, replace, or reconfigure IT systems related to this business function?
Service level agreements	Are there any service level agreements in place related to this business function? What are the requirements and metrics associated with these SLAs? How will SLAs be impacted by the disruption of this business function?	How would IT service levels be impacted by the disruption or lack of availability of this business function? How do external SLAs impact IT systems?

(Continued)

Data Point	Description	IT Dependencies
Technology	What hardware, software, applications, or other technological components are needed to support this function? What would happen if some of these components were not available? What would be the impact? How severely would the business function be impacted?	What IT assets are required to support/ maintain this business function?
Desktops, laptops, workstations	Does this business function require the use of "user" computer equipment?	What is the configuration data for required computer equipment?
Servers, networks, Internet	Does this business function require the use of back-end computer equipment? Does it require connection to the network? Does it require access to or use of the Internet or other communications?	What is the configuration data for required servers and infrastructure equipment?
Work-arounds	Are there any manual workaround procedures that have been developed and tested? Would these enable the business function to be performed in the event of IT or systems failures? How long could these functions operate in manual or workaround mode? If no procedures have been developed, does it seem feasible to develop such procedures?	Are there any IT-related workarounds related to this business function? If so, what are they and how could they be implemented?
Remote work	Can this business function be performed remotely, either from another business location or by employees working from home or other offsite locations?	Can this business function be performed remotely from an IT perspective? If so, what would it take to enable remote access or the ability to remotely perform this business function?

(Continued)

Data Point	Description	IT Dependencies
Workload shifting	Is it possible to shift this business function to another business unit that might not be impacted by the disruption? If so, what processes and procedures are in place or are needed to enable that function?	Are there other IT systems or resources that could pick up the load should a serious disruption occur?
Business/data records	Where are the business records related to this function stored or archived? Are they currently backed up? If so, how, with what frequency, where?	How and where are backups stored? Based on data provided, is the current backup strategy optimal based on the risks and impact?
Reporting	Are there legal or regulatory reporting requirements of this business function? If so, what is the impact of a disruption of this business function to reporting requirements? Are there reporting workarounds in place or could they be developed and implemented?	Are there other ways reporting data could be generated, stored, or reported if key business functions or systems were disabled?
Business disruption experience	Has this business function ever been disrupted before? If so, what was the disruption and what was the outcome? What was learned from this event that can be incorporated into this planning effort?	Has IT ever experienced the disruption of this business function in the past? If so, what was the nature and duration of the disruption? How was it addressed and what was learned from the event?
Competitive impact	What, if any, is the competitive impact to the company if this business function is disrupted? What would the impact be, when would the impact occur, when would the potential loss of customers or suppliers occur?	

(Continued)

Data Point	Description	IT Dependencies
Other issues	What other issues might be relevant when discussing this particular business function?	Are there other IT issues related to this specific business function that should be included or discussed?

Once you have collected all these data points for all your business functions and processes, you have a comprehensive understanding of your business, its key functions, and what would happen if those functions were disrupted.

5. Disaster causes: (Suggestive).

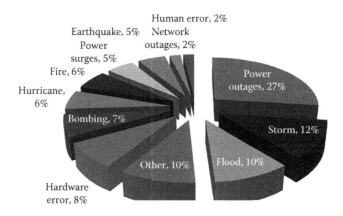

6. The following table summarizes these five questions you should ask your suppliers, as well as high-quality answers you should expect, and possible follow-up questions for each topic.

Your Question	The Answer You Should Expect	Possible Follow-Up Question(s)
1. How have you handled the scoping of your program, and how it impacts the recoverability of the products/ services you offer to my organization?	We performed a business impact analysis (BIA) that aligns our internal business operations to each of our customers' products and services. For the products/ services we deliver to your organization, we are performing risk mitigation and recovery planning.	Specific to the scope of your preparedness efforts, are you addressing all aspects of recoverability, meaning your facilities, people, technology, suppliers, and equipment/ resources?

(*Continued*)

Your Question	*The Answer You Should Expect*	*Possible Follow-Up Question(s)*
2. Please describe your strategy to recover aspects of your business that deliver my products/services.	The answer to this will be situation-specific, although the reply should describe how and where key business and technology processes are recovered, as well as supply chain risk management activities.	When will these capabilities be available following a disruptive event and at what level of performance?
3. How have you validated that your business continuity strategies work as designed?	We perform annual exercises (tests) of our business continuity strategies and involve those that will be leading the response and recovery efforts. We set exercise objectives, success criteria, and compare results to predetermined objectives.	What is the scope of your exercises—a loss of primary work locations, a loss of technology, and others?
4. How is management involved in reviewing and improving your business continuity program?	We employ a steering committee that meets on a quarterly basis to offer input on scoping and objectives, as well as feedback on our business continuity management system/program.	Does our account manager participate on this steering committee, or does he/she also receive program performance reports?
5. How do you tackle improvement opportunities in order to ensure your organization is best prepared to address my organization's needs?	We track corrective and preventative actions in a list that is reviewed and reprioritized monthly by our business continuity team and quarterly by our steering committee.	What are the sources of the corrective and preventative actions (exercises, audits, business impact analyses, risk assessments, management reviews)?

7. Table of impacts (Illustrative).

External	Environmental	Operational	Technological	Terrorist	People
Economic downturn	Floods	Stiff competition	Cyberattacks	Bomb blast	Absence of key staff
Legal and regulatory	Earthquakes	Intrusion of customer privacy and security by leaking of credit card information on Internet	Loss of data		Strikes and riots
Trade policies including foreign	Fire		Virus/Trojans		Theft unauthorized access
Political protests	Power outage		Software bugs		Disgruntled employees
Civil disorder	Lightning		Data corruption		Data security breach
	Epidemic/ pandemic		System failure		Inadequate vendor competency, vendor SLA slippage
	Building collapse		Configuration changes		
	Floods-burst pipes				

8. Types of impacts.

Impact Category	Definition
Loss of revenue	Loss of income received from selling goods or services
Additional expenses	Temporary staffing, overtime, equipment, and services
Regulatory and legal	Fines, penalties, compliance issues, contractual obligations, and financial liabilities
Customer service	Termination or reduction of service level (internal of external), live operators versus automated response
Goodwill	Public image, shareholder relations, and market share

9. Critical function analysis and recovery.

	Critical Function 1	
	Headed by...............	
A	**Potential impact on organization if function is not performed**	
	Likelihood of interruption	
	Recovery timeframe	
B	**Resource Requirement**	
	1 Staff	
	i) Number ii) Skills iii) Qualification iv) Alternate sources	
	2 Data/systems	
	i) Backup and recovery processes	
	ii) Staff and equipment required	
	3 Facilities	
	i) Potential relocation	
	ii) Work-from-home option	

(*Continued*)

4 Communications	
i) Contacting staff	
ii) Contacting customers	
iii) Contacting suppliers	
5 Equipment	
i) Key equipment recovery or replacement	
ii) Alternate sources	
iii) Reciprocal agreements	
6 Supplies	
i) Key supplies required	
ii) Provision in emergency pack	

10. Contact list of utility companies.

Name	Company	Telephone Number	E-mail

11. Contact list for local emergency services.

Service	Location	Telephone Number 1	Telephone Number 2

12. Other contacts.

Service	Company	Telephone Number	E-mail
Bank			
Insurance			
Local authority			

13. **Business continuity management** process.

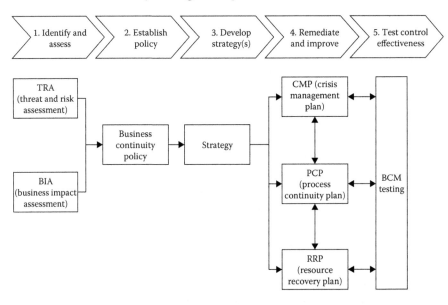

14. Some misconception on business continuity management.

We have annually tested business continuity plans that will work in crisis, and we have insurance

Organizations have misconception that they can cope with disaster by working from home

Organizations feel they do not have time to allocate for business continuity activities

Organization has misconception that they can recover operations merely on the basis of backups

Organizations are confident that probability of major loss is minimal, and insurance is the control to fall back on

Organizations plan to communicate with their employees, customers, and supply chain with their wireless capabilities for phone, calls, e-mails, and texts

15. Failure modes and effect analysis.

Function	Potential failure mode	Potential effect(s) of failure	S	Potential cause(s) of failure	O	Current process controls	D	RPN	CRIT	Recommended action(s)	Responsibility and target completion date	Action taken	Action results				
													S	O	D	RPN	CRIT
Dispense amount of case requested by customer	Does not dispense cash	Customer very dissatisfied; Incorrect entry to demand deposit system; Discrepancy in cash balancing	8	Out of cash	5	Internal low cash alert	5	200	40								
				Machine jams	3	Internal jam alert	10	240	24								
				Power failure during transaction	2	None	10	160	16								
	Dispenses too much cash	Bank loses money; Discrepancy in cash balancing	6	Bills stuck together	2	Loading procedure (riffle ends of stack)	7	84	12								
				Denominations in wrong trays	3	Two-person visual verification	4	72	18								
	Takes too long to dispense cash	Customer somewhat annoyed	3	Heavy computer network traffic	7	None	10	210	21								
				Power interruption during transaction	2	None	10	60	6								

16. Risk identification.

Sample template for risk identification

Item No.	Type of risk	Risk category		Description of risk
1	External	a.	Financial	
		b.	Strategic	
		c.	Operational	
		d.	Hazards	
2	Internal	a.	Internal process	
		b.	ICT	
		c.	Human capital	
		d.	Systems	

17. Business recovery plan simulation exercise checklist.

		Y	N	N.A.
1	Has the business recovery plan been approved by the owner of the business function?			
2	Did the recovery plan have a documented description, scope, and objective?			
3	Does the BRP specify maximum tolerable RTO?			
4	Does the BRP specify the level of service (which the business owner has agreed to be acceptable) to be provided in recovery mode?			
5	Is the simulation exercise for BRP performed at least annually?			
6	Is the corrective plan completed and closed?			
7	Did the simulation exercise meet RTO set by management?			
8	Based on simulation exercise and lessons learned, does the recovery personnel have reasonable assurance that the plan is workable?			
9	Are all changes to the BRP being approved by the process owner?			
10	Are all test results documented for each test of BRP?			

18. Significance of change management on **Business Continuity Management.**

Date	Systems Affected	Description of Change Request	Date of Change Request	Work Performed to Fulfill Change	Date Completed	Date Approved	Date Placed into Service

19. Damage assessment form.

S. No.	Name of Asset	Where Situated	Salvage Value	Extent of Damage	Cost of Repair or Replacement

20. Risk identification process.

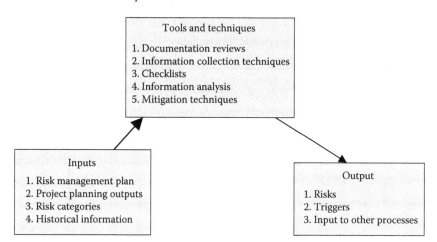

21. Business continuity plan (BCP) adequacy checklist.
The following is a list of standard ingredients for both an overall business continuity program:

S. No.	Questions	Y/N	Comments
	Program Components		
1	Do you have a clearly defined, documented, and formally approved BCP Policy?		
2	Have you assigned responsibilities for the BCP? Have you ensured it is adequately resourced? Have you designated a senior official the overall responsibility for the BCP?		
3	Have you completed a business impact analysis? Have you defined your critical business functions that must be recovered in case of an emergency? Have you ensured that your key client records can be restored (physically or electronically)? For introducers, this can be done through the service provider or the carrier.		

(*Continued*)

S. No.	Questions	Y/N	Comments
4	Have you defined your strategies for the protection and recoverability of data (electronic or physical)?		
5	Where applicable, have you established predesignated alternate sites, located a prudent distance from primary sites?		
6	Has your BCP been approved by the senior management of the firm?		
7	Have you provisioned for testing your BCP annually?		
8	Are you comfortable that clients will be able to have continued access to their assets shortly after an emergency or interruption?		
9	Has your staff been made aware of the plans? Are you ensuring that staff is kept aware of updates on the plans?		
10	Have you validated the recovery capabilities of critical third-party service providers as identified in your BCP?		
11	Is BCP awareness included in your new employee orientation?		
	Plan Components		
12	Have you drawn up emergency response procedures dealing with: Establishing the existence of an emergency Notification of staff Notification of key counterparties (including the IDA) Activation of emergency plans Are they kept up-to-date?		
13	Have you arranged for alternative means of communication in case of failure of telephone lines or power supply?		
14	Do you maintain updated lists of internal and external contacts with alternates?		

(Continued)

S. No.	Questions	Y/N	Comments
15	Does your BCP define key roles, responsibilities, and authorities with alternates?		
16	Have you designated a control and coordination (command) center location, where applicable?		
17	Do you have the minimum resource requirements for critical function recovery?		
18	Do you have clearly defined backup procedures for key applications, hardware, and data?		
19	Have you defined processes for restoration or replacement of key data (electronic and paper)?		
20	Do you review and update your plans annually?		

22. Plan for the impact of an emergency on your business.

Activities	Not Yet Initiated	In Progress	Completed
Appointment of BCM teams	O	O	O
Identifying employees and other resources such as raw materials, suppliers, subcontractor services, or logistics	O	O	O
Define and build alternate workforce and/or service providers	O	O	O
Develop and plan for scenarios likely to result in an increase or decrease in demand for your products and/or services during an emergency (e.g., effect of restriction on mass gatherings, need for hygiene supplies, disruptions to telecommunications or transport infrastructure)	O	O	O

(*Continued*)

Activities	Not Yet Initiated	In Progress	Completed
Determine potential impact of an incident on business financials using multiple scenario analysis and see impact on different products/services	O	O	O
Prepare an emergency communications plan that includes key contacts, chain of communication, escalation levels, and processes for tracking recovery status, and revise periodically	O	O	O
Find out arrangements on emergencies and sustainable solutions to contain incidents	O	O	O
Communicate BCP plans to all locations within the enterprise	O	O	O
Implement and arrange for exercise/drill to test BCP plan, and revise when changes occur	O	O	O

23. Allocate resources to protect employees and customers during an emergency.

Tasks	Not Started	In Progress	Completed
Provide necessary emergency supplies such as safety equipment, hand hygiene products, and tissues in all business locations.	O	O	O
Ensure communications and information technology infrastructures are provided to support employees in communicating and telecommuting with remote locations.	O	O	O
Ensure availability of medical facilities for employees at the time of crisis.	O	O	O

(*Continued*)

Communicate to and spread BCM awareness among employees

Tasks	Not Started	In Progress	Completed
Taking help from PR team to develop and disseminate programs and materials covering emergency fundamentals (e.g., safety procedures, evacuation, signs and symptoms of influenza, modes of transmission) to spread knowledge and awareness among employees.	O	O	O
Sharpen crisis communication methods so as to anticipate employee fear and anxiety, rumors, and misinformation, and plan communications accordingly.	O	O	O
Ensure that communication is clear, concise, and accurate.	O	O	O
Emergency preparedness plan and response procedures must be explained to employees so that they can adopt the procedures.	O	O	O
Provide for first aid and medical aid to injured employees.	O	O	O
Develop communication channels like hotlines, dedicated web sites, and building call lists for emergency communication during crisis.	O	O	O
Identify community sources for timely and accurate emergency information (domestic and international) and resources for obtaining countermeasures (e.g., specialized safety equipment, vaccines, and antivirals).	O	O	O

(Continued)

Coordinate with external organizations

Tasks	Not Started	In Progress	Completed
Collaborate with insurers, health plans, and major local health care facilities to share your emergency plans and understand their capabilities and plans.	O	O	O
Collaborate with local authorities, ambulance services, police, and so on.	O	O	O
Communicate with local or provincial public health agencies and/or emergency responders about the assets and/or services your business could contribute to the community.	O	O	O
Share emergency plans with other offices so as to share best practices for facility outages, a coordinated effort that can be made for orderly evacuation and/or emergency operations.	O	O	O

24. Monitoring social media during a crisis.

The following are best practices for preventing, mitigating, and remediating a social media public relations crisis

1. Social media to be authorized and validated by executive management.
2. Introduce transparency in stakeholder communications. Communicate what the organization does and also the rationale or reasons for doing so.
3. Proactive conversations with influencers.
4. Document all engagement in conversations during a crisis.
5. Resolve conflicting messages, and ensure crisis communication is not tangent to marketing communication.
6. Ensure consistency in all crisis communications.
7. Build a framework for crisis communication, set escalation procedures, determine type of crisis communication, and determine the spokesperson who will communicate to media during a crisis.

25. Business recovery sites options evaluation.

Recovery Option	Description	Pros	Cons	Data Delivery Method	Minimum Recovery Time Supported	Maximum Length of Message
Internal cold site	A raised floor facility with preinstalled environmental infrastructure but no server infrastructure or active communication lines. Infrastructure would be provided at the time of crisis by prearranged "quick-ship" agreements with hardware vendors.	Provides guaranteed space and defers purchase of recovery hardware.	Significant time is required to recover; it relies on third parties to provide equipment and configure communication lines. It requires effective asset management to ensure accurate recovery of applications.	All	5–20 days	Unlimited
External cold site	A raised floor facility with preinstalled environmental infrastructure but no server infrastructure or active communication lines. Infrastructure would be provisioned using prearranged "quick-ship" agreements with hardware vendors.	A contract can be purchased as a service; no additional capital expenses are required. External cold-site providers typically have nearby communication lines, which can be utilized and have experience in performing complete recoveries.	Significant time is required to recover; it relies on third parties to provide equipment and configure communication lines. It requires effective asset management to ensure accurate recovery of applications.	All	5–20 days	Unlimited

(Continued)

Recovery Option	Description	Pros	Cons	Data Delivery Method	Minimum Recovery Time Supported	Maximum Length of Message
Internal hot site	A facility with preplaced server, computer telecommunications, and environmental infrastructure. (all in standby mode).	Guaranteed availability and unlimited testing under the control of organization.	Additional data center and hardware capital expenses are required. Additional complexity is introduced into environment, which affects ongoing support and operations; additional personnel may be required at alternate site.	Tape backup Disk replication Data replication	17 hours 7 hours 0–2 hours	Unlimited Unlimited Unlimited
External hot site	A third-party facility with preplaced server, computer telecommunications, and environmental infrastructure. (all in standby mode).	Can be purchased as a service, with no additional capital expenditure incurred. Multiple recovery locations provide increased protection.	No guaranteed availability. Limited usage.	Tape backup Disk replication Data replication	24–72 hours 7–36 hours 0–24 hours	30 days 30 days 30 days
Internal warm site	A raised floor facility with full environmental infrastructure, limited server infrastructure, and communication lines are also present.	Provides guaranteed space and avoids purchase of hardware.	Requires an investment in floor space, infrastructure, and communication lines. It relies on shipment of third-party hardware.	All	5–20 hours	Unlimited

26. Comparative table-ERM, BSC, TPA.

Enterprise Risk Management (ERM)	Business Service Continuity	Third-Party Assessments
BIA emphasis on operational risks—identifying risks and gap analysis	BIA for identifying critical processes, upstream and downstream dependencies and judging severity against time criticality	BIA to inventory critical third-party service providers involved in provision of services to critical functions.
Business process focused	Purpose is to plan for incident escalation	All main suppliers of goods for conducting critical business processes to be listed.
Operational risk mitigation	It aids in estimating resource requirements	SLAs to be examined to check right o audit clause is present.
Regulatory and standards integration	Business resumption strategies	Arrange visits to third-party or arrange conference calls to discuss their business continuity arrangements.
Resilience and continuity solutions	Testing and awareness	Obtain confidence on continuity of third-party vendors by visiting installation or in some cases obtaining a copy of SSAE 16 reports.

27. Components of operational continuity/resilience.

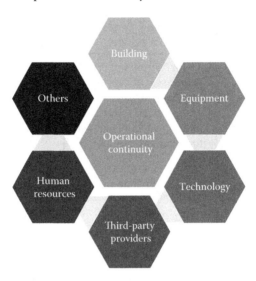

28. High availability for the enterprise.

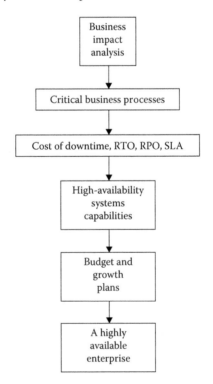

29. BCM kit.

Emergency Pack Contents
 	
Key documents, records, and equipment held at offsite location in emergency pack for recovery purposes. Contents of the recovery pack include the following:
 	
1. Documents
   a. Copy of BCM plan, including key contact details
   b. Insurance policy
2. Records
   a. Computer backup tapes/disks
   b. Financial records
3. Equipment
   a. Spare keys
   b. Torch and batteries

30. Vendor analysis questionnaire.

S. No.	Question/Query	Response/Comment
1	Do you presently have a BCM certification according to prescribed standard?	
2	Does your organization have a business continuity management system in place?	
3	Have you done a risk assessment of your business and identified risks faced by your business?	
4	Does your risk initiative cover your branch offices and cover them for specific events?	
5	Do you have a defined BCM strategy?	
6	What/who are the emergency responders during an emergency?	
7	Is your BCMS updated when there are changes in business environment?	
8	Do you have a strategy/plan for BCM exercises?	
9	Are exercise results documented?	
10	Is the plan improvised as per lessons learned from exercise?	

(Continued)

S. No.	Question/Query	Response/Comment
11	Are your senior management and operations executives trained in business continuity management?	
12	Is regular training given to staff in BCM procedures?	
13	Do you have a IT DR plan operational in your organization?	
14	Is critical data backed up, and is a copy of the backup stored at an offsite location?	
15	Are vital documents and records scanned and a scanned copy stored at an offsite location?	
16	Have you identified your critical suppliers, services, and utility providers? Are call lists prepared and available for each?	
17	Are modes of communication with staff during disruption determined and crisis communication plan is in existence?	
18	Are good PR relations with vendors maintained to ensure continued service levels?	

31. Some **business impact analysis** considerations.

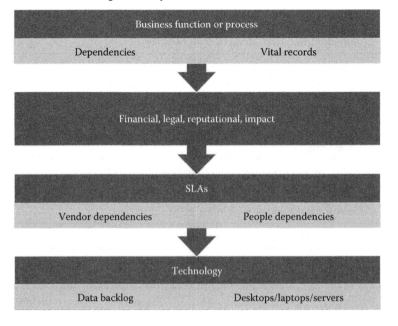

32. Action and expenses log.
    Used to record decisions, actions, and expenses incurred for recovery

Date/Time	Decision/Action Taken	By Whom	Costs Incurred

33. BCM/DR checklist.
    a. *Planning*
       i. Confirm participation, sponsorship, and buy-in from corporate executives.
       ii. Ensure BC/DR is sufficiently funded and included in the budget.
       iii. Build a team representing all functional areas for developing and maintaining your BC/DR plan.
       iv. Establish a team leader with an alternate and define roles for everyone.
       v. Create a team list with critical contact information and update it regularly.
       vi. Develop a comprehensive plan, including both business continuity and disaster recovery (Hint: Business continuity is business operations centric, and disaster recovery is data and systems centric).
       vii. Define a clear decision-making hierarchy to prevent delays when the worst happens.
       viii. Identify workforce contingencies for safety, evacuation, remote access, and communications.
       ix. Compile third-party service level agreements (SLAs) for a comprehensive reference.
       x. Make sure your plan includes scenarios for cybercrime or cyberattacks.
       xi. Keep documentation and distribution lists updated and accessible from more than one location.
    b. *Risk Assessment and BIA*
       i. Identify processes, systems, and services critical to your business and prioritize them and associate costs from disruption to them.
       ii. Evaluate your current systems for data backup and storage.

    iii. Determine recovery time, and how much downtime is tolerable.

    iv. Identify your organization's weaknesses and vulnerabilities by assessing threats (Hint: Fire, flood, hurricanes, cyberattacks are threats or hazards that lead to business risks).

    v. Perform a risk assessment to identify situations that can disrupt your ability to deliver the products or services vital to your business (include risks to your workforce, property, operations, and reputation).

    vi. Assess the readiness of your suppliers/vendors to respond or deliver during a disruption and make sure they have BC/DR plans in place.

    vii. Understand the impacts of supplier/vendor disruptions to your processes.

    viii. Use the outcomes from your BIA and risk assessments as a foundation for developing plans to ensure business continuity and disaster recovery in each scenario.

c. *Communications*

    i. Develop a crisis communications plan for internal and external communications; include your web site communications and social media.

    ii. Create an internal list of key individuals who should be contacted in a crisis and keep it updated.

    iii. Ensure the crisis communications team is aware of the decision-making hierarchy (see Planning Basics) and has a plan to access the decision-maker.

    iv. Keep a list of the audiences that need communication (employees, partners, suppliers/vendors, customers, authorities).

    v. Identify primary spokespersons during a crisis with backups for each person.

    vi. Prepare scripted communications for key scenarios and update regularly.

d. *Continuous Improvements*

    i. Maintain a regular schedule for testing disaster/disruption scenarios.

    ii. Integrate testing with normal business operations (e.g., text failover processes when your servers have to be taken down for maintenance).

    iii. Add suppliers/vendors involved in critical processes to your testing process and confirm they perform regular tests.

    iv. Establish frequent audits of more vulnerable processes and systems.

    v. Identify deficiencies in both planning and procedures. Integrate learning after each test or audit.

    vi. Evolve your plan as changes occur in processes and technology.

    vii. Train your teams and awareness for your organization's BC/DR plans through regular communication (see Communications above).

    viii. Draw upon different methods such as walkthroughs, tabletop, functional, and full-scale exercises to train, and evaluate your plans.

    ix. Assess the response capabilities of your resources, and identify additional resources as needed.

     x. Consult with local and federal agencies for guidance on your plan.

    xi. Add redundancies and backups as needed to support contingency plans.

   xii. Ensure new processes and projects include business continuity plans before implementation.

  xiii. Keep BC/DR on the annual budget to guarantee ongoing investment and support.

  xiv. Be flexible—your plan should evolve with your organization.

34. Governance cycle initiated by COBIT.

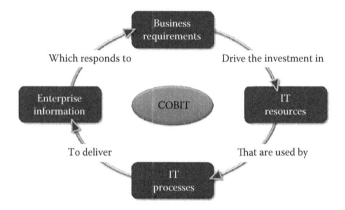

35. Alignment of business goals with IT goals and processes.

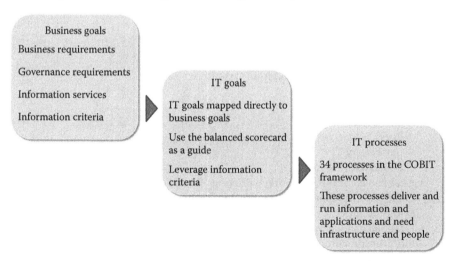

36. Tradeoff between recovery time objectives and recovery point objectives.

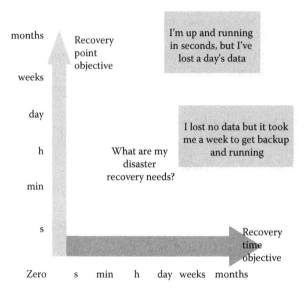

37. Incident-handling checklist.

Threat Response	Comments

• Identify incident management team members, including an incident manager and alternates
• Identify business and information technology recovery team leaders and alternates
• Update all critical internal and external contact lists. Include the following information:
  – Home address
  – Home telephone
  – Cellular phone
  – Pager
  – Blackberry
  – E-mail address
• Establish a conference bridge. Provide all incident management team members, the conference bridge number, and pass code
• Establish a voice mail box for employees to monitor for status updates
• Determine if you should place third-party business continuity and disaster recovery service providers on alert if you are a subscriber	

(Continued)

Threat Response	Comments
• Ensure that monitoring service vendors (e.g., alarm company) have current contact information • Develop procedures to account for employees • Provide employees with threat response procedures, if appropriate (e.g., bomb threat, evacuation) • Create backup tapes and ship offsite • Identify a crisis command center outside of the anticipated impact area • Top off emergency generators and arrange for additional fuel deliveries • Acquire battery-operated radios with spare batteries	
Incident Detection and Preliminary Assessment	
Follow company emergency response procedures • Conduct a preliminary damage assessment, if it can be done safely. No recovery activities should be undertaken if personnel are placed in danger • Notify the incident manager and provide a detailed report	
Activate Incident Management Team	

The incident manager will determine if the incident management team should be activated and if necessary:
 	
• Notify incident management team members
  – Provide a description of the event
  – Request that they assemble at the crisis command center or participate via a conference call
• Activate the crisis command center	

Evaluate Disaster Impact	

Determine if the severity of the impact requires implementation of the recovery plan
 	
• Determine recovery objectives including the following:
  – Priorities
  – Recovery strategies
  – Action plans
  – Assignments	

(Continued)

Threat Response	Comments
Activate Recovery Plan	

• Notify recovery team leaders and members (See personnel notification guidelines below)
• Brief recovery team leaders and alternates regarding:
  – Priorities
  – Strategies
  – Action plans
  – Assignments
  – Reporting and communications procedures
• Declare a disaster with your third-party business continuity and disaster recovery service provider if you are a subscriber	

Implement Support Procedures	
As directed by the incident manager, incident management team support personnel will provide recovery support to all affected business units	
Audit	

Consult/provide advice on changes to standard operating procedures to be implemented during the recovery effort
 	
• Ensure that the following policies and standards are maintained during the recovery effort:
  – Financial security and control policies
  – Antifraud policies
  – Information security standards
• Provide reports and recommendations to the IMT as required
• Provide additional resources to other business units during the recovery effort as needed	

(*Continued*)

Threat Response	Comments
Corporate Communications	
Establish a media briefing center • Coordinate all media communications • Review and approve all statements regarding the incident • Develop both internal and external communications • Coordinate recovery-related advertising with external vendors • Instruct employees to direct all media inquiries to corporate communications	
Health and Safety	
Ensure the health and safety of employees • Ensure that response activities to address fire, spills, and/or medical emergencies are performed in accordance with regulatory guidelines • Notify regulatory agencies of the incident as required • Enlist the assistance of vendors and agencies to assist in support activities as appropriate	
Facilities	
Conduct detailed damage assessment • Conduct salvage and restoration activities • Acquire replacement office space if necessary • Notify tenants of the incident and provide periodic updates regarding the condition of their affected office space	

(*Continued*)

Threat Response	Comments
Finance	
Ensure funds are available for recovery • Ensure that all recovery expenditures are properly documented • Set up a recovery cost center • Estimate the impact of the incident on the company's financial statement Food services • Provide foods services to recovery personnel at the alternate operating locations	
Human Resources	
• Account for all personnel • Assist public authorities in handling casualties (i.e., identification of victims, family notifications, etc.) • Monitor the condition and location of the injured • Coordinate employee communications with corporate communications • Coordinate additional or temporary staffing for recovery effort • Provide counseling services as required • Administer company personnel policies as they apply to response and recovery • File worker's compensation claims • Assist employees with incident-related benefit administration • Complete and submit HSE reports as required	
Insurance	
Coordinate with insurance broker on the preparation and filing of all insurance claims • Document proof of losses • Submit claims and monitor payments • Establish a debris management program	

(*Continued*)

Threat Response	Comments
IT	
Conduct computer system and telecommunications damage assessment • Activate alternate operating locations (for system recovery) • Recover computer systems and network environment(s) • Acquire and install replacement desktop computer equipment • Re-establish data network connections to external resources (branch locations, vendors) • Implement all telephone response plans (rerouting critical telephone numbers) • Arrange for all alternate site telephone installations • Ensure all system security devices and procedures are in place	
Legal	
Manage all required regulatory notifications • Provide legal counsel for response and recovery operations • Review and approve new contracts acquired as a result of the event, before implementation	
Office Supplies and Services	
Re-establish mail and shipping services • Redirect all mail and parcel receipts to alternate operating locations Purchasing • Manage all incident-related purchasing • Acquire office supplies, forms, and equipment for affected business units • Implement any necessary short-term financial tracking controls using designated cost centers	

(Continued)

Threat Response	Comments
Records Management	
Coordinate with information technology to ensure the recovery of the records management system • Coordinate with business units in retrieving all off-site backup records • Lead records reclamation and reconstruction efforts	
Security	
Coordinate onsite security for affected facilities and all alternate operating locations • Control access to affected facilities • Monitor equipment and records being removed from facilities	
Transportation	
Provide local transportation during response and recovery activities as required • Provide travel arrangements and accommodations for employees traveling to remote recovery locations	
Track Incident Status and Recovery Progress	
Conduct periodic debriefing sessions with recovery teams to monitor progress and determine problem areas • Reallocate and/or provide resources	

(Continued)

Threat Response	Comments
Personnel Notification Guidelines	

1. If contact is made, ask "MAY I SPEAK WITH (Individual)?" and then provide the following information:
• Brief description of problem
• Location of the crisis command center
• Telephone number at the crisis command center
• Any immediate action required
• Tell personnel to make no public statement regarding the situation
• Tell personnel that no calls are to be made to other employees
  (This will avoid premature notification to families of personnel working at the time of the disaster).
2. If not available, ask "WHERE MAY I REACH (Individual)?" If at any location other than work, get phone number, make call, and provide the above information
• If individual is at work, indicate you will reach the individual at work
  (DO NOT DISCUSS DISASTER SITUATION WITH PERSON ANSWERING THE PHONE).
• Notify the incident manager immediately
3. If there is no answer:
• Record the time attempted contacts were made
• Periodically recall until contact is made
4. If contact information is invalid (i.e., wrong number, phone disconnected, etc.):
• If person has moved, try to get new telephone number and contact the individual
• Notify the incident manager of incorrect information	

Index

Note: Page numbers followed by f and t refer to figures and tables, respectively.

Printed in the United States
by Baker & Taylor Publisher Services